THIS PLANTED VINE

DIOCESE OF

NEW YORK

THIS PLANTED VINE

*A Narrative History of
the Episcopal Diocese of New York*

James Elliott Lindsley

*Early didst thou arise to plant this vine,
Which might the more endear it to be thine.*
—GEORGE HERBERT

1817

HARPER & ROW, PUBLISHERS, New York
Cambridge, Philadelphia, San Francisco, London
Mexico City, São Paulo, Singapore, Sydney

FIRST EDITION

Designer: C. Linda Dingler

Library of Congress Cataloging in Publication Data

Lindsley, James Elliott.
  This planted vine.
  Includes index.
  1. Episcopal Church.   Diocese of Central New York—
History. I. Title.
BX5918.C4L56 1984   283',747   84-47588
ISBN 0-06-015347-4

84 85 86 87 88 10 9 8 7 6 5 4 3 2 1

To Barbara

Contents

Illustrations

Preface

When Bishop Moore asked me to write a history of the Diocese of New York marking its two hundredth anniversary, I accepted the task with an eagerness born of naiveté. If he were to ask me now, I might respond with lessened enthusiasm, despite the cordiality and warmth of those who helped me prepare this history. For the wealth of material is great, as it should be, inasmuch as here we are considering one of our largest dioceses and one of the greatest cities of the world. Anyone who attempts to tell the story of the Diocese of New York is tempted to explore byways that, however pleasant and fascinating, interfere with the principal narrative. When these pages are delivered from my desk they leave a large aggregation of material that has not been used. This includes facets of diocesan life untouched here, worthy names neglected, parishes whose rich history must go unnoticed, organizations inadequately mentioned. The lode has simply been too rich.

Therefore, let me begin by an apology to those who search in vain for specific information about a favorite person or place: its inexistence is due either to its not coming to my notice, or to the obvious limitation of page space.

As I come to the end of preparing this history and begin to think of those who have helped me write it, a great host of names confronts me. First of all, there is Bishop Moore, who conceived the history and who, with his suffragans, Bishop Wetmore and Bishop Dennis, read much of the manuscript. I cannot claim that they approved it, but their encouragement was much appreciated, and their persistence about the bicentennial of the Diocese of New York deserves the appreciation of all of us.

Two men have been helpful beyond what I had any right to expect. The first is F. Garner Ranney, Custodian of the Archives of the Diocese of Maryland, now housed in the Maryland Historical Society. Many students of Episcopal Church history are indebted to Garner Ranney, but none more than I. His helpfulness and knowledge of the material in his custody made my work not only easier, but delightful.

Nelson R. Burr is well-known for his in-depth research in American Church history. He has read much of this history when it was in its formative stage, and his valuable suggestions have been respected.

There is yet a third man whose kindness to me was more than

matched by his commitment to the Church he served, and that is Thomas Muncaster, who was clerk of the works and general factotum of the cathedral during the episcopates of five bishops. He is proof that the clergy come and go, but the laity are here always.

I have also to thank the very many other people who have helped me, beginning with my wife, who encouraged me to embark upon the work and prepared an extensive bibliography; the librarians at the General Theological Seminary; Bishops Donegan, Boyntan, and Wood; the Rev. Messrs. Edwin C. Coleman, Carl Scovel, Allen Hinman, Kenneth R. Waldron, Raymond L. Harbort, William Reisman, D. Lincoln Harter, F. Lee Richards, A. Pierce Middleton, Wayne Schmitt, William Howard Melish, Douglas Glasspool, Thomas Pike, Marion J. Hatchett, Horatio N. Tragitt, and, particularly, my predecessor as historiographer, Leslie Lang. The Rev. Frederick H. Shriver, Jr., kindly read much of the manuscript and offered valuable comments.

Thanks are also due Columba Gillis, OSH; Richard B. Morris of Columbia University; Phyllis Barr, the Archivist of Trinity Church; Denis Sennett, SA, Archivist of Graymoor; David L. Holmes of William and Mary; E. G. W. Bill, Librarian of Lambeth Palace Library; Canon Edward N. West, the Community of St. John Baptist; the Community of St. Mary; Mother Ruth of the Order of the Holy Spirit; the Holy Cross Fathers at West Park; Samuel O. Gray; V. Nelle Bellamy, Archivist of the Episcopal Church; Judy Johnson and her successor as Archivist of the Diocese of New York, James Templar; Gloria Normann, Registrar of the Diocese of New York and always ready to assist me; Clyde Griffin; Bronson Chanler; Olive Anderson; Gladden Pell Foss; James Duane Livingston; members of the Monday Club, who were encouraging while enduring two years of lectures; Andrew Oliver; Mary W. Gray; H. C. Robbins Landon; and the Rev. Messrs. George W. Wickersham, Darby Betts, and Joseph Bernardin. I am especially grateful to Thomas Newbold Morgan for hospitality in New York City while I was gathering information there; Richard H. Jenrette, for allowing us to use his celebrated Roper House on Charleston's Battery, where much of the writing was done; and my sister-in-law, Anne Newberry dePineda, who provided peace and refreshment in her house in Maracaibo for more writing.

I also thank Mary Jane Alexander, William Monroe, and M. S. Wyeth of Harper & Row.

And, finally, the people of St. Paul's Church, Tivoli (among them, my wife, Barbara): they have been very patient, and early adapted themselves to my handy excuse that writing the history of the diocese prevented me from paying them the attention they deserved.

Shewglie
Germantown, New York
November 17, 1983

THIS PLANTED VINE

1

The Beginnings

Here there bee not many people.
—ROBERT JUET

The geographical area of the original Diocese of New York was the entire state. It was not until 1838, and then only after profound misgivings, that the laws of the Episcopal Church were altered to permit the subdivision of dioceses within the state. Thus, the Diocese of New York was all that territory from Long Island's wave-washed tip to Niagara's steady roar. Within this vast space lay the Adirondack Mountains, whose forests sloped northward to the St. Lawrence plains. Further west were the high fields surrounding the Finger Lakes, where the curved horizon makes a man know that he truly inhabits a spherical earth. Below these lakes is the Southern Tier, lonely and grim-gray in winter, benign and balmy in summer. The state diocese knew all the moods and variations of nature. No citizen of the new nation would know them better than Hobart and Onderdonk, the much-traveled third and fourth bishops of the Diocese of New York.

Their predecessors, Samuel Provoost and Benjamin Moore, never saw the broad varieties of New York. They were town men, born and bred in Manhattan. It is one of the ironies of history that these men, the first bishops of the diocese, conceived their diocese more nearly as we do today: a jurisdiction flowing from the City of New York, dependent upon the metropolis, yet offering it the gifts and produce a city always requires from its rural surroundings.

The men and women who perceived the early fortunes of the Diocese of New York may have seen the state as a builder's square. The short arm is the Hudson Valley, stretching from Manhattan northward to Albany. The longer arm of the square reaches westward from Albany through the fertile valleys that summoned the white man, as they had the Indian. Except for the hamlets just beyond Brooklyn on Long Island, the Church in colonial New York was dependent upon rivers. The Dutch always preferred to settle on riverbanks or near small streams.[1] The great Hudson provided cheap transportation to Albany. The Post

Road—little more than a path in the early days of our history—was used only when necessary. At Albany, the Mohawk River led to the west; its valley would one day give the route for the canal whose commerce made the Port of New York the unquestioned mercantile capital of the young nation. Men of business would thereafter rush to the city, as their fathers had been tempted to do when the seat of national government left Philadelphia and established itself in Washington.

Our story begins much earlier, however. Indeed, it begins not on the land but on the sea. All the early voyagers and discoverers, including Columbus, shared a common goal: the enrichment of their sponsors. The financiers of expeditions to the Americas expected vast returns. Religious sentiments were, nevertheless, more in the forefront than is generally supposed; Columbus was a "proud, sensitive man who *knew* that his project would open fresh paths to wealth and the advancement of Christ's kingdom."[2] Upon his return to Spain, he addressed a letter to the Sovereigns in which he congratulated their majesties (after the manner of the age) for their being the instruments for "turning so many peoples to our holy faith, and afterwards for material benefits since not only Spain but all Christians will hence have refreshment and profit."[3] God and Caesar were to be coinheritors.

But when faith and profit set out together on a journey, faith is likely to be the tardy arrival. Religion played a conspicuous role in some North American settlements from Europe, but in other places mercantile interests were primary. And in yet other places (Jamestown comes to mind), where the principle was stated "to recover [the natives] out of the arms of the devil," religion seems to have been in fact something of a useful tool in the furtherance of the empire.

Manhattan Island is never fairer than in spring. It was, we like to think, at its very finest when, on April 17, 1524, Verrazano's *La Dauphine* came into New York Bay. He and his crew were probably the first white men to see New York.[4] They saw "the natives come toward us very cheerfully, making great shouts of admiration, showing us where we might come to land." But Verrazano didn't set foot on the land he so obviously admired. He probably feared the friendly natives might have second thoughts about the intruders. The discoverer turned about and sailed off into the Atlantic. But he marked on his map the name he had given the beautiful place he had just seen: "Angoulême," after Louise, the Queen Mother of France.

Neither that generation of natives, nor their children, need have feared white intrusion. For it was not until 1624 that the white man came into the harbor to stay.

The sailor is ever religious, at least when at sea. And, considering the dangers, it was with good reason that religious observance was steady and fervent in those early voyages. If the first services according to the Book of Common Prayer in New York were held in a military garrison, as we may suppose they were, then the first such services near New York were on shipboard, perhaps in the harbor itself. We are told that

> to avoid affronting God to the point of His becoming indifferent to a ship's fate, Sebastian Cabot charged that "no blaspheming of God, or detestable swearing be used . . . nor communication of ribaldrie filthy tales, or ungodly talke to be suffered in the company . . . neither dicing carding, tabling or other divelish games to be frequented, whereby ensueth not only povertie to the players, but also strif, variance, brauling . . . and provoking of God's most just wrath, and sworde of vengeance." Sebastian insists "that morning and evening prayer, with the common services appointed by the king's Majestie be read dayly by the chaplain or some other person learned," and "the Bible or paraphrases to be read devoutly and Christianly to God's honour, and for His grace to be obtained." As this indicates, every shipmaster provided himself with an Edward VI Book of Common Prayer.[5]

It is safe to say, then, that the Prayer Book and its observances accompanied the first English explorers and settlers in the New World.

However, the first white settlers in what is now New York City were not Englishmen, but Dutch. And, strange as it seems to us now, Manhattan Island was not the major place of settlement: it came after present-day Albany and Governors Island, as we shall see.

THE DUTCH CULTURE

Henry Hudson explored his river in 1609. He was then in the employ of the Dutch East India Company, which, on the strength of this and other explorations, claimed all the land between the Connecticut and Delaware rivers. A fort, named Nassau, was built 150 miles up the river, and when it was destroyed by flood in 1617, Fort Orange (now Albany) was built near by. The first settlers arrived in 1624: thirty families and some single men. They were Walloons and Huguenots. Most of them settled near Fort Orange, but a few remained on what is now Governors Island.

The West India Company, a newer enterprise, ordered forts to be built wherever expedient, and thus in 1625 a fort was built on Manhattan. As a precaution, and because it was general practice, Governor Pieter Minuit concluded a purchase of the island from the Indians in what has gone down in history as one of the better bargains ever made. The cost of the entire island of Manhattan was 60 guilders' worth of blankets, kettles, and trinkets. Within a year thirty houses and two hundred people were on the island.

The Dutch found the patroon system the easiest way to settle the land. Soon after 1629 large areas of land were awarded Dutchmen of good credit; their responsibility was to encourage settlement and improvement quickly. By far the most successful patroon was Kiliaen Van Rensselaer, a rich diamond merchant, landowner, and director of the West India Company; he wisely sent an able relative to New Amsterdam to develop the newly acquired property there. The Dutch were also willing to grant land patents to New England people of promise. Thus Hempstead (1643), Gravesend (1645), and Jamaica (1655) were settled and developed by families of English descent.

Dutch settlements included Esopus (now Kingston) and Schenectady; both had churches by 1657. The growth of New Amsterdam surrounding the fort there was steady, and at the northern end of the island Nieuw Haarlem was established in 1658, with an understanding that there would soon be a "good pious orthodox Minister" when the settlement numbered more than twenty families.

New Amsterdam fell to the English in 1664. The English were better colonizers than the Dutch, many of whom had chosen to return to their native land, whereas, during the middle years of the seventeenth century, troubles in England favored migration to the New World. For instance, New England grew from 20,000 people in 1640 to 50,000 in 1664; New Netherlands (which included all the Dutch settlements in and near New Amsterdam) numbered fewer than 10,000. On the whole, the Dutch in Holland had enjoyed unaccustomed religious toleration.

After the Duke of York accepted the gift of New Amsterdam from his brother, King Charles II, and renamed his possessions, there was little overt Dutch discontent. Even the Dutch Church seemed unthreatened in those first years. A steady flow of Dutch immigrants continued to enter the province, but it was noted that they preferred to live apart from the English. More interested in good fertile farmland, the Dutch spread throughout the Hudson Valley, New Jersey, northern Pennsylvania, and Long Island. The founding of churches is always a good indicator of permanent settlement, and thus we note with interest that the Dutch church in Kingston was founded in 1659, in Kinderhook in 1712, Claverack, Poughkeepsie, and Fishkill in 1716, Rhinebeck in 1731, Catskill and Coxsackie in 1732.

Two inheritances of Dutch rule were regrettable. The first was slavery. Dutch farmers employed numerous Negro slaves on their lands; 10 percent of Ulster County was reported to be slave in 1790. The other doubtful introduction was the patroon system. Though intended to be a means of quickly and profitably settling vacant land, it often resulted in the opposite. The system gave rich men great parcels of real estate and also conferred upon them certain rights and privileges. In practice, people of ability learned to avoid settling where they could never be freeholders, but only mere tenants.

The Dutch Church emphasized the importance of sermons, and these very often ran to more than two hours. The Dutch Church also took its teaching responsibilities seriously; the *voorlezer* combined the functions of sermon reader and schoolteacher. Liquor and tobacco were commonly used: "I frequently saw about a dozen old ladies sitting about the fire smoking," reported one visitor to a Dutch house. And another wrote that "it was a sad breach of politeness not to furnish the dominies when they made their pastoral visits with the choicest brew."

It has been said that the greatest influence of the Dutch upon New York was made after their surrender in 1664. As we have seen, Dutch immigration continued. "And they multiply more rapidly here than anywhere," commented one observer. Their language, in common use until after the Revolutionary War, gave household words and place-names we all know. Some are of interest in this history: Tarrytown is probably named for the wheat mill built there by Frederick Philipse soon after 1647; the Dutch word for wheat is *Tarwe*. Adrian Vander-Donck (an ancestor of Bishop Onderdonk) owned land on the banks of the Hudson north of New York City; "DeJonkheer Landt" means "estate of a gentleman"—in this case at what we now call Yonkers. The Bronx is named after Jonas Bronck.[6]

THE ENGLISH ASCENDANCY

The fort at New Amsterdam had been necessary to support the presence of the Dutch, and, subsequently, the English. It was a display of muscle, a focal center of the ascendant power. It was also the place where the people of the settlement would gather for accurate news. There they would see their neighbors in a setting that would at almost any time include the authorities of the province. Moreover, the fort, like the present day PX's, would always have the flavor of home.

This would include the Church, the Church of the Prayer Book, restored after Charles Stuart (King Charles II) "returned from his travels." The religious altercations of the Commonwealth hadn't deeply affected the colonies, which had, after all, been settled largely by people discontent with religion at home. But Restoration sentiment was apt to provide provincial governors with a piety and an enthusiasm for the Church of England that would be threatening for Puritans in Amer-

ica. The king's brother, James, Duke of York, had been far more affected by his mother's Roman Catholicism than had Charles. When the
Duke was given a large portion of North America, he knew he must
reckon with the predominant religions of the colonies there. James
insisted that the Prayer Book be available to all who might desire its
services, but there was no ducal command that those services were
required. At least for the time being, the Calvinism of the Hudson Valley Dutch might coexist harmoniously with Congregationalism of New
England, the developing Presbyterianism of New Jersey, the Quakers in
Pennsylvania, and the Roman Catholics and Episcopalians of Maryland
and Virginia. London seems to have pursued a policy of minimizing
religious differences in order to consolidate English claims in North
America. The Stuarts had indeed learned their lesson!

Richard Nicolls was the Duke's agent. His demand that the Dutch
surrender New Amsterdam was softened by the assurance that the British contemplated religious toleration. The Dutch believed this, for it
was agreeable to statements King Charles had made from Holland as he
waited to return to the English throne in 1660. We may assume that
after Peter Stuyvesant capitulated to Nicolls's demand, September 7,
1664, the usual place of worship at the fort became available to Nicolls's chaplain. This is to assume, also, that a chaplain did accompany
Nicolls across the Atlantic when the governor came to claim the Duke's
territory. Not every important voyage had a chaplain. We do know that
in New Amsterdam (now called New York) the surplice was discouraged as being too distinct from the black gowns of the Calvinists. This
and other salutary attitudes enabled the English officiants of those first
days to initiate Prayer Book services at the fort on Sundays, following
the hour of the Dutch service. This cooperative use of the fort continued until the Dutch church was built, in 1693. Thus, for more than a
quarter of a century after the English ousted Stuyvesant from New Amsterdam, the Dutch Reformed and the Episcopal services were held in
the garrison. Meanwhile, Episcopal churches were built in Boston,
Perth Amboy, Philadelphia, and Charleston, South Carolina. The only
conclusion possible is that despite royal rule in New York, the royal
Church was very weak there. This view is supported by the Venerable
Society's later declaration that "there was little sense of religion and a
most notorious corruption of manners" in New York.

The Dutch regained New Amsterdam for seven months in 1673–74,
and then lost that possession forever. The new English governor, Edmund Andros, arrived with a disciplined eye to appraise, and a memory
to correct, the faults he found. The fruits of toleration in New Amsterdam may be weighed by his statement, "Ministers have been so scarce
and Religions so many."[7] A Church of England minister's stipend of

£21.68 is recorded for 1674, but the name of its claimant is unknown. He may well have been the first priest in what is now the Diocese of New York.

English ascendance in New York was certain after 1674. The global prominence of the Dutch diminished. Britain now entered upon its great period of colonial development. The effects of this English predominance have vast importance in our history; strong English influence is to be found in the lives of New Yorkers long after the colonies won independence from Britain.

Colonial development was slow because North America was far removed across the ocean from the mother country and, once here, adventurers knew they would have a hard lot. Even so, we will see a slow but persistent trickle of English clergymen disembark at New York, and with greater or lesser success enter upon the work of their calling. In August 1678, the Reverend Charles Woolley arrived. He found a Lutheran and a Reformed minister who disdained speaking to each other. Woolley later told the story that he invited the pair, and their wives, to dinner with the understanding that whoever spoke Low Dutch would forfeit a bottle of good Madeira; they must converse in the theological tongues of German or Latin. The clergy went home late that evening good friends. (But what about their wives?)[8]

It would be false to suggest that such camaraderie between the clergy of various national churches was widely counted a desirable thing in the seventeenth century. Religious pluralism then was almost untried. When Charles II proposed a limited toleration at the eve of his restoration he was soon disappointed by a Parliament unpersuaded that it was a good—or practicable—thing. For some, toleration amounted to a weakness of conviction; moreover, it might admit Roman Catholic missionaries into Protestant territory. As early as 1584 Richard Hakluyt, a Church of England priest and author whose name we all remember from schooldays, submitted to the government of Elizabeth I *A Discourse on Western Planting,* which was mainly a proposal for presenting the Gospel to the American Indians before the Roman Catholics could meddle with them.[9] This theme of preempting Roman Catholic efforts will recur in our narrative. Until modern times the Roman Catholic presence appeared as a threat to the political and social as well as the religious settlement of the Protestant world. Thus, authority conveyed by episcopal ordination was sometimes winked at by the English missionaries: the fact that a missionary was sent over from the Established Church meant more than apostolic succession. State approval took precedence over ecclesiastic credentials.[10] Satan's politics were those of the Bishop of Rome, especially after the Scottish uprisings of 1715 and 1745.

Soon after his convivial dinner party, Woolley sailed up the Hudson and visited the English garrison at Albany. This may have been the first attempt by a Manhattan-based English clergyman to discover what responsibilities awaited him upriver. Before many more years a goodly number of Church of England clergymen would pass through the Highlands and under the "Blue Mountains" (as the Catskills were known universally until the mid-nineteenth century) en route to the frontier settlements at Albany, Schenectady, and Fort Hunter. The river was their easiest thoroughfare for nearly two hundred years.

At Albany, Woolley would have found a town of no more than 4,000 people with loyalties to their former Dutch rulers. His arrival there would have gone unremarked except for those who feared, rightly, that the Episcopal presence in this hitherto Dutch province would increase, accompanied by the authority of the new sovereign. For the Dutch Reformed Church, of course, this meant diminished prestige. The question, spoken or not, was plainly this: What would hereafter be the rights and privileges of the other churches? How far would the Church of England press its claim to be the established religion of the province?

EARLY TROUBLES IN CHURCH AND STATE

The initial difficulties did not arise from the zeal of English clergy, but from the political expediencies perceived by the royal governors. Thomas Dongan, a Roman Catholic, was appointed governor in 1683. He arrived in Manhattan with a Church of England chaplain—and also a Jesuit priest. Like any sound political practitioner of his time, the governor believed that the national Church could promote peace and unity in the province. When Dongan said, "Every town ought to have a minister"[11] he meant an Episcopal minister. Perhaps he aimed at something else, too: he may have realized that most people in the colony had no church loyalties whatever,[12] something unheard-of in Europe. It is said there were usually only twenty-five or thirty people at the English service in the fort on a Sunday morning, a poor showing considering the Church was then a social as well as a religious meeting place.[13]

Several years later, in 1692, the Reverend John Miller arrived in New York with two companies of soldiers. He reported ninety Church of England families who worshiped at the fort, certainly a significant increase over the twenty-five to thirty persons reported earlier. He further said that there were 450 Dutch Reformed families, thirty "Dutch" (that is, German) Lutheran, 200 Huguenot, and twenty Jewish families in the town. In 1686 Governor Andros had directed that worship according to the Book of Common Prayer be maintained every

Sunday and Holy Day, and "the Blessed Sacrament administered 'regularly.' "[14] It was assumed that the other churches were free to continue as long as they did not disturb the peace—words not unlike the liberal declaration of Charles from Holland in 1660. There was also provision by Andros that clergy and schoolmasters would be licensed by the Archbishop of Canterbury. Clearly, the English Church was not now merely one church among equals. The Church espoused by the sovereign was to be the preferred religion of the colony.

CONTEMPORARY CHURCHMANSHIP

What kind of religious thinking was now predominant in the mother country? With the restoration, Crown and Church had resumed their former positions but, despite the hopes and promises of both, it was a flawed partnership. The new king, Charles II, was not the churchman his father had been. For its part, the Church of England was exhausted by theological controversy. There was an inevitable reaction against Calvinism and "spiritual" preaching. Furthermore, the writings of continental theologians had come to the attention of the university faculties. By the last decades of the seventeenth century Calvinism seemed dated, out of touch. This was partly due to the subtle growth of a new discipline that came to be called science. The king was an enthusiastic supporter of the Royal Society; his interests embraced marine life, plants, and astronomy. The Calvinists disdained such preoccupations.

And there was another competitor on the religious scene. Now that all Cavalier things shone with new luster, it was remembered that many Roman Catholics had heroically supported the old king and had, in fact, even sheltered his son, the present sovereign. The country at large was fiercely anti-Roman (Fox's *Book of Martyrs* saw to that), but Roman Catholicism in the court was an open secret. Charles II received the ministrations of his old friend Father Huddleston only on his deathbed, but very soon it was clear that James II intended to foster the Roman position in England. The court was both a receiver of trends and a pacesetter for new things in the air. In Elizabethan times the Church of England had chosen a unique middle way between papal Catholicism and Genevan Protestantism. Now, in all this Restoration ferment, a restatement, a new settlement of position, was much needed. This was all the more crucial because there appeared a division in the national Church quite unlike anything experienced before. On the whole, the English country clergy were old-fashioned high churchmen of the Laudian school. Many of them had wrested their parishes from Independent clergy who had benefited by the Commonwealth proscription of

Episcopalians. On the other hand, the bishops and urban clergy tended to a wider view of the Church and its role in national life. They were much influenced by the Platonists of Cambridge, who, avoiding the rigidities of the schoolmen and Calvin, prized tolerance, advocated comprehension within the English Church, and elevated the reasoning ability of man as a useful theological apparatus.

This was to be the prevailing characteristic of eighteenth century religion and, of course, it would have an impact upon the Church in the American colonies. This new line of thought was useful in meeting the needs of the age and, in any case, was a natural development away from exhausted former loyalties. Though much maligned in subsequent generations, there were values in this peculiarly English theological stance. In a time of wide philosophic speculation (Locke, Hobbes, Descartes), exciting scientific invention (the telescope, barometer, thermometer, and microscope), and poetic humanism (Addison, Dryden, Pope), the state Church flourished partly because it appeared able happily to assimilate and rejoice in the intellectual probings of its time. In addition, there was an attractiveness about what the new thinkers were saying. The Englishman's religion had always tended to condense his belief into the "godly, righteous and sober life," enjoined by the epistle and the Prayer Book. Whichcote of Cambridge saw the Christian religion as sent to man from God "to elevate and sweeten human nature."[15] A most pleasant statement, but was anything more contrary to Calvin?

In a few years, the successors of the Cambridge Platonists would be called Latitude Men because, to many, the parameters of their doctrine were practically nonexistent. They appealed to reason as secondary only to the Bible: "To go against reason is to go against God," they said. They gladly followed the path blazed earlier by the man we know as Jacobus Arminius (1560–1609), who declared that Christ died for all, not only for the elect. But that was only part of their positive line of thought. Dismissing the Early Church Fathers, much of tradition, and the methods of the schoolmen of the past, they perceived an immanent moral law within mankind which, when consulted, vitalized the Christian's everyday life. "The Spirit of man is the candle of the Lord" was their celebrated slogan. They saw religion as a spontaneous, cheerful human endeavor, possible, even natural, for all. The Prayer Book was as good a handbook as any devised by man. And, there was no better corporate statement of God's beneficence than the English Church.

The Latitudinarians were loyal to Church order. Perhaps the combination of attendance at court and the burdens of strengthening the position of the state Church, plus the reason and orderliness they so highly valued, led them to prefer the ordinances and customs of the

Church established in England. While never exactly *champions* of Episcopacy and the Book of Common Prayer (for they disdained enthusiasm), they were *advocates* of these national inheritances. They liked
the liturgy, its "solemnity, gravity and primitive simplicity, its freedom
from affected phrases or mixture of vain and doubtful opinions."[16] The
Articles, Book of Homilies, the Three Creeds—and now, nature—
formed the reference points of Latitudinarian thinking. They assumed a
world where parts of Morning Prayer and Evening Prayer, with Bible
reading, were routine in religious households. Theirs was the Englishman's Church that

> brought little compulsion to bear on him, but it continually taught
> him the concept of duty, of personal responsibility for right decisions
> with regard to his conduct, and for a moral life.[17]

It is probably true that the Latitudinarians had jettisoned too much
history, too much of religious mystery. It is certainly true that comprehension eventually became overly cordial to Deism and Unitarianism.
If many of our Episcopal founding fathers are accused of imprecision of
belief, they can easily retort that they had worthy teachers in their religious background. Nevertheless, Norman Sykes is surely right when he
appraises the Latitudinarians as men

> called upon to face both a revolutionary change in the intellectual
> outlook of educated Englishmen and a condition of post-Restoration
> society characterized by a disregard for morality and the restraints of
> good conduct. Against this dual challenge they struggled with cour-
> age, sincerity and ability; and if the degree of their success in both
> spheres was partial and qualified, the difficulty of their task should be
> remembered in extenuation of their failure.[18]

The English Church, then, was characterized by a broad, Latitudinarian view of the world and religion in the last years of the seventeenth century and the first decades of the next. The Low Churchmen,
descendants of the Puritans, were now disorganized, their Calvinism
discredited in the wake of Restoration ebullience. The High Church
party saw their victory at the return of the sovereign in 1660 confirmed
in the Prayer Book of 1662. But these men, too, felt the sands of time
running against them as events unfolded. When in 1689 Parliament
promoted the abdication of King James II and invited his daughter
Mary and her husband William the Dutchman to take his place, six
bishops and about four hundred other clergy found they could not in
conscience acquiesce in the arrangement because they had taken an
oath to James II. They departed from the Church of England and were
henceforth regarded as schismatics—and dangerous ones at that, after

the Scottish uprisings. Their leaving the Church of England had two
notable effects upon the Church in America. First, it further weakened
the High Church emphasis in England; and, secondly, it was at the
hands of the successors of bishops of this line that Samuel Seabury
would be consecrated almost one hundred years later.

If Latitudinarianism appears to be the growing and dominant
theme in English Church life, its very drawbacks fostered remedies in
the persons of the earnest young men whose "blooming piety"[19] led
them to form small groups aimed at the bettering of religious practice,
especially in the London churches. The prevailing Latitudinarianism
placed little emphasis on missionary work, for instance; these "clubs,"
as we shall see, regarded Christian missions as of first importance.
Flourishing in the shadow of the Latitude men, the groups of laymen
(often guided by parish priests) reasserted the high traditions of the
Laudians and emerged as a force within the national Church. But there
was little friction between the Latitudinarians and these High Churchmen as, for instance, they contemplated the Church's role in the Americas. The High Churchmen simply went forth to do what their Latitudinarian friends did not care to do. Chaplain John Miller was one of the
early English clergymen who had definite ideas about promoting the
Church, and he had no illusions about what he saw in New York. He
reported that people, as we have already suspected, attended service at
the fort as a social excursion. He recognized that the frontier situation
then (1692) existing in New York province demanded more clergy
from England; doubtless, he hoped some would replace those of whom
he thoroughly disapproved.

Most novel of ideas, John Miller suggested that a suffragan bishop
be sent from England to oversee the Church in the new world.[20] We are
tempted to guess what might have happened had a suffragan arrived
then. A suffragan is another bishop who acts in the name, and at the
pleasure, of *the* bishop of the diocese. Thus, the Bishop of London
might have suffragans appointed to carry out his responsibilities in
America. Perhaps this might have been successfully managed in the
1690s. The throne then seemed safely Protestant. Stuart Catholicism
(no longer a secret) was now no threat so long as Protestant Stuarts
were closer in succession. There would have been minimal Puritan
opposition in New York at that time, though subsequent claims made
in the name of the Church of England would, in the near future,
strengthen Congregational and Presbyterian opposition in New England and in New Jersey. Before the next century was half finished the
sense of independence in the colonies had developed so that every
sign of interference from Westminster would be challenged. When,

some years later, there was a possibility that a bishop might be sent across the Atlantic, dissenting opposition in the colonies frightened the government from acting. In any event, when John Miller spoke of the need for a bishop in America in 1692, it is doubtful that the Church of England had any notion of how a bishop could be exported to America. The Church's failure at first, the government's unwillingness later on, and the inevitable involvement of the one with the other all along prevented any bishop of the English line from claiming New York until Samuel Provoost disembarked on Easter Day, 1787.

THE MINISTRIES ACT

The same year (1692) that John Miller made his recommendation about a suffragan bishop for the colonies, Governor Benjamin Fletcher of New York believed he threw down the gauntlet in a move that was nothing less than a challenge to the integrity of the other churches in New York. Fletcher was a professional soldier. He wanted things done according to the rules, especially if he made them or if they were laws congenial to him. Like many colonial officers, he flourished in the presence of the powerful and rich; thus he was content to continue Dongan's policy of granting large tracts of land in the province to favored people. He was thoroughly Church of England and was probably uncomfortable with the variety of churches he saw in New York. He planned to enact a law that would provide Church of England clergy in specified places in New York City and three adjacent counties. It has been said that Fletcher was both reckless and careless. These are grave defects in a provincial governor who is about to insist upon an unpopular act. The Provincial Assembly reluctantly passed the law subsequently known as the Ministries Act (or sometimes the Settlement Act) in 1693. It provided public support for a "sufficient Protestant minister" in the counties of New York, Richmond, Westchester, and Queens. To the governor, as to any English official, the words *Protestant minister* in an English province implied a clergyman of the Church of England. Dissenters in America thought otherwise. They, also, claimed the name Protestant.[21] The Assembly had given the governor the bill he required of them, but in his carelessness (and possibly the Assembly's wiliness) the law was fatally nonspecific. It had stated that a minister was to be settled and maintained in Westchester, Eastchester, Yonkers, Pelham Manor, Rye, Mamaroneck, and Bedford: all north of New York town, where also there was to be a Church of England minister, according to Fletcher's plan. In addition, there would be ministers in or near Ja-

maica, Hempstead, and Staten Island. Their salaries were to be paid by
tax. Two wardens and ten vestrymen for each church were to be elected
by the local freeholders.

Fletcher had hoped for a stricter act, but the Assembly's delay
forced him to gamble on what he could get. And he supposed he had
done quite well. Amazing as it seems, he thought every Church body in
the four counties would conform to the worship of the Church of England. It has been asserted that the Crown's instructions to the governor
included his appointing ministers to the churches. Since the governor
would be expected to approve only Episcopal clergy, some sagacious
Dissenters welcomed the "Ministry's Act" because it conferred the
right of appointment upon local persons.[22] As it turned out, this reasoning was far more cogent than the governor's, who was perhaps beaten at
his own game.

Fletcher was dreaming! In 1692 there were not more than one or
two Episcopal congregations in the entire Province of New York, while
the Dutch Reformed congregations may have numbered as many as
fifty.[23] Fletcher's scheme was soon shown to be faulty.

TRINITY CHURCH, GODMOTHER OF THE DIOCESE

At the New York town elections of January 1694, the freeholders elected
three Episcopalians and nine Dissenters to the vestry; the majority
claimed the right to appoint a minister of their own choice—a Dissenter,
of course. The next year's election saw only one Episcopalian elected.
By this time, it was clear that the Ministries Act would never create
Church of England parishes of the existing Dissenting ones, and so, for
a time, the law was forgotten while a far more interesting drama unfolded in New York. The town vestry, though predominantly Dissenting
in sympathy, appointed to their as yet church-less cure a man named
William Vesey. He had been educated at Harvard and was for some
years a lay leader in Congregational churches. He had also served at
Kings Chapel, Boston, and seems to have longed to return to the
Church of his "Jacobite" father. In 1696 he was lay reader in Hempstead.[24] When he was called to be the town rector in New York in
November of that year, he was eager to cross the ocean for ordination in
the Church of England. This he did, and was made deacon on July 25,
1697, and ordained priest the following August 2. When he returned for
his induction by Governor Fletcher on Christmas Day, 1697, he found
an English church formed in New York. It was named Trinity.

Fletcher's ill-conceived attempt to force the English Church on all the communities near New York town thus bore a strange (and increasingly rich) fruit. When it became apparent that the Dissenters could prevent or delay the appointment of Church of England clergy by the very provisions of Fletcher's Ministries Act, the Episcopalians of New York chose a much easier way: instead of intruding themselves into existing Dissenting parishes, they would circumvent the entire vestry provision, name their governing body "managers," and begin a new and distinctly separate church, Episcopal from its beginning. Forgetting for a moment the Ministries Act, Fletcher seized upon this plan as a face-saving alternative. He encouraged the "managers" of Trinity Church by giving them the right to collect money for a church building. He further endowed them with all "weifts, wrecks, Drift whales and whatsoever else Drives from the high sea and is then lost below high water mark" as a further aid in building the contemplated church. There was also in the governor's mind a certain farm of sixty-two acres recently escheated to the Crown, which might be leased on favorable terms to the new church. This was the Bogardus Land, variously known as the Queen's Farm or the King's Farm. In 1705 it was actually given to Trinity Church, a munificence that in subsequent years would be challenged unsuccessfully in the courts. Fletcher's generosity, which was never considered either reckless or careless by the Trinity officials, has made that man somewhat more of a hero to New York Episcopalians than he otherwise deserves to be.

This was the beginning of a church corporation whose importance in the Diocese of New York will cause us to examine its records again and again in this history. Vesey's induction as first rector took place in the Dutch church—and two Dutch Reformed ministers served as witnesses. In so doing, these dominies lent a gentle touch to proceedings which must otherwise have been abrasive to the Dutch consciousness in New York. Their presence also demonstrates again the necessary political involvement of the churches in the province.

The managers of Trinity (soon they would finally adopt the title wardens and vestry) were eager to engage William Vesey, who was "then with them." They lent him £95 for his passage to England. Perhaps the fact that he had been a year at Kings Chapel led the managers to think Vesey would be an able rector in a town situation. Or perhaps they chose a clergyman not already in the Province of New York in order to avoid entanglements with the difficulties inherent in the Ministries Act. The wardens were Thomas Wenham and Robert Lurting, and they appear to have been far wiser men than was the governor.

The new Trinity Church was something of a showplace in New York and would have been exhibited with pride by its adherents. Thus a Boston visitor recorded her 1704 stay with friends in New York, who

> are generally of the Church of England and have a New England Gentleman for their minister, and a very fine church set out with all Customary requisites. There are also a Dutch church and Divers Conventicles as they call them, viz, Baptist, Quakers, etc. They are not strict in keeping the Sabbath as in Boston and other places . . .[25]

The first Trinity vestrymen were Caleb Heathcote, William Mercet, John Tudor, James Emott, William Morris, Thomas Clark, Ebenezer Wilson, Samuel Burt, James Evets, Nathaniel Marston, Michael Howden, John Crooke, William Sharpas, Lawrence Read, David Jamison, William Huddleston, Gabriel Ludlow, Thomas Burroughs, William Janeway, and John Merret—merely a list of twenty names, some not ever significant in the annals of the Church or the City of New York, but others very much involved in the fortunes of generation after generation until the present day.

In the years 1697–1700 there was only one Episcopal church formally organized and denominated as such in the Province of New York, and but three others north of Maryland. It is probable that the Pell family had already gathered a church at their manor in Westchester. In the ten years following 1700 ten congregations were formed in the Province of New York, and they were, for the most part, at exactly those places mentioned by Fletcher in the Ministries Act. But they owed their existence not to that martinet, but rather to something entirely remote from him: the Society for the Propagation of the Gospel.

2

"Come Over and Help Us." The SPG

When I first arrived in the Province (AD 1692) I found it (Westchester) the most rude and heathenish country I every saw in my whole life.
—CALEB HEATHCOTE

The beginnings of the SPG (we shall abbreviate it, as do some of the encyclopedias) are to be found in the nagging sense of responsibility felt by cognizant Church of England people who addressed themselves to the question: What is being done by the Church in North America? By 1700 it was obvious that the future of the American coast from Georgia to Nova Scotia lay with the English. Roman Catholics and Puritans had made conspicuous settlements in Maryland and the colonies of Massachusetts, Connecticut, and New Haven. Quakers had managed to put down roots in Pennsylvania and Rhode Island, in similar efforts to evade restrictions at home. The Church of England, however, would not be expected to make such particular colonizing efforts: as the national Church it might claim *all* the American seaboard as its proper field. Whenever churchmen in England summoned imagination sufficient to consider the problems and opportunities of America, this claim, sometimes expressed by zealous churchmen, created a fear that helped put iron into the souls of the patriots of 1776.

The iniquities of Restoration clergy in England have often enough been cataloged. It may shed some new light, however, to remember that despite the jubilant return of the Church of England to its former dominance, and the restrictive laws enacted by Parliament to safeguard those rights, the hierarchy in England must often have been preoccupied by the presence of Roman Catholicism in the court during the 1660s. The Queen, many ministers and mistresses, were avowed Roman Catholics. King James II declared himself converted to the Church of

Rome and sought to promote the fortunes of his Church. Though King
Charles II was buried according to the rite of the English Church, his
deathbed conversion to Rome was no secret.

In the light of Roman Catholic presence at court, the lingering
Puritan pressures in many urban centers in England, and the restrictive
measures adopted by Parliament to ensure the privileges of the Church
of England, it is understandable that the pastoral oversight of a coast-
line three thousand miles away would not be uppermost in the minds
of those who were, from time to time, reminded that they were responsible for America. The English hierarchy has been criticized unfairly for
an apparent lassitude. The fact is that all was not as well at home as
some historians have claimed. When, in 1675, Henry Compton, Bishop
of London (1675–1713), made inquiry about America, the reply given
him (and which we may believe he suspected would be given) was that
an order from the reign of King Charles I provided that "the Bishop of
London for the time being [have] the care and pastoral charge of sending over Ministers into our British Foreign Plantations and having jurisdiction over them."[1] Compton thereafter *assumed* jurisdiction, but his
authority to do so was clouded by the fact that Charles II had commis-
sioned Gilbert Sheldon, Archbishop of Canterbury, to oversee the
Church in Virginia and elsewhere. The history and records of which
English prelate had authority—and how much authority—in America
are confusing. By 1686 the Bishop of London appears to have had jurisdiction in New York, but his powers were limited because he could not
give approval to benefices and he could not issue marriage licenses or
probate wills. It was Richard Terrick, Bishop of London, at the outbreak
of the Revolution who put the matter of American jurisdiction precisely. Though Terrick had made no extensive claim to power, he did
state that America was one of "the more distant parts, which by long
usage have been considered as having a more particular relationship to
the Bishop of London, than to any other Bishop."[2]

Even so, episcopal authority in New York, as elsewhere in the colonies, was effectively limited to withdrawing ministers from America or
sending them here.

It was one thing for an independent Puritan or Separatist minister
to cross the ocean with a shipload of emigrants. It was quite another to
send a minister of the Church of England to a land where there was
none of the ecclesiastical framework and supervision required in a
church of episcopal orders. Bishop Compton needed some kind of system, some regulatory body, and it would have to be tailor-made for the
work at hand. There must be authorities on both sides of the ocean:
sending missionaries to America without due oversight would risk

scandal. (Compton's fears were well founded, as is proved by the records in Lambeth Palace Library; but it is pleasant to record that there
are comparatively few negative reports about New York clergy there; for
some reason, Virginia seemed to attract the troublesome ones.)

In an earlier day, the New England Company had fostered a ministry. An organization composed of churchmen and Dissenters had existed, having been chartered by Charles II in 1662. The religious societies already mentioned appear to have been fairly common in
Restoration London, perhaps encouraged by a fear of popery on the one
hand, and the obvious decline of morals on the other. We are told,
further, that the societies sprang up to counteract "the infamous clubs
of atheists, Deists, Socinians." Like the phenomena which soon would
be discerned in eighteenth-century Wesleyan practices, and still later
when the Parliamentary upheavals of 1832 seemed to threaten the
Church's prerogatives, these Restoration societies used the Church's
existing customs to confront sluggards within and unbelievers without.
Daily prayers, for instance, were urged in the parish churches. Due
preparation for the sacrament was stressed. The Eucharist every Sunday
and holy day was promoted. In brief, these were groups dissatisfied
with the Latitude men.

Active in such a movement was Thomas Bray (1656–1730). He was
educated at Oxford's All Souls College, and after several curacies became rector of Sheldon in Warwickshire in 1690, a position he held till
near the day of his death forty years later. Bray seems to have been an
enthusiastic participant in the improving societies and when an appeal
came from Maryland for help in the Church there in 1696, Compton
asked Bray to go as his commissary.

Commissary? The word is new in the hierarchical appointments of
the English Church. When the governor and assembly in Maryland
framed their appeal to Compton, they asked for "a superintendent,
commissary, or suffragan."[3] Was the function of a commissary ever defined officially? And did the various men who carried the title in the
several colonies follow the guidelines laid upon them? Probably, the
frontier situation required a flexibility the Restoration Church was
strangely able to supply. The title was perhaps invented by Compton,
whose own Diocese of London was at one time in his episcopate administered by "commissories." The commissary appears to have been
the bishop's representative. His duties were to report to, and reprove in
the name of, the Bishop of London. As it developed, the commissary
probably had about as much authority as he wanted to have and his
colleagues cared to extend to him.

Due to distressing delays and the general affable inactivity that characterized the English Church's administration of its colonial responsibilities, Bray did not sail for North America for three years. (Many years later, in 1946, Archbishop Fisher graciously apologized to a General Convention for the "extremely ineffective way" his predecessors had exercised their responsibilities in the colonies.) Bray, however, was not idle during those three years. He recognized two primary needs for the Church in America: missionaries and libraries. So, during his wait, he founded, in 1698, the Society for Propagation of Christian Knowledge (SPCK: a familiar acronym). Compton gave his blessing to the society, as he would similarly approve the missionary society Bray was conceiving.

Bray remained in Maryland only a few months. Very wisely, he saw that his role should be neither missionary nor troubleshooter in America; rather, his gifts lay in organizing and promoting the work he had at heart. Thus he returned quickly to the only place where the organizing and promoting could effectively be done: England.

The first meeting of the chartered Society for the Propagation of the Gospel in Foreign Parts was held on June 27, 1701. There were four bishops, six laymen, nineteen other clergy present; the Archbishop of Canterbury presided. A splendid beginning. Successive meetings usually at St. Martin's-in-the-Fields, London, were equally well attended, says a contemporary report, "the episcopate being largely represented notwithstanding that the hour was frequently as early as eight or nine in the morning"[4]—an interesting comment inasmuch as King Charles II was known to have been up and ready for the day's activities soon after five in the morning.

At these Society meetings, in the years that followed, the members would inquire "into the religious state of the colonies, and information was sought and obtained from trustworthy persons at home and abroad." And funds were raised, again and again. In the Lambeth archives may be seen the reports sent across the ocean. They were read, discussed, resolved when possible. We can be glad that the eighteenth was a broad-minded century. And some of the bishops present may be forgiven if they rejoiced (silently) that the parson about whom they were now hearing was out of their diocese. They are not always dull reports; sin always travels with sanctity, and sometimes overtakes it. But there were the saints, too—and many of them—who faced the uncertainties of North America. New York had more than its share of them.

The SPG maintained clergy, and sometimes schoolmasters. School-teaching and the ordained ministry were then very closely associated. Many of the colonial churches had a schoolhouse nearby. Education was a Christian responsibility and taken very seriously.

THE MISSIONARY ENTERPRISE BEGINS

In 1701 the Province of New York had perhaps 25,000 people in twenty-five towns or hamlets. Ten of the settlements—one thinks of Esopus (Kingston), for instance—were thoroughly and doggedly Dutch. The only Episcopal church was the new Trinity "at New York town," although we know congregations were increasingly forming to worship according to the Prayer Book in other places: New Rochelle and Albany come to mind. And it may be that the congregation gathered at the Pell Manor predated the building of Trinity Church in New York City. Within ten years the Episcopal Church would be firmly settled in a dozen or more other places in the province. This was almost entirely due to Thomas Bray and his colleagues. In February 1702, they decided to send six priests of the Church of England to New York.

The first to arrive was promising Patrick Gordon, bound for Jamaica, on Long Island. Alas, he died less than two weeks after arriving. Soon after, John Bartow arrived, assigned to Rye, Jamaica, and Westchester. These were satellite settlements, explicitly mentioned in the Ministries Act. Manhattan was already the heart, beginning to give life and direction to the surrounding villages. Before we see how the SPG embarked upon its work in New York, however, let us make one final survey of the situation in the province. We have seen that Governor Fletcher foresaw Episcopal parishes in various hamlets in the three counties near New York town, and a major one there, too. Trinity Church in New York had been founded in 1697, and had a resident rector by the time the SPG began sending missionaries to the province. There were enough Episcopalians in the outlying settlements such as Bedford, Rye, Jamaica, Richmond, to lend a hopeful picture to the Society's directors. Further, there were prominent landowners, some even empowered to style themselves lords of the manors, to urge the Church upon their tenants (and perhaps pay for its services). The royal governors, especially Fletcher and his successor, Bellomont, saw that their interests would not be hurt by growth of the Church of England. Upriver, there was promise for a church in Schenectady. As early as 1698 Lord Bellomont was fearful that the Jesuits might implant their insidious notions among the Indians before the Church of England could get to them.[5] Business interests no longer regarded New York as a wasteland fit only for a fort guarding the river to Albany. The entrepreneurs (like the governors, with whom they worked) found the Church a potential handmaid for their activities. Moreover, a new impetus had entered the English imagination: "a vague missionary feeling for the benefits of British rule extended."[6]

All together, then, it was the fullness of time for the Church of England in New York.

MISSION TO THE PALATINES: A NOBLE FAILURE?

A peculiar instance of SPG involvement in the colonization process took place in the settlement called East Camp (now Germantown), one hundred miles upriver from Manhattan. The story is a sad one. It begins with one of the early New York magnates, Robert Livingston. Soon after settling in Albany in the 1680s, Livingston managed to gain not only a wife with a notable dowry, but also patents for huge land holdings on the east bank of the river opposite the Blue Mountains, confirmed by each governor. Land was useless to proprietors unless there were people living on it. Now, it happened that in 1709 Queen Anne had, in London, a large number of refugees from her Palatinate possessions. Governor Hunter seized this opportunity to help his Queen, his friend Livingston—and himself. He arranged for the Crown to purchase a large area of Livingston's land with a view to transporting the Palatines there. Livingston was glad to sell, especially since he was permitted to write into the bargain a provision giving him the contract to feed the Germans. The Crown was attracted by the proposition that the Palatines could produce tar for the royal navy (though few pine trees of that sort were to be found in the Hudson River Valley). The Palatines, knowing London was but a temporary refuge, probably were eager to cross the Atlantic.

It was a cruel venture from beginning to end. "Packed into quarters too limited for cattle,"[7] many of the wretched Palatines died during the long voyage. Worse, once in the New World, they were quarantined aboard ship in New York Bay for much of the hot summer of 1710, and arrived at their new upriver home only toward autumn. Their houses that first winter were burrows quickly dug into hillsides, the entrances protected by canvas flaps. The next year those who survived produced some tar, but not nearly what had been promised. By 1712 even Governor Hunter had to admit the project was a failure (and some of his investment lost). The Palatines scattered up and down the river and also in new settlements west of Schenectady, becoming in time progenitors of many a worthy Hudson River family.

As early as May 1709 the SPG determined to send "a German minister" with the "poor Palatines." By this was meant a German clergyman ordained in the Church of England.[8] The Archbishop of Canterbury and the Bishop of London wisely advised the directors not to "meddle therein" until Her Majesty's government had made a disposition of the embarrassing campers in London. But, hearing that they would indeed soon embark upon their pitch-making enterprise, the SPG inquired about sending a clergyman with them. The Society seemed unaware that there was already a Calvinist clergyman, Joshua Kocherthal, with the Palatines. Nevertheless, six of the refugees "residing at Bable Bridge in St. Clare's, Southwark,"[9] knew of a German with Church of England ordination. They petitioned the "Society of Divines meeting at St. Paul's, London [on behalf of] Mr. John Frederick Haeger, whose care and unwearied diligence in propagating of your petitioner's spiritual welfare by his constant praying, preaching and visiting obligeth us humbly to desire his presence and continuance of his ministry among us."[10]

Haeger accompanied the Palatines on their "long and tedious" voyage. In a letter written from New York town to the secretary of the Society, he wrote,

> I had hopes of transporting this people into the Church of Christ as by law established in England, but after my landing I found that the Lutheran minister in the country had made already a separation and administered the Holy Sacrament to such of his confession as arrived in the ship before ours; persuading them that they ought to stick by that, in which they were bred and born; which Mr. Kocherdal [sic] after his arrival confirmed also, in so much that the separation between the Reformed and the Lutherans is fully made.[11]

Joshua Kocherthal was granted £20 by the SPG in 1714.[12]

Not for the first time, nor for the last, had the Episcopalians supposed they could enlist the loyalties of those already persuaded otherwise. But Haeger, who was ordained deacon and priest in London just prior to his departure for the East Camp, was ever an optimist.[13] Very soon he informed the Society that he performed divine service in the City Hall of New York, and hoped a shipment of German prayer books would promote Episcopal worship, "as there is a want of liturgies in the German tongue." About the same time, Lewis Morris wrote the Society stating he had reason to think his Dutch neighbors in Fordham would "join the church in the Sacraments and other rites, had they the Dutch Common Prayer Book, and a minister who understood their language. I have taken some pains with one of their ministers Henricius Beyse, and have prevailed on him to accept Episcopal ordination."[14]

Much depended upon books. Haeger lamented that "a great many of the books bought for me by the Society have been spoiled by the seawater." Throughout his valiant ministry among the Palatines, Haeger, like Morris, believed that the simple solution of having prayer books in translation would gather the people into the Church of England. His letters also beg for a "summer gown" (that is, a lightweight Geneva preaching gown), and a surplice. He organized such congregation he was able to find in the English manner, "installing some of the oldest men as church wardens." He reported to the Society, from his temporary quarters in Manhattan, that

> I have several times celebrated the holy communion, at which occasion I counted up six hundred members; of these I instructed fifty-two in the fundamentals of our religion according to the Church Catechism; among them were thirteen papists. Since my arrival I have married four couples and by baptism incorporated eight children into Christ and his Church. Many of the people died at Sea, and here, through fever; so that the number of the survivors amount to about two thousand. At present all of the people . . . have been shipped up the river to a certain tract of land. I intend, God willing, to follow them in the near future.[15]

The Society bolstered Haeger's spirits by promising that he would "be supplied with 100 Common prayer books in High Dutch as soon as they can be procured, and that he be acquainted that his salary is duly paid his attorney."[16] The SPG was also gratified that Robert Livingston had delivered forty boards "for ye School house in ye palatyeyn town." Neither school nor church was built, however, and Haeger still looked for those German prayer books. He said his congregation numbered 150 souls—clearly, most people had either returned to their Reformed and Lutheran allegiance by 1712, or had fled the camp. Within the year, Haeger could claim forty communicants at Schenectady, sixty miles northwest, and from this time we infer that he believed his ministry in East Camp would be less successful as more and more of the Palatines forsook their assigned place and moved to places more promising: "ye people under my care disperse themselves up and down throughout almost this whole government, intending to settle some lands for themselves and posterity as the only means for their subsistence."[17]

Haeger's efforts toward a new home for his people were based on the incontrovertible fact that the unfortunate settlers could never thrive in the wilderness of East Camp. Instead of improving with time, their condition grew worse. Haeger wrote:

> The misery of these poor Palatines I every day behold has thrown me into such a fit of melancholy. . . . There has been a great famine among them this winter, and does hold on still, in so much that they boil grass and ye children eat the leaves of the trees. I have seen old men and women crie that it should almost have moved a stone. . . . I have served hitherto faithfully as Col. Heathcote and others can bear witness with a good conscience and should I now be forsaken in this remote land without any pay, or means of subsistence.[18]

Many of the Palatines moved to the Schoharie region, where Haeger visited them in 1716 and "had a large congregation. I preached several times and administered ye Holy Sacrament to seventy-four communicants." The German prayer books still hadn't arrived, however. Nor had the hoped-for church in East Camp been built. The Reformed and Lutheran congregations had built their churches, and Haeger had the governor's license to proceed with the Episcopal. The lumber lay upon the ground, squared and ready to be set up (though the SPG urged Haeger to wait until Barclay's church in Albany was completed). His optimism still in good repair, Haeger envisioned an English church at East Camp in the near future. The SPG record mentioned the "necessity for a pulpit cloth, communion table cloth, and vessel for the communion to enable him to perform the service with common decency."[19]

He proceeded to build "a little house and keep church in the same; which would hold about 200 people, the rest must stay without." Haeger was certain his efforts would meet with success because, as he reminded the SPG, his was the only English church between Kingston and Albany—a statement London might question, for there could be little reason to believe that the church in Dutch Calvinist Kingston was now English.

Perhaps because the East Camp tar-making experiment had failed, somewhat embarrassing Governor Hunter, disappointing the navy, and casting Livingston in the role of hardfisted landlord, the SPG decided to withdraw its support. Haeger was notified that his salary would not be continued beyond 1717. Even if the Society was not sensitive to the failures and disgrace involved in the Palatine matter, the fact that many of the immigrants had left East Camp made Haeger's work there peripheral to the Society's main purposes. It was suggested that "the New York establishment" might underwrite Haeger; presumably, this meant the government, not Trinity Church in New York. Haeger protested:

> being a Church of England minister, and to please God I am resolved to die so and will not turn to any other church for any offer, and I am certain that the Church of England has no less care for their ministers than any other church as to let them perish and leave them to be mocked at . . .[20]

The Society, nevertheless, stood by its decision to terminate Haeger's stipends (if not by its promises to send the German prayer books). In 1716 a committee urged he be sent £50 "for his past services," that the governor be asked about the Palatine settlement, and whether or not Haeger was (as he claimed) still working there. The inquiry was pointless: Haeger died before the SPG could reach Governor Burnet. His widow was granted the £50, paid into the hand of her new husband, SPG missionary John Ogilvie.

In his story of the Society engaged with the Palatines, we see both the strengths and the weaknesses of the SPG. Among the strengths are the regular examination (albeit from afar) of the work, the money at the Society's disposal, a certain harmony with civic leadership and, above all, the faithfulness of such missionaries as John Frederick Haeger. The weaknesses, however, are also there: the problems of long-distance oversight and the ensuing delay in communication are obvious. The East Camp experiment was a disgrace to its planners and a disaster to its participants. But could the Society lightly dismiss its missionary, or order him to abandon the miserable settlers who hadn't health or wit to move away? Haeger himself answered this query: paid or unpaid (we do not know), he remained in East Camp and from there supervised the building of the Schoharie church, whence many of his people had gone.

Finally, there is the problem of language in a Church which has always been aware of the rich inheritance implicit in its public worship. The SPG should have learned early in the Palatine affair that it was ill-equipped to compete—is that not the appropriate word?—for the loyalty of foreign-speaking people. In a notable enterprise on the banks of the Hudson River there was tried something that would, in future, become the norm of American life: people of one language entered upon a world where people of another language were ascendant, and determinedly so. In Manhattan the situation was somewhat ameliorated by usual urban customs. English and Dutch were used interchangeably for years to come. Dutch roots would always have a certain first-family dignity denied the lordly English. Stuyvesant to this day bears weight that Morris cannot. The SPG presumed for a brief time that it could make Prayer Book people out of Reformed and Lutheran Christians. Sensing what we today call the cultural gap, Haeger grasped at a very logical solution: prayer books in German. He never received them because they never existed.

While John Frederick Haeger—surely a martyr by any standard—was sharing the misery of East Camp, the Church of England was putting down stronger roots in other places.

3

An Era of Expansion in Manhattan and Westchester: Growth Around New York City

*For those places where ministers are settled I must do
the gentlemen settled there the justice to say that
they have behaved themselves with great zeal . . .*
—LORD CORNBURY, 1705

Now that the SPG provided the means for supervised missionary activity, let us see how the localities mentioned in Fletcher's Ministries Act fared. The act anticipated six clergymen deployed as follows: one man to serve New York town, one to serve Richmond (Staten Island), one to serve the villages of Westchester, Eastchester, Yonkers, and Pelham; another to serve Rye, Mamaroneck, and Bedford; one man for Jamaica "and adjacent Towns and Farms"; and one for Hempstead and "next adjoining Towns and Farms." It will be noticed that, apart from the congregation in New York town which already existed in the fort there, these are locations where the Dutch Reformed and Lutheran churches did not have well-settled congregations. Fletcher's act may have been directed at those places thought soon to see growth from immigration; certainly, Connecticut was already sending its people across the border, a border that was in contest between the two colonies. Brooklyn and Albany—both old Dutch settlements—were not to be troubled by the Ministries Act.

Trinity Church in New York had already instituted Vesey as rector when the first SPG missionaries arrived. At a very early stage, Trinity ceased receiving aid from England if, indeed, it had ever received grants. Quite naturally, the English Church in the English port took on a prominent position, promoted by Vesey's acting as commissary, which gave him an opportunity to direct SPG funds in the province. One gathers that Vesey's ambitions sometimes led him to speculate that if the Bishop of London was made Archbishop for the colonies, with power to appoint his suffragans, the name of Vesey might well be prominently mentioned, despite the fact that he was not uniformly esteemed by his colleagues.[1]

Staten Island welcomed the Rev. Aeneas MacKenzie in 1704. In a short time he was able to report that the parish possessed a parsonage, glebe, and "a pretty handsome church."[2] Queen Anne presented the church on Staten Island with a "Large Bible, Prayer Book, Book of Homilies, clothes for Pulpit and Holy Table, and a silver chalice and paten," gifts sometimes bestowed upon other churches. These were the barest necessities of Episcopal worship. Bibles were still hard to come by, and a large one for pulpit use was especially desirable. The Prayer Book would have been somewhat smaller, bound in red tooled leather. The Book of Homilies was probably limited to that published in the reign of Edward VI (a "Second Book" appeared in the reign of Elizabeth I). The homilies were sermons by eminent English divines approved to be read by less literate clergymen. The "clothes" for the pulpit and holy table were, probably, lengths of a woolen or felt material which could be tailored into a full cover for the altar, and book cushions for the reading desk. These were generally of a rich red hue, from which descends that color for carpeting and pew cushions many of us know so well nearly three hundred years later. The rubric, since 1552, required "a fair white linen cloth," but one finds few references to any linen in the early American records. (It is possible that, since linen was more available in America than wool, and more readily fashioned into altar cloths, there would be scant mention of a linen cloth covered by the imported wool.)

Much of the early history of the Church in Staten Island is lost to us, and it is perhaps worth noting that though St. Andrew's was one of the first dozen Episcopal churches founded in New York, the *Centennial History* of 1886 awards it but eleven lines, with no mention of anything prior to 1785. History seems to award the palm to those who come forward to grasp it. Take the Westchester parishes, for instance. They enjoyed the attention of the Rev. Robert Bolton of Pelham, who, in 1855, published their stories. Bolton gives much of the missionary credit to a layman, Col. Caleb Heathcote of the Manor of Scarsdale.

Heathcote was an ardent Episcopalian. He was born in 1663 in Chesterfield, England, and came to New York about 1692. By 1700 he had a house in Mamaroneck and also was hand-in-glove with New York City political, military, and mercantile persons. He served as a judge in Westchester, was mayor of New York, and an officer of the garrison forces. Commercial life was accelerating in New York, and Heathcote, already enriched by his English shipping investments, probably fared very well in the Port of New York. He was a founding vestryman of Trinity, serving until 1714, and also a member of the SPG. His name is frequently found among the earliest records and letters pertaining to the Episcopal Church. If there had been more laymen of his stripe, and fewer of the Fletcher sort, the Episcopal Church might have grown faster in the early 1700s. Which is not to say that Caleb Heathcote was not as able as any man to turn a quick profit.

It is said that Caleb Heathcote came to America because he had been jilted by his fiancée. That may be so, but he recovered sufficiently to marry Martha Smith of Long Island soon after his arrival; their eldest daughter married James DeLancey, and from that couple descended William Heathcote DeLancey, founding Bishop of Western New York. Col. Heathcote died in 1721, and was buried in Trinity Church. James Fenimore Cooper married a Heathcote descendant, and more than a century later the novelist liked to tell his friends he owned a ninety-year lease on a Westchester farm that stipulated the tenant shall "frequent divine service according to the Church of England when opportunity offers."[3] At the time of his death, each of the Episcopal churches in Westchester counted Heathcote as their benefactor.

Fletcher's Act of 1693 provided for two ministers in Westchester. The year before, a man named Mather was discouraged from beginning a ministry there because Col. Heathcote objected that he was not a priest of the Church of England. The colonel could be a patient man: he waited ten years until SPG missionary John Bartow arrived. Bartow's parish ranged across the county from Yonkers to Rye, and included the present-day "Westchester Square" in the Bronx. Very soon he was in trouble with the Presbyterians, who, quite understandably, resented the aggressive Church policies of Governor Cornbury: the governor would supplant every Nonconformist minister with a Church of England parson. One recorded episode is probably typical of the tension that then existed. Bartow was officiating in the church in Jamaica at a time when a Presbyterian minister thought he should be preaching there. Turned away at the door, the Presbyterian (according to Bartow),

> went aside to an orchard hard by, and sent in some to give word that Mr. Hobbart would preach under a tree. Then I perceived a whispering through the church, and an uneasiness of many people, some going out . . . some that were gone out returned again for their seats, and then we had a shameful disturbance, hawling and tugging of seats, shoving one the other off, carrying them out and returning again for more.[4]

A Boston visitor, stopping near Rye in 1704, recorded that

> they told me that one Church of England parson officiated in all
> those three towns once every Sunday in turns throughout the year,
> and that they all could but poorly maintain him, which they grudged
> to do, being a poor and quarrelsome crew as I understand by our
> Host, then Quarreling about their choice of Minister they choose to
> have here—but caused the Government to send this Gentleman to
> them.[5]

"Poor and quarrelsome crew" must have been a local watchword,
for in the same year, 1704, those very words were used by Thomas
Pritchard, rector of Rye, in describing his congregation.[6] Yet Pritchard
wasn't in despair. "The Minister preaches in the Townhouse," he said,
"and the parish is divided into three districts, viz, Rye, Bedford, and
Mamaroneck. . . . The number of communicants are considerably increased, since the celebration of the Sacraments . . ."[7]

The Presbyterians who carried the seats out of the church did not
discourage Bartow. He was able to report for the year 1704 that

> I have been instrumental in making many Proselyts to our Holy Reli-
> gion who are very constant and devout in, and at their attendance on
> Divine Service; those who were enemies at my first coming are now
> zealous professors of the ordinances of our Church.[8]

Bartow considered Lord Cornbury a great help to the Church, but
many observers then and since dispute that view. Nor were Presbyterians likely to be happily affected by Cornbury's posturings and questionable mode of life. For his part, Cornbury declared that the Episcopal clergy of New York, Jamaica, Hempstead, Westchester, and Rye
"have behaved themselves with great zeal."[9] Mutual cordiality between
the governor and the Episcopal clergy in a colony heretofore so thoroughly Dutch and Nonconformist was a dangerous thing. The personal
characteristics of Lord Cornbury (who sometimes appeared in women's
clothing) were not helpful to the Episcopalians, who hoped to see
their Church firmly rooted in New York soil, however much they might
bask in the favor he bestowed upon the Church. When Cornbury returned to England, he left behind a reputation for irritability, arrogance, and eccentricity that is hard for us to explain away, inasmuch as
these peculiarities put at discount the sacrifices of many Episcopal clergymen whose labors and sacrifices were sincere and devoted.

While the province was experiencing the civil administration (or
circus) of Cornbury, William Vesey in the city was exercising his duties
as Church commissary. Vesey, vicar of Trinity Church (the Bishop of
London was rector), was an assiduous servant of the SPG. He met with

the few Episcopal clergymen in New York in October 1704, and subsequently reported to the SPG the "story of the Church's introduction and progress on every side."[10] The words are important, for they suggest that until that time the Church of England was unknown in much of the province. Beginning with his own parish, Vesey relates a condition most satisfactory to himself: "The Rector of this church is maintained by a tax levied upon all the Inhabitants of the City," he declares; and an additional grant is assured "during the life and residence of the incumbent." That is to say, Vesey had friends in high places. The Assembly voted him an annuity of £60 for life. Clearly, Cornbury and Vesey worked in harmony. It is equally clear that Trinity Church was already, in 1704, in the position to be a benefactor to Episcopalians in New York. "If God pleases to continue his Excellency [Lord Cornbury] in the Administration of this Government, [Trinity] Church is a fair way of becoming the greatest Congregation upon the Continent," wrote Vesey as he listed the assets of his parish. Since "the parishioners have been, and still are at, raising the Ediface and Steeple to that perfection they designed it," the governor had urged Queen Anne "to bestow a farm within the bounds of the said City known by the name of the Kings Farm" upon Trinity Church. About the same time, June 1704, ardent churchman Lewis Morris wrote to London recommending that the "Queen's Farm" be given to Trinity Church.[11] Thus, the lands Fletcher had leased to Trinity Church were more firmly placed in the church's possession. Hastening on (perhaps because there would be questions about that farm for a very long time), Vesey assured the authorities that Trinity is working to "train up youth" and "discourage Vice in the said Province." Furthermore, the governor had contributed to the building of a French church, with hopes that a clergyman of English orders would become minister there. The Trinity report concludes with a complaint about "the pious and deserving Mr. Elias Neau who was brought up a Merchant and in good business." Vesey thought it would be better if the Society would underwrite "the worthy and ingenious Mr. Muirson, who is now going to England in the hopes of being admitted into Holy Orders."[12]

ELIAS NEAU AND THE SLAVES

In such a gloss will annals conceal a saint! Elias Neau deserves a day in the calendar, and it may be that, even after almost three hundred years, he holds some kind of record as New York's most colorful layman. Born in France, Neau had for a time been a galley slave as retribution for his Protestant faith. Like many French Protestants in New York—the Bards,

Bayards, and Lorillards come to mind—Neau had a knack for business. He did well in mercantile circles after he came to New York, but he who had once been a slave because of religious allegiance now looked in compassion upon others who were slaves because of their race: Negroes in New York. Their number was increasing; in 1715 there were 4,000 slaves in the province, and 27,000 white persons.[13] Between 1703 and his death in 1722, Neau conducted his classes, often encountering bitter opposition from clergy and church people. William Vesey allowed Neau space for catechetical classes in Trinity Church, but his encouragement was no better than lukewarm.

As long as slavery existed people who offered Negroes the amenities of a Christian civilization had to contend with others who thought their education would inevitably bring trouble. When there was a slave uprising in the city in 1712, the expected sentiments resulted. There was terror among white people, and harsh reprisals against identifiable black leaders. Of course, there were those who blamed the schools engaged in teaching slaves to read and write. The clergy generally supported Neau against criticism, but public opinion was made clear when eighteen Negroes were hanged, and the Common Council passed a regulation that Negroes must carry lanterns when walking abroad at night. Some people regarded Neau's efforts to teach slaves as an invasion of their property rights. In mid-century, religious revivals made slaveholders more amenable to education for their chattels. Neau's record cannot be acclaimed a success, as the world counts the things of success, and he knew his adversaries were powerful. He said it is hard to be a Christian when you are a slave.[14] Even some of his supporters considered it sufficient for slaves to learn the Christian religion by hearing the Book of Common Prayer read at family services at home—not a bad idea, really, if all Episcopalians undertook to do the same.[15] It is an unfortunate truth that few New York Episcopalians ever wrestled with their consciences about slavery.

Long after Neau had passed from the scene, the Rev. James Wetmore had as many as two hundred slave catechumens, but he noted the reluctance of their owners to send them to church. He also shared the common belief that to congregate the slaves together was to court danger. Nevertheless, the SPG was asked to furnish Bibles and prayer books for them.

Neau's dedication to the black slaves ran counter to Trinity's rector, Vesey, who probably reflected the views of his privileged vestry. But at first, Cornbury and Vesey supported Neau.[16] It was announced that at Trinity Church slaves would be catechized every Wednesday, Friday, and Sunday at five in the afternoon. Subsequent baptisms were rites that, it was said, made the slaves think they were free. Trouble followed. Discontent among the slaves was traced to Neau's classes at Trinity. The rector trimmed his sails, but Neau did not. In a letter to Bishop Robinson, Neau complained that the local clergy were at best lukewarm about educating Negroes.[17] It was this uneasy situation that led Vesey to encourage the SPG to support Muirson, later rector of Rye. Muirson's sympathy with the slaves may be gauged by his 1708 statement about the Indians as "a decaying people [who] say they will not be Christians nor do they see the necessity for so being, because we do not live according to the precepts of our religion."[18] Today, we read this as a prophetic statement; in that era of English ascendancy it was seen as something quite different.

FURTHER DEVELOPMENTS IN WESTCHESTER

New York's port town was beginning to be something far more than a garrison settlement. Names and events and dates flow lavishly now, as from a cornucopia. Even though New York Province in 1700 had merely 19,000 people—many fewer than Connecticut, Maryland, or Virginia— visitors began to reckon its importance seriously. "The Cittie of New York is a pleasant, well compacted place, situated on a Commodious River which is a fine harbour for shipping," wrote Madam Knight from Boston in 1704. She continued:

> The buildings brick generaly, very stately and high, though not altogether like ours in Boston. The Bricks in some of the Houses are of divers Coullers and laid in Checkers, being glazed look very agreeable. The inside of them are neat to admiration, the wooden work, for only the walls are plastered, and the Sumers and Girt [beams] are planed and kept very white scour'd as so is all the partittion if made of Bords. The fire places have no Jambs (as ours have). . . . Their Diversion in the Winter is riding Sleys about three or four miles out of Town where they have their Houses of entertainment at a place called the Bowery, and some go to friends Houses who handsomely treat them . . . Madame Dowes, a Gentlewoman . . . gave us a handsome Entertainment of five or six Dishes and choice Beer and metheglin Cyder, etc. all which she said was the produce of her farm. I believe we mett fifty or sixty Slays that day—they with great swiftness and some are so furious that they'll turn out of the path for none save a Loaden cart.[19]

New York town, then, was growing. This meant that the Church of England congregations would increase, though, as was often said, New Yorkers were not notable for churchgoing. Let us now look at an outlying community, the hamlet of Westchester.

The word Westchester means three things to us. First of all, it was, and is, a county, whose present dimensions are somewhat smaller than they were originally. Secondly, Westchester in 1700 was a hamlet: the place now sometimes called Westchester Square. Thirdly, Westchester implies a parish of perhaps as many as six church buildings and congregations under the care of one or more priests of the Church of England.

The hamlet called Westchester was far more important than its scattering of dwellings would suggest. It was the county seat, and thus had the drawing power enjoyed by all places where law courts and clerks and public meetings are centered. In 1687 Col. Heathcote exercised his capacities as magistrate and churchman by designing a "Town House built, to keep courts in, and for the publick worship of God." These plans, which included a jail, were unfulfilled. Several years later, probably in 1701, a church was built. It was twenty-eight feet square, of frame construction, and had two large sash windows on each of three sides, and a wide door on the fourth side. Its hipped roof was topped by a bell "turet."[20] This is the building where Samuel Seabury officiated during the Revolutionary War; by that time, it had much deteriorated, for in 1788 it was found unworthy of repair, and was sold and moved to a neighboring farm. We are told that while the new church was still abuilding, a Presbyterian minister named Morgan occupied it for services several times before John Bartow came from Rye to claim the church for himself.

The records state that as late as 1706 the windows hadn't been fitted in the Westchester church. It was named St. Peter's about 1710. Otherwise, the *Records of the Combined Parishes,* of Westchester, Eastchester, New Rochelle, Yonkers, Pelham, and Morrisania are of very great value to us today because they reveal one instance in the province where the civil and ecclesiastical authority were agreeably yoked together—at least for a time. From the beginning, St. Peter's enjoyed (or endured) the town vestry imagined by Fletcher. The town justices, the wardens, and the vestrymen met together, and sometimes the civil power merged with ecclesiastical matters on the same page of the record books. Thus we read on the flyleaf:

> Agreed that Warrants shall be issued to the several Constables from the Year 1702 till the present Yr 1706 in Westchester County to fetch the money due to the Minister's Rate for Morrisania.[21]

Such a perfunctory entry records for us several points of historic interest. We will not see frequent mixings of civil and ecclesiastical authority in New York. The province never experienced the domination of church over state as did say the neighboring colony of New Haven, or the Newark experiment of the 1660s. Perhaps the Arminianism born in the Netherlands had deeply influenced the Dutch Church after all, and discouraged close civil ties in New York.

Another arresting point about this flyleaf entry is the reference to Morrisania, the home place of Lewis Morris. Though originally of Cromwellian persuasion, the Morris family was now loyal to the Church of England. Morris contemplated a chapel nearer his home. He was thus reluctant to pay an assigned quota to St. Peter's, arguing that "his Mannor" was not within the boundaries of the Westchester church. The tension between Morrisania and Westchester prevailed for several years; things moved much more slowly in those days, including a predisposition to reconcile differences. It may be that the Lord of Morrisania (for such he was) expected more prominence in St. Peter's than the parish authorities were willing to grant, for in 1710 it is recited that Lewis Morris had earlier wanted to set up

> at his own Proper Charge a Convenient Seat Plan or Pew In some Suitable Part of ye Church in This Town for ye accommodation of himself and family which Generous offer was by Some (tho a deminitive number) of ye then Vestry Rejected yet notwithstanding did Conclude them all by a Tacit Aquiessency to ye have Negative voice of but two of them who not well weighing ye Consequences nor seriosly Considering ye Rationality of ye offer Did Refuse giving ye Liberty to that Worthy Gentleman which ye Vestry in yt perticular (wich Indeed Did look little Better than Black Ingratitude) Have Unanimously agreed and Concluded that ye said Mr. Lewis Morris may if he sees Caus at his own Proper Cost and Charge . . . [22]

This is neither the first nor the last time in the annals of New York that wealth and prestige won the day—and extracted an apology from those who dared deny their privileges.

Turning from the pretensions of the quality, we may note a different sort of Westchester record preserved for us. Seaman Charles Williams of the *Pink Blossom,* Mariner Captain Daskins, Commander, sued the captain for wages allegedly withheld. Churchwarden Josiah Hunt was appointed power-of-attorney for the sailor—and the affidavit is duly included in the church records. The line between Episcopal Church and state was a thin line in Westchester Square. The Presbyterians seemed to keep their distance—or perhaps the "Convenient Seat" of Lewis Morris in St. Peter's Church scared them off.

The rector, John Bartow, served the Westchester church from 1702 until his death in 1725. The Society had questioned his quick removal from Rye to Westchester, and Bartow defended his action by claiming the prior importance of Westchester. Did he also suspect there would be less trouble from the Independents farther away from the Connecticut border? He certainly stated that Lord Cornbury wanted him to be in

Westchester. The appointment by Bishop Compton hadn't specified where in the Province of New York Bartow was to minister, and most important, Heathcote approved Bartow's move. That should have ended the matter. He lived near St. Peter's, Westchester, on five acres in a house he had purchased. For many of his years there he officiated at St. Peter's only "every fourth Sabbath day, wich is Condescended to by Mr. Bartow."[23] It is perhaps revealing that, of a Sunday, he ranged about Westchester or "in the Jerseys" holding services. In doing so he was bound to meet preachers of other loyalties: "I can't repeat to you the many janglings and contentions I have had with Quakers and Dissenters, nay I may say with Atheists and Deists," he wrote to the SPG.[24] But at the same time he was glad to report that at Westchester all was satisfactory. The church was now wainscoted, ceiled overhead, "and more decently seated, and the communion table enclosed with rails and bannisters" (sic; surely he meant balusters). But there was cause to lament "that great loss we had at sea of church ornament, not knowing how it may be repaired but by the same gracious donors."[25]

Bartow's Westchester parish included, besides the church in Westchester Square, the communities of Eastchester, New Rochelle, Yonkers, Pelham, and Morrisania. Eastchester generally preferred the ministrations of Independent clergy, but with the heavy-handedness that characterized most of his Church acts, Governor Cornbury insinuated Bartow into that place in 1702. There was already a church building, which means that various clergy would have considered it a potential place for themselves. Somehow, Bartow ingratiated himself with the existing congregation at Eastchester, hitherto Presbyterian, so that (as he states) "they were so well satisfied with the liturgy and doctrine of the Church that they forsook their minister [Joseph Morgan] and conformed to the Church of England."[26] But the Presbyterian menace was never far from Bartow's door! "Some of their main agents have been with me and signified their design" for a separate church, wrote Bartow to the Society. They would have Bartow, or a Presbyterian minister: none other, he said. But he was determined no Presbyterian would preach in Eastchester church.[27]

New Rochelle, another of Bartow's charges, had much different beginnings than any other of the Westchester churches. It was established by French Protestants who were fleeing persecution, and were accompanied to New York by a minister, the Rev. David DeBonrepos. John Pell of Pelham assisted them, and by 1693 a church was built. DeBonrepos was succeeded by the Rev. David Bondet, who had been ordained by the Bishop of London,[28] but did not use the Book of Common Prayer, preferring the French Protestant services of the Huguenots. Col. Heathcote had always believed the Westchester parish required more than one parson. He hoped that Dr. Bondet might eventually be associated with the Westchester rector and be paid by the SPG. Perhaps Bondet (who preceded the SPG missionaries) thought it wise for the French church in New Rochelle to stand somewhat apart from the Church of England; certainly the English Church seemed to invite contention through its connections with the government. He sought SPG maintenance without the possible embarrassment a subsidy might bring. And in this he was successful; by 1707 Bondet was receiving SPG support. The price he had to pay was changing from the French liturgy to the Book of Common Prayer. Col. Heathcote was insistent about this, and was scheming to find "the properest ways not only for improving Dr. Bondet, but likewise at the same time think of the most effective means for taking care [of unchurched parts of the county]."[29] Two years later, in 1709, the French church of New Rochelle conformed to the Church of England; the church then numbered more than a hundred communicants. Henceforth they were expected to use the Prayer Book. Very soon, a new church was planned. The list of subscribers included the governor, twelve clergy, and names that then, or soon after, would be familiar in the annals of the Episcopal Church in New York: Laurens, Bayley, Morris, Neau, Clark, Read, Heathcote, Cromelin, Livingston ("a mayor of Albany"), Jay, and Watts. But even more important is the fact observed years later by Robert Bolton: "the first settled Episcopal minister was a French refugee."[30] Since David Bondet came to New Rochelle in 1695 and was supported by John Pell, this may give credence to the statement sometimes made that the earliest Episcopal congregation with a church in the province was at Pelham. Robert Bolton, rector of Pelham and credible historian, had no doubts: "As early as 1695 a clergyman of the Church of England was settled in the manor of Pelham," he wrote in 1855.[31]

COLONIAL CHURCH CUSTOMS

In 1702 Lord Cornbury had ordered "the Book of Common Prayer, as by law established, to be read each Sunday and Holyday and the Blessed Sacrament be administered according to the rites of the Church of England."[32] It was an instance of his lofty contempt for the other churches in the province. In light of the English minority, his order could only militate against the interests of the Church he hoped would benefit from his commands. Cornbury further said that existing churches were to be well kept, new ones were to be built, and the minister was to have a house and glebe lands. The glebe was, by English and Scots ecclesiastical law, the land belonging to the parish set apart for the maintenance of the minister. He might cultivate it himself, or lease it to a tenant. When the governor enjoined a glebe, he was simply transferring to the province the custom of the mother country. Many of the early New York parishes acquired glebe lands but, needless to say, none was as princely as that duly presented to Trinity Church in New York City.

Cornbury's order that the Book of Common Prayer be used every Sunday and holy day leads us to consider the services held in the churches he so ardently promoted. What were they like? It is safe to say that the services and the architectural arrangement of the churches followed closely those then prevailing in Britain. Most of the clergy had been educated there. In the absence of a bishop in America, all of them had been ordained there. Returning to New York, they would naturally follow what they had observed abroad, using whatever similar ornaments and "customary requisites" they could obtain. "Good Queen Anne" is credited with many gifts of silver to New York churches. Money was scarce, and the churches tended to be careful of the chalices and bread plates they received. They would be kept under lock and key in a chest, usually in the rector's house; this practice was maintained in many places until living memory. A quantity of fine seventeenth-century silver remains in the diocese. But there was much more, made in England or by the excellent New York silversmiths, that later fell victim to Victorian taste and changes in church customs. It is probable that the records of every old parish in New York tell of a vestry, influenced by the rector, ordering that the old altar service be sold or melted down in exchange for a newer sort.

An example of silver discarded because of altered customs may be of interest. The chalice of Queen Anne's time was a deep goblet, with perhaps a fitted cover that might be used separately as a bread plate. The communicant was given the chalice, which he held in both hands, and took a deep draft. He then handed the chalice back to the minister or, perhaps, to the next communicant. This practice was changed in the nineteenth century, when an increased sense of the sacramental act indicated that a mere sip of the wine was sufficient. Thereafter, less wine was consumed and chalices were shallower and wider. The "old-fashioned" goblets and their accompanying great flagons were no longer convenient.

The Word and the sacraments were held as a two-edged sword in the post-Reformation settlement of the Church of England. But in the eighteenth century, emphasis was on preaching rather than on sacrament. When Christopher Wren and his followers were engaged in rebuilding London after the fire of 1666, they designed glorious preaching halls, not somber edifices for Christian mysteries. Light flooded in through great sash windows. Gilt and light pastel tints were freely used on walls and columns. Carved putti scrambled after birds and beasts, fruits and flowers. Stalls were copied from the best Renaissance creations, and even the pulpit's sounding board could be made a thing of beauty. The floor was often a lively checkerboard of black and white marble squares. Viewed from afar, the steeple may have ascended in classic stages as orderly as the preacher's theology. This is the modish church the ordinand sought out when he was in London. Gothic architecture lingered as a possibility and never died out completely, but it was not the preferred style of Queen Anne and her immediate successors. The priest who returned from England remembered the new and wonderful churches he had seen. Who could blame him for desiring something like St. Martin's-in-the-Fields for himself and his people in America, especially when these buildings could conveniently be built of wood and brick?

Our returning ordinand would have seen in London the altars often covered by fine silk-and-tassel covers, or by a Persian carpet. This was required by canon law, but such coverings were almost impossible to come by in America. The seat cushions were often upholstered. In some English churches there were candlesticks on or near the altar. Brass branched chandeliers may have hung suspended from the ceiling. Early altars had been destroyed in the Reformation or during the Commonwealth. Archbishop Laud had expected the table altars of his time to be set apart by rails, but such emphasis on the place of the sacrament was offensive to the Puritans, and most altar rails had been destroyed. The altar could be moved. Where no rails existed, the communicants would kneel scattered near the altar. The celebrant would distribute the sacred elements for the communicants, who, at his bidding, "drew near with faith." A cross on or behind the altar was almost unknown in England and America.

The pews were no longer simple benches. Now, they were enclosed, an innovation especially welcome in cold North American winters. Somehow, the privileged people felt it their due to "sett up a Commodious Seat" for themselves. When Lewis Morris claimed the right to do so in Westchester church, he was following an honorable custom long established in England.

The celebrated three-decker pulpit set in the middle aisle in front of and obscuring the holy table is said to have been a mid-eighteenth-century development, but surely these great structures, with the altar on the floor in front, were known very early in New York. Our churches were small, and the high pulpit saved room. On the floor level there would be a seat and book rest for the clerk. It was his duty to say the responses of the Prayer Book service, and perhaps pitch the tune and "line out" the psalm, if one was sung. On the next level above was the officiant's seat and desk; the morning and evening offices, litany and ante-communion were read here, facing the congregation. Topping all was the pulpit for the sermon; an hourglass would often be attached to the wall or the pulpit rail and sometimes (often, in the Dutch Church) it was turned twice before the sermon ended. In some places the pulpit was also used as the reading desk. There were invariably hangings and upholstered cushions in the desks and pulpit for the books to rest on; these are the "pulpit cloths" so often mentioned in the early records. Crimson was the preferred color.

In front of this high desk-pulpit structure, on the floor, was the altar. Sometimes it was flanked by two or more good chairs. The altar itself was small and low, usually a table with a wood top. But sometimes it was a wooden frame on which was placed a marble slab. "A table for the communion was given me by a joiner,"[33] said the rector of Westchester in a report that was probably duplicated by a dozen other clergymen during the early days of the Episcopal Church in New York.

On Sunday, the church was opened by the sexton or a lay assistant, who was often the grave digger and the keeper of some church records. The service would perhaps be announced by the beating of a drum, or if the church was so fortunate as to possess one, the ringing of a bell.

Nowadays, we are accustomed to entering a church and waiting for the service to begin. That was not the custom of an earlier day. In the Dutch Church (which doubtless had some effect on Episcopalians), a part of the service was under way before the dominie entered.

Beneath the pulpit, in a position similar to but not parallel with the Episcopalians' clerk, sat the *voorlezer*. He was "almost as important as the minister himself in the appropriate carrying on of the service. This dignitary began the services by reading the scriptures, including the Commandments, after which he gave out a psalm and pitched the tune ... The Dominie himself entered at this point. He advanced up the aisle, bowing courteously to the right and to the left, then paused at the front of the pulpit stairs for a moment of prayer."[34]

The Reformed dominie probably was clad in the black Geneva gown. But the Episcopal minister

> would arrive in his ordinary habit (or street attire) which consisted of a long cassock, sash, gown, tippet ... He would also wear a wig and "bands"—a soft white linen neckcloth (later starched to become the modern clerical collar) with two pendent tabs. [Entering the church he would] remove his hat and walk informally down the aisle, pausing perhaps to greet parishioners and inquire of ill relatives ...[35]

Once near the desk pulpit, the officiant would put on a very ample surplice which, between services, was often kept hanging on a peg behind the wainscoting, or perhaps folded over a frame made for that purpose, and begin Morning or Evening Prayer. The clerk would lead in the responses. The congregation brought prayer books. None would be provided in the pews until Victorian piety demanded such propriety.

In the period under survey, there were no organs in most Episcopal churches. The psalms were sung, in meter:

> The Lord's my shepherd; I'll not want:
> He makes me down to lie
>
> In Pastures green he leadeth me,
> The quiet waters by

Canticles wouldn't be chanted until about 1800, and then only in the larger churches.[36] The congregation sat while singing.[37] Trinity Church, New York, adapted the Tate and Brady psalms as early as 1707; this work (which went through several hundred editions, enduring till the mid-nineteenth century) included the beloved "While shepherds watched their flock by night." But in 1720 hymnody was still far in the future in the Episcopal Church.

All musical instruments had met with Puritan wrath, but the Restoration in England was fortunate to have great musicians whose anthems enhanced the reputation of English music. Naturally, this development of music in the churches would be acknowledged in New York, and it isn't a surprise for us to learn that Trinity Church ordered an organ in 1733 from John Clemm of Philadelphia, and a better one a bare six years later. An organ at that early date was used primarily for preludes and voluntaries, and possibly for an occasional anthem. Episcopalians would wait for another century or more before hymns would be regularly included in services.

When it came time for the sermon, the rector would descend the few steps from the desk, remove his surplice and put on his black preaching gown. This was the "academic gown" of today. It is shown in most early clerical portraits. In changing vestments, it was usually necessary to remove his wig, and a wig stand would have been handy.

Since the changing of vestments is always awkward in church services, we can understand that the clergy soon insisted upon a retiring place where he could doff and don robes. The word "wainscot" which appears in so many records is a clue, for it suggests a concealed space where the officiant changed. In fact, we are told that a New York church as late as 1838, though refurbished, retained its three-decker pulpit and the "hole where the clergyman could go and change his surplice for a black gown between the service and the sermon."[38] The sermon was lengthy: "Our Colonial ancestors had stronger stomachs than modern congregations for long and meaty sermons, and they would have been deeply offended if the preacher gave them nothing more than a fifteen minute discourse."[39] The service would be Morning Prayer with Litany and Ante-Communion. The Eucharist was celebrated quarterly, or sometimes as often as once a month, in spite of the Prayer Book provisions for Epistle and Gospel for every Sunday.

"Collections" of money were rare, and only for specific, immediate needs. Everyone expected the church to be supported mainly by a few rich and dedicated persons. Much later "subscription papers" were distributed for parishioners to signify what might be expected toward church repairs, rector's salary, and so forth. The glebe was often the parson's chief income. In the first years of the Ministries Act, tax money was designated for church maintenance, as well as for the poor. The "offertory procession" we all know so well of vestrymen carrying alms basons down the aisle was unknown in the eighteenth century; "ushers" at the door would have been an impertinence.

How did the service end? We are not certain. After the sermon, the officiant probably closed the service with a general benediction. Maybe a final psalm was sung, or (in churches fortunate to own an organ), a voluntary was played as the people departed. After the regular service there was often a baptism or a marriage. Almost certainly there would be a gathering of the congregation, for many of the people had come a distance, and might not see each other again soon.

The missionary's stipend was paid by the Society in London, but it was often augmented by further sums provided by the laity in the parish. Then and later, prominent men of the locality signed a subscription paper on which they wrote the amount they expected to contribute. Such a paper, circulated for the benefit of Newburgh's missionary from 1768 to 1775, is probably typical. A group of laymen there pledged to

> the support of the Reverend Mr. John Sayre the Societies Missionary to Newburgh and the parts adjacent on Condition that the said Mr. Sayre continue to officiate in each of the divisions of his Mission, viz, Newburgh, the Orrerkill Division, and the Wallkill Division, that is to say one Sunday in every three weeks during his residence in this mission, Health and other circumstances permitting save that the said Mr. Sayre shall be at liberty to officiate one Sunday in every three months at Warwick for promoting the good of the church in that settlement.[40]

It should be pointed out that the permission allowing Mr. Sayre to take services in Warwick was a perquisite commonly extended to clergy. It gave them a chance to earn a little extra money and it promoted Church growth.[41]

The Venerable Society required its missionaries to answer and return for official perusal a long series of questions about their parishes. Thus, an approximate account of the Church in America was presented for review in London.

Between 1745 and 1781, the Bishop of London licensed at least 378 clergymen to be missionaries in America. New York Province received the least number, 17, while 20 went to New Jersey, 21 to Pennsylvania, 46 to Maryland, 142 to Virginia, 93 south of Virginia, and 39 to New England.[42]

The "frontier" situation of Westchester County in the early years of the eighteenth century was not unlike that encountered by missionaries in the West many decades later. People often lived very far from the church. At best, they could attend public services only on occasion. This led to one more novel custom for Episcopalians, as was recorded in a Victorian diary:

> The Venerable Society sent out a few missionaries who settled here and there and on occasion made tours of mission work much as our Bishops do at the present time [1889]. The good parson in wig and cocked hat, armed with his certificate of ordination and the Society's recommendatory letters, mounted his good, ambling nag, and seated on saddle bags, went through the Colony, stopping here and there, now in this village, now in that, and depending on the hospitality of the higher class Church of England families as might be found in each neighborhood he proposed to visit. Well, the good parson having arrived, a visitation was made by him from house to house, and such as had not been baptized were prepared for the rite and the children and the infants were included in its administration. In anticipation of these visits, each Church of England family owned a bowl originally obtained, carefully preserved, and solely devoted for and to this purpose.[43]

THE GOSPEL AND THE INDIANS

The original Americans whom we call Indians were frequently in the forefront of SPG concern. In the first place, there was the sincere conviction that the Indians had the right to know the Gospel. Secondly, there was the somewhat less altruistic conviction that the Gospel had best be presented by the Church of England rather than the Jesuits of France, England's traditional enemy. Let the flag and the religion of Britain be known in the farthest reaches of the province: that was the practical sentiment, and that is substantially the reason why the Rev. Thoroughgood Moore, was, in 1704, appointed missionary to the Indians north and west of Albany. He arrived with the highest ideals, but was soon discouraged because the fur traders used rum overmuch in their dealings with the Indians. Cornbury's self-serving policy was to cooperate with the merchants (as long as they cooperated with him), and so Thoroughgood Moore's complaints about the rum quickly put him afoul of the eccentric governor. He embarked for England, probably intending to give the Society a firsthand report of life among Cornbury's friends, but, unfortunately, his ship was lost and thus history was deprived of that particular glimpse into American colonial history.

Some clergy were persuaded that the spiritual health of the white man should be addressed before that of the Indians. Therefore, the SPG received the petition, "We humbly supplicate that the children first be satisfied, and the lost sheep recovered who have gone astray among hereticks and Quakers who have deneyed the Faith and are worse than Infidels and Indians who never knew it."[44] Does this better indicate a snobbish dismissal of the Indians, or an evaluation of the Englishmen's religion in the province?

Thomas Barclay, educated in New York City, was appointed a missionary to the Albany area in 1709. He soon showed much promise (but ten years later was declared to be hopelessly mad). In 1710, William Andrews was sent to assist; people complained that he was too profound. Soon thereafter, four Iroquois sachems are said to have appeared before pious Queen Anne, entreating her to promote the Church of England lest "French Priests and Presents" get the upper hand.[45] Perhaps it was this dramatic epiphany in the English court (but more likely it was the ill will generated by Fletcher and Cornbury) that led the Society to reiterate its primary aim of "conversion of the heathen and infidels," and that "a stop be put to the sending any more missionaries among Christians" such as Presbyterians and Reformed.[46]

In 1710 the Crown ordered a church built in Albany. The Queen presented the Communion plate, and the Archbishop of Canterbury supplied twelve large Bibles and the tablets of Decalogue, Creed, and the Lord's Prayer canonically required in eighteenth-century chancels. Albany was thought to be the gateway to the New York wilderness, and the Society sent missionaries to the Indians until the outbreak of the War of Independence, with varying results. "Heathen they are, and heathen they still will be," declared the profound William Andrews. John Miln was more positive about his endeavors at Fort Hunter, 1727–35. But even Miln soon wanted to leave: "the climate of Albany is too cold, the Society is crude, the work is discouraging and the salary irregularly paid."[47] Henry Barclay, son of the unfortunate Thomas, went from his Yale graduation to be the catechist at Fort Hunter in 1735. He was tutored in the Indian languages by Andrews and Ogilvie,[48] and was ordained in England three years later, returning to serve the white congregation and the Indian school at the fort. In 1745 Barclay went down-river to succeed William Vesey as rector of Trinity Church and bestow his family's name upon one of Manhattan's oldest thoroughfares. John Ogilvie, J. J. Oel, Thomas Brown, Henry Munro, and John Stuart were outstanding missionaries in the Albany area prior to the war. But it was the legendary Sir William Johnson who "probably exercized a greater influence over the Indians than any other Englishman."[49]

While the new landed magnates to the south were busy consolidating their holdings and waiting for new opportunities that might come their way, Johnson was hugely enjoying his life in the Mohawk Valley, near present-day Amsterdam, and in Johnstown. He came from England in 1738. His first wife died soon after and he purchased from a neighbor a German girl to be his housekeeper. They were married by Henry Barclay about 1740, but since Sir William maintained two houses and preferred that they both be well managed, he soon installed the distinguished Indian Mollie Brant as his mistress in Fort Johnson. This did not diminish his reputation with the Indians, and they conferred upon him the rank of a chief of the Mohawks. Johnson deserved the honor. For fair treatment of the Indian his name stands almost alone in the annals of early New York: "While frauds were being practiced on the Indians by the land-grafting officials at Albany and elsewhere, Johnson was firm in his desire that the Indians should not be cheated."[50]

William Johnson was conspicuously loyal to the Church of England, a fact that, together with his marital irregularities, did not commend him to historians of Puritan leanings. For his part, Johnson believed that Indians taught by dissenting divines usually "lost their abilities for hunting." Mollie Brant's brother, the noted Joseph, became an enthusiastic communicant and lay reader in Episcopal churches and, thanks to Sir William, there were now churches where he could officiate in the absence of an ordained missionary. Apart from offering his own houses for services, Sir William encouraged the building of churches at Fort Hunter, Canajoharie, Schenectady, and Johnstown. He died in 1774, just prior to the Revolutionary War, and was thus spared seeing his Loyalist Indians pitted against the patriots, a tragedy that Sir William might have been able to prevent had he lived.

THE QUEST FOR A BISHOP

If there was one constant problem in our colonial history it was the difficulty and dangers a candidate must surmount to be ordained in the Church. There were no bishops in the colonies, and no institution where an ordinand might be prepared specifically for Episcopal priesthood. An English youth had both university and bishop at hand, and even if he was unable to matriculate at Oxford or Cambridge, he could study with any of the neighboring clergy who were willing to be his tutor. In America, and especially in New York, Episcopal clergy were rare. Books were hard to come by and expensive, though William Bradford was publishing the Bible, the Prayer Book, and other volumes in New York City as early as 1724. Once ready to appear before a bishop, the ordinand was obliged to sail to England (where, quite probably, he would be friendless) and somehow gain the attention of a bishop after producing testimonial letters. He then had to wait until the bishop was ready to proceed to ordain him to the diaconate, and then the priesthood. The two ordinations were customarily set close together (sometimes only a day or two intervening), but the whole process was costly in time and money, and often fatal: for the voyages were perilous. A Congregationalist thought long before seeking orders in the Church of England! So did a young man born and brought up in the Episcopal Church.

A bishop for the colonies was an idea cherished by some Episcopalians. Others, such as staunch layman Caleb Heathcote, thought it just as well not to invite supervision; hierarchy would bring more discipline than many colonial churchmen desired. Furthermore, many colonists held that bishops in America would mean one more official tie with Whitehall. Political overtones were inevitable in discussions about resident bishops. The Church of England was lukewarm in promoting the idea, and Parliament was reluctant. Dissenters in the colonies declared they would actively oppose bishops in America. A contemporary cartoon shows a properly garbed bishop improperly tarred and feathered and escorted back on to the ship from which he has just disembarked. The king's Church simply wasn't trusted in colonies largely populated by descendants of men and women who had been glad to leave the land of that Church, or by others who recalled the iniquities of Fletcher and the inanities of Cornbury, or by yet others who proudly clung to the Dutch Reformed Church of their forebears and loathed Episcopal pretensions in New York. The Church and politics: it is ever a threatening combination beloved of Satan!

KING'S COLLEGE

This was the firm view of some prominent New Yorkers who participated in the founding of King's College in 1754. It is thought that the Episcopalians hoped to establish a college in the city much earlier in the century[51] but were unable to do so. Boston and the Congregationalists had their Harvard; Connecticut's Congregationalists had their Yale. Across the river, in Elizabethtown, the Presbyterians in 1747 founded the College of New Jersey (it was later moved to Princeton), and elsewhere in New Jersey the Dutch Reformed had their college—Queen's—in New Brunswick (now Rutgers). Was it not time for the Episcopalians to establish a college? Others asked quite another question: Was it not time that New York had a college?

Toward the end of 1751 the legislature authorized a lottery for a New York college. This was not entirely satisfactory to those who envisioned a college under Episcopal control, and they knew that if they were to grasp the opportunity they must act quickly. The authorities of Trinity Church were prevailed upon to step forward with land for the college, providing that its presiding officer be Episcopalian, and its chapel conform to the Book of Common Prayer. The college was duly chartered, in 1754, but the involvement of Trinity Church, and the names of the trustees (predominantly Episcopalian) "attracted attention," as a polite historian puts it.[52] In a short time, the founding and control of King's College brought to the fore two contending factions in New York life which were not irrelevant when the war came, and both are vividly represented in the personalities of two able men, Samuel Johnson and William Livingston.

Samuel Johnson was known to New York Episcopalians long before he came to King's College because he was a participant in what became known as "the Dark Day at Yale," September 22, 1722. On that day, the president of Yale and five other Congregationalist ministers of the faculty presented the college trustees a memorial in which they said they doubted the validity of their ordination and lamented that they were not "in visible communion with an Episcopal Church."[53] The Yale authorities were understandably aghast at this announcement. Four of the signers sailed to England for Episcopal ordination. One of these disturbing individuals was the Rev. James Wetmore, hitherto respected pastor of North Haven; in time, he became rector of Rye in New York Province. The people of Rye liked Wetmore because he was from adjoining Connecticut and spoke the New England "dialect," whereas the people of New York City preferred a missionary named Colgan, who was more polite. Thus there was an exchange of churches in 1726, and thereafter Wetmore flourished in Rye.[54] The Wetmores were obliged to flee New York after the Declaration of Independence (but, much later, a descendant returned to New York to serve the longest term of any New York suffragan bishop; history has its moments of rich compensation).

Another Yale dissident of interest to us was Samuel Johnson, pastor of West Haven. Together with Timothy Cutler (who became rector of

Christ Church, Boston) and David Brown (who died in London soon after ordination), Johnson had been ordained in St. Martin's-in-the-Fields (where most SPG meetings were held) on March 31, 1723. It has been said that these Connecticut Yankee Congregational ministers declared "for episcopal polity and order, which had no relationship at all to the pattern of worship they had conducted as Congregationalist and Presbyterian clergy." It says something about the strength and attractiveness of the Episcopal Church in Connecticut that these prominent ministers were led to seek ordination in England.

Samuel Johnson displays other characteristics germane to our story. He commended himself as a scholar sufficiently so that, after thirty years as rector of Stratford, Connecticut, he was called to be president of the new college in New York. *The New York Gazette or Weekly Post Boy* printed a notice on July 1, 1754, in which Samuel Johnson desired to

> acquaint whom it may concern that I shall attend at the Vestry room in the school house, near the English Church, on Tuesday and Thursday every week between the hours of nine and twelve, to examine such as offer themselves to be admitted to the college.[55]

Among those who early availed themselves of this new opportunity in New York were young men who bore such names as Verplanck, Bayard, Cruger, Johnson, dePeyster, Hoffman, Roosevelt, DeLancey, Rutgers, Lispenard, Brownjohn, Schuyler, Floyd, Watts, VanHorn, Benson, Bard, and Punderson. Every one of these would later be conspicuous in the annals of the Episcopal Church in New York. There was yet another young man who probably met with aging Samuel Johnson in the vestry room: Samuel Provost (as he then spelled his name). He was Dutch Reformed by baptism, but the family was related to Episcopalians, and while at King's College Samuel determined to be ordained in the Episcopal Church. We shall hear more of him very soon.

The Book of Common Prayer seems to have been about the only point of agreement between Johnson and Provost; in almost every other aspect they were at opposite poles. Samuel Johnson was conservative by nature, an Anglophile who found refuge in believing that New England was a corner of Great Britain, a view one sometimes encounters in surveying the Episcopal Church in America. It was said of him (as it would later be said of Hobart) that he became "very English in England."[56] He tended to look upon America as backward. Needless to say, then, he disliked evangelical enthusiasm. He decried the flamboyance of his ecclesiastical brother, George Whitefield, who, he said, "broke through all rule and order." Rule and order: these are the operative words in Johnson's life. Early on, he admired Locke and Newton and the milder Deists. Later, he found High Church rigorism attractive, possibly because it was readily adaptable in parochial life in Stratford.[57]

Johnson was one of the enthusiastic supporters of an American episcopate: "We wish we may live to see an establishment whereby the Bishop of London may become Archbishop of the American colonies, with at least three resident bishops as his suffragans in these remote provinces where the Church extremely suffers for want of her due government," he said in 1762. He thought it would be wise to have bishops in Albany, Canada, Manhattan, New England, Virginia, and the Caribbean Islands.[58] If no bishops were provided for the colonies, "the Church, and with it the interests of true religion must dwindle, while we suffer the contempt and triumph of our neighbors"—almost exactly what John Frederick Haeger had written to the SPG fifty years earlier. Always the Episcopal Church, so favorably situated in England, was seen much less favorably when contrasted with its neighbors in America because it lacked the very authority implied in its name: bishops. Samuel Johnson, however, was capable of a strange optimism, as when, in July 1760, he informed the Archbishop of Canterbury that the Church in America "is generally in a very flourishing and increasing condition, and much more so on occasion of the virulent contentions of the dissenters among themselves."[59]

He was thinking more, perhaps, of feuding among Connecticut Congregationalists. But the disruptions in Protestant thinking, the incursions of Whitefield, and intimations of diminished control of society by the clergy could be seen in New York, too. Johnson's solution was, characteristically, Rule and Order. In King's College, students were fined if they were not at morning and evening prayers. On Sunday, they were expected to attend the church of their parents' choice. There was never to be such "indecent behaviour as talking, laughing, jostling, winking, etc." in the college chapel.

But how often was the president himself in that chapel? From all appearances, Samuel Johnson spent much of his time in Westchester County in the earliest years of the college. His autobiography tells us that he came to King's College at the age of fifty-seven with the clear understanding that during periods of smallpox in town he could reside elsewhere. He moved into the college building, which he had helped design in 1760. Soon after, his wife died (of smallpox) and Johnson retired to Stratford, happy in the knowledge that he had been able to withstand William Livingston, who, as he said, "with other leading Presbyterians and free thinkers" had been his opponents when he first came to King's College.

William Livingston could indeed be a formidable opponent. Born in Albany and baptized in the Dutch Church there, he graduated from

Yale in 1741. Much later, Livingston remembered that when he came to
New York to prepare for the bar he was one of only six college gradu-
ates in the city. He joined the Presbyterian church in Wall Street, partly
in recognition of his Scotch Presbyterian minister progenitor, and partly
because the Reformed Church in New York stubbornly held to the
Dutch language (as it would do for yet many years to come). Nor was
William Livingston unaware of family prerogatives. When his father,
Philip, died in 1749,

> in the city, the lower rooms of most of the houses in Broad Street
> where he resided were thrown open to receive the assemblage. A
> pipe of wine was spiced for the occasion, and to each of the eight
> bearers a pair of gloves, a mourning ring, scarf and handkerchief and
> a monkey spoon was given. At the manor [110 miles up the North
> River] the whole ceremony was repeated, another pipe of wine was
> spiced, and beside the same presents to the bearers, a pair of black
> gloves and handkerchief were given to each of the tenants. The
> whole expenses were said to amount to five hundred pounds.[60]

It is a mark of William Livingston that, though born to privilege, he
was fully a son of the eighteenth century inasmuch as he was quick to
perceive and resent any intrusion upon human freedom. Mercurial and
impatient, he dismissed as outdated, irrelevant, and intrusive the politics and practices of the Episcopal Church in New York. The ecclesiastical ties of King's College were an affront to William Livingston, but in
view of Trinity's generous land grants he, and like-minded people,
were powerless to do much more than demand that public aid to the
college be reduced, and complain that not enough influential men had
acted to curb Trinity's ascendancy. To one friend he noted that the

> college was opened last June in the vestryroom of the schoolhouse
> belonging to Trinity Church. It consists of seven students, the major-
> ity of whom were admitted though utterly unqualified, in order to
> make a flourish. They meet for morning prayers in the church, and
> are like to make as great progress in the liturgy as in the sciences.[61]

Livingston hoped the Dutch Reformed leaders would be successful
in their request for their own professor of divinity at King's College,
which would "diminish that badge of distinction to which the Episcopalians are so zealously aspiring," he said. He was ever fearful of what
mischief the Episcopalians would inflict upon the community if their
rise to prominence remained unchecked. He wrote:

> As I sat the other evening, smoking my pipe, and ruminating in the
> elbow chair on what would probably be the situation of the province
> twenty years hence, should a certain faction succeed in their mediated
> encroachments on our liberties, I fell into a methodical dream. . . .

in which there is (horrors!) a Bishop of New York who takes "vigorous measures to reduce the obstinate clergy to the obedience of his church," there are acts prohibiting Dissenters in the provincial Assembly, the old Dutch Reformed church is reduced to 150 adults, and a professor of King's College was "deposed from his office for saying, in one of his lectures, that Christ is the supream [sic] head of the Christian Church."

His dream illustrates fears of Episcopal power, but Livingston's exuberance and energy often led him to overstate his case. He believed that the Episcopal clergy were little better than the Roman Catholic missionaries in Canada. When, in 1769, the Bishop of Llandaff preached his celebrated sermon before the SPG urging the case for a bishop in America, William Livingston quickly made much of the bishop's reference to the low moral state prevailing in the colonies. William Livingston was one of those snipers who, at the most, are a nuisance to their enemies and an eventual bore to their friends. He would have earned only passing mention in our narrative had not his agitation against the Episcopal Church been remembered when the Revolutionary War broke out. Then he climbed to heroic heights, was repeatedly elected governor of New Jersey, his adopted state, and was recognized as a man who had been in the fight long before there was a war. When we recall that sometimes the contending parties of the Revolution were known as Presbyterians opposed to Episcopalians, we see how popular a man like William Livingston could become.

REVOLUTION COMES TO NEW YORK

The uproar concerning Trinity Church's involvement with King's College might seem at first to be a footnote to New York's history, but in 1770 the sentiments of the church's opponents were still very evident. The English Church seemed similar to Mr. Murdstone: the nasty stepfather, always ready to summon to accounts after a pleasant afternoon of freedom. It was an agency that automatically blessed the civil authority. The Church was associated in the popular mind with policies emanating from London, and those policies seemed more and more intrusive. The official mercantile system restricted the selling power of colonial businessmen. Many of these merchants, or their fathers, had sought in America opportunities to ship and trade and sell freely. They were not mistaken when they believed they could do well in New York. Developing colonial business fostered a sense of independence, a proud independence based upon accomplishments of which the Crown itself should be proud. Instead the Tories, who replaced the Whigs after the

accession of King George III in 1760, enacted regulations and taxes
that hampered colonial commerce. The presence of English soldiers in
Manhattan had always been expected, even appreciated, because of
occasional Indian troubles upriver, and also because New York's harbor
was vital to commerce.[62] But by 1770 there was for some people a new
and ominous meaning to the presence of the lobsterbacks, as English
soldiers were often called. Nonetheless New York was undeniably the
Loyalist stronghold.[63]

If hostilities broke out between the colonies and the Crown, the
Church of England was bound to suffer whether or not it had the protection of government troops. In the first place, it *was* the Church of
England and most of its ministers continually made that plain. Many of
the New York clergy were missionaries supplied and supported by the
SPG. They were thus "official," part of the established order of things,
and appropriately loyal to the sovereign. It is worth noting that those
clergy who received their stipends from local subscriptions tended to
be less loyal to the king.

There were, by 1770, four centers of the Episcopal Church in the
city of New York: Trinity Church, St. Paul's Chapel (built by Thomas
McBean in 1766), St. George's Chapel (1749), and King's College. The
rector of Trinity and its chapels when war came was Samuel Auchmuty.
He was in poor health, fled to New Jersey when the patriots entered the
city, and returned only after the British had driven the Americans
upriver. Auchmuty died soon after, in 1777. In that same year, a great
fire destroyed much of the city, including Trinity Church.

The new rector-apparent was Charles Inglis and "as soon as decency permitted" he was commended to the Bishop of London, who in
response was pleased to "highly applaud" the election of Inglis to the
rectorate of a church whose principal building now lay in ashes, in a
city soon to be renowned for immorality and graft. There is something
very symbolic in hearing that the new rector "was conducted to the
ruins of the church and, placing his hands on the blackened walls, was
inducted by Elias Desbrosses, one of the church wardens."[64] Inglis was
born in Ireland in 1734 and came to America when about twenty years
old. He taught school in Lancaster, Pennsylvania, for three years and
then returned to London to be ordained. The SPG sent him to Delaware, but in 1765 he accepted a second call to be the assistant minister
of New York's Trinity Church. He was soon joined by another assistant,
the Rev. Samuel Provoost, and it is this enigmatic, gifted man who will
occupy much of our attention as the story of the Diocese of New York
unfolds. If ever two men were misyoked, it was Inglis, the High Tory to
whom was given a credulity sometimes leading to near hysteria, and
Provoost, scornful Whig, "heavy Dutch," and philosophical. Provoost

had one advantage over his colleagues and his rector, however: he was a native New Yorker, related to the most prominent families in the city, and blessed with an independent income. In 1771 Samuel Provoost left Trinity for reasons that will never be fully explained. He recalled, later, that some of the congregation were displeased because he refused to preach the "enthusiastic" sermons they would hear at the Methodistical John Street Chapel. Wesleyan piety naturally attached itself to the Great Awakening, but a Latitudinarian such as Provoost viewed those things with disdain. He said his sermons preached "the plain doctrine of religion and morality."[65]

There was perhaps another reason why Samuel Provoost departed from Trinity, and it would have taken shape when, two years after becoming an assistant there, he sailed to Ireland to attend to business with his wife's family. When he returned, he "found that there was a feeling in the Parish against him."[66] This "feeling" was perhaps because Provoost had not spared the congregation his political opinions, and in the months of his absence, the congregation—encouraged by Auchmuty and Inglis—discovered they could do without Mr. Provoost's politics. As a scion of prosperous merchants, he knew about English interference in colonial commerce. From all accounts, his studies with John Jebb at Cambridge reinforced leanings to American independence. He was early to discern the state of affairs in New York: "We are now fighting for our laws and our liberties, for our friends, family and country," he said as early as 1767. These words must have made the rector apoplectic.[67] When Provoost returned from Ireland he soon found that there was an "insufficiency of the Corporation funds to support him" and that whatever salary he thereafter received must be from "subscriptions only." In other words, if Provoost's friends wanted him at Trinity, let them pay him. Therefore, Provoost resigned in 1771. He was then twenty-nine years of age, and able to occupy himself with other concerns. His family's wealth—grandmother was a smuggler!—freed him from the necessity (if not the honor) of Trinity's stipend. His wife's health had always been poor—indeed, uncertain health runs like a fugue through the Provoost records—and the tensions in Trinity didn't help. Country life among the Livingstons, his kinsmen, seemed a logical escape from the political and ecclesiastical dilemma. The facts are not clear, but it appears that Samuel Provoost bought a farm upriver in what is now Germantown, exactly where the Palatines under John Frederick Haeger had been settled. Provoost's life there was not very much pleasanter than that of his German predecessors, for most of his income derived from city property and was terminated during the war.

Samuel Provoost was the least self-assertive of mortals. He seems to have preserved no personal records, never kept a diary, and seldom

related to his family and friends any wartime experiences. His reti-
cence, and his family's subsequent destruction of his papers, is history's loss, for in the years 1771 through 1783 he rubbed elbows with, and
was the esteemed friend of, many of the aborning nation's leading people. The Hudson River Valley was the strategic corridor of the war;
whoever controlled it would win the war, for it was the vital link
between the Middle Colonies and New England. Most of the Revolutionary army leaders passed up and down the river. New York merchants thought it wise to live quietly in the houses they found available
upriver. Provoost would have dined with Washington at Clermont in
1782 after that house had been speedily rebuilt following its burning
by the British in 1777. General Putnam had his quarters a few miles
from Provoost's house. But, inexplicable to us, Tories might also be
met at the tea table, for sometimes a leading Loyalist was "interned" in
the country. When this happened he would often be welcome in the
big houses if he was discreet about politics. No one fits this description
better than the intrepid William Smith, who, fortunately, did keep a
diary. Smith was a moderate Tory and a Presbyterian. He was persuaded
"that the Episcopal Clergy and the Zealots [should] incur Censure as
Excitors of these Troubles" and was pleased to record that Sir Henry
Clinton had even kept Tory Beardsley of Christ Church, Poughkeepsie,
waiting three hours before seeing him. This convinced Smith that even
the English military were aware of the clergy's troublemaking.[68] Early
in the war, Smith

> sent a Note to Parson Provoost desiring to know whether he will sell
> his Villa on York Island—He sends me an answer by Walter Living-
> ston last Night—That he would if he knew what to do with so much
> Continental Money. This marks the Fear of the greatest Zelot for In-
> dependency.[69]

As long as Smith was detained in "the manor of Livingston" he
complained of his clerical neighbor: Provoost "continues his attachment to Congress"[70]; "Mr. Provoost the Episcopal Minister drank Tea
here—he is greatly elated [because Burgoyne appeared to be surrounded by American forces]."[71] Smith thought Provoost was "much influenced by" Robert R. Livingston, a member of the committee charged
with drafting the Declaration of Independence.

Whatever information came to Provoost about the Church in New
York City was likely to be inaccurate (though, again inexplicably, some
of his patriot friends appear to have visited Manhattan frequently). Wartime news is proverbially biased by excitement as well as by individual
conviction. For instance, Luke Babcock, rector of Yonkers, wrote to the
Society on March 22, 1776:

Soon after the receipt of your letter the troubles of this country were multiplied. There was the fever excited in men's minds by the late battle of Lexington. Then the affairs of Bunker Hill next came, and the Continental Fast, which may be considered as a trial by ordeal of the ministers of the Church of England in America. . . . I have been threatened with mutilation and death if I go into New England.[72]

Inglis of Trinity, likewise, was led to believe all manner of wrong-doings by patriot soldiers, including the fictitious murder of a New York clergyman. We do not know if during the war Provoost was fully aware of the pamphleteering of his Episcopal colleagues, though we may be sure that eventually he heard of their writings. New Jersey's Thomas Bradbury Chandler wrote *What Think Ye Of Congress Now?* (1775). In it he postulated an incipient American nobility in those persons assembled in Philadelphia. "Oh! how we shall shine with dukes in America! There will be no less than fifty three of them," crowed Chandler.[73] Chandler, like that other pamphleteer Samuel Seabury, later learned to live at ease in an independent America, but he was far more clever in his tracts than was Seabury.[74] More conciliatory, too: in his *Friendly Address* (1774), he envisioned the American colonies as part of an English family of dominions somewhat presaging the British Commonwealth.

Seabury, who was rector of Westchester, tended to be shrill. He feared that the English court system, the mainstay of ordered society, would be overturned by mobs who would see their Loyalist opponents "tarred, feathered, hanged, drawn, quartered and burnt."[75] At the same time, Seabury wondered how "half a dozen fools in your neighborhood" could cause this war against the Crown. In a more idyllic mood, Seabury described England as "a vigorous matron, just approaching a green old age; and with spirit and strength sufficient to chastise her undutiful and rebellious children," to which Alexander Hamilton gleefully replied that, in fact, England was "an old, wrinkled, withered, worn-out hag."[76]

Chandler, President Myles Cooper of King's College, Inglis of Trinity, and Seabury had earlier agreed to write pamphlets to counter "all the publications disrespectful to government and the Parental State."[77] Inglis dashed off several tracts, but lacked the energy required to make quick replies, and soon quit the field. Myles Cooper, following the example of Governor Tryon, fled to a ship in the harbor, and then sailed to England where he took a parish. Provoost had known these men. He would have heard early that Auchmuty had died in New Jersey in March 1777, and that Charles Inglis had succeeded him as rector of Trinity. Other Episcopal clergymen were less fortunate than Inglis in 1777. John Doty of Schenectady went to Canada. John Sayre of New-

burgh fled to New Brunswick Province. John Beardsley of Poughkeepsie was arrested by the patriots for general troublemaking; he had already written that "many of my brethren are in exile."[78] After Beardsley
was moved to New York, Provoost went downriver from Germantown
for some baptisms in Poughkeepsie and, it is said, a Christmas service.
He also officiated at Catskill during the war.

Of course, Provoost had heard about the fires in the city, the first of
which had swept away Trinity Church (and probably some of Provoost's
commercial property, too). Inglis was among those who believed the
rumor that American patriots had fired the city. The blaze soon destroyed the church "and its excellent Organ, which cost £850 Sterling
and was otherwise ornamental . . . the Rector's House and the Charity
School, the two latter large expensive buildings were burned. St. Paul's
Chapel and Kings College had shared the same Fate being directly in
the line of Fire had I not been providentially on the Spot, and sent a
number of people on the Roof of each," declared Inglis.[79]

Far sadder was the plight of the Mohawk Indians at Fort Johnson.
Loyal to Crown and Church, and deprived of Sir William Johnson's wise
counsel by his death in 1774, they were firmly on the side of the Tories.
Stories of Indian outrages multiplied. Their alleged cruelties encouraged by Johnson's sons were said to even exceed the Hessians' legendary brutalities. Some Indians joined Burgoyne and went with him to
Canada. Others remained in New York and were a threat to the patriots
until General Sullivan set out with an expeditionary force bent on
slaughter readily consummated. The only positive result of this disgrace was that, after the war, soldiers who had seen those lush lands in
the Indian territory of western New York ventured back to homestead
upon them.

4

After the Peace

> *No man can build on air and the great achieve-*
> *ments of the later leaders would have been impossi-*
> *ble had there not been a certain amount of quiet*
> *repairing of the shattered foundations of the Church*
> *[prior to 1810].*
>
> —WILLIAM W. MANROSS

Many thoughtful persons in England doubted that the prolonged war with the thirteen colonies was worthwhile, and as early as February 1782 the House of Commons seemed to think further efforts would be futile. "Impracticable" is the word used by Benjamin Franklin in a letter to George Washington. Some English leaders gave credence to the notion that the colonies would again submit to the Crown after a period of "Rage and Distraction" brought on by immature independence.[1] Merchants on both sides of the Atlantic surveyed their faltering business enterprises and pleaded for peace. Conditions in occupied New York City were horrid. The city was overcrowded with Loyalist families seeking their protection from the "cowboy" marauders who preyed on them. The valleys of the Hackensack in New Jersey and the Hudson in New York were scenes of bitter fighting by neighboring patriot and Tory families, supported by whichever army was near and had the upper hand; the losers often retreated to New York, where despite its half-destroyed condition room was somehow made for them. Because of the overcrowding, goods were scarce and expensive. There was plenty of Crown money in the city (which encouraged inflation), and graft was common. "English tax money tended to end up in private pockets," writes one historian;[2] many of the Loyalists who had sought the protection of a British-held city "were living in utter poverty in roofless, burned-out rooms."[3] "Canvas-town" it was called, because of temporary roof covers. The surrender at Yorktown on September 19, 1781, was the beginning of a long waiting period, an armistice dependent upon deliberations in Paris. On February 23, 1783, Rivington (the publisher who trimmed shamelessly according to the political wind but was saved for postwar profits because, after all, he had by far the best stock of books in the city) reported that a "very important Intelligence was last night announced." But events moved slowly, and the King's proclamation recognizing American independence was not read until April 8. Ten days later Washington praised his troops for having won a war which assured "an asylum for the poor and oppressed of all nations and religions."[4]

New York received the peace news with a groan. The Loyalists there said they were betrayed by their own people. Having seen the dishonesty and philandering of military and civilian officialdom throughout the war years, they had no reason to hope for protection from His Majesty's forces now. And in any case, the English soldiers would soon be departing. Certainly the Tories in New York couldn't look for help from the returning patriots. In such cases, old scores are settled harshly. Most of the defiant Loyalists in New York elected to leave the country.

The English had the tremendous problem of vacating New York City in an orderly manner that provided maximum protection for themselves and the many families leaving with them. Ships had to be found for the 29,244 soldiers and civilians who eventually sailed down the Narrows. Houses were to be returned to their former owners. Looting and vandalism were forbidden. The peace treaty declared that no Negroes "or other property of the American inhabitants" was to be taken from the city, but (as we are delighted to discover) three thousand slaves did manage to flee with the Loyalists over the protests of their owners (some of whom were later compensated).

November 25 was set as "Evacuation Day." For many years afterward, it was an anniversary marked with particular patriotic fervor in New York State. "Close on the eve of an approaching winter, with an heterogeneous set of inhabitants, composed of almost ruined exiles, disbanded soldiers, mixed foreigners, disaffected Tories, and the refuse of the British army, we took possession of a ruined city," recalled Elkanah Watson.[5] By careful arrangement, on November 25, the Americans were to arrive in the city and the last ships carrying the English were to sail away. It seems to have gone smoothly. George Washington, Governor Clinton, and other dignitaries rode horseback down to the "barrier" on the Bowery at Grand Street. Rivington crowed, "May the Remembrance of the Day be a lesson to Princes." Thirteen shots were fired over the ruins of Trinity Church, probably as an intentional reminder of the colonies' triumph over the Crown and its Church. During these ceremonies a favoring breeze took the last British ship out of sight.

Inglis of Trinity had already departed.[6] Before leaving New York, however, he somewhat ingenuously expressed the idea that perhaps an Englishman might be found to be a bishop in the new nation. He specified an Englishman "who had never been in America, and was clear of having taken part in our unhappy Division."[7]

Inglis would also recall a meeting in New York on March 23, 1783, in which eighteen priests huddled together in shabby Tory sanctuary had planned for a bishop in Nova Scotia; Inglis himself had signed that memorial, together with Seabury and other Episcopal clergymen: Jonathan Odell, George Panton, John Beardsley, Benjamin Moore, John Bowden, George Bissett, Charles Mangan, and Joshua Bloomer. On March 28, 1783, Inglis again expressed his concern about the Episcopal Church in New York, and wondered (quite rightly) whether he could safely remain in the city.[8] The answer became obvious as Evacuation Day drew near, and he resigned on November 1. It is of interest that Inglis eventually returned to the Western Hemisphere as the first Bishop of Nova Scotia.

New York Province had not been conspicuously patriotic during the war. A historian in Boston later claimed the province supplied 17,781 soldiers for the American armies while Massachusetts sent 67,907.[9] If this is so, there must have been many tender consciences in New York at the peace. There were, on the one hand, the celebrated patriot heroes whose progeny would burnish their memory to a high luster. There were, on the other hand, those whose Loyalism had led them to make that departure of pathos on November 25, 1783. And there remained the very many others who accommodated themselves to the British occupation, and cheered the success of his majesty's forces during the war. Now these latter-day vicars of Bray found themselves unwilling to depart, and yet frightened at possible retaliation. They gambled that time could quickly heal, and for the most part they gambled well. But institutions, especially rich institutions, are more vulnerable to revolutionary wrath than people who can temporize, and nothing in New York was more associated with the discarded sovereign than Trinity Church.

There had been no services in Trinity since the fire of 1777 destroyed the church, of course, and it is presumed that Inglis and Benjamin Moore (sometimes aided by the other Episcopal clergymen who found the city more congenial than their parishes in patriot-controlled territory) officiated in St. Paul's and St. George's, both chapels of Trinity (there was also the chapel of King's College). The fact that these two churches were open during the war did not promote Episcopal fortunes later, though in fairness it was recalled that the Methodist and the Moravian churches were also open without question. The other churches were closed; the Presbyterians would be specially anathematized by the English. Closed churches were often used for inappropriate purposes—storage, sheltering horses—and few were spared casual vandalism.

On the same day the vestry received the resignation of Charles Inglis, it elected his assistant, Benjamin Moore, to succeed him. Though a Tory, Moore was an American by birth and had recently married the heiress of valuable Manhattan property. For this reason, and perhaps because of assurances received from the vestry, Moore had opted to remain in New York. Suspecting trouble ahead, the vestry planned to present their chosen man to Governor Clinton immediately "for his approbation." Their suspicions were justified. In nothing else was there a more signal lesson to be taught than in filling the position of rector of the English church, and the "Whig members of the Episcopal Church" moved swiftly. Meeting at Simmons Tavern "near the City Hall," they challenged the election of Benjamin Moore as "improper and unwarrantable." The vestry temporized and attempted pacifying proposals, but the issue was too important to be settled by amiable gestures. Moreover, personal animosities were strong. Robert R. Livingston put it plainly in a letter:

> a very great and important dispute has arisen in the church of England which is in this City a great political machine, disposing property to the amount of £200,000—the tories a few days before we came in elected as rector a man who has preached and prayed against us during the war. The Whigs insist of a new appointment and the dispute is carried on with so much warmth that it may probably draw after it serious political consequences.[10]

Chancellor Livingston's scant interest in religion was matched by his vast interest in cash and politics and, at this time, his concern that the Livingston family consolidate its position for future prosperity. Very gladly, he joined with four others who asked to meet with the Trinity vestry in Capes Tavern on December 9, 1783. The others were James Duane (soon to be mayor of New York), Marinus Willett (sheriff 1784–92), Robert Troup, and John Lawrence (both of whom had served long in the Continental Army). When the vestry refused to meet with "the gentlemen styling themselves the Whig members of the Episcopal Church,"[11] those gentlemen threatened suit and, on New Year's Day 1784, presented a petition which had been drawn up on December 10 and subsequently signed by nearly one hundred persons. Considering the precarious position of the English Church and its vast fortunes, which, surely, were envied by others, the vestry dreaded petitions and court interference. The response to the threatened suit was a sugges-

tion that there be, in effect, two ministers in charge. This was immediately rejected by James Duane, who was secure in believing the Council of the city would act in favor of the Whig petition. He was right. On
January 12, 1784, the control of the Corporation was put in the hands of
Duane, Francis Lewis, Lewis Morris, Isaac Sears, William Duer, Daniel
Dunscomb, Anthony Lispinard, John Rutherford, and William Bedloe—
all now firmly Whig. Duane had in mind a candidate for the rectorate:
Samuel Provoost, an undoubted patriot, kinsman of the Livingstons, a
son of the city. Impatient to see the thing through, Duane wrote to his
wife:

> In the mean time we are deprived of the Opportunity of doing Justice
> to the merit of our friend Mr. Provoost tho he has esteem and confi-
> dence of all the Whig interests.[12]

Duane was never during the war as notable a patriot as Provoost,
but then as now the shades of political opinion were often ignored in
the light of overwhelming tastes and personal loyalty. James Duane and
Samuel Provoost had been friends for years: Duane had been a visitor
in East Camp. He shared Provoost's delight in horticulture.[13] Provoost
himself had a capacity for friendship, and those who knew him believed his qualities and his politics should be rewarded. Undoubtedly
he had suffered financial privation during the war. Perhaps most of all,
the Livingstons saw him as a significant factor in affirming their power
in those important postwar years.

Samuel Provoost arrived in New York City on February 2, 1784, but
it is probable he had been there earlier in the winter in order to inspect
what remained of his property. Now he conferred again with the Whig
trustees of Trinity and accepted what he had been told to expect: the
rectorate of Trinity. On February 5, Benjamin Moore was informed that
Samuel Provoost had been handed the keys of the church—keys to
what building, we wonder—and that thereafter Provoost would "have
the direction" of the parish. Moore replied gracefully and insinuated
that he would await judication. But, having thus asserted his own integrity and reaffirmed the loyalty of the vestry, he stepped aside. Samuel
Provoost was the new rector of Trinity Church.

Inasmuch as Trinity was a continuing reminder of the English ascendancy and occupation in New York City, it is safe to say that had
Benjamin Moore persisted in claiming the rectorship, Whig fury might
have retaliated by alienating the landed endowments of the church.
And, if there were any selfish interests in New York that stood ready to
grasp what a discredited Trinity had failed to hold, these, too, were
disappointed in the election of Samuel Provoost. As things stood, the
Corporation of Trinity, stained with Toryism, now had at its head New

York's distinguished patriot parson, Samuel Provoost. A century later, another rector of Trinity wrote:

> It was a fortunate thing for the Parish, at that moment, that its head should be a man, not only of high repute for learning, culture, and knowledge of affairs, but also identified from the beginning with the cause of the American Revolution, and enjoying the full confidence of the State government and the patriotic citizens of New York.[14]

To this appraisal by a high Victorian, made at the nadir of Provoost's reputation, it might be added that Provoost above all others is responsible for retrieving the fortunes of the Episcopal Church in New York. What other available clergyman in New York could have done this? Benjamin Moore had indeed preached and prayed for the King during the war. This native son, now returned to the city with his wife and four children, was in almost all respects the ideal person. For, while Samuel Provoost held advanced democratic views—"a good Jeffersonian," says one historian[15]—his upbringing and manners led him to a certain Whig moderation entirely congenial to the interests of the extended Livingston family.

The Livingstons, for their part, may have regretted the departure of some of their Loyalist friends. But these were times to mend your own fortunes, and what more genteel way to do so than buy cheaply what once belonged to the King's men? Might not Trinity's properties be invaded had not the patriot parson been found and elected as rector?[16] New York City was an open field for an able man with connections to advance himself. Not all the Loyalists left the city, but those of that stripe who remained were wise not to speak overmuch about politics. Tory sympathies came in many shapes and sizes. Some families, like the DeLanceys and the Philipses, were now gone, their many lands confiscated (and often sold to their former friends). Other Tories—the dePeysters and the Kembles come to mind—remained discreetly outside the city during the war. Still others—such as Provoost's friend Robert C. Livingston—lived in England during much of the war, and when here went freely to and from occupied New York City. (The New York historian learns very soon not to inquire too closely into the movements and interests of the great patriotic families during the Revolutionary War!)

On the other side, there were those who believed Tories should be punished. Fortunately for the city and the Church, these sentiments were soon overcome by a general feeling that profit and virtue lay more surely in forgetting the past and extracting whatever advantages might now present themselves in a city waiting to be rebuilt. Ambitious businessmen saw a vast future in the realty and port of New York. It was in the immediate postwar years that a piano salesman named Astor quickly sold his London-made instruments and used New York as the center of a far-flung fur business.[17]

Samuel Provoost was the least vindictive of men (if we except his relations with Seabury!) He settled comfortably into his new responsibilities. Since Episcopal clergy were a rare commodity now in patriotic New York, he asked Benjamin Moore to remain with him as Trinity's assistant minister. It was a salutory arrangement. New York in those scrambling years needed all the refined native sons it could find to counteract both the coarse effects of the occupation and the materialism that followed. A European visitor describes the city as one of ugly small houses, most of them built of wood painted white, some of brick, green doors predominating. "You might in half an hour's walk hear French, German, Low Dutch, Scotch, Irish or English pronunciations," he said, though the "well bred" spoke English. Women were "generally handsome, very fair. In the vicinity of New York every respectable family had slaves—negroes and negresses, who did the drudgery."[18] Well-to-do men did the family marketing, carrying baskets under their arms to and from the stores, a custom prevailing in New York City almost till living memory.

ASSESSING THE DAMAGE

The Episcopal Church in the colonies had suffered much during and immediately after the war, and in the opinion of most patriots it deserved to suffer. Its clergy had a point of view that reflected their education and ordination in England. Defeated and discredited, most of them left the country. The laity were dispirited and scattered; some of them, surely, were disgusted with the Church's performance during the war and forsook it altogether. Church buildings were closed and, often, much damaged. Glebes and other endowments were frequently alienated. It is a dismal picture, but, as we have seen, immediate steps were taken to protect Trinity Church under the popular Samuel Provoost. In other places in the state the Church gradually came together under local lay leadership using whatever clergy or lay readers could be found.

After the peace, John Sayre of Newburgh realistically predicted that "country congregations will be unable to support ministries without assistance from the Society"—and then supposed (most unrealistically!) that henceforth Society appropriations must be more generous.[19] Had Sayre forgotten that there had been a war? Did he suppose the American churches were still eligible for Society grants when Seabury, arch-Loyalist, was denied consideration in London?

The condition of the Episcopal Church varied, according to location. Consider Yonkers, for instance. Its rector, Luke Babcock, had died in 1777 following a brief imprisonment by the patriots in Hartford. With Samuel Seabury, he had signed the Protest at White Plains in July 1775 against "unlawful Congress and Committees." His widow and children continued to occupy the glebe farm on the Saw Mill River. After the war they were allowed to remain there and the farm was preserved to the "Corporation of the Episcopal Church in the Town of Yonkers" by a special act on April 3, 1792.[20] The Rev. George Panton held services during the war, but quit in 1782. For some time ministers of other denominations used the church, but in 1784—that year of great good fortune for the Episcopal Church—a layman, Andrew Fowler, "collected the congregation and was the first one who read prayers and sermons in the church after the Revolutionary War." Fowler was later ordained.

"Collected the congregation"—that describes the task wherever there was an Episcopal church. An extreme example is Fishkill, where, though it was a relatively new building,

> the church was already in 1776 in a delapidated and neglected condition, unfit for use. It was hardly habitable when first occupied for the Provincial Convention in September 1777, without seats or benches or other conveniences and so fouled by doves that it could not be comfortably used . . .[21]

The rector of Fishkill was John Beardsley. He also served Christ Church in the town of Poughkeepsie, where he lived on the glebe shared by both parishes. Beardsley was firmly Tory, whereas the Fishkill-Poughkeepsie region was notably patriotic. Beardsley did little to ease tensions between his politics and those of his people; no wonder the Fishkill church was "delapidated and neglected"! "He did not conceal his sentiments," says a polite Victorian writer.[22] The Minutes of the Council of Safety, December 5, 1777, are more direct, and authorize the Commissioner of Conspiracies

> to cause the Reverend Mr. Beardsley and Henry Vandenbergh, with their families (male servants and slaves excepted) to be removed to the city of New York, and to permit them to take with them their wearing apparel, and necessary bedding, and provisions for their passage, and no other goods or affects whatsoever.[23]

Beardsley went to New Brunswick in Canada at the peace and became rector of Maugerville, New Brunswick.

The Poughkeepsie vestrymen were, on the whole, quiet Tories.

They met regularly during the war and held prescribed Easter elections, but their new stone church was closed. The glebe was rented. Samuel Provoost came downriver in August 1779 to officiate at some baptisms, probably in a private house. After Yorktown, the vestry airily forgot the war and sought a rector. They found him in the person of Henry VanDyke, a lay reader of Stratford, Connecticut. It was understood that Mr. VanDyke would not move to Poughkeepsie until he was ordained, which took place in August 1785, soon after Seabury's return from Britain. Even then, VanDyke didn't come to Poughkeepsie. The impatient vestry—without a rector for eight years—finally drew the reason from Mr. VanDyke: he would be arrested and imprisoned for debt if he came into New York State. The matter was eventually settled by the intervention of Egbert Benson, and Mr. VanDyke began his ministry in Fishkill and Poughkeepsie in May 1787. Very soon thereafter, he began occasional services as requested by "a number of gentlemen of the Manor of Livingston" in what is now Tivoli. It was the faint beginning of expansion.

What happened to other New York clergy? Inglis had reported to London that the Rev. Ephraim Avery of Rye, Bedford, and Newcastle had been dragged into the street by Whig Soldiers, beaten, shot, and his throat cut. Such a message probably reduced the Society's officers to despair, but they may have had a measure of solace in Seabury's subsequent report that the poor man was found only murdered in his woodshed. Further investigation suggested suicide. Avery's intended successor, Isaac Hunt of Philadelphia, probably never arrived in Rye. He had been assaulted by a mob in his native city, and fled to England where he became chaplain in a titled house and the father of James Henry Leigh Hunt, the essayist. George Panton, as we have noted, served Yonkers during the war, but when things began to look glum for the Loyalists he, too, retreated to the city and was one of the fifty-five who petitioned Sir Guy Carleton for land grants in Nova Scotia commensurate with those His Majesty's government contemplated settling upon officers who had served in the colonies. Epenetus Townsend of the Salems, despite his Long Island origins, fled early in the war and was lost at sea en route to Nova Scotia. John Stuart, whose long and heroic labors among the Mohwaks were matched by those of his wife, set out with her for Canada and "scarce cast a look back to the world they had forsaken."[24] Richard Mosely had gone to Johnstown in 1772, and, some safe time after the peace, turned up in Connecticut. Another priest who emerged after the war was Isaac Wilkins. He was born in the West Indies, educated in New York City, and settled in Westchester anticipating eventual ordination. He served briefly in the Assembly, but his Loyalist sympathies took him to Nova Scotia after the war. He made his own peace with the new nation, however (so many did!), and in 1799 became rector of Eastchester and St. Peter's, Westchester. He remained there till his death at the age of eighty-nine in 1830; whether or not it was a happy ministry may be gathered from the epitaph he wrote for his burial place: "He remained satisfied with the pittance allowed him, rejoicing that even in that he was no burden to his parishioners; nor ever wished nor ever went forth to seek a better living."[25] His brothers-in-law, Lewis and Gouverneur Morris, outstanding patriots, probably helped ameliorate his situation. Timothy Wetmore had remained in his father's parish at Rye as its schoolmaster, after the elder Wetmore's death of smallpox in 1760. He had declared in 1774, "It is my opinion that the Parliament have no right to tax Americans, though they have a right to regulate the trade of the Empire": a common-sense principle shared by many. But Wetmore's loyalty to the King he had heard prayed for all his life bade him depart for Nova Scotia after the war. A son, Robert, was ordained by Bishop Provoost in 1798 and died in Savannah in 1803.[26]

Joshua Bloomer, like Benjamin Moore, was to be found in his parish before, during, and after the Revolution. Educated at King's College, ordained in 1765, he remained grudgingly in his Long Island posts: "I administered the sacrament at Newtown, when I had but four or five male communicants," he stated; "the rest being driven off or carried away prisoner. I was forbidden to read the prayers for the king and royal family," whereupon he simply shut up the church until the Loyalist troops occupied Long Island.[27] It was because Bloomer did remain in his parish, and was thus an ongoing beneficiary of its grants, that in 1784 the Society sent to Grace Church, Jamaica, £30. This was the last grant sent by the Society for the Propagation of the Gospel to the Episcopal Church in New York, and it was followed by a gracious expression of hope that "the true members of our Church, under whatever civil government they live, may not cease to be kindly affected towards us."[28] Joshua Bloomer died in 1790 at the age of fifty-five.

Bernard Page, Tory rector of Peekskill, fled to England, and his substantial glebe was confiscated. Later, it was restored to the parish through the exertions of Pierre VanCortlandt, one of the lower Hudson River Valley patricians who opted for the patriot side.[29]

It is to be expected that King's College, regarded from its origins as a hotbed of Tory reaction, would attract the ministrations of the patriot soldiers during the brief time Washington's forces were in control of the city. President Myles Cooper was a "furious Tory."[30] He enjoyed pseudonymous literary debates with a favorite pupil, Alexander Hamilton—which, if the story is true, throws an attractive light on both men. Many years later, it was recalled that:

At last the mob got very ferocious against Cooper and a large body
moved at a late hour in the night [May 10, 1775] towards the college
with the intention of murdering or at least tarring and feathering its
unlucky *Praeses*. Hamilton got scent of it, and at the corner of what is
now Park Place and Broadway he made them a furious Whig address,
and in this way kept them off till Cooper got intelligence of the state
of affairs. He got out of bed, and without his breeches managed to get
out of the back gate on Chapel Street and to scramble down the steep
bank between the College and the river, and then proceeded along
shore as far as Greenwich, where he stole a boat and paddled himself
off to one of the frigates in the bay. Meantime the mob attacked his
house, smashed the furniture, ran swords through his bed, in hopes
of finding him there, and at last cleared out in disappointment.[31]

The college library, said by some to have been the best in the country,
was ransacked and "soldiers disposed of the books about the streets for
grog."

RISING FROM THE ASHES

While Episcopalians in New York State were gathering the fragments
that remained after the war, the Church in other states was engaged in
similar undertakings. The first work to be done was to find the local
congregation. There were two other main tasks: first, the Church must
be organized on an interstate level of cooperation and mutual interest.
This is not to say that a "national church" was envisioned in the earliest
postwar years. The initial aim was toward a confederation of state
churches.

The second task was to maintain the apostolic succession from the
English line of bishops. Heretofore, political considerations had made
this impossible. But now the focus of the difficulty was altered: existing
English law would not permit such consecration and, in any case, there
was no precedent in the English Church for bishops' exercising jurisdiction beyond the British Isles. There was, in effect, a great gulf fixed
between the lordly episcopate in England and the needs of churchpeople in the United States of America. The difficulty is almost unimag-
inable in our own day, where it is a familiar sight to see bishops of
various nations and traditions participating in ordinations and consecrations.

Wise William White of Philadelphia was so pessimistic about the
possibility of any American candidates' consecration in the near future
that he proposed the Church function without bishops for the time
being. White, like Provoost, had impeccable patriotic credentials; he

was rector of Christ Church, Philadelphia, brother-in-law of Robert Morris, and longtime chaplain of the Continental Congress. While his proposal was being made known to Episcopalians, other events were taking place. Ten clergy of Connecticut had met at Woodbury in 1783 and appointed Jeremiah Leaming or Samuel Seabury of New York to go to England, promising recognition as Bishop of Connecticut to whichever of them returned having been consecrated there. Leaming's advanced age led him to decline the honor thus accorded him, so the New Yorker set sail. Seabury took with him testimonials signed by Leaming, Inglis, and Moore, and word of William White's astounding idea that the Episcopal Church be nonepiscopal.[32] Seabury had, further, been advised that, should he fail to find consecration by the necessary number of English bishops, he might seek it at the hands of bishops in Scotland.

Independent of this, there was a meeting in New Brunswick, New Jersey, which led accidentally but directly to the formation of the Protestant Episcopal Church in the United States of America. The ostensible reason for the meeting was money! For some years there had existed a Corporation for the Relief of Widows and Orphans of Clergymen in Pennsylvania, New York, and New Jersey (descendant organizations still survive). The corporation had necessarily been neglected during the Revolutionary War, but it was potentially too important to forget now that the Church was looking toward renewal. Nudged by Abraham Beach of Christ Church, New Brunswick (but soon to be another of Provoost's assistants at Trinity), William White convened a meeting in New Brunswick on May 11, 1784. Clergy and laity attended. The discussions readily turned away from the corporation to matters of rebuilding the Church in the states, or, as they said with remarkable foresight, "forming a continental representation of the Episcopal Church." Sensing the importance of what they were about to do, they adjourned with plans to meet in New York City the following October. Invitations were issued to the other states, and it was directed that in "every State, where there shall be a Bishop duly consecrated and settled, he shall be considered as a member of the convention, ex officio."[33]

The autumn meeting was held in New York City, with William Smith of Philadelphia, "one of the most brilliant of the provincial clergy,"[34] presiding. That there was enthusiasm may be judged by the fact that the churches in Virginia, Maryland, Delaware, Pennsylvania, New Jersey, New York, Connecticut, and Massachusetts were represented. It was understood that each state should have a bishop, that each bishop would sit in convention, and that the first General Convention would meet in Philadelphia on the September 27, 1785, the following year.

Before that, however, New York would have its own "diocesan" (a word not yet used) convention. It met, probably at St. Paul's Chapel, on June 22, 1785. Samuel Provoost, Benjamin Moore, and Abraham Beach were the city clergy present; the lay delegates were James Duane, Marinus Willett, and John Alsop. From Long Island there was one priest, Joshua Bloomer, and four laymen: Charles Crommelin, Daniel Kissam, Joseph Burrows, and John Johnson. Staten Island produced "the Rev. Mr. Rowland" and one layman, Paul Micheau. New Rochelle sent Andrew Fowler, and Ulster, Orange, and Dutchess counties sent laymen— Joseph Jarvis and John Davis. Samuel Provoost was elected president, and Benjamin Moore was secretary. The New York City clergy were chosen to go to the convention in Philadelphia accompanied by James Duane and Daniel Kissam (from Long Island) and John Davis (from Poughkeepsie). It was further ordered that Provoost was "to call another convention at such time and place as he shall deem most conducive to the work of the Church."[35]

It was that same month, June 1785, that Samuel Seabury returned to the United States. Failing consecration in England, he had found the nonjurors in Aberdeen willing to comply with his requests, especially since Seabury agreed to use his influence to their advantage in compiling the new American Prayer Book. In doing this, Seabury doubtless enriched the 1789 Book of Common Prayer, and historians have given due credit to the concordat thus honored. But at the same time, the nonjurors themselves have never had the scrutiny they deserved.

For in truth, they were unknown to most Episcopalians, though a dim memory of nonjuror may have lingered in American minds. The politics and the Church views of the nonjurors might be embarrassing to those attempting to revive the Church in the new Republic. The nonjurors were given that name when they refused to accept the result of the "Glorious Revolution" that placed William and Mary on the throne of her father in 1689. A number of prominent Church of England clergy, including the Archbishop of Canterbury, held to the principle that, having sworn allegiance to the King, any other sovereign was a usurper as long as James II lived. In an orderly and deliberate manner, these men set up a Church in Scotland, a country where episcopacy had just then been replaced by a presbyterian form of state church.

Now that Seabury had found consecration at nonjuror hands, it was remembered that in 1724 there may have been two other such bishops in America. According to rumor, both had been consecrated by one English nonjuring bishop in 1722. Welton is said to have declared openly his enhanced status, thus making himself a pariah among those city officials who looked to the London establishment for advancement, for the nonjurors prayed for the early restoration of the Stuarts. Talbot (whose consecration is doubted by some historians) never attempted to exercise episcopal authority. He probably realized that to do so would involve him in a tangle of difficulties. Nevertheless, the possibility that there were two nonjuring bishops in America disturbed church-people who insisted on the established Church's normal orderliness. William White believed Talbot and Welton performed clandestine ordinations.

The importance to us is that the nonjurors were a discounted currency in America; two "bishops" roaming the environs of Philadelphia in the 1720s bent on drumming up interest in the Stuart cause was not an attractive scene to American minds after the Revolutionary War. It is a long cruise to England, and on their voyage to consecration there can be no doubt that William White told Samuel Provoost what he had heard about Talbot and Welton and their nonjuring politics—another nail in Seabury's coffin, as far as Provoost was concerned.

Holding to their conservative political and theological views, and thoroughly Stuart in their loyalties, the nonjurors maintained the apostolic succession but never exercised a wide ministry in Scotland. Dissensions further weakened their influence, so that by the time Seabury met their bishops, Arthur Petrie, John Skinner, and the Primate Robert Kilgour the nonjuring Church (which probably never had any church buildings) resembled a dying sect. The last nonjuror bishop died in 1805. Taken all together, the nonjurors were not what Episcopalians had in mind when they thought of their clergy receiving consecration in the apostolic line.

Certainly, Samuel Provoost didn't regard Seabury as having appropriate credentials. But then, it seems that these two men never could be congenial. The patrician Provoost resented the pretensions of Seabury, whom he had known from their days at King's College. Provoost was a Latitudinarian; Seabury's theology was nearer the Laudian standard and, once consecrated, he was not overly careful to confine his ministrations to Connecticut. Provoost had probably heard that when Seabury ordained a man he extracted the promise that there would be a personal obligation to him until the ordinand's state had its own bishop. Preposterous in a free country, one can hear Provoost exclaim. This is why Provoost later transgressed in the same manner on Seabury's territory.

Seabury's tracts during the war, his services as a chaplain, the possibility of his receiving a pension from the Crown: these rankled. Had not Provoost lost his own house and income during the war? Had not his wife's health suffered irreversibly in the wintertime harshness of East Camp? Had not Provoost been deprived of his beloved library and his scientific apparatus, while Seabury came and went in Loyalist New York? Now that the English themselves had denied him the highest honor of his career, the wily Seabury managed to extract the laurels from an obscure group of reactionary clergy in Scotland who stood for the very things Provoost hated most. When seeking the word to describe Provoost's reaction to the news of Seabury's consecration in Scotland, we can do no better than fall back upon that familiar one, apoplectic!

Furthermore, Seabury wasn't done making mischief. Upon returning from England, he and his Connecticut colleagues refused to join in the Philadelphia convention because its presiding officer wasn't a bishop (that is, wasn't Seabury himself; there were no other bishops in America). Perhaps worse, Bishop Seabury was opposed to lay representation in the councils of the Church. When the New York convention approved a bicameral national structure, he wrote to Bishop Skinner in Scotland, "I cannot but consider this a very lame if not a mischievous business. It will bring the Clergy into abject bondage to the Laity."[36]

Provoost could not agree. He owed his present position in the Church to the laity, while Seabury's election was by clergy only, and his consecration had in part been advanced by testimonials written by Tories, Inglis and Moore. Seabury was ambitious, able, vocation-minded, and contentious. Provoost was easygoing, broad in his interests, diffident about the fortunes of the Church (in the accepted eighteenth-century manner). But, if he was not contentious, he was at least able to nurse a grudge.

The first General Convention of the Episcopal Church met in Philadelphia on September 27, 1785. Sixteen clergy and twenty-four laymen were present, representing Virginia, Maryland, South Carolina, Delaware, Pennsylvania, New Jersey, and New York. Connecticut declined to attend because the Church there was still unsure about lay participation. Massachusetts found a much more Yankee-like reason not to attend: the journey would cost too much to be worthwhile. William White presided and guided the deliberations through the main business which came under the headings episcopate, liturgy, and constitution. It was determined that the states were to be ready with elected bishops when the Church of England would consent to consecrate them. A Proposed Book of Common Prayer was produced by a committee (and was never approved). The constitution of the Church on which White had spent much time began its way toward final ratification four years later.

Of even more interest to us, however, were the two New York conventions held the next year, 1786. There were four city clergy now, Provoost, Moore, and Beach having been joined by the Rev. Uzal Ogden, a difficult presbyter from New Jersey. The lay delegates were an impressive lot: Mayor Duane, Judge John Jay, Chancellor Livingston,

Richard Morris, John Alsop, William Duer, and Pascal Smith; it is perhaps worth noting that Duane, Jay, Livingston, Duer—and Provoost—were all related to one other. The united parishes of Jamaica, Newtown, and Flushing were represented, as were Hempstead and Rye; but there were many Episcopal churches unable as yet to respond to the call of a convention. Nevertheless, it was a real convention: seven clergy and fifteen laymen heard Duane's report of the Philadelphia meeting and discussed the Prayer Book for two days. The gentlemen then dispersed for a month, probably because the news they had been waiting for had not yet arrived. Gathering again on June 13, 1786, "Letters from the English Bishops and from Mr. Adams were read," earning the "thanks of this Convention . . . to the Hon. Mr. Adams and Mr. Lee for interesting themselves in so affectionate a manner for the benefit of the Church in the business of procuring for it an episcopate."[37]

5

A Bishop for New York

> By keeping the historic episcopate, the Church of
> England has preserved a visible sign of continuity
> that reaches back to the primitive church. Bishops
> are consecrated into the historic episcopate; priests
> are ordained into the apostolic succession through
> the laying on of hands by the bishop; by the bishop
> the laity are received at confirmation into full mem-
> bership. . . .
>
> —H. W. MONTEFIORE

The New York Convention in September 1786 shied away from debat-
ing the proposed Prayer Book, probably because the esteemed chairman, Samuel Provoost, wished it deferred "out of respect to the English
Bishops and because the minds of the people are not yet sufficiently
informed." Provoost disapproved any prayer book changes, having already been dismayed by those alterations that facilitated Unitarianism
at King's Chapel, Boston. He well knew that if the Church in the various states desired to continue the English line of succession, it must
be very careful of liturgical changes. In New York, only thirteen copies
of the Proposed Book were sold, and Provoost expressed his opposition
to it when he said, "We should not be able to adopt the book at present
without danger of a schism."[1] When discussing the new constitution
for the American Church, the New York delegates recommended a surprisingly High Church amendment, "That the Bishop be amenable
only to General Convention." Then came another resolution: "In com-
pliance with the direction of the General Convention, *Resolved* that the
Rev. Mr. Provoost be recommended for Episcopal consecration."

    This resolution, however, came as no surprise. Provoost himself
neither sought nor shirked it. Who else in New York was eligible, especially in a city that had suffered the troubles of enemy occupation?
Samuel Provoost was in 1786 the only candidate who could win unani-
mous approval in a diocesan convention whose members would ask
each other, "Who is completely above suspicion?" Provoost was popu-

lar with the city's Episcopalians, and respected by all others who knew him. His wartime retreat added a touch of gallantry. He was intelligent and able (but a dull preacher). He was social and well-connected. His patriotism bade him dine at Washington's table, and his scientific and agricultural studies probably led him to more than one hearty conversation with Jefferson. His classical learning was a formidable and ongoing avocation. He had the means to live well, was much respected by the clergy of other churches, and, above all, had already shown a capacity to preserve and improve the fortunes of Trinity Church—and thus those of the Church in the entire state. For it was Provoost who began the practice of Trinity's generosity to needy churches. What other man in New York approached him in those abilities?

The New York convention of June 1786 appointed Provoost, Joshua Bloomer of Long Island, and Benjamin Moore the clerical delegates to the next General Convention. The laymen elected were Provoost's friends and onetime East Camp neighbors, James Duane and Robert Cambridge Livingston. Other lay delegates present were John Jay—"a sensible man and good churchman"[2]—Robert Crommelin, and a "Mr. J. Farquhar." This delegation was "instructed not to consent to any act that may imply the validity of Dr. Seabury's ordinations"—for, Seabury, upon returning from Scotland in June 1785, had proceeded to ordain four candidates almost immediately. The New York Convention, either by their own knowledge, or tutored by Samuel Provoost, knew that plans to obtain consecration in the English Church would be jeopardized by an overcordial reception of Seabury and his nonjuring line.

The delegates at that New York Convention in September 1786 signed Samuel Provoost's certificate of election (where is it now?), and the parishes were asked to help defray the expenses of his voyage to England. William White, the Bishop-elect "for the State of Pennsylvania," and Samuel Provoost set sail from New York Harbor on November 2, 1786, on what would be the fastest crossing then known.[3] They were greeted as important old friends in London (which says something about British halfheartedness in fighting a war that produced no more determined opponents than the two men they now welcomed). But when the Archbishop of Canterbury sought to delay the consecrations, Samuel Provoost ingenuously declared it was absolutely necessary that he return to New York by Easter because of a "peculiarity in the charter of his church."[4]

The consecration document, as found in the Act Book of the Archbishop of Canterbury,[5] records the event on one page, naming White and then Provoost. This explains why, in the American succession, Provoost is listed as third, following Seabury and White, though it is said that Provoost was actually consecrated first at the ceremony in Lambeth

Palace Chapel on February 4, 1787, because his ordination was prior to White's.[6] The Provoost section of the consecration certificate reads:

> ... And at the same time, The Reverend Samuel Provoost Doctor in Divinity, Rector of Trinity Church in the City of New York, and a subject or citizen of the United States of America, having been elected to the Office of a Bishop by the Convention of the State of New York, One other of the said United States, was consecrated by the said Lord Archbishop of Canterbury in his Chapel aforesaid, Bishop of the Protestant Episcopal Church in the State of New York; the said Lord Archbishop having first obtained His Majesty's Royal License authorizing and empowering him to consecrate the abovenamed William White and Samuel Provoost to the Order of a Bishop respectively, according to the Tenor of an Act of Parliament passed in the Twenty Sixth year of his Majesty's Reign; which Act of Parliament, and the several other instruments used on this occasion are hereafter transcribed at large.
>
> His Grace, the most Reverend William Lord Archbishop of York, primate of England and Metropolitan, the Right Reverend Charles Lord Bishop of Bath and Wells and the Right Reverend John Lord Bishop of Peterborough assisted in this consecration.
>
> Mem^dum Mr. Robert Jenner, Noty Publick, attended as Deputy Registrar and read the King's License; the Attendance of the Vicar general, or of any other persons from Doctor's Commons, besides the Deputy Registrar was not thought necessary.
>
> So I attest
Wm. Dickes   Secretary[7]

White and Provoost embarked, after some brief festivities in England, and after heavy Atlantic seas arrived in New York on Easter Day, 1787. They could look back upon a pleasant London sojourn, filled with meetings with old acquaintances (including Inglis), many of the prominent clergy, and even King George III himself. With perhaps less pleasure they could look forward to the work they would assign themselves in their respective places. Both men knew that, instead of adopting the titles and respectabilities obtaining in England, it would be their duty to transplant an episcopacy "simplified according to the original intention as much as possible."[8]

When Samuel Provoost returned to New York after his consecration, the Episcopal Church there numbered six clergy, and perhaps twenty-six parishes. King's College, renamed Columbia, was a place dear to the new bishop; the college was about to install layman William S. Johnson in the president's chair once occupied by his father, the Rev. Samuel Johnson. The college remained nominally, and by a courtesy that saluted its foundation, a Church institution; those ties, however, were strong enough to lead Jeremiah Leaming of Connecticut to sound out the new president about having Seabury join White and Provoost in consecrating David Griffiths, thus saving the Church in Virginia the expenses of a transatlantic voyage. Johnson demurred.[9] He probably sensed this was a Seabury-inspired maneuver aimed at gaining approval of the Scottish consecration.

This seemingly innocent approach to Columbia's president was only one of the difficulties entailed in putting the Church on a sound course, one that White of Pennsylvania, though he too insisted upon descent in the English line, regarded as a thing trivial when compared with other problems. White and Provoost certainly discussed these matters in their voyages together, and had agreed that the prayer book and a constitution for the Episcopal Church in the United States merited priority. The Church in America would never realize consolidation until these matters were settled. Sectional antipathies must be recognized. Connecticut, for instance, still abhorred the principle of lay participation in the highest councils of the Church, though this was already the practice in the South and in the middle states. New England also opposed the Proposed Prayer Book, all the more since a few deft alterations had been enough to remake King's Chapel, Boston, into a Unitarian church. For their part, the middle and southern states would block any move that sought to enlarge the powers of the bishops at the expense of the laity. Provoost was very firm about this, and could point to what he considered to be the ecclesiastical posturings of Seabury.

These, however, were problems peculiar to transplanting the Church. In due time they resolved themselves so that, miracle of miracles, Samuel Provoost would invite Samuel Seabury to dinner, a genial moment that ended their public quarrels. Provoost grew accustomed to Seabury's presence in Connecticut, and William White (as always) was adroit and patient.

NATIONAL SKEPTICISM

For there were greater problems. The country was experiencing that constant phenomenon of postwar periods, an examination and reassessment of religious thought. In those postwar years there was a distinct unfriendliness toward revealed religion,[10] and an exuberant swing toward what has been called rational, natural religion. Ethan Allen's *Reason the Only Oracle of Man* (1784) was a direct attack on Christianity. More general was the notion that God is a force seen best, and perhaps solely, in creation. A corollary insisted that all good aspirations may readily be found already residing in the human spirit. True reli-

gion, then, required no cultic elaborations. A very popular book that
stated this philosophy was the novel *Paul and Virginia*, published in
New York City by Evert Duyckinck. Its characters, a boy and girl cast
ashore on a desert isle, find ethics to be natural, not requiring their
application by a sponsoring society. This book was widely read (and,
boosting its popularity, gloried in the woodcuts of the first American
illustrator, Alexander Anderson). Thomas Paine's *Age of Reason* (1784)
had, at least, the imprimatur of the author's patriotism and war career.
Paine has always had a place in the American pantheon and one must
agree that the treatment he eventually received at the hands of churchpeople in New Rochelle justly earned them his contempt, and that of
his followers. (But it is fair to add that staunch Episcopalian James
Duane was one of those who found a home for Paine.)[11] Deism was
popular in colleges that had hitherto been exactingly Christian. Lodges
and secret societies sprang up at this time—the Masonic Grand Lodge
was formed in New York in 1781. These tended to offer a substitute for
the churches. Chancellor Robert Livingston, for instance, supported
Samuel Provoost and was a Trinity churchwarden; but he was a religious skeptic all his life. The Chancellor was pleased to be installed
Grand Master in 1784, and "because of the respect in which he was
held contributed much to the reputation and growth of the Fraternity
during his administration," which ended in 1801.[12] During that time
sixty-six Masonic lodges were established in New York State.

PROVOOSTIAN ORTHODOXY

It cannot be said that Samuel Provoost, now in his fortieth year, was
prepared to sally forth and wage battle in the name of Christian orthodoxy. But neither can he be accused of vague rationalism. His sermons—practically the only holograph material known to survive him—
are ponderous after the fashion of the day. And they are sound. We
have, for instance, a sermon he preached at St. Paul's Chapel in the
morning, and repeated in St. George's in New York City that same
afternoon, the Fourth Sunday in Advent, 1789. His properly liturgical
subject is repentance, and having announced the topic the bishop proceeds:

> Let us enquire into the nature of Repentance and consider it as the
> first step to be taken as the preparation of the day of the Lord—for if
> we do not keep Duties apart and treat them with distinctiveness; if we
> do not range them in their proper place, and according to their re-
> spective Subordinations, we shall never know how to proceed, where
> to begin or end—(we shall fight as those who beat the air). [Stating

> that repentance begins with "an Appeal to the natural conscience of
> every sinner," the bishop continues:] Let us, my Brethren, never de-
> ceive ourselves by trusting to anything but a good life or a Sincere
> and timely Repentance, for nothing else can with the least shadow of
> reason be trusted to—nothing else can give as rational comfort and
> assurance in the hour of Death and in the Day of Judgment . . .

Many years later, the very orthodox Morgan Dix of Trinity Church declared Provoost's sermons to be most commendable for the age, but
William A. Duer is probably equally close to the mark when he recalled
that the bishop's popularity in the city never depended upon his
preaching.

PREVAILING ANGLOPHILISM

If Bishop Provoost managed to walk with rationalism without compromise, and in other ways commend the Episcopal Church to New
Yorkers, his troubles with the prevailing mood were softened by factors
definitely favoring the Church. First of all, there was the orderliness,
the cadence—the *reasonableness*—the beauty and stateliness of Prayer
Book worship. These appealed to a people who, having cast off the
moorings of their political past, still felt a need for the sound and
acceptable things of that past. Also, implicit in English religion was a
tender reluctance to require much more than credal assent. Other denominations might demand catechetical certainty from their adherents,
but the Episcopal Church (because of its to-and-fro swings long experienced in politics from the Tudors through the Hanovers) shied away
from dogmatic demands.

Another factor (and perhaps the most decisive one) militating
toward a quick revival of Episcopal Church fortunes in New York is the
undeniable fact that things English had an irresistible glamour after
Yorktown. Those who win are often quickest to forget the war they
have won. Samuel Provoost knew that many of his acquaintances (indeed, some of his own kin) had trimmed to both the Whig and Loyalist
winds, and were now as content to be in an independent New York as
they would have been content to be in a city still royal. Provoost maintained his integrity and was respected by those who read Paine and
Allen and joined the lodge. This sophistication was fruitful. Broad-
mindedness was very much in the air.

There was, however, a drawback to this casual Episcopalianism: it
was ill-prepared to meet the challenge of that American phenomenon,
the American frontier. The Book of Common Prayer does not easily
adapt to informal usage (one of Hobart's gifts, it was said later on, was
that he could use the ancient forms in remote places; or was it that

pioneer people hungered for what they thought they had left behind?).
"Those denominations that took seriously the challenge of the West
and developed methods of meeting it were to become the giants," explains one historian.[13] The Methodists, Presbyterians, and Baptists met
frontier demands by such singularly American forms as lay preaching
and revivalism, modes entirely alien to the traditional Episcopal spirit.
Can one imagine any Bishop of New York at a camp meeting?

Religion in America may well have foreseen a dismal future had
not news of the French Revolution shown what the "logical result" of
Deism and Rationalism might be.[14] Americans who remembered Lafayette's timely arrival here announcing help on the way during their
own Revolution were disillusioned by developments in France, especially when French politics came to threaten American commercial interests.

Bishop Provoost's first convention following his return from Lambeth convened in New York, June 27, 1787. He was elected, according
to the General Constitution of the Church in New York then prevailing,
its president. Six priests and twenty-four laymen were present, representing congregations in New York City, Staten Island, Long Island,
Eastchester, North Chester, Rye, New Rochelle, Philipsburgh (Garrison), Fishkill, and Poughkeepsie. Letters from the churches in Albany
and Balltown (Ballston Spa) asked that they be recognized as belonging to the union of Episcopal parishes in the State of New York; the
word "diocese" was still not in ordinary use in 1787.

REASON FOR OPTIMISM

When the delegates of that 1787 convention began making mental lists
of where Episcopal congregations might exist, they might arrive at a
total as high as thirty-five. One historian has claimed there were
twenty-six Episcopal churches in New York in 1774 and the same number in 1789.[15] It is probable that no one knew for sure in 1787 where all
the New York Episcopal congregations had once gathered, or still existed, but if the delegates put their heads together they might come up
with encouraging statistics. In the city, of course, there was Trinity. The
building lay in ruins, and the congregation of the mother church had
joined with that worshiping regularly in St. Paul's Chapel, which had
been built twenty years earlier. There was also St. George's Chapel,
built in 1752, for a congregation recognized by Trinity's vestry as early
as April 1748, because "accessions from the Dutch Church had become
so numerous, and the seating capacity of Trinity Church was so utterly
inadequate."[16]

In the convention, Trinity and its chapels were represented by the rector-bishop and his assistants, Benjamin Moore and Abraham Beach. But what about those other places not represented in the convention but known to have congregations? Prayer Book services were held in Pelham Manor as early as 1695, and John Pell, Sr., was elected in 1702 as first "Vestry-man" for this part of the Westchester Parish provided by the Ministries Act of 1693.[17] In nearby New Rochelle John Pell and his wife, Rachel, had given a large parcel of land for "the French church erected, or to be erected." This was probably in the year 1696, for the church was built the next year, and conformed to the Episcopal Church in 1709. St. Paul's, Eastchester, represented in the 1787 convention, is said to have been founded as a result of "the settlement by the Ten Families from Fairfield";[18] services were held there as early as 1707. St. Peter's, Westchester (1702), was still scarred by the war (and since Seabury had been its rector, perhaps the people preferred not to appear at a Provoost convention!). St. Anne's, Morrisania (1703), was known to exist. Mamaroneck (1704) and Scarsdale (1724) might be expected to be present. Lewisboro (1725) and North Salem (1725) were known to exist and, given the current Yankee trend of moving across the state line, must be promising. St. Andrew's in Walden (1733), St. Thomas, New Windsor (1733), and St. David's, Otterkill, could count upon the ministrations of St. George's in Newburgh (1729). As far as was known, there was now no congregation in Kingston, which had been burned by the British and, in any case, had always been a very Dutch town. Patterson (1744), South Salem (1759), and Croton (1756) might also find their lot improved by the Connecticut immigrations. The Peekskill congregation (1744) could look to the rector of Philipsburgh (1768), who was present in the convention. And there was the congregation in Beekmantown (1766) revived as St. Ann's in 1793. Bishop Provoost himself would have added Catskill to the list, for he had held services there during the war; and, of course, he had heard that services were now required "in the Manor of Livingston."[19] And, it was said, St. John's in Yonkers (1702) would soon be strong enough to support services in Tuckahoe.

Long Island delegates to that first convention could count nine congregations there: St. James', Newtown (Elmhurst); St. George's, Flushing; Grace Church, Jamaica; St. George's, Hempstead; Christ Church, Oyster Bay; St. John's, Huntington; the two congregations farther out, in Setauket and Islip (Oakdale); and St. Ann's in Brooklyn, founded during the recent war.[20] Bedford, (1704), Newcastle (Mt. Kisco) (1722), White Plains (1724) in Westchester County each held promise of revival. The church building at Fishkill (1755), though new at the war's outbreak, was now in ruinous condition, having been used as a barracks and hospital by patriot soldiers; Christ Church, Poughkeepsie (1759), had been closed during much of the hostilities and there were probably many in the town who remembered that its rector had profited by some questionable land grants under the old government. By 1787 both congregations showed marked signs of growth.[21]

In what is now the Diocese of Albany, there were two churches: St. Peter's, Albany (before 1708), and St. George's, Schenectady (after 1750). Just before the war Sir William Johnson had built a fine church near his home, Johnson Hall, but the church had not been used very long. Much more unfortuante was the plight of the Mohawk Indians. There had been Indian congregations at Fort Hunter and Upper Castle, and their strength was due not only to energetic missionaries but, as we have seen, even more to the landed Johnson and his Indian counterpart, the distinguished Joseph Brant.[22]

This, then, is the picture that may well have appeared to the knowledgeable delegates of the 1787 convention. If they were allowed to lapse into that optimism that has always informed Church statistics, they might well count more than forty congregations that could be expected to attend future conventions. This is a scene much brighter than has customarily been thought to be the case and perhaps its most important aspect is that, in the present Diocese of New York, all but one of these congregations exist to this day; the sole exception, Beekmantown, after a very brief post–Revolutionary War renascence, lapsed into oblivion soon after 1800. Yet, that is the very neighborhood from which came all the Potters!

If the delegates were glad to be able to count to forty, imagine their delight had they been able to foresee the very near future. For, within fifteen years, four new churches would be firmly established; two in New York City (Christ Church, 1793, and St. Mark's, 1799), and two congregations in rural villages: St. James', Goshen (1793), and St. Peter's, Lithgow (1801). There was indeed much reason for hope, and it was heightened by the election of a blue-ribbon Standing Committee "to advise with the bishop in all matters in which he shall think proper to consult them"—an amazing role description when one considers Bishop Provoost's insistence against Seabury that the laity share powers equally with the clergy in Church councils.

On the third day of that initial convention there was a ceremony of the sort that delighted the eighteenth-century New Yorker. The convention lay and clerical delegates proceeded with the students of Trinity Charity School, congregation, and vestry to the bishop's residence, where he met them at the door and joined them in a procession to St. Paul's Chapel. There they heard an address in which the bishop was congratulated on his return from England and recovery from "a painful and dangerous illness." The theme of Provoost's many maladies runs through the remainder of his days, and it is hard to escape the fact that he did indeed suffer poor health—and allowed that fact to curtail his duties as bishop. He always considered his role primarily as rector of Trinity Church. There is every reason to believe he was a superb rector, rebuilding both a destroyed church and setting it on its great role in New York. The speaker at this convention ceremony, however, alluded to the importance of New York's having a bishop—"a Church complete in all its parts"—to which Bishop Provoost later replied (perhaps it was a swipe at Seabury) by praising the English bishops for "their benevolent and paternal exertions in our favor."

There was yet another New York Convention that year, in November. Now the bishop and eight priests were joined by twenty-five laymen. The bishop "expressed his satisfaction to the Convention on account of the increasing state of the church and informed them that he had ordained several persons," and made a visitation to several churches on Long Island, for confirmation, and "hoped that the other churches here represented would be equally prepared for the reception of that sacred rite, as he intended to visit them next spring."[23] Represented in this November 1787 convention were the congregations in New York City, Jamaica, Newtown, Flushing, Hempstead, Staten Island, Rye, White Plains, Brooklyn, Phillipsburgh, Poughkeepsie, Eastchester, "Upper Salem," North Castle, Bedford, and New Rochelle.

The next year, other parishes were represented: Huntington, Oyster Bay, "Ulster County," and Albany. Bishop Provoost noted the "prosperity of the church in the State," and regretted that he had failed to "visit the congregations in distant parts," due to much business in the city. Among other matters, the convention considered the request for ordination of Theodore Bartow, reader at New Rochelle, and recommended more study. Preparing their delegates who would soon attend the General Convention in Philadelphia, the New York Convention agreed to stand by the promise Provoost and White had made in London "to preserve the Episcopal succession in the English line." When this was discussed Provoost had yet another opportunity to fault Seabury for that irregular consecration in Scotland. The nonjurors, he said, were the enemies of freedom; "their slavish and absurd tenets were a disgrace to humanity, and *God grant* that they may never be cherished in America [which], as my native country, I wish may always be saved to liberty both civil and religious."[24] Anyone who supposed that Samuel Provoost was lethargic need only mention the nonjurors to see the sparks fly! Unfortunately for him (if not for the Church at large), the New York delegates were insufficiently informed of the nonjuring iniquities, and they eventually disregarded instructions and approved Seabury's consecration. Understandably, this angered Provoost, who inexplicably had not managed to attend the great General Convention of 1789 in Philadelphia.

THE NATIONAL CHURCH

There were two General Conventions that year. The first convened on July 28. Bishop White presided. Perhaps Bishop Provoost absented himself because he sensed the tide was running toward approving Seabury's consecration. The General Convention might recognize that consecration, but no legislation could force Provoost into participating with Seabury in the consecration of Edward Bass of Massachusetts. Provoost was somewhat appeased when he heard that the delegates provided for a bicameral General Convention. At least that was a proper defeat for Seabury! And perhaps Provoost wished he might have gone to Philadelphia after all when he learned that the convention had extended greetings to newly elected George Washington, adding, "We anticipate the happiness of our country under your future administration." How did Seabury like *that*?

The second session of the Philadelphia Convention was William White's triumph. A constitution was adopted, along with accompanying canons. There was, also, agreement about a prayer book for the Episcopal Church in the United States. It would be much like the English book of 1662 except for substitutions for words considered antiquated, the deletion of some holy days and the ornaments rubric, changes in Morning and Evening Prayer, Holy Matrimony and Visitation of the Sick, the omission of the Athanasian Creed, and the addition of some services and occasional prayers. Seabury was present, and was able to fulfill his promise to the nonjurors that he would see that an Invocation was included in the prayer of consecration in the Holy Communion.

It was exactly two weeks prior to the first of these General Conventions that the mob in Paris stormed the Bastille. Very soon, Church property in France was confiscated. The American public's applause of these first events of the French Revolution turned to revulsion when, several years later, new riots brought about the infamous Reign of Terror. Americans, depressed by what they saw as the low estate of the churches in America, might well despair of what was happening to Christianity in places where it had long been established. The Episcopal Church in New York, however, was fortunate in having the eager help of men notable in the rebuilding of society after the war. No layman was more loyal and useful than James Duane. He had been a moderate Whig during the war and, upon returning to the city after the

evacuation, opposed baiting the defeated Tories who remained (many
of them were his friends, some his relatives).[25] Duane was the first
postwar mayor of the city and was "a skillful administrator and an able
leader in the work of municipal reconstruction."[26] The Hamiltonians
were in power in New York until 1800, and thus it was entirely agreeable to Duane that he accept Washington's offer of a federal judgeship
in 1789. He then resigned as mayor of the city, but remained a governor
of New York Hospital, vice-president of the Society for Promoting Useful Knowledge, and active in the Society for the Relief of Distressed
Debtors. Throughout the 1780s, and until he moved to his large holdings near Albany, Duane was a conspicuous member of Trinity's vestry
and the diocesan Standing Committee.

No less notable was John Jay, also related to Provoost by marriage.
As we shall see in due course, several generations of Jays were passion-
ately concerned with the sad and cruel situation of black people. As
early as 1777, John Jay tried to secure emancipation by law. Failing in
that, soon after the peace he worked for a law prohibiting the importa-
tion of Negroes for sale in New York. At the same time he helped found
the Society for Promoting of Manumission (of which he became active
president). Thanks largely to John Jay, gradual abolition was voted in
1799, but in fact slavery existed in New York until 1841.[27]

DEVELOPMENTS IN NEW YORK

The city's population in 1790, 33,131, made it larger than Philadelphia.
Ten years later, the figure would be doubled. Immigration was the
cause. In the years 1789–94, there were 1,500 immigrants from Boston
alone each year.[28] Immigration from Ireland was already notable: "Too
many United Irishmen arrived here within a few days," complained
Federalist Hugh Gaine toward the end of the decade.[29] The importance
of the harbor and the increasing China trade attracted families to New
York City. Some of them were New Englanders sighting faster rewards
in the city's maritime trade than Boston or Providence could offer.
Other New Englanders, especially Connecticut Yankees who thought
their taxes too high, spread across the border westward to the Hudson
and beyond, looking for richer farm lands, better mill seats, or greater
fields for the Merino sheep that were the new rage. Not a few of these
Connecticut newcomers carried Prayer Books with them, and they were
often glad to help revive old or establish new Episcopal churches. We
will not be surprised to see many Yankee surnames appear in Diocese
of New York records.

Samuel Provoost was aware of upstate developments, but he was essentially a man of New York City. In a life of eighteenth-century benignity he enjoyed the prestige the rectorship of Trinity conferred upon him, and he returned the compliment by preserving the fortunes of the parish and making them often available to other churches so that, long after his lifetime, Trinity Church would be the bountiful bestower of riches upon many places. This was not always an easy thing to do, for there were churchfolk who maintained that Trinity's endowments belonged to all Episcopal churches in the city, possibly the state. One of the more vexing situations of Provoost's rectorship occurred in 1794, when a fair number of Trinity people separated to form a new parish, Christ Church, in a building they proposed to build very close to Trinity itself. Because there were signs that the new congregation might make claims to a share in Trinity's endowment, both diocese and parish acted together in denying Christ Church admission to convention until 1802, when the new parish formally relinquished whatever claims it might have to Trinity's wealth.

Apart from Provoost himself, the man most insistent that Trinity Church use its endowments to help other Episcopal churches was James Duane. When he resigned in April 1794 because of his removal to Duanesburgh, he wrote to the rector and vestry:

> I am happy after our hard struggles to leave you in the quiet enjoyment of your valuable temporalities . . . [b]ut less fortunate brethren of the same communion who are establishing new settlements have still every difficulty to encounter and demand a share of your sympathy and attention. Be entreated to be mindful of them.[30]

That Trinity Church was mindful of the needs of the churches is indicated by a letter written in the spring of 1796 by a New York City parson to a friend in Maryland:

> The country parishes in this State are badly off. Our church in the city has lately distributed among them £7000. This may animate them a little. We have lately erected a new church in the vicinity of the city [St. Marks-in-the-Bowery]. When it is finished another clergyman will be wanted. Are there any clever fellows in your quarter?[31]

Duane further hoped to see "the establishment of one or more itinerant ministers to visit congregations which are destitute [and] supply the poorer members and youth with Prayer Books."[32] Provoost's gracious reply to James Duane's letter implies that Duane had written what the bishop had all along been telling the vestry and other prominent Episcopalians in the city.

Who were some of these prominent church members in the last years of the eighteenth century? Apart from Duane (whom John Adams characterized as "very shrewd, very sharp"),[33] there were Richard Harrison, city recorder; Chief Justice Richard Morris; Isaac Sears, assemblyman; Marinus Willet, alderman, sheriff, and mayor; Robert Troup, judge; John Alsop, president of the Chamber of Commerse; John Jay; Morgan Lewis (who later was governor); William S. Johnson, president of Columbia College and United States Senator from Connecticut (at the same time); Rufus King; Thomas Randall; William Bayard; Wynant Van Zandt; Jacob LeRoy; Nicholas Carmer—most of these latter on the Common Council of the city.

Most of these men were well-known to Levinus Clarkson, one of New York's import merchants and member of Trinity Church, whose cash book contains the names of many other New York families: Van-Horne, Haviland, Nichols, White, Gilcrist, Duffie, Bowne, Crommelin, Verplanck, Egbert, Hazard, Johnstone, Woodhull, Stilwell, Classon, Hamilton, Talman, VanBuren, Van Cortlandt, VanSinderin, Watson, Greenleaf, Schermerhorn, Bogart, Childs, Stewart, Merrill, Laight, Dunlap, Bond, Fullam, Ludlum, Lefferts, Smith, Kissam, Cromwell, Levy, Rankin, Storm, Suydam, Staats, Hunter, Billings, Ward, Pell, Seton, Judah, and Ludlow. These men (by no means all of them Episcopalian) often did the ordering of household necessities, and might be seen sauntering homeward with three yards of "flemmish Linnen" under their arms. Or "Camphire for the Cloths," 200 quills, or a ream of writing paper. Or wheeling home a pipe of gin (at five shillings a gallon, probably the best quality from Holland). Merchants like Levinus Clarkson preferred to range widely, buying wholesale at the dock whatever imports looked salable. They dealt in blankets, tea, and ivory combs from China, wheat, casks of gunpowder, waffle irons, nutmegs, linseed oil, slates. Clarkson dealt in bills of exchange, discounted notes, and somewhere in his cash book noted that he had paid John Lewis, the appointed collecter for pews in the new Trinity Church, the sum of £34[34].

The fact that Levinus Clarkson and so many of his acquaintances were members of Trinity Church or its chapels suggests that whatever animosity they bore that old citadel of Toryism was now forgotten. The Episcopal Church seemed already to be on a much firmer basis than it had enjoyed—or suffered from—when New York was a province. Then, the political ties were between church and state, and could be embarrassing. Now, church and state were formally separated, and officials of both sat together on a voluntary basis, a most happy arrangement that continued for some years.

If city merchants like Clarkson were careful to keep records of their dealings, the Church should do the same. After the 1790 diocesan convention Bishop Provoost "enjoyned upon the Churches belonging to his Diocese to present the State of their respective congregations, thro' their deputies, at the next Convention. The writing to be delivered in under the hands of the Minister and Churchwardens . . . He has in contemplation to visit the churches on the Hudson whenever circumstances will permit." In such a way were the first "Parochial Reports" required of the churches in the Diocese of New York. Bishop Provoost probably had little interest in these reports other than insofar as they indicated the satisfaction or the disappointment of his clergy.

Much pleasanter were his occasional confirmations, his renewed friendship with George Washington (whom he probably first met at Clermont in 1782) when the President lived in New York City, the rebuilding of the burned church in 1788–90, and the gradually improving state of the Church. Since very little is left of Samuel Provoost's personal papers—a few letters and books and some sermons—and since his family seems to have gone on to successive generations without undue attention to a distinguished progenitor, we know very little of his personal life except that it was attended by much illness and sadness. Therefore, William A. Duer's description of Provoost is important to us. It was written in 1847 when Duer, retired president of Columbia College, was in the midst of churchmanship troubles, which served to enliven his pen when he wrote of Provoost:

> In character and appearance, he was every inch a bishop—not, indeed, according to modern notions and exemplars, but after the model of the fathers of the reformation in the English Church. Devout without ostentation, stately without pride, dignified without austerity, he commanded the respect and esteem both of his clergy and the people—and he won the friendship and affections of all admitted to his intimacy. Like his saintly fellows in the Episcopacy, White and Madison, he was the follower of Cranmer, Latimer and Ridley—not the follower of Bonner, Laud and the non-Juring Bishops of Scotland, like some of his successors. He was truly Catholic, both in his principles and in his feelings; nor was his charity confined to his own denomination. It comprehended all who confessed "the Lord that bought them," within the pale of that universal church which is defined to be a "congregation of faithful men." One of the few among the Episcopal Clergy who adhered to their country at the Revolution—he sought an asylum when the British took possession of the city among his relatives in the manor of Livingston, where he resided during the war. Upon the evacuation of New York by the British he returned, with the rest of the inhabitants who had fled at their approach; and when his Whig friends gained the ascendancy in the vestry he was chosen for its Rector instead of Dr. Benjamin Moore,

who had remained in the city as an adherent to the Crown. Nor was the preference given to Dr. Provoost merely on account of his political principles—but for qualifications essential and germane to the office. He had received his education at the University of Oxford [sic], and brought from it acquisitions more valuable than the tory principles she more usually dispenses. Besides being a learned and sound divine he was a polite scholar and accomplished gentleman. He read the noble Liturgy of his Church with critical accuracy, without impairing the devotional spirit it is so well calculated to excite. As a preacher he was not so happy. His deliberate and sonorous declamation was better adapted to the reading desk than the pulpit. Although his enunciation was distinct as well as forcible, yet his sermons were delivered so emphatically—*ore rotundo*—that the exertion thus induced, together with plethoric habit, rendered the public services of the Church tedious and laborious to himself and to his hearers. But it is by no means certain that these circumstances did not tend to the improvement of his sermons by rendering them shorter. In private life the bishop, though studious and retired in his habits, and in mixed companies oppressed by diffidence, was certainly more agreeable, and a greater favorite, than in public. He possessed a vein of genuine humor, which gave zest to his conversation without infringing upon clerical or conventional propriety—and the playfulness of his manner when surrounded by his family and intimate friends was quite captivating. He was particularly condescending and attractive in his intercourse with the young; with whose tastes and feelings, from the simplicity of his own character, he could more easily sympathize. I shall ever gratefully remember his kindness to me as a boy, and the companion of his sons. He would frequently admit us all to his study—the upper room in the back building of the house which stood at the corner of Nassau and Fair (now Fulton) street, when he would show us his rarest and most valuable prints, exhibit to us the objects of his microscope, and divert himself with our youthful wonderment; and sometimes of a bright starlight evening he would display to us the more fascinating wonders of his telescope, and from his serious and impressive explanations he seemed to derive a graver and more holy pleasure from our curiosity and admiration. I thought, at that time, that Bishop Provoost was perfection itself; but before many years had elapsed, I discovered he was but a man. His faults, however, were those of one whom he resembled both in character and station. Like Eli of old, he was ever indulgent to his sons—and like Eli, he was punished by their loss.[35]

Those last cryptic words refer to the profligacy of Provoost's sons. Their troubles, and the prolonged illness of the bishop's wife, made it impossible for him to enjoy the improved fortunes of the Church.

APPROACHING A NEW CENTURY, A NEW ERA

The diocesan convention of 1798 was canceled when yellow fever broke out again in the city. Had the convention been held, there would have been general satisfaction at news of the Church's growth upriver. The Connecticut migrants often included the Book of Common Prayer in their baggage. In 1795 Ebenezer Dibble (related to Punderson of Trinity Church, New Haven, and Christ Church, Rye) was missionary in Delaware County; Stamford there is named after the town of the same name in Connecticut.[36] Perhaps earlier, another Yankee had initiated services in Claverack, Athens, and Catskill. Two names are outstanding, however: Gideon Bostwick, and Daniel Nash, his protégé. In his labors as rector of Great Barrington, Bostwick must often have followed his flock as they and their friends settled new lands in Columbia County. From Bostwick's vantage point on the Berkshires, the distant Catskills would soon be a field white for the harvest. And that region, though forty miles from his own parsonage, was much closer to him than it was to Trinity in New York City. Young Daniel Nash caught the vision. After his ordination by Bishop Provoost, he set out to the country J. Fenimore Cooper would one day romanticize in his novels. Like Stuart before him, "Father" Nash had the help of a wife no less devoted than himself. Together for nearly forty years, they endured the privations of what was frontier life. Churches in at least nine counties owe their existence to Daniel Nash and his wife.

Yet another star was on the horizon: Philander Chase. Born in Vermont, tutored by Ellison, the unreformed Tory rector of St. Peter's, Albany, Chase was ordained deacon by Bishop Provoost in 1798, and with help from the new diocesan Missionary Society organized congregations from Troy to Lake George. This was the beginning of a life work that took him to New York City, Poughkeepsie, New Orleans, and eventually the episcopate in two dioceses in the midwest—Ohio and Illinois.

The Episcopal Church was destined to grow. Samuel Provoost could see this, and being a man of intelligence he could see that now the role of Episcopal Bishop of New York was far different from what it was in 1786. Then, it seemed that the rector-bishop had one task: to conserve the fortunes of Trinity Church and regain goodwill toward a church whose clergy, during the Revolution, had, perhaps rightly, lost the respect of the public. Provoost was fifty-six in 1798—by no means an old age—but his private troubles were heavy upon him. Maria Bousfield Provoost, his wife, died, after a very long illness, on August 18, 1799. Both his sons disappointed him. When George Washington died,

just as the splendid century was drawing to a close, Provoost could see
another portent: ill, tired, depressed, and very possibly aware of new
demands that must soon come upon him, he and his circle of heroes
would not be men for a new century. Perhaps, then, it is fitting that
Provoost's last extraordinary public appearance was at the "funeral" of
Washington in New York City. Nothing more appropriately characterized that century's sense of public stateliness:

> The Reverend the Clergy walked in full dress, with white scarfs, and
> twenty-four beautiful girls, in white robes, scarfs and turbans, strewed
> laurels as they went along. The Funeral Urn and its decorations was
> supported by eight soldiers upon a Bier, in form of a palanquin, six
> feet by four . . . As soon as the procession have been seated [in Trinity
> Church] music suited to the occasion was performed, a prayer was
> offered up to the most High by the Right Reverend Bishop Provoost,
> and an oration on the character and history of the deceased was deliv-
> ered by the Honorable Gouverneur Morris. After the solemn services
> of the temple had concluded, the bier was deposited in the ceme-
> tery.[37]

Difficulties for Provoost multiplied in those last months of the century. His celebrated assistant minister, John Bissett—an "eloquent and
powerful preacher," especially popular with the ladies—was far gone
in alcohol, and resigned in disgrace in March 1800. This was something
of a *cause célèbre* in the parish because the man had won an impressive election in the congregations of Trinity and the chapels several
years before. While Provoost and the vestry were seeking a replacement
for Bissett—they had their eye on a man named Hobart—the bishop's
younger son, John, committed suicide and, in accordance with the custom of the day, was buried perforce under the sidewalk outside St.
Paul's churchyard; even the very humanitarian Bishop Provoost would
not read the service.[38]

The next month, Provoost "nominated the Reverend Mr. Hobart"
to be an assistant clergyman at Trinity Church. That done, the rector
intimated, September 8, 1800, his impending resignation from Trinity.
A biographical sketch written by the bishop's sons-in-law, and published in 1844, states that Samuel Provoost was "induced" to resign.
Whether this was a careless choice of word, or whether Provoost was
strongly encouraged to resign for the sake of his health, or whether
there was already strong pressure from younger clergy and laymen, we
cannot know. Each is possible, but circumstances appear to opt for the
latter. Why else did he deliberately prove himself to be as lethargic as
his critics said he was? The rector was slow to leave the stage. Morgan
Dix, Trinity's historian-rector, asserted that Provoost waited "for the
completion of the transaction" of Hobart's acceptance, and thus an

assurance of Trinity's future welfare. A generous assessment. The rector remained to nominate Benjamin Moore to be his successor, and lingered yet longer until the vestry granted him an annuity of $1,000 a year beginning August 1801. The instrument of resignation (why was such an elaborate document thought necessary?) was signed December 22, 1800. But, since the annuity did not commence until the following August, and since Provoost remained Bishop of New York, there is no reason to suppose he was not often to be seen in Trinity Church or St. Paul's Chapel. The church historian will always regret that no one was present to record what conversations Provoost and the young assistant minister, Hobart, might have had in the vestry room.

Bishop Provoost now planned the next step: retirement from the episcopal office. If his leaving Trinity had been accompanied by appointments and documents and agreements, this time Samuel Provoost would exit in his own style. Nevertheless, the resignation was somewhat expected; no one in the 1801 convention was very much surprised when the bishop simply announced that "ill health, afflictive occurrances, and an ardent wish to retire from all public employment" led him to resign his "jurisdiction as Bishop." The convention delegates were, however, nonplussed when, after his statement, the bishop walked out of the church. The General Convention then meeting in Philadelphia viewed the move as most disconcerting, if not irresponsible, because bishops simply didn't enter into "the design in question." Had Provoost been coerced? If so, the House of Bishops stated that, though prepared to consecrate an elected successor for New York,

> this house must be understood to be explicit in their declaration, that they shall consider such a person as Assistant or Co-adjutor Bishop during Bishop Provoost's life, although competent, in point of character to all the Episcopal duties.

Having declared this, the House of Bishops proceeded to do just the opposite: they approved the consecration of Benjamin Moore as "Bishop-Elect of the Church in the State of New York." Eleven years later, the right reverend gentlemen would be glad they made the mistake.

6

Benjamin Moore:
Benign Bishop

*The varied knowledge and classical attainments of
Provoost, the piety and beneficence of Moore, and
the talents, zeal and ceaseless activity of Hobart . . .*
—J. W. Francis [1]

Though Samuel Provoost was sufficiently sensitive to the significance
of dates, it could not have occurred to him that his resignation in 1801
marked far more than the passing of the old century. It symbolized
nothing less than the disappearance of the New York he had known all
his life. The years immediately following the peace probably revealed
to Provoost himself that the views of Church and society he shared with
an enlightened eighteenth century left him ill fitted to meet the demands of a new century. A century later, a successor was to allege
(without sufficient citation) that Bishop Provoost

> had no very sanguine expectations as to the growth of the Church or
> its mission to his age and countrymen. He is said, indeed, to have
> expressed the opinion that the Church in the United States would die
> out with the old Colonial families; and with such views it is not to be
> expected that he should do much to promote its growth or advance-
> ment.[2]

The mild, patrician, Latitudinarian stance of Provoost frustrated
those clergy and laity who believed the Church was of divine origin
and by providence had now been presented a great opportunity in the
State of New York. The bishop's policy of presiding over the corporation of Trinity Church, dining out as a sought-after table companion,
and making occasional visits to confirm or consecrate churches was
unacceptable to those who believed the Episcopal Church should be
expanding its efforts in the city and in the countryside. An eighteenth-
century bishop was inadequate in a city eager to greet new things.

Such is the well-worn appraisal of Provoost. It needs some modification. We must bear in mind that in Philadelphia William White was in 1800 much the parallel to Provoost. Apart from the fact that White seems to have enjoyed presiding over the House of Bishops, and was blessed with good health during a very long life, his views of the episcopate evolved only slowly toward that which was later thought to be appropriate.

Provoost and White shared an unquestioned patriotism, but the Bishop of New York could not claim that he had actually taken part in the contest (apart from that caper on the banks of the Hudson in East Camp in 1777). William White had long served as chaplain to the Continental Congress. In any event, Provoost's loyalty to the American cause was, in the last decade of the century, a coin of little value. Despite the threat of renewed hostilities, there was strong pro-British sentiment in New York. If ever there had been a sharply drawn line between Tory and Whig in the city and its environs, it was obscured now.

Provoost lived another fifteen years after his retirement, almost entirely forgotten by the Church—perhaps himself even unmindful of the Church. Years later, this was held against him. The ascendant High Churchmen excoriated him, and his memory has had few defenders. Many years after his death, Provoost's eclipse was thus stated by a Presbyterian:

> Our Episcopal brethren have too much overlooked the man, his learning, his liberality, and his patriotism. He had the bearing of a well-stalled Bishop, was of pleasing address, and of refined manners.[3]

Exactly! But the Church in New York needed more than these delightful qualities.

Immediately after Provoost's sudden resignation, Benjamin Moore was elected president of the diocesan convention. It is thought that Provoost left the chair in order to free the convention of any restraints his presence may have imposed. We may also assume that he shied away from the dubious compliments every retiring parson must receive. He would be especially sensitive about this because of the recent ordeals of his wife's death and his son's suicide. Perhaps it was these tragedies that moved the convention to its delicate farewell next day, in which Samuel Provoost, their bishop, was thanked "for his kind wishes, and whilst they regret that he should have judged himself under the necessity of quitting so suddenly beg leave to assure him of their sincere and fervent prayers."[4]

THE FIRST BISHOP MOORE

The day after the resignation, September 5, 1801, the diocesan convention unanimously elected Benjamin Moore to replace Provoost as
Bishop-acting in the State of New York. It must be thus stated because
the resignation of a bishop was novel and, in fact, the General Convention (then meeting in Philadelphia) refused to accept Provoost's resignation but permitted New York to elect Benjamin Moore as acting bishop.

Everything presaged Moore's election. He had long been prominent in the Church. His former Tory sympathies were now no barrier to
promotion. So general was the satisfaction that Benjamin Moore was
consecrated in St. Michael's Church, Trenton, just six days after his
election. The consecrators, who crossed the Delaware River from the
General Convention in Philadelphia, were Bishop White, Bishop Claggett of Maryland, and Bishop Jarvis of Connecticut. As far as we know,
Bishop Provoost was not present. But it is probable that he had anticipated the convention's quick approval and Moore's consecration when
he suddenly resigned.

If Samuel Provoost had been precisely the right man to identify
patriotism with the Episcopal Church in 1783 (and by doing so make
the future of the Church much more secure), Benjamin Moore was now
the right man to bridge the gulf between the eighteenth century and
what would be expected in the nineteenth. First of all, there was still a
dearth of leaders in the New York clergy (though Hobart was one of
Provoost's last appointments). More important, however, was Benjamin
Moore's sympathy with demands that the Church vigorously expand
upstate.

Benjamin Moore was born in Newtown, Long Island, in 1748; his
family recognized his academic qualities and sent him to King's College, from which he graduated with honors in 1768. He prepared for
orders under the supervision of Dr. Auchmuty of Trinity Church, and
was ordained in London in 1774. He returned to assist in Trinity parish,
filling the place Provoost had vacated not long before. A mild degree of
competition and mutual suspicion that arose then may never have quite
disappeared between these two men, especially since Moore (despite
his New England ancestry) was a thorough Tory during the Revolutionary War. Their relationship could not have much improved when Provoost was called back to Manhattan to displace Moore as newly elected
rector of Trinity. But Provoost had been sufficiently large-minded to
reinstate Benjamin Moore as first assistant at Trinity. By 1800 the two
were apparently congenial, and it was Provoost who nominated Benjamin Moore to succeed him as rector of Trinity in 1800.[5] Morgan Dix

later believed that Moore's "quiet behaviour and modesty" won the approval of the patriot bishop.[6]

During the Revolutionary War, Moore married Charity Clarke. Her father was an English ship captain who invested in land some distance north of New York City. He named his new holding "Chelsea"—a name still well-known in New York, and in the Episcopal Church. For, not many years after Moore was made Bishop of New York, his son, Clement Clarke Moore, would induce the fledgling General Theological Seminary to settle in Chelsea by offering it an entire square of land.

When Benjamin Moore became Bishop of New York he was greeted by overt anti-Christian sentiments reminiscent of the reputed excesses of the French Revolution. "The typical symbols of Christianity were sometimes outrageously profaned, and the holy sacraments prostituted to the vilest ends," wrote a commentator some years later.[7] Into this ferment Bishop Moore entered at the age of fifty-three; perhaps exactly the best age for the task ahead. If a man will ever be wise he will be so when fifty-three; if ever of a strong constitution, he will have that, too. The record shows that Benjamin Moore was precisely the man of the hour. Like his predecessor and successor, he retained the rectorship of Trinity Church, for that salary maintained the Bishop of New York. There was as yet no adequate state-wide manner of providing for a bishop. In addition to presiding over Trinity Church, Bishop Moore was responsible to perhaps as many as fifty churches and twenty-five clergy and an uncounted number of laypersons in a rapidly growing state. Though it is arguable that Moore was bishop for only one year (since Provoost died in 1815, and Moore in 1816) he was de facto Bishop of New York from the day of his consecration in 1801. Bishop Provoost never interfered with his diocesan administration, and the contretemps of 1811 (which will soon be discussed) was brought about by enemies of Hobart, not opponents of Moore. In fact, the episcopate of Moore perfectly blended the gentle viewpoint of his own heritage with the exuberance of his gifted assistant, John Henry Hobart.

CHURCH LIFE IN THE GROWING STATE

As Benjamin Moore assumed the responsibilities of the Bishop of New York, the city itself still retained much of the intimacy of a small town. A prominent New Yorker later wrote:

> Trinity and St. Paul's Chapel marked the populous centre; around the Battery, and in Wall Street (where but one bank yet existed), and the

parallel streets, dwelt the aristocracy; and the bridge where Canal
Street now is formed the usual boundary of evenings walks. . . . Harlem was a distant village; mails from New England and Albany arrived
and departed only twice a week; there were but two newspapers published; water was a marketable commodity.[8]

This was the city Moore knew well. As a landed gentleman whose
holdings in Chelsea promised rich increase in value, his mind must
often have turned to New York's destiny to grow and grow. He and all
knowledgeable Episcopalians were aware of awakening commerce and
building upriver where the Mohawk, emptying into the Hudson,
seemed to invite restless men and women to enter upon the promising
fields of the western valleys.

The death of Alexander Hamilton provides us with a vignette of
life in the Church and city. When Bishop Moore was told that his
neighbor Hamilton was fatally wounded by Aaron Burr, in July 1804,
and desired the sacrament, the bishop refused to comply immediately
because Hamilton (not among New York's more fervent Episcopalians)
had probably thought about it insufficiently. Also, there had been a
duel. Later, the bishop relented and celebrated the Holy Communion
at Hamilton's bedside, and the dying man showed "unmistakeable grat-
itude." Bishop Moore was present when Hamilton died, and later testi-
fied to the coroner against Burr. The funeral oration was delivered from
the porch of Trinity Church by Gouverneur Morris.[9] Hamilton was buried near the church door.

Following the New York customs of the time, his body was probably carried in a small hardwood coffin resting on a footed bier borne by
four intimate friends. Family, physicians, business associates, and other
friends followed on foot, or in carriages. Churches were often draped
in black for funerals. A lengthy sermon might be expected. There being
no tolling hammer in the early days, the church bell was wrapped in a
blanket or carpet, its sound thus muffled and lugubrious. Its tones
would be heard before the service, and again while the body was carried to the grave nearby. The English custom of ringing out the number
of years of the deceased's age, preceded by six tolls for an adult
woman, and nine for a man, may have been common in New York in
the early years of the nineteenth century. Certainly the professional
clerk was employed at that time to lead the responses in the service; it
is said that the first city church to discard the clerk was Grace Church,
and when the rector, Jonathan M. Wainwright, did so, he faced some
opposition.[10]

The first call upon the new bishop was from the distant parts of the
state. Several Episcopal churches had long been established in the
Albany-Schenectady area. In the Hudson River Valley, whose agricul-

ture supplied the city's markets, there were a number of growing towns and river hamlets. There had been Episcopal churches in Newburgh, Walden, Fishkill, and Poughkeepsie since the old century. Now in the first years of the nineteenth century there were new ones in Catskill, Hudson, and Red Hook. In the year after Bishop Moore's consecration, the Rev. Davenport Phelps was "employed as a missionary on the frontiers of the State" by the Society for the Propagation of the Gospel in New York under the direction of Bishop Moore.[11] Mark this event well, for it is the first practical diocesan-wide missionary effort we know. Daniel Nash had already begun his heroic work upstate; twelve parishes today owe their foundation to him.[12] Soon, Troy, Lansingburg and Waterford were added to their number. By 1810 there were twenty-five parishes in and near Albany—twenty of them established since 1801.

These facts make two things clear: there was increase in population upstate, and an awakened appeal of the Episcopal Church. Even so, Bishop Moore did not visit those upriver places until 1809.

Later on, energetic Victorian churchmen would fault Bishop Moore for his failure to visit far-off places in his diocese immediately. Bishop Provoost had been similarly excoriated. We will do well to remember that the role of Bishop of New York was seen by these men as complementary, perhaps subsidiary, to their position as rector of Trinity Church. If we praise Trinity for its diocesan-wide munificence, we must recall that its impulse to such generosity was immeasurably encouraged by these rectors, who, as bishops, were responsible for those distant places. No less a high Victorian than Morgan Dix credits Samuel Provoost with the foresight of garnering Trinity's wealth to ensure future generosity. Between 1800 and 1868 Trinity aided at least forty-five churches alone in the wide area now the Diocese of Albany.[13]

Bishops then were not expected to travel to distant places. Seabury had done so, but then he was always somewhat peripatetic (and sometimes a nuisance to his brother bishops). White of Pennsylvania preferred to restrict his ministrations to the Philadelphia area until the last years of his episcopate—by which time his protégé Hobart had set an example many later bishops (including Hobart himself) found lethal. Qualities of one era must be shrewdly assessed by succeeding generations. Their contemporaries in New York admired Provoost's scholarship and Moore's piety, and this went far to sustain those men in their day. Soon, much more would be expected of a bishop in New York.

More would be expected of the other clergy and of the laity, too. In the diocesan convention of 1803 there was pointed discussion about the failure of delegates to appear. The next year, lists of clergy present and not present were published (Samuel Provoost appears in neither column; was it supposed that he had resigned his orders as well as his position?). Again, in 1805, there was poor attendance, but this time with reason: the convention met in Poughkeepsie. The place is significant. Now the Church beyond Manhattan island is formally recognized. Another reason was one more severe outbreak of yellow fever in New York. The clergy gave their parochial reports verbatim this time, and fellow delegates heard the communicants statistics of the Church in Albany (80), Brooklyn (77), Catskill (12), Hudson (15), Trinity and its New York City chapels (1,000), Christ Church, New York City (300), St. Mark's (20), St. Esprit (12), New Rochelle (18), Newtown (23), Flushing (20), St. Andrew's in Walden, Orange County (50), Rye (30). Of course there were many parishes not reporting. And we must not be confused by the low number of communicants: when bishops were not expected to travel beyond their own city they simply did not confirm many persons belonging to outlying parishes. Thus Trinity (where the bishop resided) could report a thousand communicants, but Christ Church in the fast-growing city of Hudson a mere fifteen. Also, sometimes only confirmed *men* may have been reported as communicants because only men were allowed to cast a vote at parish elections. These reports soon changed, for in 1808 Bishop Moore visited ten churches (none far from New York City) and confirmed 692 persons. The next year he reported to an admiring convention that he had gone as far as Lansingburg and Schenectady, had confirmed 304 persons, had ordained seven clergymen (and deposed one). It is important to notice those ordinations. The fact that seven men had undertaken preparation for the ministry in a time when the church seemed weak and was unable to provide the benefit of a divinity school doubtless weighed heavily upon the delegates gathered for that convention.

It is equally remarkable that one reads little about money in the early records of the diocese. This is partly because the convention needed very little income. It had minimal diocesan expenses. There was, of course, no diocesan office, and no diocesan program requiring funds. At Moore's election, the diocese (by this time the word *diocese* was in increasing use) had about £1,000 invested, a most respectable sum, one would think. Provoost's style hadn't been expensive. He spent freely from his own inheritance—too freely it was said—and at the same time had husbanded Trinity's investments. Bishop Moore relied upon the munificence of Trinity Church, but like Provoost, he enjoyed a comfortable inherited income that he probably used for church purposes on occasion. The expectations of the eighteenth century didn't disappear after 1800.

The American bishops had to forge their individual manner for the work in their several jurisdictions. Bishop Madison of Virginia saw his lifework fulfilled as president of William and Mary; he gave modest attention to his episcopal duties. William White was First Citizen of Philadelphia, and lived long enough to adapt to and even be enthusiastic about the requirements of episcopacy in America. Benjamin Moore, unlike others, had been privileged to study closely Provoost's failures and the needs of the Episcopal Church in New York State. Not dynamic by temperament, he began almost casually the work of a bishop. Two years after his election his report to the convention delegates "congratulated them on the flourishing state of the diocese." By gradual steps his reports foreshadowed the work of later bishops in New York and elsewhere; he directed missionary activity; he exercised right of appointment to vacant places (as many as eighteen in 1807); he assumed chairmanship of ecclesiastical organizations such as the Society for the Propagation of the Gospel. Upon this broad understanding of a bishop's responsibilities Benjamin Moore's immediate successors had at their command various established agencies and precedents, and these provided money and policies for church growth. This novel strengthening of an executive bishop lent facility to expansion of the Church's interests. But the disasters of the 1840s may be traced directly to those decisions which, early in the century, provided the Bishop of New York with power to express by means of Church organizations his personal preferences in opposition to a sizable and resentful minority within the diocese. The benign Benjamin Moore could easily endorse young Hobart's New York Bible and Common Prayer Book Society in 1809, and the Protestant Episcopal Tract Society the next year, never supposing these organizations would very soon be controversial among New York Episcopalians.

SIGNS OF GROWTH

All the evidence suggests that the revival of Episcopal church life in New York came soon after the Revolutionary War, and that prejudice against the former Church of England was quickly forgotten. The difficulty lay in finding clergymen available to minister in the now-independent Church.

An excellent example of Episcopal renascence is found in the story of St. Matthew's Church, Bedford. As we have seen, this was part of the Rye, Mamaroneck, Bedford triad envisioned as one of the two Westchester parishes mentioned in Governor Fletcher's Ministries Act back in 1693. Bedford was to be served by the rector of Rye. As early as February 28, 1694, a Rye Vestry was elected having two representatives from Bedford. An early rector was Thomas Pritchard, who was remembered because he "totally ruined the interests of the Church" in Bedford. When James Wetmore became rector of Rye things improved markedly in the Bedford congregation, but nevertheless there were no great stirrings there. But there was promise enough to induce the ardent churchman St. George Talbot, then in his one-hundred-fourth year, to bequeath £600 to the Bedford church. That was in 1766. When in the next year Talbot died, his executors were slow to pay the generous bequest. It is a sign of life in St. Matthew's that, thirty years later, in 1796, the congregation demanded an accounting and a remittance from Talbot's executors and their successors. Eventually, Alexander Hamilton was engaged as a lawyer for St. Matthew's, and he was concluding successful litigation at the time of his death.

The fact that the congregation was impelled to seek its elusive inheritance is enough to indicate that the people of St. Matthew's, Bedford, meant their church to prosper. They used the Talbot bequest to purchase a glebe and land for a church building, which was built 1807–1808. In 1810 the parish was declared to be in a very flourishing state—certainly better than it had ever been under the Crown. Reasons for this are easy to discover: a definite easing of animosity toward the Episcopal Church, population growth in Westchester, including perhaps Episcopalians from Connecticut, and the prestige attached to the Jay family, who belonged to the Rye and Bedford parish. (There is yet another note important to this history: a century after its church was built, the three-decker pulpit was still in use—perhaps the last such in the Diocese of New York.)

In the ten years between Moore's consecration in 1801 and his virtual retirement in 1811, the Bishop of New York found himself in an ever widening sea of concerns and demands for a number of reasons. First of all, the never-absent English ascendancy in Manhattan provided, after the Revolutionary War, a firm and, yes, patrician base for the Episcopal Church. Then there was the growing importance of New York's port, rapidly overtaking Philadelphia and Boston as the commercial shipping center of the nation. This meant immigration from Europe to New York City, and thence upriver toward Albany. The immigrants were very often from England.[14]

The record of Bishop Moore's ten years' activity is clearly a record of growth and laying foundations for future growth for the Church in New York State. But there is one thing conspicuously lacking in those ten years: leadership. Bishop Moore was benign; everyone respected his gentle, quiet, blameless life. The city, however, was an increasingly tough place. Everywhere there was an aggressiveness which was seen as part of the American ideal. Episcopalians were perhaps disappointed in the pacific gentility of their Church. There was, also, a stirring of American Christianity, the opening tremors of what became the Second

Awakening. A younger generation was impatient to improve the performance and correct the outlook of the fathers.

These younger men had, after all, never had a chance in New York. Provoost was the man of the hour in 1783, but, thanks largely to his generous spirit, Benjamin Moore was regarded as heir apparent. "In Case Bishop Provoost should resign it is not supposed there will be any choice at this time of a successor," wrote the newly appointed assistant minister at Trinity, John Henry Hobart, in September 1801. He continued in the letter to a friend, with an archness that is amusing to all who know that Hobart was not above playing politics,

> You must come forward to aid us in conciliating unanimity and harmony—I trust that the party spirit that both disgraced and injured us is near expiring. Had I my will, I would crush it, I was going to say, to the nethermost hell, its congenial habitation.[15]

This was written when the tired Provoost was about to retire. The ensuing ten years saw gratifying growth in the Episcopal Church, but the younger people questioned whether it had been a growth as rich in doctrine as it had been in numbers.

The concerns of the Diocese of New York and its bishop increased steadily. The burden proved to be too great for Bishop Moore. He suffered a stroke in 1811 and was thereafter partly paralysed and much confined to his house. He declared "the utter improbability of my ever being again able to perform my episcopal functions."[16] His son, Clement, wrote to the diocesan convention on behalf of the bishop, asking that a special convention elect an assistant. That convention was called for May 14, 1811, and when it convened there were representatives from thirty-eight congregations and other delegates from mission stations. Now there arose a possibility and a problem. The possibility was that, for the first time since 1786, the diocese could elect a man without circumstances dictating who would be the choice. Despite the appropriate regrets at Moore's misfortune, it was seen as a hopeful springtime for the Church in New York. But there was the problem, too; who, in 1811, was the Bishop of New York? The House of Bishops had displayed reluctance to accept Provoost's resignation in 1801, because it was unsure how to handle the resignation of a bishop. Therefore, it was made clear then that Moore would be considered "Assistant, or Coadjutor Bishop during Bishop Provoost's lifetime."[17]

One bishop who declined to serve, another bishop unable to serve—and a third man who very much wanted to be bishop. For one thing was clear in New York in 1811: John Henry Hobart would be Benjamin Moore's successor.

7

The Heritage of a Great Bishop: Hobart

Evangelical truth and Apostolic order
—John Henry Hobart

The traveler who passes through any number of New York State hamlets is likely to spy a venerable Episcopal church. Upon inquiry, he is told the building dates from 1825, but Prayer Book services commenced in the village in 1817. Eighteen seventeen! Ah, yes: Hobart.

These words summarize that man who will ever be a leading character in American Church history. In remote places, among people not congenial to the religious and political predispositions of the Episcopal Church, one finds Hobart or someone sent by him. Be it a solidly Presbyterian town near his home in New Jersey, or a staunch Congregationalist village near the Connecticut border, a logging camp in the Catskills, an Indian settlement in the Adirondack foothills, or a city church: Hobart was there, and his presence was recalled generations later.

This seems strange, for he was the opposite of glamorous. He was of small build, had an unpleasant swarthy complexion, was much afflicted with stomach distress, and had poor eyesight that made necessary spectacles that gave him an owllike appearance. He was frequently rendered inactive by mental fatigue. Throughout the extant letters of his contemporaries there runs the consistent theme of their anxiety about his health. Strangers found him memorable: "Heard Bishop Hobart preach a very excellent sermon. He is an orator, but unfortunately too much confined to book or notes, which is constantly interrupting the action, of which he has considerable," noted a European auditor in 1815.[1] Despite awkwardness and a very keen predilection to controversy, Hobart was seen by many as "a sort of shining knight, the ideal husband, brother, son and friend."[2] One can imagine the myopic bishop earnestly preaching orthodox Christianity as he understood it, well aware of his own personality. Passion and control, character and belief, determination and facility: that is the picture John Henry Hobart leaves of himself.

He was born in Philadelphia on September 14, 1775, the last of nine children of Enoch and Hannah Hobart. His great-great-grandfather came to Massachusetts Bay Colony in 1633. There were several Puritan clergymen in the family. Grandfather John moved to Philadelphia and became an Episcopalian. John Henry's father was a merchant and ship captain whose success in life was cut short by an early death. The future bishop was still an infant, but Captain Enoch's estate was adequate to enable his widow to send the boy to good schools. He went to the new Episcopal Academy, and later spent two years at the University of Pennsylvania. Then he attended Princeton for two years, graduating in 1793 at the age of eighteen. His family expected young Henry (as he seems to have been called) to become a businessman. He dutifully entered a kinsman's office for a brief time, but then returned to Princeton, where he was a tutor for four years. During this time he became certain of a calling to the Episcopal ministry. We may be certain that he consulted with Bishop White (who had baptized him) during those tutorship years. Princeton was not congenial to Episcopalians who had a high opinion of their Church. It is pleasant to think that Bishop White was a surrogate father, not only in the crucial time of determining vocation, but in Hobart's earlier years. The bishop suggested books for young Hobart to read, but one suspects his real theological training was in the halls of Old Nassau, where his natural combativeness led him to debates with his Presbyterian colleagues. He later said his views were "obnoxious" to his fellow tutors. Here is another attractive facet of Hobart's personality: he was quick to enter controversy, and yet he retained the friendship of his adversaries. Princeton gave Hobart solid biblical background, and a broad knowledge of Church history. One suspects the college of Signer Witherspoon also lent a fierce sense of American national destiny, which Hobart remembered as he later traversed the broad expanses of his diocese.

He was a very able man. Made deacon by Bishop White in 1798, in the next two years he became, successively, minister of several churches in Philadelphia, rector of Christ Church, New Brunswick, and rector of St. George's, Hempstead. By late 1800 he was an assistant minister at Trinity Church, New York. In May of that year he had married Mary Chandler, whose late father, Tory Thomas Bradbury Chandler, had been rector of St. John's in Elizabeth, New Jersey. Whatever books from Chandler's library came along with the bride would further encourage Hobart's High Church views. As an interesting sidelight to our history, this author possesses a Chandler book inscribed "Revd

Dan[l] Nash from his friend and brother John H. Hobart."

Such clerical mobility—five changes in two years, while yet a deacon—would be unacceptable today, but in the Episcopal Church then it betokened a man making his mark. He was ordained priest in Bishop Provoost's last ordination. It has been suggested that Provoost resigned the rectorship only when he was "secure in the knowledge that Trinity had another competent minister on the staff."[3] At Trinity Hobart found himself yoked with the aging Abraham Beach as the other assistant under Benjamin Moore, the new rector. Indeed, since Beach had been rector of New Brunswick, he may have been the one who brought Hobart to the notice of Provoost and the vestry. Four months later, the Rev. Cave Jones joined the Trinity Church clergy, with duties primarily at St. Paul's Chapel.

While Jones very soon became much esteemed at St. Paul's, it is Hobart who became the prominent minister at Trinity. Reasons for this are easy to discern. First of all, he had (and knew he had!) a winning personality. Secondly, he gave the appearance of great energy such as would enthrall those who were impatient to see the Episcopal Church bestir itself from stolid eighteenth-century decorum. Lastly, Hobart's preaching provided an unwonted "order and system" to religious devotion such as Provoost's sermons had failed to give. Very soon this man, who had moved from Pennsylvania to New Jersey to Long Island and then to Manhattan, knew he had come into the harbor where he would be. The Trinity congregation filled the new church for the young assistant; if another preacher mounted the pulpit steps, there was an almost audible groan from people who expected to hear Mr. Hobart.

He would always begin his sermons with a biblical text. Like most of his contemporaries, he wrote his sermons. He tried to memorize them, but he often depended upon the manuscript on the pulpit desk. "He appeared in the pulpit as a father anxious for the eternal happiness of his children," wrote an admiring Canadian visitor to an English friend.[4] No admirer of the new assistant was more fervent than Elizabeth Bayley Seton, daughter of "the most eminent surgeon in New York."[5] Her grandfather was old Dr. Charlton, rector of St. Andrew's, Staten Island. "Betty" Seton had long been conscious of reaching out to God, whom she sincerely and devotedly sensed as present in her life. What she now longed for, apart from a security not vouchsafed by her husband's uncertain business pursuits, was a consolidation in worship of the various Christian traditions she found satisfying. She wore a crucifix and responded to Wesleyan hymns. Along with many of her well-bred friends, she was accustomed to stately Morning Prayer in Trinity Church, with a fervent anticipation of "Sacrament Sunday." Her sense of duty, submission, and perhaps even of deserved punishment was at least partly a response to the Calvinism that was never very far away from early America. And she, like her new minister, was influenced by overtones of Christian revival in New York. For "revival" was very much in the air.

But why must Christianity depend upon occasional revivals? Does not God desire a sustained, systematic relationship with his creation? Must religious affirmation by cyclical; should it not be a linear encounter leading back directly to the faith once delivered? There were some, and John Henry Hobart was one, who said Yes, it is to be found in the visible Church of apostolic foundation, the Church of primitive practice and intellectual integrity, the Church of Mrs. Seton's own forebears, saved from papist accretions and Protestant innovations by the peculiar English Reformation, and now transplanted in the United States of America. Here it is, and you are already part of it. This was the message from the new curate who wasn't yet thirty years old, and it exhilarated those who crowded the aisles at Trinity.

Mrs. Seton was particularly in need of such substantial fare. Her husband, as yet unimpressed by Mr. Hobart, was obviously suffering from tuberculosis. His business affairs continued to falter, and the children were unwell. Mr. and Mrs. Hobart were loyal friends, and as the Setons' fortunes worsened, the Hobarts did their best to make things easier for Betty. Perhaps it was at this time that Hobart gave his friend a *Commentary on the Psalms* which she treasured all her life. They also asked Elizabeth Seton to be a godmother of their daughter, Rebecca. When, in a desperate attempt to seek a better climate, the Setons decided to sail to Italy, the Hobarts agreed to store some of their furniture; perhaps Hobart would hang their painting of *The Redeemer* on his own wall until they returned.

During these early years in New York, Hobart's energies were spent in ways that would extend the influence of the Episcopal Church beyond the pulpit of Trinity Church. He became a trustee of Columbia College at an early date, was a founder of the Protestant Episcopal Society for Promoting Religion and Learning in the State of New York, and was busy compiling a devotional manual for laypeople. He was not an average parish assistant and, naturally, this caused some animosity among his fellow clergy in the city. He was ready for whatever challenge, whatever opportunity, came his way. It does no injustice to the man to suppose that he hoped the see of New York might eventually fall to him.

Mrs. Seton could be something of an irritation, if not an embarrassment, along the way. Hobart suspected trouble when he heard that she and her dying husband were sailing to Italy. Knowing the depth of her religious outreach, and fearing that Seton would die in a Roman Catholic country, Hobart warned Elizabeth that she might be overly impressed by the ardor and multitudes at worship in Italy (where he had as yet never been). It happened exactly as he suspected: William Seton died in Italy. The widow was treated very kindly by enthusiastic Roman Catholics, and by the time she returned to New York, her spirit was aimed toward the Roman Catholic Church. Hobart warned her to beware of that "corrupt and sinful communion." He recommended John Newton's account of his conversion to Evangelical Christianity. He thought his friend could still respond to the robustness of "Glorious things of thee are spoken" and the piety of "How sweet the name of Jesus sounds." Hobart was not an unwise man, but wise men can be mistaken—and impatient. After Mrs. Seton became a Roman Catholic there was that decided coolness between them which is to be expected of people who have disappointed each other. It cannot be denied that Hobart, busy with many things, appeared to abandon Elizabeth Seton in the final months of her quest, while her Roman Catholic friends supplied the support the sensitive widow required.[6]

It is interesting that Elizabeth Seton became (on the two-hundredth anniversary of Hobart's birth, September 14, 1975) the first native-born American to be declared a saint by the Church of her adoption. But to us there will be additional salient factors. Hobart's prominence at Trinity Church is one. His early concern for a particular, gifted parishioner is another; we may suppose countless other men and women questioning the Episcopal Church's authenticity similarly occupied his time. Yet another factor is Hobart's loyalty to his church as truly catholic, and his belief that the Church of Rome was not nearly so. Perhaps more important to us is Hobart's early involvement in what soon became a cause célèbre: the conversion of a prominent Episcopal lady to the Roman Church. In this connection, other facts bear historic weight. The first is that a relative of William Seton's, Martin Hoffman, successfully sought to prevent further Roman Catholic invasions upon the family; Hoffman was a progenitor of the great dean of the General Theological Seminary, Eugene Augustus Hoffman. And it may be of further interest to our story that the Setons' next-door neighbor in New York was Joseph Corré, who became father-in-law of Henry Anthon, a clergyman who would in time seek to undo much of the Hobart "system." New York was still a small town in those days. Also, it was at this time (1805) that Hobart's "Essays on Episcopacy" began to appear in the Albany *Centinel*. These essays provoked a spirited pamphlet warfare among several Episcopal and Presbyterian clergy and laymen—and did much to bring the name of Hobart before the public.

Soon John Henry Hobart became very much the man of New York. Later, it would be said that Hobart and Dr. Hoosack and DeWitt Clinton were "the tripod on which New York stood." The diocesan journals make it clear that Hobart's star began to ascend as soon as he became an assistant at Trinity Church. He was almost immediately elected secretary of the convention, and was the preacher at some subsequent conventions. His conviction that the Church needed various organizations to fulfill definite tasks meant that able people were enlisted. Perhaps most important, he sounded a certain trumpet in a time of nationwide heightened religious activity. "Evangelical truth and Apostolic order" was the reasonable phrase people heard from Hobart, and they found the man and his message impressive. Thus, when the stricken Bishop Moore asked for an assisting bishop, Hobart's election was a clear indication of the new climate prevailing in New York. Hobart was the champion of those who restlessly sought the end of the lethargy characterized (as they thought) by Provoost and Moore. Furthermore, the party idea in Episcopal Church life was by now, 1811, respected in America. Cliques and inner circles enlist human loyalty, but never more than in the first half of the nineteenth century. We will never know exactly what lines might have been drawn by Episcopalians in that era. In his dealings with his neighbor Mrs. Seton, Hobart had already shown that the claims of the Church would be firmly stated. Bishop Provoost's idea, almost certainly unaltered by Bishop Moore, was that a certain sort of New Yorker preferred to worship according to Episcopal form. But now there were those who said that Episcopal worship had a divine and historic basis that made it preferable to all others.

It was later said that in Benjamin Moore's time, the New York clergy were

> more orderly than zealous—more orthodox than evangelical—more distinguished for attachment to the ritual of the Church than for a fervent and edifying mode of performing it—more intent upon guarding their folds against the inroads of enthusiasm than upon the conversion of sinners.[7]

And this estimate, written in 1842, might be said to characterize much of the Episcopal Church's image in New York through the years. How perfectly the Church suited the needs of seaboard Americans who desired orderliness and decorum!

When Bishop Moore requested an assistant bishop in 1811, he bared a dilemma. His poor health made the assistance imperative, but at the same time the Episcopal Church was wary of the concept of "assisting" bishops. There was an additional troubling aspect to the situation: was not Bishop Moore himself an auxiliary bishop? The first Bishop of New York was alive, and now suddenly displayed an unaccus-

tomed lively interest in Church affairs. He had doubtless heard that
though Bishop Moore's health was said to be "mending," John Henry
Hobart would "no doubt be chosen Assistant Bishop."[8]

Of course, Provoost had observed John Henry Hobart's rise at Trinity Church (though the Provoost family preferred attending St. Paul's
Chapel, whose minister, Cave Jones, had been entirely acceptable). It
may be expected that there was a degree of rivalry between the congregations meeting only several blocks apart. Hobart made many public
statements, and his activities were well marked. Bishop Provoost, now
nearing seventy years of age, may have been amused by some of Hobart's Old World peculiarities—his use of "ye" in writing, for instance;
Provoost eschewed that sort of archaism. Nor would the retired bishop
be persuaded by Hobart's notions that the Church would more quickly
"revive" if all the Prayer Book feasts and fasts were observed; these,
said Hobart, were a perfect safeguard against "ye dangerous extremes
of lukewarmness and of enthusiasm." Perhaps even worse for Provoost
was Hobart's assessment that Methodism was not as dangerous to Christianity in New York as were the Presbyterians. One of Provoost's most
esteemed public friends was the prominent Presbyterian the Reverend
Dr. John Rodgers.[9]

RISING TO POWER

Nevertheless, Hobart was the obvious choice for assistant bishop. He
was still secretary of the diocesan convention, the confidant of many
Episcopal clergy and laymen, and the man whose ability clearly led
toward the episcopate. And, it is safe to say, he was Bishop Moore's
choice. Not everyone concurred, however. The Rev. Cave Jones, popular and efficient minister at St. Paul's Chapel, was one of those who
viewed Hobart's rise with misgivings. It was a matter of conviction and
also a matter of personality. Hobart and Jones had quarreled over what
appeared to be Hobart's ambition and high-handedness, and they had
been unable to make up their differences. Therefore, when it was certain that Hobart would be the chief nominee for assistant bishop, Cave
Jones wrote and circulated a tract of eighty-five pages entitled *A Solemn Appeal to the Church*. It appeared ten days before the election.
The *Solemn Appeal* is a list of personal grievances which may have
concealed deeper diversity; some people have seen the real difficulty
as being one final struggle between Tory authoritarianism on the one
hand and Whig liberality on the other. Surely, Hobart was often impatient and lofty. Believing himself qualified for great things, he arro-
gated to himself responsibilities which might better have been dele-

gated to him by an aging rector-bishop. His colleagues naturally chafed when Hobart outpaced them. Now, according to Cave Jones, Hobart caused trouble for Evangelical Richard Channing Moore, rector of St. Stephen's Church (and soon to be Bishop of Virginia). More to the point, Jones accused Hobart of sidetracking the episcopal hopes of Abraham Beach—not a very cogent argument inasmuch as Beach was then in his seventy-first year. Worse, Hobart had used "every electioneering device possible to obtain votes" (which was probably true!).

Hobart was easily elected. In a confidence nourished by victory, he or his supporters succeeded in having the bedridden Bishop Moore bar Cave Jones from the Holy Communion. This was a blunder, for it appeared to be persecution and won friends for Jones. Tension increased. John Jay, the great jurist, and his family were among those who rose to defend Jones. They would thereafter bear a grudge against Hobart and his successor, Benjamin T. Onderdonk. Very soon, St. Paul's Chapel parishioners desired to be independent of Trinity, that Hobartian hotbed. The vestry sidestepped the request and began negotiations with a view to dismissing Cave Jones from his position in the parish.

Jones felt himself treated unjustly by people much more powerful than himself, and in desperation he turned to the resigned bishop, Samuel Provoost. He sought reinstatement. The kindly bishop, removed from ecclesiastical matters, and never much interested in party pressures, advised Jones to "disregard" the deposition proceedings of "Benjamin Moore and his presbyters" as not "sanctioned by the principles of our religion or humanity." What words of the Enlightenment, those! Furthermore, the patriot bishop probably saw in the Cave Jones affair the same injustice he himself had resisted in 1776, and the same authoritarianism he had discerned in Seabury now revived in Hobart. The imbroglio was an effective tonic, for (as was soon reported) "Bishop Provoost is remarkably reinvigorated both in body and mind, and is in better health than he has for many years enjoyed, insomuch as to be able to attend public worship regularly, and funerals when called upon."[10] Clearly, at this late date Samuel Provoost was indicating that he was taking an interest in the affairs of the diocese he had so summarily resigned ten years earlier.

There were several reasons for this. Provoost's family (especially son-in-law Cadwallader Colden) and some friends urged him to thwart Hobart's ambitions. More directly, Provoost may have thought Hobart's supporters irresponsible. Certainly, their having the paralyzed Bishop Moore inhibit Cave Jones from the Communion was reprehensible. For his part, Hobart probably never doubted that he would be elected third Bishop of New York, but this unexpected reentrance of Provoost on the scene *was* awkward.

Just before the election, Hobart wrote "from my little country retreat in the neighborhood of [the present Short Hills, N.J.] I have left
my family in New York. I have come out here for a few days to attend to
my garden, etc. In fact the country has always charms for me." And then
he proceeded to state that retirement in the country was often more
appealing than "the arduous duties and awful responsibilities of ye
office [of a bishop]" to which his undoubted abilities would soon bring
him.[11] If we are skeptical about Hobart's sincerity in these sentiments,
we may at least grant that he had reason to believe there would not be
the necessary three bishops present to consecrate him. James Madison
of Virginia and Claggett of Maryland had declared their unwillingness
to travel as far as New York. Bishop Provoost resided in the city but
seldom officiated and, in any case, disapproved of Hobart. Bishop
Moore was unable to participate in any services. The consecration of
Hobart was scheduled to take place on May 25 in New Haven, where
the General Convention was meeting. Alexander Viets Griswold was to
be consecrated Bishop of the Eastern Diocese, the name given a temporary merger of several New England states, at the same time Hobart
was to be consecrated for New York. So serious was the problem of
finding participating bishops that William White feared "that the American Church would be again subjected to the necessity of having recourse to the mother-church for the episcopacy."[12] Finally Bishop Provoost agreed to be present if the consecration was moved to Trinity
Church in New York. Morgan Dix later related, perhaps fancifully:

> At the last moment Dr. Provoost had a serious attack of sickness.
> When therefore the vast congregation assembled in Trinity Church to
> witness the ceremony it was moved by but one thought, "Could Pro-
> voost attend?" After moments of almost intolerable suspense, the
> news that the venerable bishop had arrived and was actually in the
> vestry room was whispered from one to another. Audible thanks-
> giving ran through the assemblage. "He's come! Thank God!" was
> echoed throughout the sacred edifice. Bishop Provoost remained in
> the vestry room till the conclusion of Morning Prayer, entering the
> chancel for the Holy Communion service. He read the Epistle in a
> low but distinct voice. Dr. Hobart and Dr. Griswold were consecrated
> together.[13]

Bishop White reported in a letter to the Bishop of Maryland that "it
affected me much to see Bishop Provoost brought out in his debilitated
State, altho I trust it has not been injurious to him."[14]

This was probably Provoost's last participation in a crowded service, and it was the beginning of a sad final chapter in his public life.
He had perhaps been urged to take part in the consecration of Hobart
by the very people who most disliked the bishop elect. Why? Because it

would be a dramatic reentry into diocesan life and enable Provoost to make the startling but plausible claim that he was the de facto Bishop of New York. This is precisely what happened, and there is reason to think John Jay, as well as Provoost's son-in-law Cadwallader Colden, were among those who encouraged him to circumvent Hobart's ambitions. For, though Hobart was in name the assistant bishop, he was in fact practically the Bishop of New York. This was a fulfillment of wise William White's prediction early in 1811: "I consider it as very improbable that [Bishop Moore] will ever be able to take an active Part in ye Concerns of ye Church."[15]

It was commonly understood, then, that the new assistant bishop would direct the affairs of the diocese. And some people were unhappy about the prospect. None was more fearful of what the elevation of Hobart presaged than Provoost, who sent a message to the 1812 convention signing himself "Bishop of the Protestant Episcopal Church in the State of New York, and diocesan of the same." He stated that though poor health will not "enable me to discharge all the duties of a Diocesan, and for that reason I cannot attend now the Convention," he claimed to be the bishop of the Church in New York and "bound to consider every Episcopal act as unauthorized." If the diocesan convention were to accede to this claim, then every act of Bishop Moore since 1801 could be questioned, and as Bishop White with his usual good sense opined, Bishop Moore had acted as *the* Bishop of New York for ten years without any demur from Provoost; how could those ten years now be invalidated?[16] The diocesan convention took the same view, with a mildness calculated to soothe the respected retired bishop. Events unfolded as predicted: the helpless Bishop Moore turned all diocesan matters over to John Henry Hobart. An unfortunate footnote is that the usually magnanimous Hobart refused thereafter to take part with Samuel Provoost in any ceremony, fearing this would confirm Provoost's dubious claims.

THE HOBART EPISCOPACY

Given his ebullient personality, Hobart appeared to dismiss the affair of Provoost's threatened reentry into the diocese. But did he? Despite his personal fame, the unquestioned loyalties gained even from erstwhile opponents, and the statistical gains of his episcopate, tragedy always seems to stalk Hobart. From the beginning, he was at pains to defend his consecration; Bishop White had omitted a crucial Trinitarian formula during the service.[17] Then, there was the seductive attraction of the place in Short Hills: "Our brother," wrote a friend, "has too much

to do and is too often absent from New York. He has purchased a farm
forsooth in New Jersey and is there when he should be at his station."[18]

This was written just prior to the election, but would be heard
again and again throughout Hobart's episcopate. The farm was within
the limits of Springfield, New Jersey, but lay closer to the village of
Summit. The house was of an ample size, and Hobart liked to think he
could be signaled from the steeple of Trinity Church if his presence in
the city was urgently needed. The place was purchased in 1810, and the
location was chosen probably because it was close to old friends of the
Chandler family. It remained in the Hobarts' possession for many years,
and though the house has disappeared, the old road traversing the land
retains the bishop's name to this day. We can discern a certain dissatisfaction on the part of New Yorkers that their bishop chose a Jersey
residence, but in fact it may be that a retreat removed from his own
jurisdiction was exactly what was needed. For, in his episcopacy of
nearly nineteen years, Hobart was at least twice on the verge of emotional collapse.

Short Hills may be accountable for part of the bishop's fabled career, lending the nonecclesiastical setting often required by an overly
active clergyman. Hobart's impatience and nervous energy, even a certain arrogance, were well-known prior to the election. But these were
overshadowed by qualities equally known: intellectual brilliance,
readiness to admit a mistake, firm belief in God's guidance, and an
amazing capacity to endear himself to his colleagues. The times were
with Hobart, too. First of all, immigration from England continued
strong. The growing city needed skilled and unskilled laborers. Factories were springing up along the Hudson River and its tributary
streams. Immigrants from England would be welcomed in New York by
a congenial Anglophilism—and none admired England more at this
time than the Bishop of New York. Revolution in France, the Napo-
leonic Wars, and the puzzling unsteadiness of current French sovereigns set much of American loyalty where it always really wanted to be:
toward England. As early as 1810, Hobart listed recent English victories
over the French in a letter and ends, "Hurra for Old England."[19] A
climate preferring English life was, of course, helpful to the Episcopal
Church.

The romantic revival also was helpful. In part a reaction against
Enlightenment ideals, its outward signs were often seen in adornment
associated with "Gothic" styles. But "its imaginative transfiguration of
the past was not merely an aesthetic fad, but an inspiration to political
and social action."[20] Above all, for our present discussion, there was
borne along in the romantic revival a "feeling for the still potent allure-
ments of a traditional and authoritarian faith."[21] Hobart was among

those who would look back and grasp for his day things of the past. No wonder Mrs. Seton and her friends found much to admire in the new assistant's sermons and teaching.

ROMANTIC PIETY

In another, subtle way the romantic revival aided the Episcopal Church. While Gothic motifs had never completely disappeared, they had much declined in the wake of classic simplicities now so much associated with early America. Classic "orderliness" and "visible reason" were to be seen in architecture, heard in music, and experienced in worship. On the other hand, Gothic forms encouraged the human imagination, suggested freedom (at least for the well-born), and praised the products of nature. Both the classic and Gothic modes claim to be essentially "natural," as perhaps they are. And a part of the genius of the Prayer Book is that it can be used with equal force in either setting. If the Western world was now bored with an eighteenth-century espousal of classicism and was ready to indulge in the luxury of romanticism, the Prayer Book was ready to go along, especially now that churchgoers were reading Walter Scott and beginning to require furniture and dwellings appropriate to his characters. If there is hidden meaning in Provoost's remonstrances to the convention, it may be that he was attempting to stop the flow of a tide.

The Episcopal Church readily adapted to the new mood as the nineteenth century progressed. This began with a point of view, for churches are generally wary of tangible changes. Hobart's "high" ideas about the Church, however, were acceptable to many New York Episcopalians because they were based on what seemed to be a new interpretation of history, at the beginning of a century quite ready to adopt a sense of history that could complement its own fast pace. Eventually, this altered point of view began to find expression in the ceremonies of the Church, and that is when great troubles came. But this was after Hobart's death; changes during his time seemed to suit the national feeling. One of these was the romantic revival, with its Gothicisms and reaching back to the supposed benignities of the Middle Ages. Another was the definite religious revival which began just prior to Hobart's ministry, and extended beyond his death.

The "Second Awakening" is the name popularly attached to a new attention given the churches in America in the early years of the nineteenth century. In 1800 no more than 10 percent of the American people were church members.[22] As we have seen, influences said to emanate from atheistic France effectively challenged Christianity in America.

At the same time, a postwar conservatism manifested itself. If gifts of the past were to be treasured, none was more important than the religion of Jesus Christ. One form of religious revival may be seen in the career of Timothy Dwight (1752–1817), grandson of Jonathan Edwards, and educator, farmer, and Congregationalist pastor. Dwight directed his pen and voice to counteract inroads of Deism and infidelity. In 1795 he became president of Yale College, which gave him a prestigious platform to continue his intellectual, reasonable arguments entirely appropriate in the eighteenth century.

But more was required, especially as a new century dawned upon a frontier country. If parts of New England and New York could utilize old-style metaphysics, other places found more satisfaction in an emotional approach that blended romanticism and religion.[23] If a heightened sense of history had much to do with the Hobartian triumph, it also led the bishop to stand apart from the conspicuous events of the Second Awakening while at the same time his Church reaped a plentiful harvest from it. Hobart's insistence on the apostolic origins of the Episcopal Church prevented him from appreciating rebirth experiences and the Low Churchmanship of the revival. As a matter of fact, while the Second Awakening was notable in western New York—that "burnt-over district" of religious frenzy and inventiveness—it was decidedly less remarked in New York City. The Awakening lasted many years as a recognizable movement, punctuated by particular events and satisfying increases in church membership; "A state of religious excitement prevails in many neighborhoods through our Diocese," said John McVickar in 1831.[24] Indeed, it would be difficult not to trace the devotional piety and church activism of the Second Awakening to the present day. The striking advancement of the Episcopal Church under John Henry Hobart must be seen as a peculiar expression of the Second Awakening in New York.

The times always seemed right for Hobart. And he had the ability to find the right solutions to problems. Very early he elucidated three difficulties that faced the Episcopal Church: education in the Church, missionary expansion in the diocese, and a popularizing of a Church that seemed yet to be the preserve of the privileged. In the first year of his priesthood, Hobart was a leader in organizing the Protestant Episcopal Society for the Promotion of Religion and Learning in the State of New York. Two years later, in 1804, he edited *A Companion for the Altar*. This was a communicant's seven-day preparation for the sacrament (though, of course, no Episcopal church in New York had a weekly Eucharist). The *Companion* was borrowed from "divines of the Church of England, who imbibed their principles and their piety at the pure fountain of the primitive Church," as Hobart truly believed.[25] The theological approach is soundly redemptionist:

> We are saved from the guilt and dominion of sin by the divine merits and grace of a crucified Redeemer; and the merits and grace of this Redeemer are applied to the soul of the believer in the devout and humble participation of the ordinances of the Church administered by a priesthood who derive their authority by regular transmission from Christ, the Divine Head of the Church.[25]

Redemptionist, yes. But could there ever be a more concise premise for "high" ideas about the Church? No wonder John Henry Hobart called himself a "high Churchman."[26]

Hobart had also founded the Protestant Episcopal Theological Society in 1806 and, deprecating Bibles circulated without Prayer Books, he established the New York Bible and Common Prayer Book Society in 1809. This, of course, was in direct competition with the American Bible Society, against which Hobart warned his people. Later, he edited *The Christian's Manual,* which approved ejaculatory prayer, outlined mental prayer, and enjoined churchpeople so to familiarize themselves with the Book of Common Prayer that they could use its words automatically: "Episcopalians have been so much in the habit of praying in the language of the Prayer Book that they cannot make bad prayers," Hobart wrote. "It is more difficult for an Episcopalian to make a bad prayer than a good one."[27] Such statements did not always endear Hobart to people of other churches, nor did his idea about "familiarizing" the Prayer Book make him a favorite to those of us who were later required to learn the collect of the day by heart on Sunday mornings.

MAKING THE EPISCOPAL CHURCH KNOWN

The second recognized need in the Episcopal Church was missionary expansion. Hobart had the gift of sensible strategy, and the complementary ability to inspire clergymen he sent to remote places in the diocese. In the year after his consecration, he sailed upriver and, apart from calling at some of the landing towns in Dutchess and Ulster counties, he visited Milton, Charlton, Stillwater, Albany, Fairfield, Richfield, Unadilla, Stamford, Troy, Lansingburg, Butternuts, Waterford, Athens, Hudson, and Catskill. Succeeding years saw Hobart in much wider swings throughout selected portions of New York State—and sometimes northern New Jersey, where for a while he had jurisdiction in the absence of a Bishop of New Jersey. Each journey was enthusiastically reported to the diocesan convention as being a normal concern of that body. In 1813 he suggested a diocesan canon requiring parishes to contribute toward missions in the state. That was in his convention address, in which his call for mission labor supported by an annual offering was considerd with his appeal for liturgical faithfulness as a barrier against fanaticism, and for a "learned and pious ministry."

Hobart's most lasting contribution was his popularization of the Episcopal Church and removing it (as far as ever could be done!) from its reputation as being the church of wealth in New York and an enduring vestige of English colonization. By means of his vivid personality, inexhaustible drive, pleasing speech, and readiness to debate, Hobart made Americans aware that the Episcopal Church was now a native church, and could offer rich gifts from its historical treasury. Hobart's "Evangelical truth and Apostolic order" became a celebrated slogan for the Episcopal Church. As we have seen, he spoke an Evangelical's theology, but departed from it when he insisted that the Church, by God's design, is the dispenser of his grace. Those Evangelicals who failed to note this insistence could warmly embrace Hobart. When he clashed with them, it was usually because he would not join in services with other churches or societies. He stood aloof from Masonic exercises and, toward the end of his life, was much criticized because he refused to take part in the obsequies for popular Governor Clinton.

Hobart's *Companion* would have marked him as a High Churchman, for he had an exalted view of the Church, as we have seen. We must repeat, however, that "High" ceremonies were hardly known in his time. The Episcopal services throughout Hobart's life remained about as they had been when Samuel Provoost was a student at King's College. Hobart distrusted the word "sacrifice" as applied to the Holy Communion, repudiated what he understood to be transubstantiation, and spoke earnestly against auricular confession. Unlike his successor, Hobart was singularly uninterested in clerical garb or church architecture, or the dozens of peculiarities that expended Episcopal energies after 1830. He stressed the invisible structure of the Church, its liturgy, and particularly its ministry, so that critics were likely to retort, "All Church and no Christ."[28] No wonder Samuel Provoost and his friends feared another Bishop Seabury had been set loose in New York. But this was another age. The door of the past century was firmly closed and the Georgian Church was, at least in America, gone forever. In Hobart, various strands were intertwined. There was the old-fashioned and moderate theology he had learned in Bishop White's library. Then there were the books of his father-in-law, Thomas Bradbury Chandler. From the one man he would have learned the practicality demanded by the real situation in a pluralistic America. From Chandler he would have found the answers needed by his own nervous and active personality: a toughness and yet a tenderness and (perhaps best of all) a reverence for the claims of the old high churchmen, now seasoned by intimations of the romantic revival. It is a conservative political and ecclesiastical viewpoint, exactly what Provoost detested. But it was a conservatism maintained by a man of free-wheeling charm and genial manners: hard to place in the scheme of things. Those who looked to one extreme called him an "enthusiast," mused his staunch admirer John McVickar, while "those who looked to the other styled him a 'formalist,' and 'bigot.' It was not every one whose intellectual grasp could take in both points at a single view."[29]

When Hobart's abilities were activated in expanding the Episcopal Church in New York, the results were immediate. We have seen that he promoted various Church organizations long before his consecration, and published books for communicants. Other Church societies followed: the Young Men's Auxiliary Bible and Prayer Book Society (1816), the Missionary Society (1817), and the New York Sunday School Society (1817). Hobart knew he needed these organizations to strengthen his work, and was always optimistic about the future. "Our Church," he wrote to Rufus King in 1815, "in this country has, I trust, passed through her worst days and better times await her. The interest of lay gentlemen and influence is not one of the least and most gratifying circumstances in encouraging this hope." It has been said that at Hobart's death in 1830 "nearly every important town in the State had an Episcopal church and rector."[30] It has also been stated, rightly, that Hobart's great achievements were in the rural areas of his diocese; to his successor was left the mounting problem of New York City's growth gone berserk.

Until 1815 there were three Episcopal bishops of New York. Samuel Provoost sulked in his tent because General Convention declared him to be a "resigned" bishop. Bishop Provoost is "very justly indignant at certain conduct in relation to himself at the late general convention and refuses to take any part whatsoever in the affairs of the Church [in New York] until the House of Bishops shall have decided on his claim to the Diocesanship," wrote an observer in 1814.[31] Nonetheless, Provoost was, at least in title, Bishop of New York.

The second bishop resident in New York in 1815 was Benjamin Moore. But since 1811 he had been confined to his sickroom; "Dr. Moore is a nonentity in the Church," wrote a critic of Hobart, who added, "Dr. Hobart is a man from whom I never will ask a favor, and from whom I never expect any."[32] Hobart, of course, was the third Episcopal bishop in New York. There was no question that he was de facto bishop of the diocese, but he carefully avoided joining Provoost in any ceremonies, still fearing the older man might claim diocesan authority.[33]

A "retired" bishop, an incapacitated bishop, and an energetic bishop—all in the same city, and all with arguable rights to be acknowledged as diocesan: this was the situation in New York until September 6, 1815, when Samuel Provoost died. The funeral procession formed at his house in Greenwich Street next day, and included "all Episcopal clergy of the city . . . the pall, covered with the Bishop's robes was borne by the elder of the Clergy" to Trinity Church, where the principal officiant at the evening service was Cave Jones. The Provoost family was charged one pound for candles to light the church, which was thronged. In the procession were the lieutenant governor of the state, judges of the federal courts, the mayor of the city, the recorder, members of the bar, the bishop's physicians, the trustees of Columbia College, the vestrymen of Trinity Church—all led by children of the parish school. The interment was in the vault of William Alexander (Philip Livingston's father-in-law), but later, probably when the present church was built, the bishop's coffin was transferred to the Colden plot in Trinity Cemetery.

Provoost died in the year peace was declared after the War of 1812. The United States was now decidedly independent of the mother country. It was an appropriate time for the old bishop to die. His earliest years had been spent in New York, a large town already known for its outstanding silversmiths and cabinetmakers, a place where itinerant artists knew rich sitters awaited them, a city where the English Church had pretensions never fully substantiated. Provoost, knowing the difference, disdained the sham and allowed himself the luxury of choosing what he thought was the best of the world in which he lived. Perhaps therein lay the failures posterity would attribute to him.

Provoost's death meant that now, at last, Benjamin Moore was second Bishop of New York. Though "able to reason and converse"[34] Moore continued unable to act as bishop. Hobart was very much in charge of the Episcopal Church in New York, and also New Jersey, where, though the province was of Quaker and Presbyterian origins, the Church of England flourished in at least twenty-four congregations prior to the Revolution.[35] Hobart and William White shared responsibility for the Church in New Jersey until 1815, when Bishop Croes was consecrated for that state.

The next year, 1816, Bishop Moore of New York "expired on Tuesday evening, the 27th of February, 1816, at his residence at Greenwich, near New York, in the sixty-eighth year of his age."[36] Another prominent link with pre-Revolutionary America was broken. The Church paused to remember this gentle man who "never made display of talent, of learning or of station." Bishop Hobart preached the funeral sermon, and said Benjamin Moore loved the Church, was steady in principle, and "lived until he saw her . . . raised from the dust, and putting on the garments of glory and beauty."[37]

THE GENERAL SEMINARY

With Provoost gone in 1815 and Moore the next year, one might expect a significant event in 1817. The General Theological Seminary calls that the year of its origin, but a theological training school was in Hobart's mind much earlier. Of all the needs that his various organizations were intended to meet, none was greater than that of a seminary. Presbyterians and Congregationalists and Dutch Reformed candidates could prepare for the ministry in famous places equipped with appropriate faculties. Episcopalians were obliged to find a clerical tutor. Hobart probably imagined an Episcopal theological department at Columbia College, but the tide began to run against Episcopal domination of the college when Bishop Moore resigned as president in 1811. The head of the college should be an Episcopalian because of Trinity's land grant—so ran the agreement—but now not even staunch Episcopalians were prepared to contend for full Episcopal management. Not even Hobart. The appointment of Episcopalian William Harris as president and Presbyterian John M. Mason as provost made it clear that too many influential trustees were prepared to argue for neutrality in the college. Hobart's influence at Columbia was therefore considerably diminished. But he nursed the hope that if the college abandoned its buildings to move elsewhere, the land could be reclaimed by Trinity and used as a seminary.[38]

New York was only one diocese looking for a seminary. Other Episcopal dioceses needed places where candidates for the ministry could study. Bishop White and Bishop Hobart thought of diocesan seminaries, but other Church leaders envisioned a main seminary controlled by the General Convention. The idea of control aroused Hobart. Predictably, he opposed such a seminary, arguing with cogency that "the direction and superintendence" of theological studies was the responsibility of the ordaining bishop, not the responsibility of the General Convention. Hobart was not likely to share these important duties with others—and certainly not an impersonal legislative body such as General Convention. Nevertheless, the move toward a "general" seminary grew stronger, and Hobart perceived possibilities in the enterprise when the General Convention, on May 27, 1817, proposed that "this seminary be located in the city of New York." Perhaps Hobart

also found encouragement in knowing that his views might be dominant in the seminary if the Diocese of New York could furnish an
impressive wherewithal. He already knew that his predecessor's son,
Clement Clarke Moore, was ready to give an entire block of his Chelsea
estate if the seminary would build there. Early in 1818 he met in Philadelphia with other members of the "theological school committee and
agreed on certain measures for collecting funds."[39] This particular
committee did not do its work very well, for the General Theological
Seminary was a most impecunious institution for many years to come.
Nonetheless, there was enough optimism to induce two able priests,
Samuel Farmer Jarvis and Samuel H. Turner, to become the first full-
time professors when the seminary began in the spring of 1819, with six
students meeting in a corner room of the gallery of St. Paul's Chapel.

Fortunately for those who feared that Hobart would dominate the
General Seminary, he appears to have been too busy elsewhere to en-
force his will upon the seminary; furthermore, in Jarvis and Turner he
would encounter wills as strong as his own. Like many men who must
control any venture to which they put their hand, once Hobart discovered he could not rule the General Convention's seminary, his lack of
interest in it was manifest. Bishop Brownell of Connecticut was more
encouraging, and at his invitation the seminary forsook the school-
rooms offered by Trinity Church and moved to space above a bookstore
in New Haven. This further displeased Hobart, who regarded New
Haven with the contempt customarily reserved by a Princetonian for
Yale; was not Old Eli in 1820 still a bastion of New England Congregationalism?

Now that the General Seminary was removed from New York City,
Hobart resumed his efforts for a diocesan seminary. Part of his plans
included a regrettable attempt to undermine whatever progress the
New Haven seminary might enjoy. Hobart called upon Clement Clarke
Moore for the Chelsea land the old bishop's son had promised, and he
had in hand certain funds with which to proceed with his theological
school. As far as Hobart was concerned, there could now be two seminaries: the doubtful one in New Haven, and the other safely under his
control in New York. (Another seminary was beginning, in Virginia, at
this time.) The resourceful bishop was also thinking of an "Interior
School" upstate, in Geneva, where men from that part of the diocese
could be trained for the ministry. Meanwhile, the New York Diocesan
School in New York City opened on May 18, 1821, with four students;
later in the year, there were nine students at the Geneva School.

Then Jacob Sherred died. Of German Lutheran background, he
had been a successful merchant and a vestryman of Trinity Church. Not
long before his death, Sherred had been induced by John Pintard to

leave a handsome bequest for the establishment of a seminary "within the State of New York, under the direction or by the authority of the General Convention of the Protestant Episcopal Church." *Within the State* and the *authority of the General Convention*! Within days, both the New Haven and New York seminaries were claiming the bequest; both had attorneys assuring them of their rights. Bishop White called a special session of the General Convention. The result was that the General Theological Seminary was relocated in New York City, on the Moore land that was eventually named Chelsea Square on the road that has become Ninth Avenue. Hobart's control was somewhat limited by the absurdly large number of trustees provided by the General Convention. The resettled and redefined seminary pleased most people, though one churchman wondered if "the evil of the undue influence of New York" (meaning, of course, Bishop Hobart) might not pose a threat to sound theological education.[40]

Throughout these proceedings, which have been admirably told by the seminary's historian, Powel M. Dawley, Hobart's whole personality may be seen: his need to control, his occasional pettiness, his ability to conciliate, and his final magnanimity. "Scholarship was not his stronghold,"[41] declared John McVickar, who thought his god's greatest personal gifts lay in the ability to grasp a situation and give it practical application. Hobart is described variously as "affectionate," "child like," "warm and gentle and kind."[42] Charles Finney, the Abolitionist preacher who designed and had built the Broadway Tabernacle after the Tappen brothers invited him to New York, left in his autobiography an appealing vignette of Hobart. A young girl of the street responded to a revival meeting. Later, she told Finney she had stolen a shawl belonging to Bishop Hobart's daughter. Finney declared the shawl must be returned. So the poor girl took herself to the bishop's doorstep. Whoever responded to the knock ushered her into Hobart's presence, and the crime was confessed. "When I told him, he wept, laid his hand on my head, and said he forgave me."[43]

RECORDS OF SUCCESS

One New York City parish that entered upon a flourishing existence in the Hobart years was St. Stephen's Church, then on the corner of Broome and Chrystie streets. The church had been founded by English Lutherans in 1805 and by 1816 was reported to be the largest congregation in the diocese. It was said to be composed of "merchants, grocers, butchers, wheelwrights, shoemakers, watchmakers, sail makers and bricklayers."[44] When Hobart was consecrated, his friend Richard Chan-

ning Moore was rector of St. Stephen's. The church then had the customary high pulpit in the aisle "with velvet cushions and silk tassels."
The choir of men and women found the note by means of a tuning fork,
though a pipe organ was soon purchased. In winter the church was
warmed by four great iron stoves that burned hickory; the sexton (for a
fee) would help the people fill their portable footwarmers with coals
from these stoves. There had been a Sunday school at St. Stephen's
from its beginnings (it was, possibly, the first Episcopal Sunday school
in New York), but Hobart's enthusiasm for religious education and the
effects of the Second Awakening practically assured a Sunday school in
every active parish by 1825. The fact that its rector, Richard Channing
Moore, was a noted preacher and soon to be Bishop of Virginia promoted
the fortunes of St. Stephen's Church, and it enjoyed much prosperity
until its congregation joined in the uptown hike which proved to be
disastrous to all but the most resilient of parishes.

Another church that traces its prosperity to the Hobart era is St.
George's, Newburgh. This was a parish of Royal Charter (1770), whose
first building dated from prior to 1750. St. George's had fallen on hard
times in the Revolutionary War and had failed to make the recovery
other churches enjoyed. Bishop Hobart persuaded John Brown, rector
of Fishkill, to go to Newburgh in 1815; within four years, a new church
was built and St. George's was on the way to being one of the Hudson
Valley's prime parishes. Such a rapid recovery suggests the growth of
Newburgh, then a port of increasing prosperity. It also illustrates the
improved fortunes of the Episcopal Church in the metropolitan area.
John Brown was rector of St. George's for sixty-two years, his ministry
there being a long link between the era of Benjamin Moore and that of
Henry C. Potter. In that time, Brown founded several missions that
grew into independent parishes and a hospital. In his time, too, old St.
Thomas's, New Windsor, was revived. This was another SPG mission,
reaching back as early as 1731. When the old chapel burned in 1845, it
was immediately replaced by one of America's significant "correct"
stone Gothic country churches, copied from St. James the Less, Philadelphia (which was itself a replica of St. Michael's, Long Stanton, Cam-
bridgeshire).

These accounts of quickened growth might be repeated again and
again in this history. Churches of all major denominations prospered in
the Era of Good Feeling. The Episcopal Church in New York was particularly able, for reasons already outlined, to utilize all the favorable
breezes of those times—especially with a man like Hobart at the helm.
The statistics are impressive: assuming the beginning of Hobart's episcopacy to be 1812, his first full year as Moore's assistant, there were in
the Diocese of New York twenty-five clergy, forty churches, and 2,345

communicants. When Hobart died, the were 168 clergy, sixty-eight congregations, and 6,708 communicants.

Given the strain upon a man of the bishop's temperament, the
responsibilities he saw attending upon such growth brought their own
warnings. A prolonged European tour seemed to ward off an impending breakdown. But once back in New York, the bishop gathered again
all the strands in his own hands and resumed the control that was his
wont. In all probability he was dissatisfied at the manner in which
affairs had been managed in his absence. Above all, there is a sense of
the *loneliness* the man must have felt: even his fellow bishops seemed
wary of him. They were often irritated by his eagerness to command the
situation. He had myriad admirers, persons of all walks of life. Proud
parents conferred his name upon their children. But were there many
friends?

His death came, most appropriately, while he was on a visitation in
a far-off corner of the diocese. The bishop arrived in Auburn the evening of September 1, 1830. He said he had a slight cold with some chills,
but appeared to be well the next day when he preached in St. Peter's
Church and confirmed nine candidates. But when he returned to the
rectory he complained of "coldness and oppression of the stomach."
No one seems to have become alarmed. The bishop had shown similar
symptoms for twenty years, and in any case had been indisposed in that
same house four years earlier. Several days later, it was apparent that
Hobart was very ill. His son, a physician, was summoned from New
York. Hobart died September 12, 1830, at the age of fifty-five. The route
from Auburn to New York City became one long funeral procession by
means of horse-drawn wagon, canal barge, and the river steamboat *Con-
stellation*. A crowd met the coffin at the dock in Manhattan and conveyed it to Trinity Church, where the burial service was read by Hobart's Evangelical friend, Bishop Moore of Virginia. Benjamin T.
Onderdonk, long the bishop's trusted lieutenant, was the preacher at
the service.

8

Onderdonk: Triumph and Tragedy

... was half talked into the belief that there was
something in all this. But I can't and won't believe
it. But I'm too much mystified and astonished and
disgusted to discuss the matter. One thing I'm sur-
prised at, I confess: the very general feeling of sym-
pathy for the Bishop that seems to exist even in quar-
ters where one would least expect it.
                              —GEORGE TEMPLETON STRONG

Any man elected so quickly to take the place of the renowned Hobart must have possessed considerable popularity, ability, and the implicit benediction of his predecessor. And so it was. Benjamin Treadwell Onderdonk was a native son, born in New York City on July 15, 1791. His older brother, Henry Ustick Onderdonk, was a student in medicine before he, too, decided to enter the ministry. Both men studied under Hobart and were ordained. Henry served as missionary in Canandaigua and subsequently became rector of St. Anne's in Brooklyn; he was elected Assistant Bishop of Pennsylvania in 1827. He thus came to work with William White, the now aged mentor of Hobart. Benjamin Onderdonk's entire ministry had been as an assistant at Trinity Church and a teacher at the General Theological Seminary. He was often considered a surrogate for Bishop Hobart.[1]

"The opinion of his own friends is, I find, that the Bishop is a little Dutch," wrote James Fenimore Cooper.[2] If the novelist meant that Onderdonk tended to be tenacious and stubborn, the judgment can be sustained by a hundred proofs. Thoroughly committed to the principles of his tutor and benefactor, Hobart, Benjamin Onderdonk never hesitated to seize an opportunity to promote New York High Churchmanship. He was not one to soften his importunities. A letter he wrote to John Henry Hopkins of Pittsburgh as early as 1828 is an illustration: he wanted Hopkins (who would one day sit in judgment upon him) to come to the vacant St. Stephen's Church in New York because the rector there should be a man "of sound Church principles who will keep that church in unity of sentiment and operation with the Bishop and the great body of Clergy in this City and diocese."

The letter is forthright and does not hesitate to equate the "good cause" with Hobartian High Churchmanship.[3] It is quoted here not only because it reveals Onderdonk's bluntness but also because it shows us that the assistant at Trinity was very much in the corridors of influence. He was the hardworking, loyal servant of Hobart and, like the bishop, was liable to quarrel with his associates. But alas, he lacked Hobart's celebrated grace and charm. One suspects he also had little of that other most endearing Hobart quality: a ready ability to apologize when shown to be in error. Nevertheless, he was friendly, often child-like, and despite his capacity for politicking there seems to have been an otherworldliness about him. He was speedily made the fourth Bishop of New York in an election that met with general approval, though some of Onderdonk's best friends regretted a certain coarseness of manner and an unfortunate habit of openly "fondling" his students at the seminary[4] or "often caressing" people he knew well.[5]

The years between 1830 and 1840 were ones of continued great advance for the Episcopal Church. Even by the beginning of that decade Greene County was "well sprinkled with flourishing missions."[6] One reason why the Episcopal Church was to be found in such remote hamlets is that between 1830 and 1840 the number of its clergy doubled.[7] Another reason is that, in New York State, Hobart had prosecuted an energetic missionary strategy. And perhaps there is yet another reason why the Episcopal Church began to thrive in these burgeoning years of the nineteenth century: having passed through an era of unpopularity caused by the politics of the Revolutionary War, the Episcopal Church tended to avoid involvement in the many parties and pressure groups that were springing up in the young nation. The Church stood aloof from, and seemed untouched by, the antislavery and anti-Masonic movements. When Temperance became a nationwide issue, some notable Episcopalians were its exponents, but they tended to make it mainly a household virtue, avoiding political formalities. Even so, the Temperance question had an emotional and economic appeal, and there is no doubt that the drinking habits of Americans were profoundly altered in the 1830s. It is arguable that the Temperance movement led to the downfall of both Onderdonks. One other national political movement probably had a certain influence upon Episcopalians, though the Church itself wasn't officially involved: the nativist Know-Nothings, who deplored the influences brought to these shores by the increasing numbers of non-British immigrants.

NEW YORK IN THE 1830s

When Onderdonk was consecrated Bishop of New York in 1830, there were 128 clergy, 68 congregations, and an undetermined number of missions, and 6,708 communicants in the state. By the end of his active episcopate (1845), there were 198 clergy, 165 church buildings, and 13,486 communicants: a remarkable increase. Much was due, of course, to continued immigration from England, which tended to fill Episcopal churches while old-timers in Manhattan were lamenting the disappearance of the Knickerbocker families. Changes were, as ever, carefully noted. "Everyone is driving after money," said James Fenimore Cooper in 1833 (forgetting for the moment that his own Quaker cum Episcopal family had done rather well in that line). Cooper also thought he could see a new "coldness" about New Yorkers, and he wondered if the city fathers were capable of controlling a municipality where "there is an alarm of fire every half-hour, as usual, and the pigs have the freedom of the city, as usual."[8] Cooper counted among his relatives the Jays, Watts, Laights, Kearneys, and dePeysters; his brother-in-law, the Rev. William Heathcote DeLancey—note the middle name—would soon be the first Bishop of Western New York.

The diarist Philip Hone was another knowledgeable New Yorker who was dubious about developments. He wrote in 1833 that "emigration to America [is] in numbers so great as to cause serious alarm . . . 49,569 emigrants have arrived in Quebec since the opening of navigation of the St. Lawrence the present year. Of these, a large proportion find their way into the United States, destitute and friendless."[9] "All Europe is coming across the ocean," he wrote later.[10] Nevertheless Hone was not a Know-Nothing or much in sympathy with the exclusionists; he reserved his disdain for the American parvenus he discerned about him. For, as the port grew, fortunes were rapidly made and, often, as rapidly lost. John Bernard, an English actor visiting New York City about this time, left a memorable glimpse of

> the habits of New York merchants [who] breakfasted at 8 or half-past, and by 9 were in their counting houses to lay out the business of the day; at 10 they are on their wharves, with aprons around their waists, rolling hogsheads of rum and molasses; at 12 at market, flying about as dirty and as diligent as porters; at 2 back again to the rolling, heaving, hallooing and scribbling. At 4 they went to dress for dinner; at 7 to the play; at 11 to supper.[11]

THE CHURCH IN THE 1830s

When Benjamin T. Onderdonk became the Bishop of New York, the growth of the Episcopal Church nationwide was thought to be "very much in the Evangelical direction."[12] By this is meant that what became known as the Oxford principles were generally unknown, or ignored. We have seen that Hobart favored certain embellishments in the churches, and yet spoke often of the "apostolic purity" of the Episcopal Church. Hobart however was quite at home with, and uncomplaining about, the familiar arrangements of church interiors. But his successor Onderdonk urged changes that, though they might be already in the air, were subsequently blamed on him.

And indeed, in a fast-growing nation and Church it was time to question some of the old ways of doing things. Church buildings in the 1830s were very plain, inside and out. No crosses were to be seen, and little interior color. The officiant clung to the old custom of changing vestments in mid-service: at sermon-time he would slip out from under his great floor-length surplice and don a black silk gown with sleeves looped or folded back above the elbows. In cold weather, he would wear gloves, with the forefinger snipped so he could turn the pages of his long sermon. (Those gloves might be colored, even if the walls were not; one congregation long remembered the sight of the rector's new lavender kid gloves; that morning he preached a sermon on "Humility.")[13] The "little ceremonies" of today were unknown: no entrance or exit ritual, no "passing the plate" and presentation; alms were collected (if at all during the service) in bags or boxes and placed at the head of the aisle. Preaching was confined to "pro-virtue and anti-vice,"[14] which was, at least, a change from the continual emphasis on adoption that had prevailed in an earlier, Calvinist-inspired age.

Even so, the thought pattern of most Episcopal clergy expressed itself in distinctly Evangelical language. Both Hobart and Onderdonk preached in a solidly redemptionist style. Their "theological stance" (as we would say today) led them to emphasize the atoning work of Christ. They seem to have seldom referred to the Incarnational point of view that is thought to be more characteristically Anglican. The language these High Churchmen used when they exhorted each other reveals their understanding of God. "Keep near to the throne of grace," wrote Levi Silliman Ives to William R. Whittingham.[15] Whittingham had succeeded Ives as rector of St. Luke's in-the-Fields; the pair had made that parish a bastion of New York High Churchmanship. Ives bade his friend pay special attention to the Bible class there, whose members were "often in my heart before God."[16] Whittingham speaks the same way; of a penitent, he wrote, "He has thrown himself at the foot of the cross and he has known Jesus to be precious."[17] Of himself, Whittingham noted, "Sadly wasted time, What but the blood of Christ can bring it back!"[18] Or, revisit the death chamber of Hobart, the most noted of all High Churchmen, the man credited with turning the Church away from the "Evangelical direction." The words he uses to the anguished visitors to his bedside are these: "I have no merit of my own; as a guilty sinner would I go to my Savior, casting all my reliance upon him—the atonement of his blood. He is my only dependence—my Redeemer, my Sanctifier, my God, my Judge."[19] Finally—after the man has lain there desperately ill for more than a week!—someone suggests the Communion, and it is almost as a revelation to himself that Hobart replies, "The Sacrament—the Sacrament, that is the last thing, that is all, let me have it."[20]

Both Evangelicals and High Churchmen could use the same language, because they saw the contest not as one between what soon came to be a High Church and Low Church difference, but rather one that was High Church opposed to Latitudinarianism. Hobart had labored long for apostolic order and evangelical truth as he understood it. He and his successor, Onderdonk, cherished the prerogatives, the exclusiveness, they believed attached to a church of apostolic succession. They adorned the Church of the Prayer Book with an elaborate, pious language unknown to the Caroline divines, and disdained by the Latitudinarians. This partly explains why Samuel Provoost, and others of his age, were swept into oblivion.[21]

Changes were brewing, however. The poetry of John Keble was popular with many Episcopalians about the time Onderdonk became Bishop of New York. Hobart had visited Keble's friend, Hugh James Rose. Several clergymen in America corresponded with Keble, whose *Christian Year* was well-known and struck the right note for an age just dawning. A quotation from Keble's "Holy Innocents Day," for instance, was to be found on many an infant's grave marker in years to come: "Just born, baptized, and buried." Was there ever a better alliterative line for an age devoted to the bittersweet?

Another cause of change was the effect of the Episcopal seminary in Alexandria, Virginia, founded about the same time Hobart settled the General Seminary under his own watchfulness in New York City. "The seminary in Virginia has made Evangelicals dangerous," declared Hobart to a friend in Maryland in 1826.[22] Prior to 1817 an Episcopalian preparing for ordination studied under a knowledgeable, able presbyter or bishop who shared with the young man what books and time he had at his disposal. When new ideas arrived, they came by way of the ocean, from England. American theological training had usually been managed through tutors. Now there were two seminaries, in New York and Virginia. Each of them was under a separate, often contending, influence, for one sought to retain and improve what it found in the Evangelical heritage of the Episcopal Church while the other with equal determination sought what was precious in the writings of the Oxford divines and their predecessors. The Virginia Seminary tended to a lack of interest in the ancient claims of the Church, stressed the Bible, used the Prayer Book, and urged foreign missions. The General Seminary, on the other hand, had a "higher" view of the Church as descended by means of bishops from the days of the apostles, protected the Church by preferring not to cooperate with other religious bodies, and believed mightily in the spiritual value of outward and visible things. It is easy to see that in this division of emphasis, the Evangelicals would mark themselves hereafter with the language and piety hitherto shared by all.

Hobart's sudden death also played a part in fixing future events. Though not young according to longevity of his own time, Hobart's death bore the sure marks of heroism. He died hard at work, in a distant place, without warning, worn out (as they said) in the Church's service. It is tempting to imagine what might have happened to the Church in New York had Hobart lived to an old age of diminished powers such as plagued his two predecessors. And, had he lived, would he have reaped the whirlwind eventually visited upon Onderdonk? Probably not. Hobart's facile grace would enable him to withstand the more advanced High Churchmen while yet retaining their loyalty. His integrity, and surprising readiness to admit mistakes, would have kept the respect of Evangelicals and Low Churchmen. To be succinct: Hobart probably could have carried off the Carey ordination in 1843; Onderdonk could not.

THE ONDERDONK STYLE

This compounds the tragedy, for there could never be a bishop more well-meaning and hardworking—*plodding* is a better word—than Onderdonk. Whereas Hobart was given to great bursts of energy and accomplishment followed by nervous exhaustion or disappearance into the remoteness of his beloved Short Hills, Onderdonk seems to have labored steadily, day after day, month after month, for the fifteen years of his episcopate. In addition to the indefatigable traveling made necessary by the growth of the Church and the growth of the state, Onderdonk was a superior administrator. (In those days that meant that he managed to journey, write, plan, and pray without any assistance.) In only one area does he seem to have failed, and that is in meeting his classes at the General Seminary—an irony, since his High Church influence was later declared to be perilous to the students there.

The Onderdonk years formally began with the diocesan convention in "old" Trinity Church on Broadway. (Though not yet forty years of age, the church was already showing signs of inferior workmanship and would be pulled down toward the end of Onderdonk's episcopate.) In the diocesan convention of 1830, eighty-two clergy represented 182 congregations in the diocese. There were 122 laymen present at the opening ceremonies, which included Morning Prayer, the bishop's charge to the clergy, an ordination, and the Holy Communion. It was the custom in New York, and probably in other large dioceses, for visiting bishops to attend; it was also customary in New York to have a formal roll call and a procession of professors and students from the General Seminary. This latter was a Hobart-Onderdonk touch and, as the High Church reputation of the seminary increased, was much resented by some of the convention members.

In his initial convention, Bishop Onderdonk gratefully referred to his predecessor and then reported his visitations: upriver, May through June (1831) he visited parishes as far north as Hudson. In July he went to Albany, and in the following weeks was in Troy, Saratoga, Ticonderoga, Plattsburgh, Schenectady, Amsterdam, Geneva, Auburn, Skaneateles, Ithaca, Batavia, Rochester, Oswego, Cazanovia, and Pompey, ending with the Indian congregation at Oneida and the church in Utica. He returned to New York City on September 12 having, in this year, ordained eight deacons, five priests, and confirmed 1,350 men, women, and children. He had spent one-third of the year traveling, and it was a story to be repeated with even more intensity in the years to come.

The rigors and inconveniences of episcopal travels were a necessary duty for the American successors of the apostles. When Whittingham became Bishop of Maryland he asked Onderdonk to advise him about planning his travels. The bishop wrote, from Sandy Hill in Washington County, somewhat wryly:

> On setting aboard the steam boat, at Newburgh, on Friday night at an unusually late hour, it was my lot to find it completely booked— every berth settled, mattress, table, etc. occupied by slumberers. My night was therefore spent in the rather comfortless posture of sitting with my hand as the only pillow for my head. Thus refreshed, I had double duty on Saturday and was obliged to devote the rainy evening in making calls that could not with propriety be omitted. Then there was before me twelve or thirteen miles travel and three preachings, for the following day. Will you not excuse me, under these circumstances, from begging to be excused from my promise to sit down and prepare memoranda of my week's service? Sunday night I was some-

what similarly situated, but now, being here, weatherbound, for the night, on my way to Whitehall, I will tell you what, by the divine goodness, I have been enabled to do of episcopal duty since leaving home . . .[23]

Bishop Onderdonk then proceeds to say that on the previous Monday he had been in North Salem, Westchester County. On Tuesday, he was at Christ Church, Patterson. Thursday found him in Garrison, and on Friday he was at St. George's, Newburgh, but in the afternoon he crossed the river to lay the cornerstone for St. Anna's Church, Matteawan. It was that night he found no accommodations on the steamboat; next day he instituted Horatio Potter rector of St. Peter's, Albany. On Sunday he consecrated the new church in Cohoes, and the next day there was a confirmation at St. John's, Troy. Today, a bishop might keep these appointments with comparative ease, but in the 1830s public transportation was unreliable. There was no Hudson River Railroad connecting New York City with Albany until 1854. Travel was rough, time-consuming.

Apart from fulfilling the travels that then took so much of a bishop's time and energy, it was, of course, necessary that the Bishop of New York be aware of public trends. Like Hone and Cooper and others, Benjamin Onderdonk was aware of the effects of immigration upon New York City. In his first convention address he warned those present that the Church had a special responsibility for the many immigrants arriving from England and Ireland. In 1832 he was able to report that "the first fruits of the New York Protestant Episcopal Mission Society" had been the consecration of the Church of the Holy Evangelists in Vandewater Street. Here was a free church for immigrants, where visitors to the city could be welcomed, for the other churches had assigned or rented pews that were off limits to strangers. "This enterprise has been crowned with signal success," the bishop exulted, and then he proceeded to that sort of abrasive remark that so often marred his public utterances: the Mission Society's constitution, he said, "recognizes the general supervision of, and responsibility to, the ecclesiastical authority of the Diocese, and the most marked and respectful consideration has been paid to my feelings and wishes."[24] Everyone present knew there had been difficulties with the clergyman in charge of Holy Evangelist Church, but with such lordly remarks, repeated many times, lay the beginnings of the bishop's downfall. His gratuitous pronouncements must have been offensive to some of the delegates to convention, or to some of the rectors in whose churches he spoke. Much later, a commentator upon the City of New York asserted that Bishop Onderdonk had "great executive talent, and ruled the diocese, it is said, with a rod of iron. In personal appearance he resembled Napoleon the First, of which fact he was quite proud. . . . He was decidedly the ablest man that has ruled the see of New York for many generations."[25]

In the better months of the year the bishop made his western tours. It was a rigorous life for a man in his forties (an older age then than now). Tedious rides, interruptions, the inconveniences of long waits— then a service, a meeting, perhaps a confrontation with parish leaders, a meal, and then a bed in a strange chamber—all to be repeated the next day, and the day after: this was Onderdonk's life through the summer. History has not awarded him the praise it bestows upon Hobart. No portrait of Onderdonk was ever hung in diocesan halls. But he, more than any other bishop, was responsible for the growth of the Church in the State of New York. This is not to say that Hobart is undeserving of the laurels offered him but, rather, that the pressures of population growth, immigration, and undeniable vibrancy of Church life—an acceleration of all factors—bore more heavily upon Bishop Onderdonk. The Erie Canal was a significant part of Onderdonk's problems because it moved people far away from Manhattan, where a Bishop of New York naturally resides. After 1830 the fertile fields that General Sullivan's men had appropriated from the Indians became the city's breadbasket. The thinner, worked-out soil of the Hudson Valley might be adequate for the lawn of a gentleman's "villa," but a growing port demanded more hay and wheat and corn and beef, and these would hereafter arrive by canal boats plying the new Erie. Coal, slate, and cement would soon come to the city by way of the new Delaware and Hudson Canal, which had its terminus in Roundout, near Kingston, and was the cause of rising hamlets along its waterway; soon churches would be needed there, too. And, even in Bishop Onderdonk's time, people began to long for a respite from civilization such as might be provided by the Catskill wilderness and the breathtaking views from the mountain escarpments. The tanbark men killed the hemlocks, leaving them lying where loggers could cut them for sheathing New York City dwellings— and Catskill Mountain boardinghouses.

Beginning in 1832, Bishop Onderdonk tried to have annual confirmations in the city churches because of "the many strangers sojourning among us."[26] He would continue "the usual triennial" visitations in all other places. That year he went northward as far as the Canadian border, on to Utica, and then to the Oneidas. This would have been a poignant visit, for Onderdonk was familiar with the Indians' long attachment to the Church. He reported

> Holy Communion was, of course, administered, when a large number of Indians were among the recipients. The *Gloria in Excelsis* was chanted by the Indians in their native tongue [but] that portion of the Oneidas which professed attachment to our Church removed soon after, to the vicinity of Green Bay.[27]

That July the bishop made a wide circuit through the Catskills and on up to Watertown, and having done this he could say he had visited every parish in the diocese at least once. In 1832 alone, he had traveled 3,000 miles "to almost every extremity of the State," and in that year he had ordained nine priests and twenty-two deacons, consecrated twenty churches, and confirmed 1,101 persons in a diocese that now numbered 10,030 communicants with 183 clergy.

Onderdonk's liturgical opinions, as we have seen, were delivered with more freedom than wisdom. He consistently upheld the prerogatives of the clergy, which is probably one reason why the majority of them remained loyal to him after 1845 when the laity of the diocese knew his was a lost cause.[28] Once, he reminded the convention that the priest is "supreme in the school or schools of his parish"[29] and arranged for the clergy and laity to sit separately in diocesan conventions. It was long the custom for the professors and students of the General Seminary to have assigned seats in the conventions, and in the diocesan *Journal* graduates of the seminary were denoted by an asterisk. This attention shown General Seminary was not likely to appeal to clergy who were not its graduates, or to laymen who opined that Romanism was rife in Chelsea.

It is probable that Bishop Onderdonk never realized in those middle years of his episcopate how offensive his pronouncements could be. Was it wise for him to speak, in convention, of the "proper position" in Holy Communion service?[30] Should he have declared incorrect the rubric that then expected the celebrant to stand at the north end of the Holy Table?[31] Surely, he was showing his customary tactlessness when he criticized the shallow chancel of one church and the dubious placement of the altar in another. He was a trifle overbearing in his recommendation that the people should comply with the House of Bishops' recent preference that the people join the minister in the General Confession rather than repeat it after him. And was it worthwhile to insist that there be no prayer before the sermon?[32] Or that chancels be at least two feet above the nave?[33] In the diocesan convention of 1841 the bishop elaborated on the appropriate preparation for the Holy Communion. The bread loaf was to be cut in moderate slices, and then cut again, half through, at right angles (and thus the more easily broken into pieces, the bishop explained). One quart of wine should be allowed for every hundred communicants—none of your late Victorian sips—and silver vessels should be used.[34]

Now, in so advising, Bishop Onderdonk believed he was doing the work of an apostle's successor, and since he was "a little Dutch" he would argue for that right, unaware that neither the parish priest nor his laymen cared to come all the way to New York City to be thus lectured. Some of the delegates preferred to hear how their churches were to pay for the elements and the priest in those terrible years of depression that followed the 1837 Panic. We may well imagine the gentlemen's frustration as they talked to one another on the sidewalks or strolled in St. John's Square during recess. The wiser of the delegates would have said that the shame of it was that the able bishop managed to swamp himself in these edicts of Church life when at other times he showed himself so competent and so faithful.

The bishop's closest friends feared the disasters his naiveté could bring on. "I should feel extremely anxious about your convention," wrote George W. Doane to a city presbyter in 1836[35] and added in a later letter, "he suffers solely from faults of manner, the impulses of a kind and loving nature uncontrolled by sound judgement."[36] As the 1830s proceeded, it seems that every one of Onderdonk's good friends held his breath until the diocesan convention was past, wondering what gaffe the poor bishop would conjure up for his own embarrassment and his enemies' delectation.

DIVISION OF THE DIOCESE: WESTERN NEW YORK

Nonetheless, the greatest single accomplishment of Onderdonk's episcopate took place in those very forums which later determined his disgrace: the House of Bishops and the diocesan convention. Church growth and New York's phenomenal population increase made it necessary to divide the diocese of New York. It was still known as the "Protestant Episcopal Church in the State of New York" in 1837, though the word "diocese" was in common use. In 1834, Bishop Onderdonk tested the waters by telling the convention that "the time must soon come, and perhaps it may not be long distant, when this diocese will be too great for unshared supervision."[37] That remark was calculated to elicit questions. Everyone knew Bishop Onderdonk was overworked. Did he now want a bishop to assist him? Or did he advocate splitting the State of New York into more than one diocese?

Either alternative would draw impassioned argument. Assisting bishops were still not deemed suitable in a church whose very name implied *a* bishop presiding over his diocese. There was the memory of Provoost's attempted intervention, and the awkwardness of Hobart's being an assistant in name but in fact very much the leader while the invalid Benjamin Moore remained "Bishop of New York." Assistant bishops were an unsure thing in those days. On the other hand, the Episcopal Church prized its present stance as the Church in the several states, corresponding to the federal government as it applied itself in bicameral houses with the union of the states. This is what the early

General Conventions had in mind. Moreover, no state had as yet ever been divided into more than one diocese, and there was no canon enabling this to be done.

The bishop let the matter brew and meanwhile helped steer canonical adjustments in the General Convention. His best arguments were the plain facts: 239 clergy and 232 parishes in 1836. In that year pressures of work made it necessary for Bishop Onderdonk to resign as a minister of Trinity Church. It was a position that had been necessary as a source of salary and, luckily in this year before the Panic, Trinity Church found ways to continue providing for the bishop through the new "Episcopal Fund" of the diocese. "The connexion with the parish of which for nearly a fourth of a century I was one of the ministers has ceased," he informed the convention in 1837.[38] The bishop said he hoped the Episcopal Fund would soon be great enough, thanks to Trinity's largesse, so that the diocesan could be supported by it and not depend upon a parochial stipend. Perhaps this was the first time many of the delegates realized that all along Trinity Church had been responsible for paying the greater part of the salary of the Bishop of New York. The bishop's optimism was meagerly rewarded and in the future he often found it necessary to mention his "inadequate temporal support." This, too, in times of depression became a matter of diocesan friction and contention, especially when there were those who had seen the "splendid residence and the most splendid furniture" at the bishop's Murray Street address.

The bishop's careful preparations for dividing the diocese included planning a special diocesan convention in Utica on August 22 and 23, 1838. The main purpose was to consider division of the diocese, and so the bishop chose a town which would be in the center of the new diocese. General Convention had amended the Church's Constitution so that the dioceses might be divided if the proposed area contained not less than 8,000 square miles and thirty priests. It was also necessary that the original diocese and General Convention consent to division. Bishop Onderdonk also wanted to be sure that the clergy in the western part of the state attended, but many men from downstate also appeared; Washington Irving was there the second day, a delegate from Zion Church, Greenburg (now Tarrytown). A committee of laymen and clergy had conferred with the bishop to determine the boundaries of the new diocese. It was reported that the line would be the eastern borders of Broome, Chenango, Madison, Oneida, and Lewis counties, and the northeast corner of Jefferson. The dividing line was said to split the population and area of New York State almost equally. (1,016,245 people and 21,463 square miles in the west and, it was said, 1,158,273 people and 21,750 square miles remaining in the Diocese of

New York). Such a division would make the "western portion compact
and of easy communication" by means of canals, projected railways,
and crossroads. "Very few persons would require more than a day to
travel from the remotest part to the centre," it was said.[39] There were
about fifty mission stations in the western area, and one of the thorny
tasks of those favoring division was convincing those missionaries that
their salaries would be guaranteed. There were also about forty self-
supporting parishes. The bishop declared to the delegates at Utica,
"Depend upon it, the eye of the world and the Church is now very
especially upon you,"[40] but many of the delegates remained unpersuaded that division was wise. There was a last-minute attempt to re-
scind the motion to divide, but the convention ultimately sustained
what had long been Onderdonk's hope, and he was the man of the
hour.

General Convention, meeting in Philadelphia the next month, approved New York's course. Bishop Onderdonk anticipated this, and
had arranged for another diocesan convention in Trinity Church on
Tuesday, September 11, 1838. The business of the day was to facilitate
the work of the Utica convention, setting a date of actual division (November 1), and receiving the formal permission of the diocesan bishop.
It was also necessary to appoint a committee to discuss how the new
diocese would share in the Episcopal Fund, a most sensitive matter.
The new diocese would be named in its organization convention in
October. This, also, was a sensitive matter, for High Church preferences led a diocese to choose the name of its key or see city, while Low
Churchmen preferred them named after areas. Bishop Onderdonk was
chairman of that organizing convention, and presided over the elec-
tion of his favorite candidate, William Heathcote DeLancey, as the first
Bishop of Western New York (for that was the name chosen).

TROUBLES WILL COME

The next year—it was perhaps Onderdonk's finest year—he was able to
refer in diocesan convention to the successful separation accomplished
in 1838. He was also satisfied to remind the convention that in the
eight years reviewed in his address he had ordained 148 deacons, 112
priests, consecrated 96 churches, and confirmed 8,896 persons. Hobart,
he said, in nineteen years ordained 150 deacons, 113 priests, consecrated 80 churches, and confirmed 11,678. The bishop had the grace
not to state that his statistics compared very favorably with Hobart's.
But, surely, everyone present was quick to see the point.

While Bishop Onderdonk was reviewing diocesan statistics, he might have tried to add up the myriad of independent organizations that had been formed in the diocese. Even in Bishop Moore's time tract and educational societies had begun to do what the parish church and the diocese could not undertake. Bishop Hobart had used organizations and able directors to promulgate his aims and views, a practice maintained by Onderdonk. He also founded other organizations to assist him. The most notable was the New York Protestant Episcopal Mission Society, at one time known as the Education and Missionary Society of the Protestant Episcopal Church in the State of New York. It was firmly established in 1832 with the bishop as president and vice-presidents including such clergy as John Reed of Christ Church in Poughkeepsie, Henry Milnor of St. George's, John McVickar of Columbia College, Henry Anthon of St. Mark's, and such able laymen as Peter A. Jay, Lieutenant Governor Edward P. Livingston, and William A. Duer, president of Columbia College. Other members were Berrian of Trinity, Wainwright of Grace, William Richmond, Manton Eastburn, Luther Bradish, William Bard, Cyrus Curtis, Jacob LeRoy, Matthew Clarkson, William A. Muhlenberg, and John C. Spencer—all of them, clergy and lay, a galaxy of opinions and great capacities. One of the aims of the Society was to assist men preparing for Holy Orders. Another was to support missionaries among the poor of New York. In later years, of course, the work of the Episcopal City Mission Society would find wider fields for work. One of the original purposes of the Society was to establish churches in New York City. The first was the Church of the Epiphany, others were the Church of the Holy Evangelists in Vandewater Street and St. Matthew's, Christopher Street. It must be emphasized that Onderdonk was keenly aware of work needed among the poor and unchurched in the increasingly teeming city. A fast-growing city meant developing slums, a problem scarcely known to Hobart but at least partly recognized by his successor. Why, then, was Onderdonk silent when an organized mob, at least partly encouraged by James Watson Webb, an Episcopalian and editor of *The Morning Courier and New York Enquirer,* sacked St. Philip's Church? As far as we know, the bishop's sole response to the outrage was a hand-delivered letter to St. Philip's rector, the Rev. Peter Williams, Jr., calling upon Williams, himself a black, "to resign at once, your connexion in every department, with the Anti-Slavery Society, and to make public your resignation."[41] The bishop implied that God, in his own time, would make all things right. Williams complied with the bishop's directive and resigned his leadership in the Anti-Slavery Society.

Unfortunately, the early days of the City Mission Society were plagued with dissension. Manton Eastburn believed, quite rightly, that the bishop intended to insinuate High Churchmen into the Society's work. He led a rebellion in the group which, as we have heard the bishop report to convention, was unsuccessful. The details of the matter will be forever lost, but Doane, among others, feared a repetition and wrote to William Whittingham:

> I have written in the plainest English to Bishop Onderdonk. The City Mission is the most dangerous post in your diocese. An artful, unprincipled man of ability and address could do the Church more harm in it than in any other rectorship in the city. So I have written my excellent friend and brother. I do hope the gate may be kept closed against the wooden horse.[42]

Since Low Churchmen feared they would be outmaneuvered by the bishop, or outnumbered by his friends, other organizations were founded to counteract the prevailing influences. One of the more sinister of these was the "Association for Promoting Christianity," gathered at St. Thomas Church at the time of the trouble in the City Mission Society. John Duer was a member, and Evert Duyckinck a leading spirit. The object of the association was to raise funds for existing Episcopal organizations, and dispense them only after careful scrutiny. In need of funds—and also in need of watching!—were the Domestic and Foreign Missionary Society, New York Episcopal City Mission Society, General Theological Society, the Sunday School Union, New York Bible and Common Prayer Book Society, and the New York Episcopal Tract Society. Duer and Duyckinck would ferret out any High Church malefactions in those and other Episcopal organizations.[43]

Apart from their obvious drawbacks of searching for trouble in the Church, there was probably a certain advantage in the diocese's having various groups of churchpeople engaged in charitable efforts. Nevertheless, the question remains: did loyalty to the "little" societies and associations militate against a united diocese in the 1830s? It would seem so. In a collection of Church archives one will find an unidentified "Rule of Life" dating from about this time. It tells us a very great deal:

> I will never speak disrespectfully or unkindly of or to my Bishop.
>
> I will not expose the faults of my brethren of the Clergy unless duty requires me so to do.
>
> I will always vindicate my Bishop or an absent brother when slandered.
>
> I will never urge upon my guests the indulgence in intoxicating drinks.
>
> I will as much as possible keep my family from attending theatres, and operas, and make it an example of a Christian family.[44]

THE BISHOP AND HUDSON VALLEY WORSHIP AND SOCIETY

The High Churchmanship of Hobart and Onderdonk increasingly expressed itself in the physical arrangements and appearance of the church building, and again, one's attention is turned to what Episcopal churches looked like.

There had always been considerable latitude in the interior arrangement of the churches. Thus, a visitor to Trinity Church in New York City in 1744 described the building as being

> above one hundred feet long and eighty wide. At the east end of it is a large semi-circular area in which stands the altar [structure, probably including pulpit and reading desk], pretty well ornamented with painting and gilding. The galleries are supported with wooden pillars of the Ionic order, with carved work of foliage and cherubic heads gilt betwixt the capitals. There is a pretty organ at the west end of the church, consisting of a great number of pipes handsomely gilt and adorned . . .[45]

All this was swept away in the fire of 1777, but the church built on the site in 1794, though somewhat smaller, was much like the original Trinity.

The bishop of the diocese, however, never knew what awaited his gaze as he approached a church on the visitations the diocesan constitution of 1787 required at least once every three years. St. Paul's, Eastchester, for instance, had a dual orientation, in a building that had

> stone walls, rough and unplastered. The roof with its immense rafters is plainly visible. The pews are of pine, the divisions as well as outside work being in panels with doors hung with knuckle hinges and capped, high-backed, capacious—and unpainted. To your surprise you find beside the present side aisles an additional main passage, at right angles with them, extending from the middle door to the Clerk's seat, behind and above which is at the east end of the building and within it the new Communion Table, surrounded by a rail.[46]

This was prior to the changes of the 1840s and '50s which brought St. Paul's into conformity with most other Episcopal churches (and conformity with Bishop Onderdonk's oft-expressed preferences).

St. Stephen's Church in New York was one of the many churches here and abroad where the visitor would find a heavily embellished pulpit sounding board. There was also a statue of Stephen, with the text "And they stoned Stephen." Christ Church in Poughkeepsie rejoiced in a gilded dove perpetually alight on a screen behind the pulpit. This is the screen that figured in reminiscences about when

the clergy lay aside the surplice, or sacramental vestment, when entering the pulpit to perform their teaching function in the academic
gown. . . . From 1834 to 1854, while this screen was in existence, the
children of Christ Church used to watch eagerly for what they considered a delightful Jack-in-the-Box performance. The Rector would
leave the reading desk just before the sermon, disappear through the
door at the north end of the screen wearing his surplice, and suddenly reappear, in the high pulpit, in his black gown.[47]

A fuller account of this standard Episcopal performance describes the
fashion-plate appearance of the clergy:

The officiating clergyman wore a surplice, gathered with fine pleats
in a yoke around the neck, and reaching to the ground, with scarf of
broad black silk, and bands made of lawn (and tied around the neck
with small strings), which hung in front of the collar. It was the
custom for the clergyman to retire during the singing of a hymn, after
the Gospel had been read, and to return arrayed in an academic black
silk gown, to enter the pulpit and preach the sermon. On the first
Sunday of each month, at which time the Holy Communion was administered, the clergyman retired to the vestry-room after the sermon,
and resumed his surplice. He then proceeded in the administration
of the Lord's Supper.[48]

The long, full surplice was used in some places in New York as late as
1900. The black preaching gown with accompanying bands was discarded much earlier, though for many years there were those who
recalled Episcopal clergy "thus attired [in] the streets on official occasions."[49]

St. George's in Schenectady had, after 1798, an arrangement
whereby the Communion table shared the east end with the pulpit on
one side, and the pew of the patron's family on the other. Pews for
honored persons were common in the churches. They were richly upholstered in crimson, and might have a suitable canopy overhead. Such
a pew was set apart for George Washington at St. Paul's Chapel, and was
shown to him by his friend Samuel Provoost. The old box pews lent
themselves to whatever alterations their owners cared to bestow upon
them. Sometimes chairs and tables were set in these enclosures. The
substitution of "slip" pews for the older box affairs was a step toward
the uniformity Bishop Onderdonk desired, but personal tastes were
asserted long after the bishop's day. Many churches can recall the pec-
cadilloes of assertive parishioners, but it would be difficult to surpass
those embodied in St. Paul's, Tivoli, where, when the new church was
built in 1868, the eccentric General John Watts dePeyster had built for
himself and his brother-in-law Johnston Livingston an apse with separate door, richly furnished with sofa and four armchairs; the whole was

fenced off from the main body of the church so the general might bring his dogs with him when he attended service.

Most Episcopal churches built after the Revolutionary War were the white-painted boxlike structures that, to this day, dot the American landscape. They used the severe, straightforward lines of classic architecture. Hobart mildly preferred Gothic because it looked English and he was, at least for the first part of his episcopate, very much of an Anglophile. Onderdonk preferred the Gothic style because he deemed it best suggested what the Church of God is, having a long past reaching back to divine origins. "The great faults which prevail throughout the country," he said in 1832, "are small and low chancels and the want of comfortable vestry rooms." [50] Onderdonk idealized soaring, arched ceilings, and it is one of history's ironies that when his architectural notions were sublimely realized in New York at Grace Church and Trinity Church his suspension from office prevented him from consecrating them. He took pains to promote Gothic architecture, and lost no opportunity to praise Gothic accomplishments in the diocese. Thus he rated the "brick Gothic Church" in Westfield as a fine new landmark in Chautauqua County. [51] In 1836, he was overjoyed by the new church in Medina

> . . . a platform running nearly across the church and raised above the level of its aisles three or four steps. The Communion table is against the center of the wall in the rear of the platform; and in front of the platform, on the extremity at the left of the altar, is the reading desk, and on that level at the right, the pulpit; the three standing on the same level, and the desk and pulpit being exactly alike. [52]

He was describing exactly what soon became the normal arrangement of Episcopal churches.

But if the nearsighted bishop had once peered over his spectacles while delivering these lectures on proper chancel arrangements he might have noted restlessness and sideward glances among his auditors—perhaps even a groan when he declared the ideal church was one surmounted by a cross. Did the bishop ever realize how disturbing his remarks could be? Again, in 1839, he commended crosses on steeples and reported to convention that in the new church in Troy "the altar holds its proper distinguished station, having suitably provided places, on its right for the daily prayers, and on its left for preaching," [53] and urged that Ante-Communion, "which the Church requires to be read on all Sundays and holy days" be read from the altar. "It is a great mistake," he declared, "and one coupled with serious misapprehensions of the Christian system, to represent the pulpit as the chief and most honorable part of the Church." If the younger men out of the

General Seminary applauded these lessons in chancel arrangements (with their implied preferences for sacerdotalism), many of the older clergy were annoyed that the bishop used public occasions to promote his partisan preferences. They may have been all the more irritated when the majority of younger men solemnly agreed with the bishop's pronouncements. The clergy do not like to be publicly lectured, especially from their own platforms, or in convention when their leading laymen are present. Onderdonk's requirements for "proper" chancels were offensive to those delegates who were quite satisfied with the present arrangements of their churches.

OXFORD MOVEMENT PERILS

It is necessary to emphasize Onderdonk's aggressive opinions about chancels because it was a constant theme during his episcopate. Since he had never seen a medieval church we may be sure that it was theology more than taste or aesthetic preference that led him to dictate what constituted the ideal chancel. Moreover, as a reader and active churchman, he was aware of and sympathized with the coming wave of ecclesiastical life. His active episcopate, 1830 to 1845, almost exactly parallels developments in England that came to be known as the Oxford Movement.

By 1830 it was clear that Parliament would exercise political prerogatives which would drastically affect the state Church. Contemplated changes included acts which would permit Nonconformists in the universities and the disposition of some dioceses in the Church of Ireland. Some English clergymen regarded this as dangerous and irresponsible Erastianism—the state dictating to the Church—and they disputed the state's right by notable sermons and tracts. Eventually (for Parliament proceeded to do what it threatened), the business of "the Oxford men" became a rediscovery and publicizing of the traditional teachings and beliefs of the Church of England. Some of this had long been in the air in America. It has even been claimed that the new emphasis on tradition was less novel here than in England. But the British developments had dramatic aspects lacking in America. Keble, for instance, was officially silenced for a time. Pusey functioned in the great universities and had the advantage of Oxford's prestige, if not always its sympathy. It was his name that was lent to Church doings that were sometimes thrilling, and often suspect; "Puseyism" had an aura of daring, of ivy-covered walls in old England—exactly the things that intrigued many Americans. Then, there was John Henry Newman. He soon assumed leadership, wrote most of the Tracts for the Times, and possessed the authority belonging to the vicar of St. Mary's, Oxford.

"Young men were all enthusiastic about Newman in those days," recalled Arthur Cleveland Cox when he wrote about his days at General
Seminary.[54] Then, "like a thunderclap," it was said, in 1845 Newman
forsook the Church of England for that of Rome.

   Such, in brief, was the Oxford Movement as it appeared to American Episcopalians. They met it with opinions ranging from fervent approval to dark fear. New York was as quick to receive news from abroad
as it was to receive immigrants, and in some minds the events in Oxford
were as threatening as were the newcomers. At the seminary, however,
where Onderdonk was a leading influence as trustee and professor, he
was now seen as also a protagonist of the "Oxford Divines," whom he
praised, though (he said) "they may sometimes push their zeal too
far."[55] When the bishop asked the convention delegates to discern the
difference between "catholic and Romish systems," he forgot that some
of the clergy and laity were apt to be suspicious of *both* "systems."[56] As
the 1830s progressed almost every pronouncement of Bishop Onderdonk's made him vulnerable to future attack. It may well be that the
man's energy, friendliness, and patent goodwill postponed his ultimate
downfall.

   No one could deny him that excellent record of unrelenting work
and ability. An admirer wrote of him:

> How the bishop acquits himself in his services, his sermons, and his
> social intercourse! The gentleman in the parlor, the plain parish
> priest, fatherly, affectionate, and at home in the plainest farmhouse.
> And so sound, so edifying, so consoling in his pulpit exercise.[57]

And this is the impression most people had of him while he was active
as Bishop of New York. He never displayed Hobart's flamboyance and
charm (or wiliness!). He had no social ambitions (though his house
was said to be opulent). He seems not to have walked easily with prominent people. His notable characteristic was, simply, hard work: city
work in winter, rural in summer. His diocese was, until 1838, the entire
State of New York. Transportation was, as we have seen, by Hudson
River sloops and steamboats and, west of Albany, by the new Erie Canal. He probably knew the dirt roads in the state better than any other
New Yorker; it was common for him to jog along slowly all night in a
wagon.

THE USUAL YEARLY SCHEDULE

The year would begin in New York, where the bishop may have in-
dulged in his ancestors' pleasant custom of the New Year's Day calls.
By the time winter began to fade the bishop would have made tentative

plans for visitations in distant parts of the state. Very likely, such schedules were only approximate because the bishop would never know
what exigencies would detain him in one place, or what transportation
troubles would prevent his on-time arrival at his next appointment. It
was only after railroads were built that the timetable became an episcopal reality. But this was after Onderdonk's time, and it may be said that
his successor bishops of New York were railroad experts until the day
Bishop Burch bought his infamous motor car. With Bishop Onderdonk
dependent upon water and rough road transportation, the rector in, say,
Batavia, would prepare his people for a visit from the bishop sometime
in the third week of August. Then they would await his appearing, and
be quite understanding if a message arrived saying the bishop would
arrive the following week—or not at all that year because he had been
summoned elsewhere. But Onderdonk probably canceled few appointments. People remembered how he had faced inconvenience and dis-
comfort to reach them. No wonder that, when his troubles came, the
bishop found far more support upstate than in New York City.[58]

The Brooklyn and Westchester parishes would be visited in late
winter, or in late autumn. Transportation there was easier, and Bishop
Onderdonk was able to spend the night and proceed next day to another church, another meeting. Upriver arrangements were more complicated, and perhaps made an interesting puzzle for an otherwise serious and prosaic bishop. His letter to Whittingham quoted above
shows that the bishop accepted the vicissitudes of travel as they came.
Of one thing he might be certain: if the rector or warden knew he was
coming, there would be a delegation from the local church waiting to
greet him at the landing, and another to wave him off as he departed. It
was a courtesy that persisted as long as the bishops of New York used
public transportation on their long-distance visitations. The Bishop of
New York was a familiar celebrated personage on the Hudson River
landings and on a hundred railroad platforms.

Bishop Onderdonk, following the canon, expected to visit each
rural parish at least once in three years. After the diocese was divided
he aimed at annual visitations. Not all stops had church buildings, of
course, and very often the bishop preached and confirmed at inns,
fraternal lodges, borrowed churches, or dwellings. There were about
eighty "missionary stations" in the diocese when Onderdonk was consecrated. It happened then, as it does now, that an established parish
had come to grief and was trying to regain its wonted prosperity. St.
Mark's, LeRoy, was an example, as Bishop Onderdonk told the 1832
convention. The Rev. Francis H. Cuming had recently gone there and
"found the parish in somewhat of a depressed state in consequence of
having been for a long time destitute of regular ministerial services."

The able Cuming's name shows up frequently in American Church annals; he was, for instance, a founder of Calvary Church in New York, missionary to the Oneidas, and an unofficial chaplain to the bishop—it was he who accompanied Hobart's body to New York. Cuming soon had a large Sunday school in LeRoy, a Bible class with fifty-five members who met Tuesday evenings and handed in written assignments on the Fourth Gospel, and the inevitable "Female Benevolent Association" that met to make articles for sale. Throughout his career, Francis Cuming was an enthusiastic organizer of fund-raising women's organizations in the Church, and if not the founder he was at least the patron of what became a dependable and lucrative feature of the Episcopal Church.

When Bishop Onderdonk thought of the upriver Hudson, his imagination needed to take him no farther than what is now midtown Manhattan. That is where the "country" began, and in the bishop's day it stretched from there infinitely northward. In Bishop Provoost's time many fine Federal style houses were built in the fields toward the northern extreme of Manhattan Island; Gracie Mansion is a significant survivor of those houses that provided escape from city heat and disease in summer. But now that steamboats and their docks had improved, men and women of comfortable means were enabled to go farther upstream. The Hudson River entered upon its halcyon days when huge houses were built along its banks. Washington Irving was one of Manhattan's sons who settled on the riverbank after his return from Europe and, like many of his friends, he helped the Episcopal Church prosper in the Hudson River Valley. Other New Yorkers were also conspicuous in settling the Church in neighborhoods they adopted. The pattern was likely to be this: a wealthy New Yorker, who had more leisure than his father had ever enjoyed, was able to retire early on former earnings, and would build a summer "villa" on the river. Once the house was built, the proprietor might turn his attentions toward "improvements"—and by that he had two things in mind: the condition of his lawns and the morals of his neighbors.

There were precedents and books to guide him. The precedents were (apart from the enviable English custom of squire-with-chapel) what had already happened in upper Manhattan. There, St. Michael's (1809), St. James' (1810), and St. Mary's (1820) had been established to minister to the summer families who had built houses on the Hudson and East rivers. Now that estates were developing in or near river hamlets there was a broader scope than Manhattan provided. Up in Newburgh, there was a nurseryman's son, Andrew Jackson Downing, whose ambitions embraced improvements and cultivations whether architectural, agricultural, or social. Soon, Downing had a wide circle of friends and clients, north, south, and in England. But his native Hudson River Valley remained his favorite place. He concentrated upon developing houses and landscape there, insisting that the best mode was what he termed the "picturesque," which was in fact an adaptation of Gothic. Bishop Onderdonk was pleased, and had he been a wiser man he would have left the popularization of that favored architectural mode to Downing.

We shall hear more about the Gothic revival, but for the present discussion it is only necessary to say that Downing found it worth his time to include mention and designs of chapels and churches in his writings. Since he was an Anglophile and formed a literary partnership with the celebrated London writer about gardens, Mrs. Loudon, and brought Calvert Vaux to New York to be his office partner, it is easy to see that Downing was an asset to the Episcopal Church in New York. No man could better encourage the rich New Yorker to become a squire whose duty was to provide uplift in the neighborhood.

Hobart had fostered this attitude of educational and spiritual noblesse oblige which proceeded to build and manage for the rest of the century. Vestiges of this ecclesiasticism wed to manorial paternalism are still to be found in Hudson River towns, and, as we will soon learn, its most outstanding offering to public life is probably present-day Bard College. The pattern of a rich Manhattan merchant moving to the country to build his house, his church, and its school was seen as a boon to the rural people who worked in the brick plants, the ice houses, or the textile factories. In the annual diocesan *Journal* it accounts for the rise, or rebirth, of many parishes, beginning with Yonkers. Peekskill, Garrison, Wappingers Falls, Annandale, Tivoli, Beacon are only a few of the places where the Episcopal Church enjoyed reinvigoration due to a superimposed squirearchy delightfully applied. A clear result of this proprietal management was that the rural people were induced to forsake their Reformed, Presbyterian, or Lutheran faiths and become Episcopalians. It is a safe bet that the impressive confirmation statistics of the nineteenth century were, in part, the results of pressure from the big house.

Bishop Onderdonk saw only the beginning of these developments and he cannot be blamed for their offensive aspects. In any case, he had neither the time nor inclination to linger at any man's villa.

CAREY AND CONSEQUENCES

The Carey ordination July 2, 1843, was the undoing of Bishop Onderdonk. An ordination is always a poignant event: a Christian asks to be set apart for extraordinary work; parents and friends circle round, joyous and yet awed by the weight of a thousand and more years of history. It should have been so for Arthur Carey: young, innocent, earnest—and very High Church. At the General Theological Seminary Carey was viewed as holding "advanced" views, which, to many, seemed indistinguishable from those of the Church of Rome. The General Seminary was thought to nurture and encourage this point of view, and not a few New York ministers kept a watchful eye (and a ready ear) to discern erroneous doctrine in Chelsea Square. Was popery not already strong enough in New York now that immigration from Ireland was so accelerated? Hadn't the General Convention investigated the seminary because of peculiar goings-on there? What about those prominent Episcopalians who had become Roman Catholic? While still a seminarian, Arthur Carey was marked as a man who appeared to be sympathetic with Catholic things. This brought him to the attention of Henry Anthon, rector of St. Mark's-in-the-Bouwerie. Anthon's friend, Hugh Smith, rector of St. Peter's in 20th Street where Arthur Carey taught Sunday School was also exercised. But perhaps the most critical watchdog of all was Manton Eastburn, rector of the Ascension, the Careys' parish. Eastburn had gone off to be Bishop Coadjutor of Massachusetts, but he later implied that he had kept an eye on Arthur Carey, whom he declared to have "imbibed the deadly poison of the Tracts for the Times."[59]

On the other hand, nothing seemed to deter Bishop Onderdonk from a triumphal pursuit of what he believed to be right for the Diocese of New York and the Church at large. Therefore, when it appeared that Arthur Carey's ordination to the diaconate would be opposed by prominent Manhattan rectors, the bishop appointed a committee to question him. The fact that Bishop Onderdonk assigned assessors on the whole favorable to Carey is of little historic importance, for those men probably were representative of the diocese. But they did not reflect the thinking of some New York clergy, or of many Episcopalians elsewhere. "New York Churchmanship" was exactly the pivotal concern.

The committee appointed to examine Arthur Carey recommended that he be ordained. Though Anthon and Smith had been among the examiners, and had been outvoted, they were yet convinced that the man should not be made a deacon. Therefore, at the ordination, when Bishop Onderdonk asked the traditional question embodied in the service, whether or not there might be any impediment known so that Arthur Carey ought not be ordained, Dr. Smith, and then Dr. Anthon, advanced from their pews and read protests. There was a terrible tenseness in St. Stephen's Church. Then Bishop Onderdonk, who clearly had expected the protest, declared that these same complaints had already

been heard and dismissed by a committee: he would proceed. Whereupon Bishop Ives, Bishop of North Carolina, who was in the chancel
and appears to have been equally clued, began the Litany. Anthon and
Smith strode out of the church, vowing that they would have their day.

Theological divergences and personality differences: these set
some people against Benjamin Treadwell Onderdonk. But there was
further abrasion: many people thought he was coarse. The word comes
up again and again. It is something weightier than whether or not the
man was likable to those who deferred to him—countless people dis-
agreed with Hobart but were captivated by the man. If we say Bishop
Onderdonk was a victim of theological differences we will not be telling the whole truth. More accurately, he fell because his undoubted
abilities and successes had insulated him from correctly gauging the
integrity and dedication of enemies who must find a solution to their
frustrations.

The story has become an epic in the Episcopal Church, and we will
merely summarize the events. First of all, Judge John Duer, scholar,
member of the state's 1821 Constitutional Convention, noted jurist, kin
of the state's oldest families, was in the convention of 1844. He was one
of the ablest judges in the state, and a very influential member of the
Episcopal Church. He was not friendly to the bishop, and the bishop
knew it. Duer arose to address the convention. The bishop refused to
hear him and ordered him to his seat. Duer was not accustomed to such
peremptory commands, and he insisted upon his right to the floor. The
bishop thundered out, "Sit down, sir! Sit down." To this imperious
command the judge submitted. The convention was greatly excited,
and all knew that the matter would not end there.[60]

Even before this, however, an ugly matter had arisen before the
Church at large. Francis Lister Hawks, formerly of New York, was elected
Bishop of Mississippi in 1844. He was at that time residing in the South,
having found it wise to move there after the failure of St. Thomas Hall,
the school he had founded in Flushing, Long Island. It was no secret
that the bishop elect was hiding from his creditors. The question was,
in these unpleasant circumstances, would the House of Bishops concur
in his election? Given the tender sensibilities of the Episcopal Church
at this time, people began to line up one side or the other: should, or
should not, Francis L. Hawks be the Bishop of Mississippi?

Henry Anthon was a friend of Hawks, and wrote to warn him that
Muhlenburg (who had conducted a competing school), and Bishops
Whittingham and McCoskrey would oppose the consecration, as would
Onderdonk and "the North Carolina Prelate," Bishop Ives. Just at this
time Benjamin Onderdonk's brother, Henry, Bishop of Pennsylvania,

was accused of indecent behavior while under the influence of alcohol.
If Henry Onderdonk's case, wrote Anthon to Hawks,

> is put upon the shelf without an impeachment our B[ishop] will prob-
> ably lift up his horns on high and speak with a loud mouth. But if the
> ecclesiastical horizon there [in Philadelphia, where General Conven-
> tion was about to meet] gathers blackness before we assemble [in the
> New York diocesan convention] we shall experience during our ses-
> sion the very quintessence of Amiability from a certain quarter. *I won-
> der if he has heard what we have heard?*[61]

What we have heard! Anthon meant nothing less than sordid talk
about Bishop Benjamin Onderdonk's improper conduct with women.
Specifically, it was said the bishop had molested an ordinand's wife
during an all-night carriage ride at which her husband was present, in
the central part of the state (prior to division of the diocese); it was
further said that Bishop Onderdonk had similarly made indecent approaches to "the Rudderow girls" in a carriage ride after service in St.
James', Hamilton Square; and there was another story, about another
clergyman's wife. In fact, Bishop Onderdonk had become something of
a stale joke in New York's drawing rooms. If, at a party, the gaslight
failed, there was always some wag whose voice would be heard in the
darkness, "Ladies need not fear: the bishop is not present." Stories had
gone the rounds, as they will, and were an affront to many Episcopalians, because no one could dispute that Bishop Onderdonk did have
the habit of unconsciously touching people when he spoke to them.

Unfortunately, an eccentric but credible clergyman, James C. Richmond, began to collect stories about the bishop. Richmond had earned
Onderdonk's disapproval, and had a score to settle. Francis Hawks, too,
"gathered together all the testimony bearing against the powers that
be, and if opposition is made to his consecration [as Bishop of Mississippi, he] will declare war to the Knife point."[62] The fact that Hawks
was well-known throughout the national Church lent credence to whatever "testimony" he might share with Onderdonk's foes. When the
General Convention met in Philadelphia in the autumn of 1844, everyone but Benjamin T. Onderdonk was aware of the scandal about to
break over his head. Calvin Stowe wrote to his wife, Catherine Beecher,
about the Episcopal bishop who "while half boozled has caught young
ladies who were so unfortunate as to meet him alone, and pawed them
over in the most disgusting manner . . . and now it all comes out against
him."[63] So persuasive were the stories—and so persuaded in their own
Low Churchmanship?—that three bishops determined to go to New
York City after General Convention to ascertain to their satisfaction the

extent of Onderdonk's culpability. Needless to say, there were men in New York who were glad to entertain them. It was these three—Bishop Elliott of Georgia, Meade of Virginia, and Otey of Tennessee—who proceeded to make a formal presentation against Onderdonk.

The hearing—for such it was—took place in St. John's Chapel, the scene of many Onderdonk triumphs. The bishop was not present, and made no defense other than a broad denial. The House of Bishops considered testimony of alleged "immorality and impurity." There was no accusation of adultery. On January 2, 1845, the Bishop of New York was adjudged guilty, by a vote of eleven to six.[64] The verdict was not entirely along party lines: disgust of sexual irregularity was stronger than religious orthodoxy. The question, then, was the degree of punishment to be meted out; the new canon providing for a trial of a bishop was singularly unclear about this. Three sentences seemed possible: deposition, suspension, or admonition. Onderdonk's friends on the bench sought to save him from outright deposition by agreeing to a sentence of suspension. It was a fatal mistake, for in doing so they doomed the man. There was no time-limit to suspension. Presiding Bishop Chase merely signed an order suspending Benjamin Treadwell Onderdonk "from the office of a Bishop in the Church of God, and from all functions of the sacred ministry."

9

Interregnum

*Never have I so desponded with regard to the Church
as I do now.*

—WILLIAM ROLLINSON WHITTINGHAM

The Diocese of New York was crippled by the suspension of its bishop, and the dismay of the convention that met in September 1845 would have been disastrously compounded had the delegates known how long the diocese would remain without a leader. "In the absence of the Bishop"—the words were not only fact, but prophesy as well—William Creighton of Christ Church in Tarrytown was named chairman of convention. This man deserves a prominent niche in the iconography of the Diocese of New York. Year after year he would be led to the convention rostrum, overwhelmingly elected to preside. He had been Anthon's predecessor at St. Mark's, but was not marked by anti-Onderdonk partisanship. He, like his friend Washington Irving, had moved to the country near Tarrytown but often traveled to the city to participate in Church affairs. He earned the trust of all (a rare commodity those days in the Diocese of New York) and maintained considerable order in the contentious diocesan gatherings that followed the bishop's suspension. (If it is true, as was charged, that the convention later developed into a "gentlemen's club," its earlier years resembled how those same gentlemen would have behaved in a poorly run house of correction.) Creighton was often obliged to use the gavel. Once, he ascended to the desk and his optimism led him to hope that "Christian courtesy will continue to lighten and make pleasant the discharge of duty to which you have called me,"[1] only to have it otherwise reported that "everybody was very acrimonious, ill-tempered, and excited."

The ill temper of those conventions following the suspension was caused by the delegates' striving to maintain the dominance dictated by their opinion about Bishop Onderdonk. The voting roll calls indicate that the clergy were in sympathy with the bishop and the laity opposed to him. The facts are more complicated, for many of the clergy and laymen who favored the bishop's cause soon realized that he could never again function as the Bishop of New York. On the other side were a few extremists, who attempted to jettison Onderdonk altogether. It was the chairman's task to keep the business of the convention proceeding beyond the sloughs of hero worship on the one hand and nasty vindictiveness on the other. "The Chair would impress upon members the necessity of abstaining from any remarks calculated to create excitement," Creighton would say; but there would be yet one more catcall which might bring on the "much disorder," "a little amusement," "great uproar," or the "disorder and tumult" which reporters used to describe the proceedings.[2]

Many of the delegates were lawyers and judges. They were accustomed to the thrust and parry of public meetings. Sometimes their long speeches dominated, and one wonders if they would have permitted in their courts what they allowed themselves in the convention of the Diocese of New York. Other speakers also produced chaos. Imagine, for instance, how the Onderdonk opponents greeted the words of novelist James Fenimore Cooper when he declared in convention, "We all know that this trial has been alleged to proceed from a party spirit, and that the prosecution was the result of party in its inception, and in its prosecution."[3] (But it should be noted that Cooper's early sympathies for Bishop Onderdonk were later replaced by a belief that he was guilty and should be permanently relieved of all responsibility. Quite possibly, Cooper had heard the fresher opinions of his brother-in-law, Bishop DeLancey.)

In the years immediately following the suspension the people of the Diocese of New York began to see the Onderdonk affair in a new perspective. Cooper reflected the general opinion when he alleged that "party spirit" caused the trial. Church historians have usually accepted this view, but it seems too simple an explanation. The cultural forces of the day were complex and, more to the point, there were too many new forces at work, especially in the port city of New York. Think, for instance, of the well-documented fear of strangers, the Yankee disdain of their elaborate religious practices, and their latent threat to a system operating for the benefit of the existing ascendancy. Consider, too, the popularity of the new temperance movement, which, among its other aims, hoped to curb the appetites of the alleged hard-drinking immigrants. Other New York Episcopalians (though, alas, not many) were caught up in the abolition movement and were disappointed that leaders such as Hobart and Onderdonk in their Church were cold to the cause that had already begun to tear apart the congregations of their Presbyterian neighbors. Why did the Episcopal Church in New York fail to produce even one abolitionist minister like the Presbyterian Samuel Hanford Cox, whose Laight Street Church was wrecked by an antiabolitionist mob? (Cox's son, Arthur Cleveland Coxe, later became the Bishop of Western New York, adding an "e" to his name but retaining moderate abolitionist views when he changed churches.)

Public issues, then, played subtle parts in Bishop Onderdonk's downfall, but the attacks upon him focused on his personal mannerisms. As early as 1825 a close friend had said that Benjamin Onderdonk was "easily gulled."[4] Other friends described him as "coarse."[5] He lacked tact, and his naiveté led him to public contretemps. "Do keep the Bishop's affairs out of the convention, and him in the city," wrote his friend George W. Doane to William Whittingham in 1836.[6] But now his enemies had struck him at the most vulnerable areas of Victorian sensitivity: sex and liquor. When the diverse convention assembled in September 1845, Onderdonk, because he had been suspended by his brother bishops, was prevented from attending.

Almost immediately in that first convention chaired by William Creighton it was apparent that the anti-Onderdonk men were determined to rid themselves forever of the suspended bishop. First of all, Hamilton Fish of Anthon's St. Mark's Church asked that the list of attending clergy and laity be scrutinized, for he was convinced that many of the delegates favorable to the bishop possessed insufficient credentials. The second prong of the attack came from a most respected source, Luther Bradish, sometime lieutenant governor of the state and a valued, prominent churchman hitherto believed to be a friend of Bishop Onderdonk's. Bradish declared what, in time, came to be the opinion of most people when he said, in a motion debated in convention, that since Bishop Onderdonk had "been pronounced guilty on certain charges of impurity and immorality . . . he can never perform episcopal functions in this diocese with any prospect of usefulness to the Church."[7] The motion was tabled—overwhelmingly by the clergy, and just barely by the laymen. But the words stood, printed for all to see in the *Journal,* and they contained a cruel and certain prophecy. To make matters nastier, it was soon revealed that the trustees of the Episcopal Fund had not paid Bishop Onderdonk a large portion of his salary since the sentence was passed nine months earlier. Whether or not the suspended bishop should receive a salary, and how much, was frequently mentioned in those first conventions after his downfall. In the end, however, he was assured of a regular stipend from the Episcopal Fund because, even if suspended, he would remain *the* Bishop of New York until his death or resignation.

When Bradish made his motion stating that Onderdonk's "usefulness to the Church" was past, his aim was to induce the bishop to resign. It was the first of many moves and countermoves by those who wanted the bishop's resignation and those who believed he should be reinstated. It was suggested that he resign, with the understanding that the diocese would provide a pension.[8] On the other hand, the Report of the "Committee of Twenty on the State of the Diocese" held that Onderdonk should not be asked to resign, that "he is yet the Bishop of this Diocese, so that no other Bishop can be elected in his place."[9] The committee further recommended that he be granted "an income not more than adequate to his support." Six members of the committee refused to sign the report, and in a minority statement denied that Benjamin T. Onderdonk "is the existent Bishop of this Diocese; that he should be paid his salary arrears, be comfortably maintained, and that he should voluntarily resign as conducive to the peace, purity, and influence of the Church and the best interests and dignity of the suspended bishop."[10] The 1845 convention voted to pay the suspended bishop the salary then owed him, and approved the Standing Committee's decision to ask other bishops of the Episcopal Church to perform episcopal acts in New York. Just before adjournment, a time when (then as now) many delegates had departed, there was another motion (which was defeated) that Onderdonk could never again serve as the Bishop of New York.

The Standing Committee, then, could look forward to another year of tense and exacting duty, often dealing with affairs for which that body is not canonically intended. Bishop McCoskry of Michigan and Bishop DeLancey of Western New York seized the opportunity to spend some months in New York. Twenty-one men were ordained, seven churches (including the new Trinity) were consecrated, and more than 2,000 people were confirmed in the first year these two visiting bishops served the diocese. The 1846 convention reported many new clergymen attached to the diocese, but there was no significant discussion of Onderdonk's dilemma. Clearly, the delegates knew that nothing could be gained by further discussion in convention. Onderdonk stubbornly refused to resign and assured his supporters he was prepared to return to his duties. He looked forward to the time when the House of Bishops would remit his sentence. Others shared this view, and it may have been the possibility of such a remission that led the kindly, optimistic William Creighton to express in 1847 the hope that in the next convention a bishop would be in the chair. The delegates proceeded then to address a memorial to the forthcoming General Convention asking that the diocese of New York "be relieved from its present anomalous position.[11]

The General Convention was not cooperative and the stalemate continued. Reuben Sherwood, rector of St. James' Church, Hyde Park, moved in the 1848 diocesan convention a declaration that the suspension was unfair to the diocese, and that since the House of Bishops had now repudiated the principle of indefinite suspensions but declared the probability of Onderdonk's reinstatement "slender and remote," the House of Bishops should immediately terminate its sentence or "specify on what terms the suspension shall cease.[12] The motion was tabled but taken up again the next year, with additional comments about Bishop Onderdonk's sufferings, and was carried.

Had there been a strong central party in the diocese during these crucial years, the matter might have been settled. The record suggests that there was little effort at arbitration. The inducements offered by each side signified defeat to the other. Bishop Onderdonk himself was immovable: he was the bishop, he would die the bishop. It was reported that he scrupulously avoided the discussions carried on in his behalf (though one doubts that he did not often confer with Seabury and his other ardent supporters). His opponents were equally plain about their requirements: they wanted Onderdonk out of the picture entirely. A pension, yes; a functioning bishop, emphatically no.

When the General Convention of 1847 abandoned the principle of an alternative sentence of suspension, the decision was declared not applicable to the case of Benjamin T. Onderdonk. Thus, New York found no relief from its memorial. It was now almost four years since the House of Bishops had deprived the diocese of its bishop when Whitehouse of St. Thomas' Church (formerly an opponent of Onderdonk, and future Bishop of Chicago) moved in the 1849 diocesan convention a most peculiar resolution. It provided for the bishop's resignation, a pension, and a petition to the House of Bishops to permit him whatever functions "are allowed to a Bishop who has resigned his jurisdiction."[13] Such a resolution was doomed before it was ever moved. Bishop Onderdonk might, somehow, be persuaded to resign, but there was no guarantee that his hitherto implacable brothers would ever permit their disgraced colleague any exercise of his ministry.

In any case, the situation soon changed. A special diocesan convention met in 1850 to implement in New York the General Convention's recent legislation which provided a "provisional bishop" for those places where a diocesan bishop was unable to function. In cases of reinstatement after suspension, the provisional bishop automatically became an assistant, with right of succession. It might be an awkward situation, but New York hastened to grasp the opportunity.

Bishop Onderdonk doubtless approved this measure, for his friend and advocate Samuel Seabury of the Church of the Annunciation allowed his own name to be put in nomination. It was a spirited contest. Seabury nearly won, but then (as George Templeton Strong recorded it) was "thrown overboard, and Southgate taken up, on trial, by the

High Church men; today he was dropped and Creighton was the candidate." After another day spent voting, "both parties concluded that any more ballotting would be a waste of time and temper," and the special convention adjourned.[14] For yet another year, the Diocese of New York would be without a bishop.

THE COST OF SUSPENSION

It was now recognized that, in suspending Onderdonk indefinitely, the House of Bishops had made a blunder that cost the Church in New York dear. When his friends on the bench panicked at the possibility of his deposition after conviction and thus agreed to the lesser sentence of suspension, they had unwittingly led Onderdonk into a trap from which he would never escape. Even if party spirit had prompted the trial, it was *not* High Churchmanship that convicted him; it was the charge of immorality, and now, six years later, his brother bishops were unlikely to restore to their company a man they believed rightly judged. The resulting hiatus was disastrous to a Church ministering in such a fast-growing state.

The Standing Committee continued to ask visiting bishops to take services in the New York diocese for perhaps three months of the year, when weather was unpleasant in their own dioceses. Nevertheless, the traditional *persona,* the head of the diocese, he whom the Prayer Book addressed as Father in God, was absent. Added to this was the implied shame attached to the reason for having no bishop in what should have been the most prominent diocese of the Episcopal Church. Surely, New Yorkers saw themselves in a prolonged season of Lenten humiliation.

The statistics prove that invited visiting bishops were inadequate. Bishop Onderdonk had traveled 4,750 miles in 1843 and confirmed 1,540 persons. In 1846, the visiting bishops reported 2,028 confirmations, but that number represents the classes for two years. Not until after 1850 did the number of confirmations equal those of Onderdonk's episcopate.

All this time that there was no acting bishop of New York, the state was growing rapidly. Improved transportation on Hudson River sloops and barges encouraged the growth of many small riverbank communities. Many of these hamlets had as seigneur an Episcopalian who had a summer house on the river and was glad to sponsor the beginnings of an Episcopal Church for the handful of year-round residents. His wife doubtless encouraged him, and arranged for a Sunday school because she knew the community had many unchurched children and would have more as these hamlets grew. The great sprawling city downstream required products the Hudson River Valley was prepared to send. Think of the red bricks needed in Manhattan and Brooklyn, where today's country lane was sure to become next year's city street, lined with rows of brick houses! (Jersey brownstone was, in the 1840s, just beginning to appear on the more stylish houses.) Think of the ice needed for the thousands of kitchens, and the hay needed for the thousands of horses in the city! Fruit in season, beef on the hoof, vegetables, shad and herring, tanbark, lumber, cement and bluestone—all these had long been Hudson Valley offerings to the maw of a never satisfied, always demanding, city. Now, further north, Troy sent its ironware and finished cotton goods to the port city, while the improved Erie Canal supplied a steady procession of barges creaking under their loads of western grain and hay. Just north of Albany, where the canal met the river, all the way to slips in the East River past the Battery, the Hudson swarmed with busy boats. There is Tivoli's *Harvest Queen* laden with strawberries, and there is Catskill's *Golden Store* maneuvering to pass her and to arrive first at the Manhattan market. And there is a wide-beamed sloop, specially designed for sailing on a river whose northeast gusts can be treacherous, catching the wind and darting ahead of the Anderson Taylor and Company's newest star, *Emerald,* just out from Newburgh and itself determined to catch up with its rival *Norwich* and race to the city. The passengers on another boat, *Telegraph,* are amused at the game they see, and grateful that their captain is known to refrain from a dangerous pastime. In the year just past irresponsible captains racing each other cost fifty lives in one explosion and fire. Having the promise of a safe and pleasant journey, they consult their penny guide and map to identify that new steeple they see jabbing up above the treetops. It may well be an Episcopal Church, but if so not consecrated by the Bishop of New York, for he was in a disgrace not discussed in mixed company.

And so the river traffic made its way to New York Harbor. A forest of masts and furled rigging met the eye. The great ships of many seas were docked in the two rivers and pointed their bowsprits far over the streets below. "The broad quays are covered with the produce of every clime; and barrels, sacks, boxes, hampers, bales and hogsheads are piled in continuous ridges along the streets," a visitor noted.[15]

The interior streets of New York City were quick to absorb the fruits of what was, unquestionably, the nation's leading commercial center. Layman George Templeton Strong abandons his customary suavity when he assesses the city's development in 1850:

> How the city marches northward! The progress of 1835 and 1836 was nothing to the luxuriant rank growth of this year. Streets are springing

up, whole strata of sandstone have transferred themselves from their ancient resting places to look down on bustling thoroughfares for long years to come. Wealth is rushing in upon us like a freshet.[16]

But Strong took another look the next year, and was less pleased:

We have our Five Points, our emigrant quarters, our swarms of seam-stresses to whom their utmost toil in monstrous daily drudgery gives only a bare subsistence, a life barren of hope and enjoyment; our hordes of dock-thieves, and of children who live in the streets and by them. No one can walk the length of Broadway without meeting some hideous troop of ragged girls, from twelve years old down, brutalized already almost beyond redemption by premature vice, clad in the filthy refuse of the rag-picker's collection, obscene of speech, the stamp of childhood gone from their faces, hurrying along with harsh laughter and foulness on their lips that some of them have learned by rote.[17]

Another historian asserts that in the 1840s the New York City

rich and poor scarcely inhabited the same universe . . . sewers over-flowed, privies fouled wells, streets went uncleaned; and the poor, crowded in tenements, cellars and shanties sickened and died with fearsome rapidity.[18]

Yet that consummate Knickerbocker, Washington Irving, returning from Europe to his native city in 1848 and feted as the New World's first cultural deity, was bound to note happier things: "New York is wonder-fully improved in late years," he said. "The houses are furnished with great luxury, the tone of society also is greatly improved and the opera house which is the fashionable assembly place in the winter is giving quite an air of refinement to the city."[19]

This was the greatest period of Irish immigration.[20] Most of the Irish immigrants were Roman Catholics, but many were members of the Church of Ireland. When these Episcopalians inquired about their bishop in New York, they would be told that he had been suspended indefinitely, for "impure behaviour." And neither these newcomers nor the Episcopalians they found already resident in New York would see a bishop of their Church until 1852.

JONATHAN WAINWRIGHT: "BISHOP AFTER ALL!"

It was in 1852 that Jonathan Mayhew Wainwright was elected Provisional Bishop of New York. "Everyone talks of Wainwright, but he is never elected," noted the diarist Strong. In fact, able and endearing William Creighton had been elected by the convention and, after prolonged

A noteworthy record of liturgical transition in St. Philip's Church, Garrison, about 1860. The church is decked with hemlock for Christmas. A semicircular chancel rail is surmounted by a "rood" of similar shape whose cross is probably the only such symbol in the church. On the wall and rood are seasonal mottoes. The font may be seen in the left of the picture. The brass vases on the altar are filled with holiday greens, not flowers, but are nonetheless a daring innovation at this early date. The alms basin and a Prayer Book are also on the altar. The rector, Charles F. Hoffman, stands in the reading desk, which is equipped with Bible and Prayer Book and the upholstered, tasseled cushion referred to in many old documents. The stairs to the pulpit above can be discerned to the right, and the pulpit also has a cushion with Bible and Prayer Book. Mr. Hoffman wears a floor-length surplice and a "preaching stole," for he is among those who by this time had ceased using the black gown at sermon time. In a year or two, St. Philip's would build a new church, designed by Richard Upjohn, and one of the last "triple deckers" would pass into history.

Courtesy: William S. Reisman.

consideration about his age and family cares, decided he must refuse what must have been the crowning honor of his long life of devotion to the Church. So, almost in desperation, the delegates turned to Wainwright and, on October 2, 1852, Strong wrote in his journal, "Wainwright is Bishop after all!!—elected by a small majority at last. People were worn out with waiting and balloting . . . nobody is quite satisfied, and a good many are quite savage, but I suppose it's the best thing that could have been done." [21]

As we have already seen, George Templeton Strong was a realist. He lived the life of a very proper New York gentleman, but as a shrewd attorney he was not blind to facts. His education for the law, and not his natural impulses, led him to discern what was the issue and what was the best expedient. Originally a supporter, and always something of an admirer, of Onderdonk's, he early knew that the bishop's usefulness was past, and his imposing presence an embarrassment. Even more, Strong resented the spirit of anarchy and partisanship that prevailed in the diocese following the bishop's suspension and (as so delightfully often!) he pleased himself by writing in his diary that he would have preferred the election of Alexander Vinton, because Vinton

> would have bred an earthquake in the diocese within three months after his Consecration. He would have invaded the next meeting of the Pastoral Aid Society in person, kicked out the members if necessary with his own episcopal foot emphatically applied . . . silenced Tyng and bullied down Anthon, and ruled the flock committed to his keeping with a thick rod of red hot iron. [22]

There could be no better description of diocesan dissension, and as an informed layman Strong longed for the discipline Hobart enjoyed and Onderdonk attempted. Jonathan Mayhew Wainwright was not the leader Strong hoped for. Strong was especially convinced of this when he heard that Wainwright of Trinity had definitely identified himself with the Low Church party.

Wainwright passes across our sky as a brilliant meteor of force and charm and (because of the circumstances) reconciliation. Then, in less than three years, he is gone: burned out, they said. He was not an American by birth; he was born in Liverpool, England, on February 24, 1792. His father, Peter Wainwright, was an English merchant who arrived in Boston soon after the Revolutionary War; his mother, Elizabeth, was an American, a Mayhew of that Martha's Vineyard family that produced a line of sturdy public officials and clergymen. Her father was a Congregationalist minister tending to Unitarianism; it is said he was a resourceful opponent of any notions that the Crown might entertain about sending bishops into New England. For reasons not now clear,

Peter Wainwright resettled in England. Young Jonathan went to two schools there, one kept by a Nonconformist minister, and the other by a Welsh clergyman. When he was eleven years old the family returned to Boston, and in 1808 he entered Harvard College.

It might be said that Wainwright entered the ministry by means of music. Music and literature were always compelling forces in his life. He was for some years organist at Christ Church, Cambridge; he was also an instructor at the college, and for a while read law in a Boston office. From all that we can gather, however, he moved steadily toward the Church, and then studied for the ministry with the rector of Trinity Church, Boston. He was made a deacon in St. John's, Providence, by Bishop Griswold, and ordained priest in 1818 by Bishop Hobart in Christ Church, Hartford, whither he had been called while yet a deacon. Bishop Hobart was taking occasional episcopal duties in Connecticut that year, as Bishop Jarvis had died in 1813. Later that year Wainwright married Amelia M. Phelps of New Haven, and after a brief time as an assistant at New York's Trinity Church, he became rector of Grace Church, then practically next door to the older church. It is a mark of Wainwright's ability that he was able to minister in one and then the other without leaving a sense of rancor in either.

As might be expected with this man in this age, Wainwright concentrated on improving choral music at Grace Church. It was a time of musical experimentation. Few colonial churches had (or wanted!) pipe organs, but now an expanding social and cultural life in New York permitted—even required—a development in church music. Wainwright was glad to oblige. In 1824 he was reported as personally undertaking to pay the five choristers at Grace Church. It is worth noting that one of the five was also responding clerk, whose duty was to make the Prayer Book replies to the officiant's prayers and suffrages: the past died slowly! Wainwright also attempted, unsuccessfully, to establish a school "for the promotion of Psalmody." It is worth a guess that he hoped to proceed toward a choir school of boy choristers such as he had seen in England, but the idea did not at that time take hold in Grace Church. Nevertheless, very soon Jonathan Wainwright became a notable rector in New York:

> The impressive chants were given in a perfected style not equalled by any choir in the city. Miss Emma Tillingham was the leading lady of the efficient choir, whose rich tones had been cultivated by Sconcia; and she was not infrequently assisted by Charles E. Horn and Austin Phillips, two of the sweetest singers New York ever had. The aid afforded by these cultivated songsters was a powerful adjunct to the Doctor's polished efforts for the spread of Christianity, and Grace Church was always filled to the utmost capacity, while wealthy, pre-

tentious Trinity, "the mother of us all," could fitly be compared to a
"banquet hall deserted" . . . Dr. Wainwright was for many years the
beloved pastor than whom a more respected genial Christian gentleman never entered a New York pulpit.[23]

The "many years" of Wainwright's rectorate at Grace Church were
in fact twelve, for in 1833 he was called to be rector of Trinity Church,
Boston. Again, he expended his efforts toward the betterment of music
in church services, this time traveling as far as England in order to
purchase the right pipe organ for Trinity Church. To this day, Boston
(which has a long memory) preserves the fact that Wainwright, as rector of Trinity Church, was in the chair at the meeting which founded
the Harvard Musical Association, from which, it is said, all present-day
Boston musical blessings flow.

But New York always had a compelling appeal for Wainwright, and
we may suppose that he was glad to return there when again called to
be an assistant at Trinity Church. Now he was promised more responsibilities than those usually allotted to an assistant minister. He remained
at Trinity and, more especially, at its fashionable St. John's Chapel—in
truth the most prestigious (and loveliest!) Episcopal church in New
York City for many years, despite its poor acoustics—until 1852, when
elected provisional bishop.

Those seventeen years were heady ones for the city, and for the
future bishop. Wainwright was able to indulge in the city's cultural life,
which burgeoned so remarkably in those years. "The literati of New
York were predominantly Episcopalian," we are told.[24] Wainwright belonged right with them. He had written books, edited sermons, published a biography of Bishop Heber, books about travel, about prayer,
about the proper use of Church music. Very early, he had produced *The
Book of Chants,* followed in 1828 by *Music of the Church;* some years
later, he would collaborate with William Augustus Muhlenberg in a
Choir and Family Psalter. New York in the 1840s was rampantly Anglo-
philic. The Gothic revival was firmly rooted and coming into full flower.
Why should a man of Wainwright's taste and ability not be urged into
the city's various literary clubs and groups? Most of them were "Federalist and Episcopalian and all but abjectly respectful of the mother-
country."[25] His companions at such meetings would be from old New
York families, or rising notables gravitating to them; men, in short,
"who survived either by their own wits, or by husbanding inherited
wealth, dined at four in the afternoon, told good stories, dressed well,
and managed, despite the muck of New York's streets, to act as though
Gotham were London."[26] It was still a small town for those privileged
persons who were able to grasp what was offered.

Christianity has long been influenced by the printing press, and as New York City approached mid-century the Episcopal Church was particularly able to utilize the printed word. Hobart had been a genius at realizing this, and in their time his publications did their work, which was decidedly "churchly." Now, however, we find several New York magazines casting a favoring glow upon the Episcopal Church though they were not ostensibly ecclesiastical in intent. One of these was the *Knickerbocker,* founded in 1833. Charles Fenno Hoffman was the editor; Washington Irving's lamented Matilda was his half-sister, and both were related to Gulian Verplanck, the "essential New Yorker." As an assemblyman, and General Seminary professor, he had obtained the incorporation of the seminary in 1821, and almost immediately thereafter joined its faculty at the urging of Bishop Hobart.[27] The *Knickerbocker* magazine set was apt to be "high church Episcopalians" who were partisans of Bishop Hobart; they were also likely to be conservative Whigs.[28] While embracing the heritage of the Europe they deemed worthy, they denounced as unacceptable the likes of Madame de Staël, George Sand, Balzac, and Hugo. Perhaps more important to our history, Wainwright and his friends were pleased to see New England's discredited radicalism replaced by the conservative cultural preferences of an enlightened New York.[29]

Wainwright's friend Evert Duyckinck, of an old New York publishing family, was a vestryman at St. Thomas Church, and regularly submitted items to that "organ of Episcopal scholarship," the *New York Review.* Perhaps Wainwright also offered articles, under a pseudonym, as was so often done. He was accustomed to the limelight and savored the highbrow company he kept. Why not? He must frequently have met with the literary and artistic names of the day. Herman Melville was then in the city; Washington Irving was by now practically beloved, if not always appreciated by New Yorkers who took their history too seriously. James Fenimore Cooper, upstate, treasured memories of people who knew Sir William Johnson. There were also John James Audubon, Thomas Cole of Catskill, and Asher Durand of New Jersey, William Cullen Bryant, who had come down from Great Barrington, and Samuel F. B. Morse (less remarked by the literati perhaps now that he had turned from art to inventions). There were Fitz-Greene Halleck, Nathaniel Parker Willis the dandy, Philip Hone and James K. Paulding, perhaps even Edgar Allan Poe and, certainly, John Lloyd Stephens, the traveler-writer who transported exotic stone figures back from Yucatán.

These, and probably many more, were cultural giants who greeted Wainwright often on ground compatible and rewarding to them all. It is important to remember that those forces that a later age would call "uplift" now met and were assisted by, marks that are readily seen in literature, art, and especially architecture. Andrew Jackson Downing could write in *Rural Essays:* "The leading idea of the Gothic arch is found in its upward lines—its aspiring tendencies."[30]

These, then, were the pleasant colleagues and rewarding thoughts with which Jonathan Mayhew Wainwright was summoned when elected Provisional Bishop of New York. Let it be said, to his credit, that the brief life yet allotted to him was spent fully in the work of diocesan bishop. He was consecrated in Trinity Church on November 10, 1852. "How beautiful he was as he knelt in his meekness to receive the trust of an apostle, " says his biographer; "and what an 'Amen' went up from that subdued and melted multitude that God might grant it all." For at last, New York again had a bishop.

Not, of course, *the* bishop. Benjamin Onderdonk would retain that honor till his dying day. Jonathan M. Wainwright and, for some years, his successor, Horatio Potter, would be styled "provisional" bishops. This is emphatically recorded in the records of the Church, but in fact Wainwright's task from the beginning of his episcopate was to make up, as far as possible, what had been lost. Parishes not visited, rectors who had never met their bishop, persons not confirmed, churches not consecrated, diocesan direction absent, partisan spirit deep and ubiquitous, opportunities gone or slipping away—all these and much more were the immediate problems the new bishop faced.

A LINGERING IMPASSE: BLACK CHURCHPEOPLE

To us now, but apparently less so at the time, no problem was greater than the admission of St. Philip's Church, Manhattan, into union with the Diocese of New York. The whole matter is an embarrassment to New York Christians, and yet it is not without its heroes. It is for this latter reason that the situation cannot be explained away as due merely to contemporary cultural forces. There *were* some white, well-connected, prominent, and reasonable Episcopal laymen who were zealous for nothing less than decent, fair treatment of Negroes. They fought year after year for equal participation in the diocese, and particularly in the diocesan conventions. William Lloyd Garrison founded *The Liberator* in 1831, and it was thereafter clear that a growing number of people demanded that a policy of immediate emancipation should replace the older idea of gradualism.[31] Slavery must be abolished, now! Garrison was neither the first nor the final abolitionist, but his vivid personality publicized a cause that had hearers in the Diocese of New York. There had been a long history of antislavery agitation in the city, but it must be admitted that the Episcopal Church was never notable in the cause.

One entire family that had earned the fury of proslavery people was that of John Jay of Bedford. His sons, William and Peter, carried on the father's insistence on full rights and emancipation for all Negroes. William Jay was particularly active in the cause, and, once enlisted, he was a persistent adversary.

William Jay was born in New York City in 1789 and was educated in the school of Dr. Ellison, rector of St. Peter's, Albany. He then attended Yale College. His classmates there included John Calhoun. He married Augusta McVickar, and she proved to be a noble support throughout Jay's long battle for emancipation. They lived in the Jay house in Bedford, attending to their extensive farm there. By the time William was twenty-six he was deeply engaged in various "philanthropies." He was a founder of the Society for the Suppression of Vice in Bedford, and an organizer of the Westchester Bible Society. He thus clashed with Hobart when the bishop tried to discourage Episcopalians from participating in Bible societies.

One of the Jay interests had been emancipation, but William was aroused to new passion after the Gilbert Horton case of 1826. Horton was a free black man found in Washington, D.C., and jailed for vagrancy. When it was advertised that Horton would be sold to pay for the "expenses" of his incarceration, there was an uproar, and, of course, funds were immediately raised for his release. But Jay, who by this time was a judge in Westchester County, realized that the question of selling a free man hadn't been resolved. He recognized that the North needed almost as much education in the matter as did the South. Jay tended to avoid the various abolitionist societies, though he had worked with Peter Williams in the New York Anti-Slavery Society. He often noted that Episcopalians were rarely seen in such groups, and he once wrote a diatribe to Bishop Levi Silliman Ives about "clerical efforts to sanctify slavery and caste."[32] When no one could be found to publish Samuel Wilberforce's *History of the American Church,* William Jay gave the reason: the Englishman had exposed the Episcopal Church's tacit support of slavery and class distinction. On another occasion, Jay noted that the Fugitive Slave Law was "approved by many clergy who preach in fine churches to rich and fashionable city congregations." He doubtless had New York in mind.[33] He opposed the idea of colonization, and when he published his *Inquiry* in 1835 conservative men such as Alonzo Potter, Peter G. Stuyvesant, and Chancellor Kent were impressed and converted by the reasonableness of William Jay's approach.

Many northerners were slow to sympathize with the abolitionists because they feared extremism. It seemed extraordinary for aristocrats like the Jays to be involved in Negro emancipation. Furthermore, in that time of utter conformity, there was the horror produced by rumors that black ministers performed marriages for couples of mixed race.[34]

St. Philip's was a "colored" congregation, founded about 1809, incorporated in 1818, its church consecrated in 1819—but still, in 1852, not admitted into union with the diocese, and therefore not entitled to a place in its conventions. In 1819 the Standing Committee approved the ordination of a black man with the understanding that he not be admitted to the diocesan convention. This appears to have been the policy of the Diocese of New York for some years, and there is no record that it was ever questioned by the bishops or the convention— or by anyone other than the Jays. "It is one of the most melancholy circumstances of the condition of the colored people that so many of the ministers of the Lord Jesus Christ are among their most influential enemies," wrote William Jay to his rector.[35] "Look at the conventions of New York and Pennsylvania excluding ministers and disciples of the crucified Redeemer merely because they are poor and despised." Jay loved the Church and believed its conventions could promote ideals he knew to be close to the Mind of Christ. "I, as a private member of the Church, am in no degree responsible for the heresies of Puseyism nor the more disgusting heresies of cotton-divinity," he wrote to a friend who wondered how he could remain a churchman.[36]

A convenient sentiment in the diocesan conventions was that eventually there should be a separate African Episcopal Church with "a council of their own for their peculiar government."[37] When, in 1846, the Jays and their few friends in convention claimed the Church in New York "degraded" the black man, the convention's retort was that Negroes "*are* socially degraded and not regarded as proper associates for the class of people who attend our conventions."[38] Considering the disorder and coarseness so manifest in those recent all-white conventions, Negroes in New York may forever accept that statement not as criticism, but as an encomium! When a committee reported that blacks were unfit to converse and debate with the high-toned gentlemen usually found in diocesan conventions, a minority report was spread upon the minutes asking the potent question, "Was not the Gospel vouchsafed to all of us?"[39]

Now another Jay, John Jr., joined the battle. He was William's son, a graduate of Columbia in the Class of 1836 and principal founder of the Parochial Fund. He wrote "The Dignity of the Abolition Cause as Compared with the Political Schemes of the Day" (1839), "Caste and Slavery in the American Church" (1843), and "The American Church and the American Slave Trade" (1860), all brief treatises offering no comfort to tender consciences. In the diocesan convention of 1850 John Jay, Jr., attempted once more to have St. Philip's admitted. His sentiment had become strong enough in the North to make it seem proper enough to admit St. Philip's. This was not the end of the Jays' struggle for Negro rights. Peter A. Jay had died in 1843; William lived till 1858, leaving in his will $1,000 "for promoting the safety and comfort of fugitive slaves." Arthur Cleveland Coxe said of him, "There was much of the Huguenot in the piety of the Judge, but nothing of the Puritan."[40] The surviving Jay, John Jr., took umbrage when in 1863 he heard that the rector of Christ Church, Rye, refused to read prayers for the President. Jay wrote the reverend gentleman a long (and probably public) letter, stating that "the loyal families of that ancient parish are being driven from their seats." The rector of Rye, stunned by the attack, wrote a letter (probably also public) to the Bedford postmaster inquiring if "this person is *sane.*"[41]

WAINWRIGHT VINDICATED

It was perhaps salutory for Bishop Wainwright to encourage the idea that he was sympathetic to the Low Churchmen. It assured him his election and tended to pacify those who were still hounding Onderdonk and his High Church minions. And since Wainwright carefully refrained from being found in the forefront of any of the battles about the old bishop, the High Church people would have no firm reason to distrust him. If some churchpeople thought he vacillated, others could reasonably claim this was nothing less than ecclesiastical statesmanship—just what the Diocese of New York needed, they said. Indeed the very brief time of Bishop Wainwright's leadership may be considered, like the episcopate of Benjamin Moore, a time of preparation for what lay ahead under the direction of a successor. Mildness and ambition were nicely combined in Wainwright, and it may well be that (except for the election of 1921) there was never again such an outright contest between the High Church and the Low Church in the Diocese of New York: his all-things-to-all-men manner was useful, after all.

But vigorous partisans of both sides might chafe under Bishop Wainwright's apparent indecision. One vignette of the bishop was recorded by George Templeton Strong, who was a member of the committee charged with building Trinity Chapel in 25th Street. Richard Upjohn was the architect and, as usual with his larger churches, he envisioned a stone altar. The committee readily concurred, and so the diarist (whose sense of humor is by now well-known to every New York antiquarian) gleefully recorded the bishop's monologue in his journal:

> I hope, Mr. Strong, that your committee will adopt a table instead of an altar for Trinity Chapel. The Communion table should be a table in the literal sense of the word.

[A week later, after the building committee had firmly settled upon
Upjohn's limestone designs] oh—ah—it is to be of *stone?* Then of
course I can have no objection to the design the committee is in-
clined to adopt—That settles the question—yes—precisely—to be
sure—certainly—the form of an altar is of course the proper one—
ah—hum—I hope your family is well . . . his principal subject of talk
was the magnificence of this house—the good taste of the Dining
Room decorations—the agreeable shade of the green paper hangings—and how much would the premises probably bring at private
sale.[42]

Not a complimentary glimpse of Bishop Wainwright, but then
Strong hadn't ever much liked the man and suspected that his real aim
was to be president of Columbia University: "a convenient sinecure
after two or three years of an overworked episcopate."[43]

Those last two words are significant: it *was* an overworked episcopate, of less than two years. Think of the task Wainwright had accepted!
There had been no episcopal visitations of the parishes since Onderdonk's last full circuit in 1843. The next year's General Convention
prevented his usual full swing around the diocese. Bishop Wainwright
was indecisive, something of a literary dilettante, and certainly caught
up in New York society. But he was also a man of conscience, and he
sought to fulfill the duties of the office he coveted—Bishop of New
York. He began to unravel the knotted strands he had inherited, and
restored to the diocese a sense of respectability and mission. Perhaps
he was not able to minister to Paddy on the Erie Canal, but his "all
mildness and grace" noted earlier by Philip Hone was pure gold in a
diocese so long troubled.[44]

THE CHURCHES: SUBTLE CHANGE

Aftershocks of the Onderdonk troubles were still felt in the 1850s. The
Low Church firebrands saw their suspicions vindicated by the Episcopal clergy who forsook their Church for that of Rome. John Murray
Forbes, prominent rector of St. Luke's, Hudson Street; Homer Wheaton,
once rector of Christ Church, Poughkeepsie, and much spoken of as a
candidate for Provisional Bishop in 1852; Preston of the *Ecclesiologist;*
Samuel Roosevelt Bayley (Mother Seton's nephew); Bishop Ives, son-
in-law of Hobart: all these had "gone to Rome." Good riddance, said
the more philosophic churchmen. But their brethren who tended to be
more truculent chafed at the damage they thought done to the
Church's Protestant integrity. For instance, William A. Duer, former
president of Columbia College, could write of the new Trinity Church
in 1847,

that lifts its tall spire to the skies, but mocks them with the gilded toy that tops it. We will not enter, lest the solemn mockery within should repel, instead of excite, as in charity we may suppose it intended to excite—that pure spirit of devotion which sanctified the humbler edifice from whose ruins it has risen.[45]

Sentiments ran high. Both the Catholic- and Protestant-minded had able, vocal champions. But something new became apparent—a middle group unattached to prominent names of the old battles. Many Episcopalians were tired, even embarrassed by the long quarrels that had prevailed before and after Onderdonk's suspension. They were also favorably impressed by some of the novel things said, sung, and done in the churches. Unlike Duer, they did not bristle at the sight of a gilded cross on a church steeple. They had become accustomed to a central holy table, and didn't mind looking toward the pulpit corner of the church during the sermon. The vestryman tended to listen appreciatively to the sung chants when his daughter had been enlisted in the choir, and he was glad enough to see flowers in the chancel at Easter when he could mention to his fellow worshipers that they came from his own hothouse. He might be somewhat proud that the celebrated Upjohn was a devout Episcopalian as well as a successful architect of the Gothic taste. And it mattered that James Renwick, an amateur architect whose Grace Church was admired by everybody (except Philip Hone), was related to most of the old families of New York. Renwick added to his fame when he proceeded to design twin-towered Calvary on Fourth Avenue, St. Patrick's Cathedral on Fifth Avenue, the Smithsonian Institution and, somewhat later, St. James' on 72d Street. Upjohn's country churches dotted the upstate landcape, and they were appealing, available to the humblest congregation because they could be built so easily. Such a wooden church, designed by John Priest of Brooklyn, was built in the city for St. Michael's on 99th Street, and a brick one, St. John's, in Cornwall. Its architect's premature death deprived the Episcopal Church of a gifted designer.

What Duer and his friends never realized was that churches now were larger, and large churches require some ornamentation and ceremony. Grace Church, for instance, under Thomas House Taylor had been in the vanguard of Episcopal Low Church persuasion. But once the congregation moved into its new Renwick edifice there would necessarily be a gradual enrichment of decoration. Carvings and stained glass suggested medieval times. Once the holy table and the pulpit were separated, movement during the service from one place to the other became a ceremonial moment. In mid-century, each church found its own best way to surround the worship of the Book of Common Prayer with a sense of dignity and gravity. And churches tended to borrow each other's usages, so that after a time of experimentation and adaptation there seems to have emerged a sort of uniformity that lasted until our own time. But it was created by the Victorian's demand for propriety as well as by some possible theological predispositions. And ceremony associated with the Holy Communion, colored stoles, candles and flowers on the altar, processional crosses, and alms basons were still scarce in the early 1850s.

THE NUCLEAR CHURCH

About this time, something appeared in the Episcopal Church that was very much in harmony with the age. It was, equally, dissonant with much that had hitherto characterized church life in America. Since no name has been quite able to describe this phenomenon let us call it the nuclear church. Before this, the local church had been, on the Sabbath, a place of assembly for worship: virtually a meetinghouse. During the week it stood as a mute symbol of an authority locally defined.

The romantic age fostered something quite different, and it needed those gifts the Episcopal Church was able to offer to a young republic. Current literature—Walter Scott comes to mind immediately—told of ancient glories. Civic and domestic architecture began to evoke a mystic past. Music showed its ability to range the ages freely; Mendelssohn was "discovering" J. S. Bach. The painters turned away from classic themes and depicted a creation very much satisifed with its Creator. The Hudson River School became a prominent exponent of man's harmony with nature.

These forces were in the air, as was a compelling American desire for a legitimate past. Though it was the Centennial in 1876 that brought about a decided reevaluation of the *American* heritage, the romantic revival persuaded the new nation to dig among the treasures of a European past and claim whatever was found to its liking. The search brought the respectability that long-standing institutions always lend, and nothing was more available than the Episcopal Church. Herein lay its appeal in the mid years of the nineteenth century. The longings of a parvenu populace were met by those gifts that had always been the stock-in-trade of the Episcopal Church. There was the Book of Common Prayer; it bestowed upon Americans an acceptable sort of worship in a language much like that of the King James Bible they all knew so well. There was a European flavor, a certain sophistication, a congeniality with the Old World.

The nervous, creative, searching, visionary impulses of Americans fostered an improvement in the fortunes of the Episcopal Church. Moreover, conspicuous personalities played an invaluable part. In New

York, there was the impressive, even romantic, figure of John Henry Hobart, who had died at the apogee of his powers. In his mind's eye there was a picture of what the local parish church should be. Hobart's successor, Bishop Onderdonk, was even more convinced, and it is the church we here call nuclear. For it gathers to itself the longings and aspirations of the people; it calls upon them to find here, in this place, the good things that shall be promoted throughout the country. It is a church on a public street (though Victorians often preferred it secluded among weeping willows or dark pines). The architecture is Gothic because that is the idiom best able to remind Americans of a bygone time redolent of strength and security. If possible, the church is built of stone, but even the local carpenters, thanks to the new design books, could now run up a Gothic sort of wooden church.

In mid-century the rector in the Diocese of New York is likely to be a graduate of the General Theological Seminary, and he regards its two new stone-buttressed and crocketed buildings as splendid examples of all that is churchly: enduring and solid in a fast-moving and somewhat secular-minded society, ready to forsake completely the Puritan past. He will desire in his churches the correctness implied by a Gothic church, just as his leading parishioners will opt for Gothic-style dwellings. *Parishioners:* surely a new word in the Episcopal vocabulary, and another sign of the nuclear church, creating in itself what might be considered the ideal nation writ small: a perfect commonwealth in miniature. The renewed mind of the Episcopal Church concerned itself with the widest spectrum of human life. Here you would find the "correct" (that is, ancient) design for a baptismal font; and here, too, you will find as correct a graveyard; was it not so in England? Inside the church, enriched music complemented worship; the canticles were readily adapted to music provided by the much-improved melodeons.

The church was no longer a mere auditory. It was an organization (now said to be of divine origin) that upheld the verities of religion. In a future day parochial "guilds"—is there a more medieval word?—would enhance the centripetal force of the parish church. Hobart's High Churchmanship championed a wide range of activity in the nuclear church, and the bishop was untiring in encouraging parochial schools. In the next generation this was no longer the mark of the High Churchman; in New York, the extreme Evangelical Church of the Holy Trinity on 42d Street would sponsor a myriad of satellite organizations—schools, lodging houses, and tradesmen's club rooms. It is arguable that the institutional parish of the century's end owed its origin to Hobartian High Churchmanship, for in those great city churches we see the nuclear parish in full flower.

It is manifest that the nuclear parish provided abundant opportunity for many talents: scholarship, craftsmanship, artistry, music, even horticulture could be embraced and lifted as an offering to God. In New York, where Washington Irving, James Fenimore Cooper, the Duyckincks, and others participated in the counsels of the Episcopal Church, it is no wonder that a similar mind, informed by contemporary trends and graced by social approval, Jonathan Mayhew Wainwright, should be elected to the episcopate in 1852.

Perhaps the most celebrated example of the nuclear church was William Augustus Muhlenberg's Church of the Holy Communion on Sixth Avenue at 20th Street in Manhattan. It is well-known that here Muhlenberg envisioned a parish church that would concern itself with education, help for the poor, and, in short, be an oasis of Christian activity in the city. From this church St. Johnland and St. Luke's Hospital eventually developed. Muhlenberg treated Gotham as if it was a family ("family" was a Muhlenberg ideal; he wanted each patient in St. Luke's to be treated as a member of the family). Muhlenberg invented parochial festivals, freely adopted pictures of the Nativity and Crucifixion at the altar, flowers and music, sunrise services, and customs of his Lutheran background to the uses of the Episcopal Church.[46] He was the founder of a sisterhood, and the building next to the Church of the Holy Communion was a forerunner of what would soon become a necessity for every up-and-coming Episcopal Church: a "parish house" (words that suggest the ambitions of a nuclear church).

Much less known, but yet a perfect example of the new mode of parish life, was the Church of St. John the Evangelist in Stockport (now in the Diocese of Albany). St. John's was built by Joseph Marshall, an Englishman who set up cotton printing mills on Stockport Creek and encouraged many of his countrymen to come to work in New York. The exquisite church—it remains untouched by "improvements"—was built in 1838, just about the time mills failed after the Panic of 1837. Marshall died a debtor, but left a parish church that amply fulfilled his visions. It is a magnificent, unfussy, stately frame church, painted brown (to resemble stone). Inside, the walls are grained to simulate rich woods. The font was placed on a platform, near the door, where the Tractarians said it should be (because baptism *is* the entrance of the Church). There is a gallery for organ and octet, and the "east" wall displays the canonical Creed, Commandments, and Lord's Prayer. There is a comfortable vestry room, adequate for parochial meetings, and the church is surrounded by a cemetery complete with a lych-gate that seems transported from rural England. Once there were a rectory and a greenhouse that supplied flowers for the chancel and, probably, protected tender tubbed plants in winter. Some years later, a parish school was organized, but from the beginning the north transept of the church formed a Sunday school room (under which the founder is buried). All this was established within a few years' time. Think how exciting, how attracting, such a picturesque center could be in a mill hamlet never exceeding 500 souls. Then multiply Stockport by, perhaps, one hundred and you will see how the Episcopal Church fitted in the New York landscape. True, few churches were as well equipped as Holy Communion or St. John's. But many were in larger towns and, with their guilds and music and proper Victorian attitudes, they were able to have a much wider influence. If you would capture the spirit of the Victorian church as illustrated by the settings and ambience of church buildings, a visit to, say, St. Barnabas', Irvington, or Holy Innocents, Annandale, to Holy Innocents, Highland Falls, or Zion, Wappingers Falls, will furnish lasting impressions, as will the earlier St. James', Hyde Park, the later St. Paul's, Tivoli, and, supremely, St. Philip's, Garrison (Richard Upjohn's parish), and St. Luke's in Beacon, designed by Withers. St. James', Fordham, is another successful attempt at reproducing what people were commonly seeing in lithographs such as Nathaniel Currier made popular. These are village churches, and the idea of a village church still lingers in the American mind. Their architecture repudiates the rationalism implicit in the eighteenth-century church; all of them quiver with a fervor dear to the romantic mind. The Currier and Ives pictures fix the ideal: men and women wending their way to an ivy-covered Gothic church. This was the ideal Victorian scene, and no American body was so able to actualize all it suggested as was the Episcopal Church.

One of the seminal publications promoting the nuclear parish was Richard Upjohn's *Rural Architecture* (1852). Though some wary Episcopalians still bore a grudge against the architect for what they considered to be his high-handed promotion of the High Church ornaments at Trinity Church, his book set a reliable standard for all schools of thought. The Victorian tide was running strong in favor of arts and architecture evocative of an earlier time. Upjohn was the perfect publicist for the new mode of church building.

Richard Upjohn was born in England. In Boston, he met Jonathan Wainwright, who recruited him for work in New York. He was a faithful Episcopalian, was known by leading churchmen, and was congenial with building committees. Often he was generous in supplying plans where the church had no money to pay him. Most important, he was able to produce drawings that "any intelligent mechanic will be able to carry out."[47] His book of plans included a church, a parsonage (the word rectory wasn't much used then), a chapel, and a schoolhouse—in brief, all that our nuclear parish needed. If you will look carefully at the plans for the church you will see exactly what was happening in the Episcopal Church at mid-century. First of all, you will see three crosses on the church roof, one at each end, and a cross surmounting the pointed steeple. The church door is sited at the southwest corner of an oriented building, just as was common in old England. Inside, the chancel is raised fifteen inches above the nave, and its furniture is described by names hitherto unfamiliar in the American Church: "sedelia," "fald-stool," "stalls." There is an "altar" (of wood), and a "bishop's chair." All of these would have been unknown in an earlier time, and were even now often offensive to the embattled Low Churchman. A closer look would have made our astonished Evangelical dismiss Upjohn as an irresponsible Romanizer, for there was a credence table (always a sure sign of sacerdotalism), and a font supplied with a drain (implying an innovative baptismal theology).

Our by now apoplectic Low Churchman will flee the scene, but we may linger in Upjohn's church to perceive one or two more signs of change. There is, for instance, a shelf for books under the pew seats indicating that sometimes the parish provided prayer books; this meant the end of the centuries-old custom of bringing your own book to church. And now the pulpit, a modification of the graceful "wineglass," was reached by way of the "robing room." Upjohn would never have gone so far as to use the word "sacristy," and he may not have intended the gentlemen of the vestry to assemble in this tiny room. It was exactly what he said it was: a robing room in which the preacher might, en route from chancel to pulpit, change from surplice to gown (if such remained his practice). In other words, a pulpit reached only by way of a robing room was a nice concession to old or new custom. Upjohn had tact.

His book had a wide influence, as did pictures of the new churches then abuilding. If a building was to "look like a church" it must be in the Gothic style. No man was more responsible than Upjohn for this American idea which, despite change in taste and theology, persists to our own time. And the fact that his designs made churches look like churches so attached itself to the popular mind that even Low Church vestries (doubtless promising themselves to beware of the man) sought Upjohn's help when they built their new church. Nor were all rectors appreciative of Upjohn's attempts to introduce new furnishings in the church. One clergyman for whom he had designed a church wrote to him, about 1850:

> I *will* not use a lectern, and I *will* not hold a book in my hand. I want a good serviceable Reading Desk . . . erected in front of the Chancel pointing west, not less than six feet in width, three feet six inches high from the floor on which the minister stands, with a board in

front wide enough to hold a folio Bible of the largest sort, and a folio prayerbook.[48]

The same man insisted on a closed box rector's pew, and no credence table ("it is a perfectly useless thing").[49] And the Bishop's chair "*must* be on the north side of the altar, and face not *in,* towards *it,* but *out,* towards the people," and to summarize his demands the irate rector flung at Upjohn, "I do not know what medieval usage may recommend, and care as little."[50]

Even though he encountered this kind of opposition during his practice, Richard Upjohn and his son (who succeeded him in the firm) accumulated an impressive list of New York churches. Beginning with the early Trinity, Holy Communion, and Ascension in the city, Bethesda in Saratoga Springs, Christ Church and Grace Church in Brooklyn, St. Thomas, Amenia Union, they proceeded to complete more than thirty-eight churches in what is now the Diocese of New York.

10

Horatio Potter: From Farm to Fifth Avenue

*A spirit of earnest Christian activity seems to be re-
viving among us.*

—HORATIO POTTER

Horatio Potter was born February 9, 1802, at LaGrange, New York, a
farming hamlet southeast of Poughkeepsie. That area had been settled
by Quakers at the end of the eighteenth century, and among them were
the Potters, who moved over from Rhode Island. It is not irrelevant to
this history to note that Horatio Potter was the first Bishop of New York
to have grown up in rural America, for when, much later, people tended
to be overly optimistic about small churches supporting themselves,
the farm-bred Potter knew better. He was the last of ten children—his
immediately older brother, Alonzo, became Bishop of Pennsylvania,
and was father of Henry C. Potter—and while the Potters were not poor,
they must needs be prudent. *Prudent!* That is a key word to understanding the Potters.

He was educated in the country schools, we suppose, to a level that
enabled him to enter Union College in Schenectady, from which he
graduated in 1826. He was made a deacon in 1827, without benefit of
seminary training, and priest the next year. He looked forward to life as
a teacher, but spent the first year of his ministry as rector of Trinity
Church, Saco, Maine. He then went to Trinity College, Hartford, where
he was professor of mathematics and natural philosophy for five years.
In 1833 he was called to be rector of St. Peter's Church in Albany,
where he remained until elected Provisional Bishop of New York on
the eighth ballot in 1854.

Many years later, the bishop is recorded as saying he "never med-
dled with other people's affairs" while rector of St. Peter's. Here is
another key to understanding him, for this suggests hard work in his
own appointed duties and an avoidance of the strife that had beset the

diocese since his institution at St. Peter's by Bishop Onderdonk. Potter's name is not prominent in diocesan affairs until shortly before his election, but his abilities had already commended him to other dioceses searching for a bishop, and he was "several times" mentioned for vacancies.

What was this greatest city of the nation like when Horatio Potter was summoned from Albany to be the second Provisional Bishop of New York? Perhaps the new bishop already knew about the busy department stores: A. T. Stewart's, Lord and Taylor, R. H. Macy, and Lewis and Conger. He might also know about the prominent commission merchants who received fruits and vegetables sent downriver for sale in the city. And he would also know about the auctioneers, important men who managed the sales on the vast imports coming from Europe, Asia, South America. But now that railroads augmented the river's supply of American-made goods that came into the city, businessmen were specializing. Gone were the days when an up-and-coming city merchant paced the dock waiting for ships that would bring his firm sugar, rum, coffee, flour, pimento, oak staves, Indian meal, bread, onions, mahogany, linen, potash, beeswax, bamboo blinds, and "sattin Breeches."[1] Now he might deal specifically in, say, the mahogany the many able cabinetmakers in the city required. By 1860, two-thirds of the country's imports and one-third of its exports passed through the Narrows. American seamen had earned a worldwide reputation as able and hard-driving.

Croton River water came to the city by way of bored logs, fitted together. Wells were practically forbidden, poisoned because the city had not yet found a mode of sewage disposal. There were no uniformed police until 1845, and only then were the constables made to wear uniforms so that they could not so easily join in the brawls they were sent out to subdue. The Irish immigrants had occasioned fierce street fights (though, on the whole, the Irish showed a remarkable ability to conform to the ways of the older Americans). It had been fairly easy for the recent immigrants to arrive in New York; bunk passage was about $20 (but luxury cabins might cost as much as $150).

New York City was especially strong in two mercantile areas: textiles and metal products from England. By 1860, most Americans bought their clothes through New York firms. The merchants in Manhattan had a virtual monopoly on English woolens and finished cottons, on German and Irish linens, and silk and laces from France. Since much southern cotton was transshipped in New York—thus giving New Yorkers a double chance at the business—many southern businessmen spent part of their time in the city or its suburbs. Their collective influence on New York's commerce goes far to explain the city's reluctance to support the first administration of Abraham Lincoln.

Metal products from Birmingham in England were cheaper than similar American goods, and when the Crimean War used many ships hitherto in the American trade, these imports could be shipped in American bottoms. Albany and Troy, however, seemed to reserve unto themselves the prominence in stove manufacturies. And then there were the shipyards across the East River, using more and more hardware until the day when entire hulls would be sheathed in metal.

From the days of Provoost and earlier, New York City had its centers of speculation. By 1840 the stock exchanges were firmly established (if not always as firmly controlled), and many a shrewd lad came in from the country and made his fortune in the environs of Wall Street. And many lost their riches in the Panic of 1857, which, as it happened, introduced yet another set of new men who bought, sold, scalped and were scalped, retired rich or fell into the already congested streets. Whether a man was wealthy or starving, he could be sure of one thing: there was a great deal of money in New York. By 1855 there were an estimated 214,000 workers in 24,000 places making goods worth more than $317,000,000.

All this material prosperity demanded a corresponding spiritual development. One historian finds reason to assert that "the religious history of New York between 1825 and 1860 is one of the most fascinating chapters in the history of Christian expansion."[2] The Episcopal Church was a major beneficiary of this restless searching as, at another extreme, were the adherents of Mormonism, Millerism in the 1840s, and Spiritualism in the 1850s. It is arguable that John Henry Hobart was but the Episcopalian symbol of the Second Awakening of the 1820s which saw significant revivals in all the manor churches leading to "active" parishes, Sunday schools, enthusiasm for spiritual reform, and a new interest in promoting missions domestic and foreign. We have already seen the Episcopal Church's application of these Second Awakening ideals. Less obvious in the Episcopal Church, however, were the concomitant movements that inevitably followed. The temperance movement began to succeed when some of the churches took it seriously; it has been wondered if Onderdonk's miseries had been occasioned by a general repugnance for liquor that took hold in the mid-1840s when the first local option law was enacted. Abolition and the rights of women were also subjects openly debated in the wake of the Second Awakening. (Only after 1848 did married women in New York share the same inheritance rights as were allowed single women.) As for abolition, by the 1850s there were divisions in the Methodist and Presbyterian churches over the subject.

The wily Horatio Potter may have regarded these as "other people's affairs" and taken care to avoid them. Perhaps we should excuse him on the grounds that his primary task was to be a bishop—and only a provisional bishop at that—in a diocese long disturbed by the suspension of one bishop and saddened by the premature death of another. Also, the man had undergone a rough transplanting. He could remember pleasant days in a parish rectory with a wife (now dead) and children (now also gone) in provincial Albany, where laurels came naturally to a prominent city minister.

He was consecrated in Trinity Church on November 22, 1854. It is said that eleven bishops were present, and that seven participated in the laying on of hands. As far as we know, Onderdonk was not present; nor was he listed among the clergy in the diocesan *Journals*. Potter seems to have had a reputation for poor health, and it may well be that many of those present in Trinity Church that morning wondered if he, like his predecessor Wainwright, would go to an early grave. As it turned out, they need not have worried on that score!

Horatio Potter was the first of New York's bishops who hadn't ever had official ties with Trinity Church. All his predecessors had been assistant ministers at the old church, and three—Provoost, Moore, and Hobart—had been rector there. The rector at this time was the aged William Berrian; it was under his leadership that Trinity Church, now in a neighborhood decidedly unresidential, further developed its policy of parochial chapels. Richard Upjohn had recently completed Trinity Chapel in 25th Street; the rectory would be next door. The northward move is a steady theme in the nineteenth century. "Old Trinity" (scarcely twenty years up, in 1855) would serve less and less as the church where significant diocesan ceremonies would take place. Other churches, notably St. John's Chapel, were preempted. This was a beautiful, large edifice, designed by Isaac and John McComb and built facing a park named Hudson Square. Morgan Dix remembered that

> the place became the Court end of the town. St. John's Chapel faced a charming pleasure-ground in which grew noble trees, representing almost every variety found in our native forests. This park was surrounded by the residences of the wealthiest and most fashionable members of New York society; and on the east side was one of the noblest ecclesiastical edifices in the city with lofty spire, and deep porch receding from its massive colonnade of stone, a building still [in 1900] imposing, and admired even in its slow delapidation and decay.[3]

It is, perhaps, necessary to say here that when the "most fashionable members of New York society" began to desert the St. John's neighborhood, Trinity Church sold it and its bucolic park to the New York Central Railroad. A freight terminal was built there and, as Dix indicates, St. John's Chapel fell into gradual disintegration. But it was still beautiful when it was razed in 1918.

St. John's Chapel was for many years the central meeting place for New York's Episcopalians. It was abandoned in the city's northward march, leaving unanswered a moot question: should not the Diocese of New York have a permanent, central church, perhaps a cathedral? Horatio Potter would answer that question, but not as early as 1855.

The episcopate of Jonathan M. Wainwright had healed beyond the proportion of its brevity. Now it was clear that Horatio Potter must proceed to lead the diocese. He must familiarize himself with its strengths and weaknesses, point new paths. A man of fifty-three can well do this, especially when empowered with Potter's wisdom and balance. But first, he must find the materials at hand. To begin, there were 20,000 communicants in the diocese and 304 clergymen. Independent funds promoted various Church agencies and causes. The bishop of the diocese was, ex officio, a participant in most of these although, as we have seen, some funding groups had been established precisely to thwart the dominance of Onderdonk. We are speaking about a time prior to the day when there would be a definite organization on a diocesan level. Horatio Potter needed the help of semiautonomous well-disposed forces. The Society for the Promotion of Religion and Learning, for instance, helped support forty-nine students in the General Theological Seminary, and provided them with books, as it would do for generations to come. Diocesan missions were at this time financed by means of a "missionary agent" who, under the direction of the bishop, went about appealing for funds to support seventy stations in twenty-seven counties. The results of his efforts were gratifying, it was said. Grants ranging between $100 and $300 were allotted the clergy in the missions. (This would not include James Starr Clark and George Seymour in Dutchess County, for they were employed by John Bard of Annandale.) The bishop's salary was to be paid from the Episcopal Fund, and it was hoped that the principal would one day amount to $150,000. Trinity Church offered $20,000 on condition that another $50,000 was subscribed by other churches. When this didn't happen, it was determined to assess "the churches in all portions of the Diocese."

Some parishes offered "interest" on what they supposed they ought to pay, and this was a help. But there arose the question, which bishop should receive the money? For there were two: the unresigned Bishop Onderdonk and the Provisional Bishop Potter. Bishop Potter's salary was set at $6,000—a very lordly sum. But there was the prior claim of Bishop Onderdonk. The diocesan convention of 1855 was considerably upset when it was discovered that there was only $1,900 in

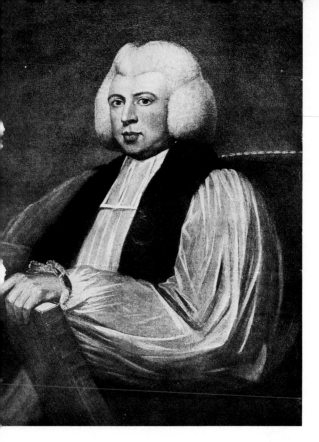

Samuel Provoost, first Bishop of New York (consecrated 1787 in London). His abilities and services as citizen and churchman were to be discounted as the nation and Church entered a century whose ways would be far different from those of Provoost's youth, yet he is the man who saved Trinity's wealth and guided it toward its future generosity.

Benjamin Moore, second Bishop of New York (1801–1816). Though he "preached and prayed against us" during the War of Independence, his prominence at Trinity Church and his gentleness made him the natural successor of Provoost; nevertheless, the younger clergy chafed under his mere benignity.

John Henry Hobart.

John Henry Hobart, third Bishop of New York (1816–1830). His energies were lavished upon popularizing the Episcopal Church throughout the growing regions of New York State in an era of religious revival.

Benjamin T. Onderdonk, fourth Bishop of New York. Consecrated in 1830 to succeed the celebrated Hobart, he supervised the growth of New York to becoming the premier diocese of the Church; unfortunately, his obstinate naiveté was turned against him when his enemies sought redress.

*Benj. T. Onderdonk
Bishop of New York*

Horatio Potter, sixth Bishop of New York (1861–1887). Respected for "minding his own affairs" as well as for his obvious ability as rector of St. Peter's, Albany, he was elected Provisional Bishop in 1854 and proceeded to administer the diocese longer than any other man.

Jonathan M. Wainwright, Provisional Bishop (1852–1854). A compromise choice, his single-minded labors for the recovery of the diocese after its eight years without a bishop astonished his friends, silenced his detractors, and resulted in his early death.

Henry Codman Potter, seventh
Bishop of New York (1887–1908).
He was considered the city's First Citizen and enjoyed the reputation of
metropolitan prelate; but in fact he
preferred to be in the small churches
of upstate New York.

David Hummel Greer, eighth Bishop of
New York (1908–1919). A resourceful
preacher and thinker considered a peer of the
great Phillips Brooks, and an administrator
of wide ability, he spent his last years somewhat unwillingly overseeing the development of Cathedral Close.

Charles Sumner Burch, ninth Bishop of New
York (1919–1920). He was ordained at an age
when most of his contemporaries were considering retirement, and his abilities quickly
brought him into prominence in New York.

William Thomas Manning, tenth Bishop of New York (1921–1946). He seemed to play the role of medieval prelate in Gotham, but those who knew him best recognized the rightness of his judgments.

Charles Kendall Gilbert, eleventh Bishop of New York (1947–1950). He served sixteen years as Suffragan and then surprised everyone by choosing to become Manning's successor. It was a wise decision.

Horace William Baden Donegan, twelfth
Bishop of New York (1950–1972).
During his episcopate, Church and society
experienced incredible changes.

Paul Moore, Jr., thirteenth Bishop
of New York (1972–   ).

St. Paul's Chapel of Trinity Parish was barely ten years old when it survived the fire of 1777, and it was the site of the first diocesan conventions. In those days the pulpit was centrally located under the chancel arch.

St. Luke's Church, Somers, was organized about 1830, and the church built in 1842 in a style that usually pleases American churchgoers—and always dismayed Bishop Onderdonk.

The second floating Church of Our Savior, berthed in the East River. It was launched by the Seamen's Church Institute in 1846, and transferred to the Archdeaconry of Richmond in 1910.

St. Thomas Church, New Windsor, was built in 1848. It is a significant landmark in American ecclesiastical architecture because it quickly followed St. James the Less, Philadelphia, in attempting to copy exactly an English parish church. The plans may have been furnished by John W. Priest, a neighboring architect who also designed St. John's Church, Cornwall.

St. Thomas Church, Amenia Union, built 1849–51 from innovative plans provided by the elder Upjohn.

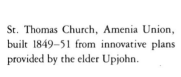

St. Barnabas' Church, Irvington. The original design was by Richard Upjohn at the urging of John McVickar, who organized the parish in 1858, hoping to establish a pre-seminary college there.

St. Luke's Church, Beacon. Designers Vaux and Withers were careful to place the main door in the "correct English" location on the south side, and the arboreal-minded Sargent family completed the perfect mid-Victorian setting by planting specimen shade trees in the churchyard.

The Free Church of St. John the Evangelist, Barrytown, was built because its donor believed that those who lived within two miles of her estate should never "suffer for want of the necessities of life, and that they should be encouraged to worship." She therefore sent a carry-all such as is described in Edith Wharton's *House of Mirth* to transport parishioners to service, and engaged Bishop Henry C. Potter's brother to design the church.

Manhattan's Church of the Epiphany, located on York Avenue where Bishop Manning said it should be. Architects: Wyeth and King.

St. Gregory's Church, Woodstock, a contemporary church design such as was fostered by the Cornerstone Campaign after the Second World War.

Nave of the Cathedral of St. John the Divine, opened for use just before Pearl Harbor after fifty years of building; the change in architectural styles is manifest in this photograph, as is the trend in liturgical practice suggested by the two altars.

the Episcopal Fund. Predictably, Henry Anthon moved that all of it should go to Bishop Potter; let Trinity Church undertake to support Onderdonk, read the motion, since he had "for so many years been a faithful minister there."[4] The motion was lost, but the sarcasm was not. John Jay, no supporter of Bishop Onderdonk, rose to speak about the insufficient support of the "clergy generally in the rural districts, and for a smaller number in the cities." This, he said, was "unjust to the Reverend Clergy and unworthy of the laity." The result of the pro-longed discussion was a potpourri of pleasant intentions: each parish should purchase a "glebe and parsonage," insure the rector's life, increase his salary, and pay him in advance, quarterly.

When Horatio Potter rose to address the convention, he could review with considerable pride the accomplishments of his first year as provisional bishop. To begin with, the sense of peace bequeathed by Wainwright still prevailed. And Potter's energies had about equaled those of his lamented predecessor. He had traveled perhaps 9,000 miles and visited two-thirds of the parishes. More than 1,800 persons had been confirmed. In a moment most politic, Bishop Potter stated that the episcopate is a task "at which we must remain until summoned away from it by death." That ever-so-innocent statement served to grasp the offensive away from any who held Potter to be a usurper. The man was very canny. He proceeded to speak to those who would divide the diocese: "For a person possessing a fair amount of energy and facility in the dispatch of business and correspondence, there is nothing in the administration of such a Diocese as this that need, of necessity, greatly oppress the mind or exhaust the strength" of its bishop. It was John C. Spencer of Potter's own St. Peter's Church, Albany, who had first proposed again dividing the diocese in 1851; had the erstwhile rector once encouraged his leading layman to do that which he now opposed? Whatever Potter's secret ambitions had once been, he could be proud of his first year's accomplishments.

He had no staff, no secretary, no tried-and-true helpers at hand whose perfect judgment of all things from Staten Island to Canada, Montauk to Syracuse, would save him from grave blunders. In that first address he mentioned only two prevailing problems: the predicament of smaller churches, and the deleterious effects of the Oxford Movement in New York. He said that there would always be churches so small that they could not support themselves, and therefore they would require funds from other churches. As for the Oxford troubles, the bishop said that no "great movement" in the Church was ever without its excesses. He praised Tractarianism as "energetic" and "important," and (to calm those who feared yet more defections to the Church of Rome) he had reason to believe that "large numbers of Roman Catholic clergy and laity have now conformed to the Anglican Church." This is perhaps the first use of the word *Anglican* in a diocesan address, and astute auditors may have wondered where these "large numbers" who had joined their Church were.

It was a salutory address. The bishop minimized the burdens of his office, and he dismissed the dangers of the Oxford Movement because, as he rightly declared, there were much larger concerns at hand. The next year he was more direct. He related the expected statistics about visitations (200 during the preceding year), and confirmations (2,496), and then unburdened himself of his thoughts to this

> grand Council of the Church, consisting of scarcely less than a thou-sand persons, *when all are present,* convened in the great central city of the Union representing a Diocese long since become conspicuous not more for her magnitude and position than by the amount of abil-ity usually found among her members.[5]

While those delegates were still preening their feathers at these com-pliments, they heard the bishop say that Church extension was not keeping up with the growth of the State of New York. "Luxury and extravagance are growing apace," said this scion of Quaker forebears. "Can we say that we are doing all we ought to do to supply this city with houses of worship, with faithful ministers? Can we say that we are doing all we ought to do to uphold the hands of the Missionary Com-mittee of the Diocese?" The diocese had been most casual about for-eign missions, too: "We in this country are indebted, under God, to a foreign Church—we have robbed Africa of its sons and daughters—we have sent our pestilential commerce to corrupt and half-depopulate some of the islands of the ocean—we are debtors to all on foreign shores." Church missions, domestic and foreign, were important and deserved more support than that provided by "a few general collec-tions loosely made."[6]

There was a General Convention in the year 1856, and for the Diocese of New York its primary importance may have been the report of a special committee appointed earlier to consider the "Memorial" presented by the Rev. William Augustus Muhlenberg of Sixth Avenue's Church of the Holy Communion in the preceding General Convention. Muhlenberg, as we know, was the charming and innovative rector who, with some of his friends, believed the entire nation required a tradi-tionally ordained ministry that would function in a manner more com-prehensive than that presently afforded by the Episcopal Church. Could not men be ordained who, assenting to the Scriptures, the Creeds, the two Gospel sacraments, and the "Pauline" understanding of grace, might find a God-given work beyond the confines of the Episcopal Church? Let them be ordained, said the Memorialists, and let them report every third year to the bishop who had ordained them.

The Memorial was vaguely worded, and many Episcopalians who were impressed by the names of the signers tried to take it seriously but failed to grasp exactly what was proposed. The result was a series of recommendations by General Convention aimed at what we today would call Church renewal. These included suggested improvements in Sunday worship and Christian education in the parishes. Significantly, the ministry of women was recognized as an unused, even unwanted, resource in the Church.

Horatio Potter was as vague about the proposal as was the Memorial itself, but the possibility of women working in the Episcopal Church fixed upon his practical mind. Muhlenberg's Sisterhood at the Church of the Holy Communion was already a celebrated thing in the Church. Patterning them after the Kaiserweith Deaconesses, Muhlenberg's Lutheran background enabled him to take ecclesiastical risks—and get away with it! When he founded St. Luke's Hospital in 1850, his women workers in the parish became notable pioneers in that important enterprise. Potter watched the Muhlenberg experiment and waited. The field was new, untried and, frankly, vulnerable to the same Protestant hostilities that had wrought punishment upon the Onderdonks. Except for occasional bazaars where needlework was sold, women had never been called upon to do much in the American Church. It had been thought noteworthy, even shocking, when Wainwright appointed a Board of Ladies to help oversee the Charity School established at Grace Church in 1824. Perhaps Horatio Potter was already aware that now, in the 1850s, shops and stores were offering many goods hitherto available only through the distaff in their homes, that more women now had more free time. If he and other Church leaders had thought deeply about this nineteenth-century phenomenon, they would have realized changes the Church could have utilized as well as graced.

Let us move further, to 1859. Here we will find one opportunity and two problems that would require future settlement: the opportunity was St. Stephen's College; the problems were division of the diocese and the perennial awkwardness of the Onderdonk suspension. We will consider the college in greater detail in subsequent pages of this history, but it must be said here that the college was an outgrowth of the Society for the Promotion of Religion and Learning. In 1859, the Society was helping to support men studying for Holy Orders in the General Seminary, Hobart, Trinity, Columbia, and New York University. Other men were enrolled in secondary schools and with private tutors. The Society, it was announced, was assisted "in carrying out the plans" of a Training School for men preparing to enter General Seminary by a "warm hearted and liberal churchman of the Diocese," John Bard, who had given land and buildings at Annandale on the Hudson River.

There were as yet no clear plans for a college. The idea was mainly an outgrowth of independent missionary activity in the Hudson Valley. The Memorialists, and many other Episcopalians, believed education desirable. John Bard's devotion led him to found schools and churches near his riverfront estate. He was encouraged to do this by a neighboring rector, Henry DeKoven, who will now detain us for a moment, not only because he was older brother of the saintly James and father of the composer Reginald but, more to the point, because after building Christ Church in Red Hook village he engaged a curate, Frederick Sill, who perhaps overmuch shared DeKoven's enthusiasm for Church extension. For, after "the Reverend H. DeKoven, family and servants took their departure from Boston for Europe" for a two-year grand tour, Sill initiated services in Clermont, Rock City, and Pine Plains. Thus, when the rector of Red Hook returned from Europe he was shocked to find himself in charge of not one, but four congregations. He very soon parted company with his energetic curate, and then, perhaps overwhelmed by the prospect of work awaiting him, resigned Red Hook in the year we are considering, 1859. It should be added that two of the four congregations survived.

This digression suggests that the growth of the Episcopal Church in even the smallest hamlets was regarded as something feasible. Expansion of the Church was "in the air," and statistics are quite to the point: thirty-four congregations were gathered regularly between 1855 and 1860 in the present Diocese of New York. Add to that number nine congregations in the present Diocese of Albany, an estimated twelve on Long Island, and a modest five in what is now the Diocese of Central New York, and the total is sixty new congregations in a span of five years. The evidence increasingly pointed toward a division of the diocese and, to many, it convincingly pointed to the reinstatement of Bishop Onderdonk.

Bishop Potter spoke in his 1859 convention address to the one possibility, and obliquely to the other. He approached the matters with stealth, beginning with an account of the flourishing Church in New York City: new Trinity Chapel was thronged; Holy Apostles, Transfiguration, the Church of the Incarnation, St. Peter's, Christ Church were all enlarged, or reporting much growth; there were encouraging signs at St. John Baptist, Advent, and at St. Timothy and Zion. Lest New York Episcopalianism be identified too much with the frivolities of the "Court side of town," St. Luke's Hospital should be considered, for there might be seen suffering every hour of the day: "Go, ye giddy sons and daughters of pleasure and see what human life is in another of its

aspects," said the bishop. He acknowledged increased Lenten attendance in Episcopal churches and the "excitements in other bodies"
due to the current religious revival and then, having said what everyone
present wanted to hear, he proceeded to say what many men present
did *not* want to hear: "What the Bishop has to do in the way of visiting,
in summer, in the interior of the Diocese is little more than an agreeable change and refreshment after the town work of winter and spring
[and he had] done each year an amount of work which, I venture to say,
has been fully equal to any done in the same by any of my very laborous
predecessors." [7] If the diocese seemed overlarge, the answer wasn't
more bishops, but more money, and the bishop warmed to his subject
by saying that five or ten new missionaries could be used immediately
to work under his personal direction if the money was forthcoming.
Since no such funds were in sight, there was no reason to think that
northern New York would prosper as a separate diocese as had Western
New York after 1838. There! he had said it: Horatio Potter remained
firmly opposed to carving a northern diocese from what was left of the
Diocese of New York. He was certain such a diocese could not survive.

He was, necessarily, less candid about the specter of Bishop Onderdonk. The suspended bishop had borne his long punishment in a
stoic manner. Except for his circle of very loyal friends, he was conveniently forgotten by much of the diocese, though it must be admitted
that the Onderdonk case itself was indeed well remembered.

We come, then, to the final phase of the Onderdonk tragedy. After
the bishop's suspension the contest had been between those who believed the man guilty and justly ousted and those who, with equal
conviction, believed him innocent and the victim of partisanship. A
middle shade of opinion not immdiately discernible when the sentence was imposed in 1845 eventually appeared, but very soon it was
obvious that none but his most die-hard supporters thought that Onderdonk could ever again act as the Bishop of New York. General Convention's new canon allowing the election of a provisional bishop
further weakened Onderdonk's prospects. Wainwright's mediating
mildness and Horatio Potter's tactful statesmanship put an end to any
hopes the suspended bishop might still entertain. But yet *he* was the
Bishop of New York and whoever else might function in his place was
obliged to use the style "Provisional."

There had been informal discussions about the anomaly, and they
surfaced at the diocesan convention in September 1859. For reasons
not now clear, Francis Hawks, Henry Anthon, and Alexander Vinton
agreed to work toward Onderdonk's restoration. Not surprisingly,
Anthon soon withdrew from the undertaking and stated Onderdonk
should cease hoping for the impossible: "Persistence cannot restore

public confidence and reputation," he declared.[8] George Templeton Strong shrewdly guessed "it is part of the old scheme" of dividing the diocese, with the understanding that Potter would take the Albany area.[9] The diarist, loyal to the bishop but sensible about the situation, probably confided to his journal the clearest summary of the affair ever given: the bishop had been guilty of "certain ill-bred familiarities and caressings that meant nothing," but now, since "nine-tenths of the community" acquiesced in the suspension it "would only be a scandal and an offence" to restore him at this late date.[10]

Not everyone could have been as dispassionate as this diarist who so often noted the Trollopian affairs of the Episcopal Church he loved and served so well. Certainly Bishop Potter wasn't now relishing a return to Albany, and in a sense it was the provisional bishop who closed the door on Onderdonk. For, encouraged by Hawks, the aging bishop made one final, pathetic gesture of appeal. He stated that, if reinstated, he would turn over to Potter all administrative duties of the diocese, and he would refrain from visiting any parishes where he would be unwelcome.[11] He would do all in his power to make Potter's delicate position easy. These were the general agreements between Hawks and Onderdonk in July 1859. The next month, Hawks and William Eigenbrodt of the General Seminary conferred with the bishop, whom they had not seen for some time. Hawks reported that he was "very subdued and Christian-like, he seemed to me to be a different man from what he was years ago."[12] In his irenic mood, Bishop Onderdonk agreed to make his own renewed plea to the House of Bishops.

So he played his last card. He wrote the House (some of whose members had been his judges and jury) that his conduct had indeed been censurable. He said he knew he had brought reproach upon the Church and, of course, deserved to be disciplined. He expressed "sincere, penitent sorrow" for any wrong he might have done. Nevertheless, the House of Bishops declined to lift the sentence. In the ballot, Horato Potter did signally what he had all along done inferentially: he abstained from voting. It is a safe guess that, had Potter argued in favor of the remission, Onderdonk would have been reinstated.

Bishop Onderdonk lived on. "Often have I seen him on his churchward way," said an observer,

> walking with a downcast look, as if unwilling to attract attention, and saluting only those who spoke first to him; but then the salute was returned by him with a genial warmth, tinged with sadness which went at once to the heart.[13]

To someone requesting genealogical information, the bishop wrote:

... The years of severe trial which have been allotted to me, have yet, through the mercy of my Heavenly Father, often seen me greatly comforted and cheered by the kindness of friends, whom I continue to find every now and then, in unexpected quarters, and often in hitherto unknown persons. It is an unspeakable consolation to have reason to believe that many prayers are offered in my behalf, for I indeed feel that I need them.[14]

He died, quite unexpectedly, in his seventieth year on April 30, 1861. His funeral at Trinity Church was attended by crowds "that filled the church and overflowed into the churchyard and into the public streets."[15] Ever loyal Samuel Seabury of General Seminary preached at the service and used as his text the words Onderdonk himself had chosen at Hobart's obsequies: "He was a burning and a shining light, and ye were willing for a season to rejoice in his light." But George Templeton Strong wrote it plainer in his diary: "Died this morning, poor old Bishop Benjamin Treadwell Onderdonk who just missed a great career and an honored name."[16]

SISTERHOODS

We have seen that William A. Muhlenberg at the innovative Church of the Holy Communion on Sixth Avenue envisioned a band of women workers who would visit tenements, seek out and help the poor and sick, and teach in the Sunday school. It may be said that the charming rector's wisdom did not equal his energy, and the Church is all the better for that. Always ready to formalize his schemes before they were well thought ought, Muhlenberg had, in 1845, conducted a service of "Dedication" in which Miss Anne Ayres pledged herself to Christian service. She was joined by several other women, and in 1852 a "Sisterhood" was formally acknowledged. When Dr. Muhlenberg disclaimed any intentions of founding a convent, Protestant apprehensions in the Episcopal Church calmed. His "Sisters" were to make none of the traditional vows and, in particular, it was made known that there was to be no profession of lifetime commitment. It was this vow that so aggravated Protestant convictions.

By 1856 the Sisters of the Holy Communion (as they were often called) had added to their work a dispensary and infirmary. This caught the public's imagination and, the next year, the indefatigable Muhlenberg was able to gather enough support and money to build a four-story hospital on Fifth Avenue at 54th Street; it was named St. Luke's Hospital. The architect, John W. Ketch, followed Muhlenberg's ideas of what *this* hospital was to be: the wards opened into the central chapel, the institution was to be the ideal Christian family writ big, with Dr. Muhlenberg himself the paterfamilias, and the Sisters of the Holy Communion, well—sisters. The hospital grounds were like those of a Victorian mansion; there were shrubs and flower beds and shade trees and a gazebo. There was a small conservatory but, in time, it became the pleasant custom for New Yorkers to inundate the hospital with flowers for the patients, so that children carrying Easter flowers to St. Luke's on Fifth Avenue is said to have been the origin of New York's "Easter Parade." The hospital was demolished in 1896, after the new St. Luke's was built north of the cathedral on Morningside Heights.

When Dr. Muhlenberg moved into his quarters at the hospital, he was fulfilling his stated role as head of the St. Luke's family. The Sisters were also in residence there, and for a year or so all went well enough under the direction of Sister Ann Ayres. Then, problems inherent in Muhlenberg's scheme for the Sisterhood emerged. Some of the Sisters, notably Jane Haight from Catskill and Harriet Cannon from Connecticut, desired a formalized conventual life; Sister Anne Ayres opposed them in what must have been, at least partially, personal differences arising from the stress of responsibilities in the hospital. Muhlenberg, apparently fearing he would have irreconcilable squabbles on his hands and probably lose capable Sister Anne in the bargain, suddenly terminated the Sisterhood. In fact, he had never contemplated lifetime vows for those Sisters!

Four Sisters were thus forced to withdraw from St. Luke's. For a short time they dispersed; a providential situation reassembled them. Whether they appealed to Bishop Potter, or whether their plight and hopes were generally known, we cannot tell, but it happened that in the spring of 1863 the House of Mercy needed new leadership. The House was the former Howland mansion, a ponderous Greek revival structure somewhat the worse for disrepair and neglect. Mrs. William Richmond (sister-in-law of James, Bishop Onderdonk's adversary) had established there a home for neglected, derelict girls. Unfortunately, Mrs. Richmond's abilities did not match her enthusiasms, and when her health failed even she realized help was necessary. Who could be better than the deposed Holy Communion Sisters? On the first day of September 1863, the "Sisters of St. Catherine" (as they then were called) took charge of the House of Mercy. They were then Jane Haight, Harriet Cannon, and Mary Heartt. Sister Jane, their de facto leading spirit at this time, insisted that Mrs. Richmond leave the House of Mercy entirely to the Sisters. In doing this, it was made clear that henceforth the Sisters would be an independent group. The report of the House of Mercy for 1863 reads:

> This institution furnishes a home for girls in need of attention; is situated on the banks of the Hudson River at the foot of 86th Street, being in possession of ten lots of ground and a commodious house. There are accommodations for eighty inmates, although the largest number yet cared for has been about forty. Mrs. Richmond, the founder and long the superintendent of the Institution, has recently resigned her charge to a Sisterhood, who take the internal management of the House. A committee of ladies from many of our City Churches render valuable assistance.[17]

About this time the Rev. Edward Folsom Baker offered his assistance and, apparently at the Sisters' urging, compiled a service for their forthcoming profession.

This quickly brought Bishop Potter into the picture. He had watched, cautiously, the developments that took the Sisters from St. Luke's Hospital to the House of Mercy. He was probably quite undecided in his mind as to whether the Sisters should adopt a conventual life, or whether the role of women Church workers was preferable. A pragmatic man, Potter never ventured on unsure ground, and his wisdom led him to wait and see what happened. But now rumors said the Sisters contemplated a lifetime profession, with vows taken in a semipublic service. The bishop may already have had fears that the Sisters were interesting themselves in rites not entirely congenial to most Episcopalians; perhaps the rector in Catskill had informed him that Jane Haight had left St. Luke's Church there because its services weren't sufficiently "High." So Bishop Potter wrote to the Rev. Edward F. Baker, "I now hear that something very formal and somewhat peculiar is proposed to be used on occasion of the introduction of a new member into the Sisterhood, and that a number of persons have been invited to be present ... The question of a form of initiation has occupied the anxious attention of other Bishops." But when Bishop Potter was shown the order of service, he agreed to all "the Christian Ladies now in charge of the inmates of the House of Mercy propose."[18] In fact, the bishop "performed the service of Reception" himself, in St. Michael's Church in 99th Street, having been assured the event would be "kept very quiet."[19]

Perhaps to further protect himself, Bishop Potter appointed a committee of five city rectors to advise him. None of the five could be expected to oppose a Sisterhood. First of all, there was Isaac Henry Tuttle of St. Luke's, Hudson Street; he would for a time serve as the Sisters' pastor—hardly an opponent. Morgan Dix of Trinity Parish was considered the enfant terrible of High Churchism, and Arthur Cleveland Coxe was sometimes considered the High Church poet laureate. Abram Littlejohn of Holy Trinity, Brooklyn, was not known to oppose, and Thomas McClure Peters of St. Michael's was the prime agent of the

Sisters' going to the House of Mercy, and it was he who lent St. Michael's for the "service of Reception." This committee, then, would strengthen Bishop Potter's conviction that the Sisters would be a significant help in the Church in New York and, in addition, provide him with the counsel such a committee could give. The result, in response to questions the bishop himself had asked, was that Bishop Potter should be visitor of the new community, that he should appoint a chaplain for the Sisters, that a "suitable and uniform habit be adopted," and a "code of Rules subject to the Bishop's approval" should be speedily drawn up. In this way, and with these recommendations, the Church in New York sought to find a solid path for its indigenous Sisterhood. As we shall see, several years later another community would seek its foundations from the Community of St. John Baptist at Clewer, in England.

The Community of St. Mary, as it was soon known ("St. Catherine's" being discarded), shortly felt itself qualified to assume work beyond the House of Mercy. In October 1864, the Sisters took charge of the Sheltering Arms of Jesus; eight months later, they added St. Barnabas' House to their responsibilities. These might have been the beginnings of vast growth but, as it happened, so many Episcopalians were said to object to the "practices and usages" of the Sisterhood of St. Mary that work in the Sheltering Arms was given up in 1870, and at St. Barnabas' House even earlier. Thereafter, the Sisters concentrated on the House of Mercy and St. Mary's School in 46th Street. In 1872 the convent property on Mt. St. Gabriel was purchased, and there architects Henry M. Congdon and Ralph Adams Cram would in time design convent and school respectively.

Bishop Horatio Potter's lengthy convention address in 1864 included mention "of several of those Christian women who were formerly so well known and so esteemed for their good works in St. Luke's Hospital . . . [That confirmation service] which interested and touched me most deeply was the confirmation administered to twelve weeping penitents in the hallowed little chapel in the House of Mercy." [20] Speaking of the Sisters' innovative role in the Episcopal Church, the bishop warmed to his subject, making it quite clear that he stood behind them. What critic stood ready to undertake this work? he asked.

> The care and responsibility rests now mainly upon these Christian women. Shall they be chilled and discouraged for lack of sympathy and support? Shall they and their poor inmates be starved for want of some of the crumbs which, in this great city, fall from the Rich Man's table? Shall they be neglected and forgotten because they lead a recluse life, devoted to their anxious and trying work? . . . We have in that House every element of success, if efforts in such a work ever can be successful. [21]

This was no apology for the conventual life; it was a practical man seeing a task assumed by women who, with their previous experience at the Church of the Holy Communion and at St. Luke's Hospital might succeed.

CIVIL WAR

Potter was perhaps less emphatic in the one paragraph about the Civil War then raging. He observed that "persons whom I met had been made not worse, but better, while perilling their lives in the sacred cause of their country"—an utterance probably accepted reluctantly by convention members who already had friends and relatives killed in the war. The previous year, 1863, the bishop had marveled that the diocese prospered so markedly during wartime. The Episcopal Church had not been much agitated by either southern or abolitionist points of view until just prior to Fort Sumter. Some prominent Episcopalians supported slavery, none more conspicuously than New York's Dr. Seabury, rector, editor, and seminary professor. There were also laymen who, late in the day, joined the Jays in demanding emancipation. Abolition had a long and heroic history in the Presbyterian and Congregational churches, but the Episcopal Church seemed aloof from the struggle. When the South seceded, Episcopalians there sensibly organized the Episcopal Church in the Confederate States of America, so the General Convention of 1862 was much smaller than its immediate predecessor conventions. New York was much heard from in that convention. Murray Hoffman (long a member of New York's Standing Committee) rose to second a motion condemning the Rebellion. Milo Mahan of General Seminary (and father of the admiral-author) opposed any censure of the South. Francis Vinton made sure there was adequate seating in the House of Deputies for deputies from the southern dioceses; let no one say the South had been repelled from the convention. Vinton's gesture was not forgotten in General Convention of 1865 when the few southerners attending found places awaiting them.

It may be that there was sparse mention of the war at diocesan conventions because, in the nature of things, the delegates there were likely to be wealthy, and thus their sons able easily to pay a substitute to enlist. At the time, it is well to remember that no sensitive bishop would use a convention to harangue churchmen about this tragic war that, seen as "the irrepressible conflict," left bitterness in so many homes. Bishop Potter had seen firsthand what wartime chauvinism could do, for his colleague of Washington College days, the Rev. Francis Lister Hawks, had run afoul of city patriots soon after hostilities began. No New York rector was abler, or more ill starred, than Hawks.

Celebrated as rector of three New York City churches in succession—
St. Stephen's, St. Thomas, and Calvary—and propietor of St. Thomas
Hall, a school whose failure prevented Hawks from accepting a bishopric, he had been rector of Calvary Church since 1850. However, as everyone acknowledged, he was

> known to be a Southerner; and when the Union flag was not dis-
> played at the Church, suspicion was aroused. One day the Church
> was threatened by a mob, demanding that the flag be displayed. This
> Dr. Hawks refused to do. The temper of the mob became so danger-
> ous that the sexton rushed to Mr. William Scott [a vestryman] with the
> information that the mob was about the burn the Church. Mr Scott
> went at once to Dr. Hawks, and in a few minutes the flag was flying
> over the building.[22]

Dr. Hawks was obliged to resign. He moved to more congenial Baltimore, where he was briefly rector of Christ Church (a successor there
would be Horace W. B. Donegan). But even before the Civil War ended
he was back in New York, founding a new parish; it would have been
his fourth in the city, but he died before he could fully enter into its
work. His return to the city implies the antisouthern sentiment wasn't
as dominant as might be expected. Some of the seminary professors
were known to be Copperheads, a fact that might not have helped the
fortunes of that "impecunious institution." On the whole, however, the
Civil War was seldom mentioned in the records of the diocese except
for Bishop Potter's brief references to the hostilities in convention addresses.

Postwar growth in New York State, and the prosperity of upstate
towns, revived the idea of again dividing the diocese. Bishop Potter
was opposed to small dioceses because he doubted they could support
themselves. His views might have prevailed had not another area begun to agitate for separation: Long Island, now no longer a rural appen-
dage to Brooklyn. The diocesan convention of 1868 appointed Hamilton Fish chairman of a committee to look into division of the existing
diocese. The committee immediately began to study the possibility of
two new dioceses. In Long Island, the clergy were overwhelmingly in
favor of division, the laity slightly less so. A new Diocese of Long Island
would immediately become the seventh largest in the American
Church, it was said.

If there should be a new upstate diocese its prospects, too, seemed
promising. Most of the clergy there were in favor of a separate diocese,
with the life-belt hope that "some connection with the mother diocese
can be retained." There were nominally ninety-six parishes there, but
twenty were thought to be moribund. If a new diocese were created, it

would be the tenth largest (New York would remain greatest of all: 166 parishes, 271 clergy, and at least 20,000 communicants). There remained the question, Could a new northern diocese support itself? Since Bishop Potter was attending the first "Pan-Anglican Council" at Lambeth, the New York convention adjourned until November so that he could preside over the important deliberations.

The result in that adjourned convention was the decision to set apart Long Island and the area north of Dutchess and Ulster counties as two new dioceses. It was understood that no part of the Episcopal Fund or the Fund for Aged and Infirm Clergy would go to either of the new jurisdictions. But the new northern diocese would be given $50,000 by New York, a gift unbestowed for many years. Long Island immediately raised an endowment from wealthy Brooklyn Episcopalians. General Convention approved the divisions in October 1868, and it was then Bishop Potter's pleasant responsibility to preside over the election of bishops for the new areas. In the Church of the Holy Trinity, Brooklyn, the organizing convention for Long Island elected the rector, the Rev. Abram Littlejohn, November 18, 1868. In St. Peter's, Albany, Potter's old parish, on December 21, 1868, the rector, William Croswell Doane was chosen first Bishop of Albany, for such was the name chosen. It was the first diocese in the American Church to be named after its see city.[23]

From 1868 onward, despite periodic urgings for further alterations, the Diocese of New York has been that area south of Columbia and Greene counties. "Beloved brethren, today we begin a new history as a Diocese," said Horatio Potter to the 1869 convention.

RITUAL AND OTHER CHANGES IN THE CHURCH

While the General Convention of 1868 neatly divided the Diocese of New York, it was less successful when wrestling with demands that ceremonial prohibitions regarding worship be made explicit. Of course, it is impossible to devise ironclad rubrics for every moment and movement, but for a time the House of Bishops considered a canon that would outlaw the use of incense, crucifixes, processional crosses, lights on the Holy Table ("except where necessary" for the officiant to see the written page), bowings at the Holy Name, genuflections, choral services and vested choirs (unless the vestry or bishop consented). The bishops, exhausted, realized any such canon would be unenforceable. But the fact that the bishops were engaging in a Ritual War skirmish pointed to divisions in the Church far more profound than the simple carving up of geography. Some Episcopal leaders argued for "comprehension," a Church able to contain a wide variety of ceremony. But most Episcopalians were doubtful that this could be done.

In the very year that the House of Bishops discussed the prohibitions, the Rev. Ferdinand C. Ewer, rector of Christ Church (then on Fifth Avenue at 35th Street, in the immediate neighborhood of at least four other Episcopal churches), left that traditionally Low Church with 116 parishioners in order to found a parish that would from the outset use whatever "catholic" practices were found to be desirable. The name of the new church was St. Ignatius: a most un-Episcopal name, said some critics, who probably didn't know which saint by that name was honored in the new parish, where the word "Mass" was used at once. Incense followed in 1877. When Arthur Ritchie became rector, he "introduced" (as they said) full colored vestments, candles, wafer bread, the mixed chalice, holy water stoups, the Reserved Sacrament, and the service of Benediction.[24]

Elsewhere in the diocese there were signs of practices and ceremonies that would have puzzled Hobart and astounded Onderdonk. Confessions had been heard by Dr. Houghton at the Church of the Transfiguration in the 1850s,[25] and in that church might be found altar candles and a processional cross, too; this is the church that claims to have had the first vested choir in America.[26] But then, the Transfiguration was thought to be a peculiar place, which is why, in 1870, a neighboring rector directed an actor to see the rector of "the little church around the corner" about burial arrangements for another actor—for "they do that sort of thing there."

Liturgical embellishments came fast in the post–Civil War years. To us they may seem harmless, perhaps a trifle fussy; but to a large segment of Episcopal people they were nothing less than a denial of the Protestant martyrs who had died at the stake. One observer barely disguises his disapproval of the new mode at Trinity Church in 1868:

> The choral service is one of the specialties of Old Trinity. It was introduced in its present order by Dr. Cutler, who succeeded Dr. Hodges as organist. A choir of boys was introduced in connection with the voices of men; the whole dressed in white surplices make quite a show in the chancel . . . The choral service is very taking. Everything is sung that can be sung—the Psalter, the Creed as well as other parts of the service. The people are mere spectators . . . The service opens on Sundays with a thronged house—aisles and vestibules full. The crowd remains till this singing is over and the sermon begins. Then it disperses, as if the performance was complete . . . At the opening of the service the leader of the music comes out of the robing room dressed in a black gown, followed by about forty or fifty boys and men in surplices. The rector leads [a successive procession] followed by a train of clergy in white robes. At the opening of the

vestry door the audience rises and keeps on their feet till the procession moves into the chancel and are seated. The priest intones after the manner of the Catholic Church. The preacher of the day is escorted from the vestry to the pulpit by the sexton. The rector of Trinity is thoroughly High Church . . .[27]

The "catholicity" of Trinity is equaled by the elegance of Grace Church, where the "intelligence, wealth and fashion of New York" congregated. "To be married in Grace Church has been regarded as the height of earthly felicity." Brown, the sexton there, "has the air of a boatswain. It is worth a visit to Grace Church to be ushered into a pew by Brown. He shows you into a seat and impresses you by his condescension as he closes the door."[28]

The formalities of Trinity, and the fashion of Grace, never troubled Potter, for these were part of ongoing Episcopal Church life. The processions of Trinity would soon become standard practice. Potter's difficulties—and he managed them with a Potter's accustomed adroitness—lay in the extremities that came to his attention. He had a High Church mind, but was skeptical about the accoutrements of worship. Once, seeing a crozier in the church, Potter told the incumbent "that unless he removed that implement from the chancel the service should proceed no further."[29] He may have seemed to be a "timid" man who dreaded confrontations,[30] but perhaps that was an ingredient of his statesmanship. He said he saw himself as a "harmless drudge." If there were complaints that the Sisters of St. John Baptist were encouraging auricular confession, the bishop would be appropriately exercised. "But we always had Dr. Houghton to straighten him out," reads a note in the Community's archives.[31] Knowing something of the man, we can believe Potter readily allowed himself to be "straightened out" when the trouble was a preferred practice of a Sisterhood, for he knew the worth of their community to the Church of New York.

In 1868, however, there occurred a more troublesome situation that attracted so much publicity that soon every Episcopalian had heard of the "Tyng Case." Stephen H. Tyng, Jr., was the able, earnest founding rector of the church of the Holy Trinity in 42d Street where parish life was fully developed in schools and lodging houses. Tyng had already have several brushes with ecclesiastical authority when, in July 1867, he held a service in a Methodist church in New Brunswick, New Jersey. There was at that time a firm custom, reinforced by canon law, prohibiting Episcopal clergy from speaking in other churches. The canon was probably violated on occasion, but Tyng was such an inveterate rebel for the Low Church cause (as he saw it) that the two New Brunswick rectors saw themselves forced to make formal complaint to Bishop Potter. A court of five New York clergy found Tyng guilty of "intrusion," with mitigation, and recommended public admonition. This was carried out, deftly, by Bishop Potter on March 14, 1868, in the Church of the Transfiguration, a site chosen perhaps to satisfy High Church people that Tyng had at least seen the inside of one of their places.

This would have been a tempest in a teapot had not some of Tyng's supporters believed that verdict yet another signal advance for un-Protestant things. The Tyng Case became a cause célèbre in the so-called Ritual War that saw yet another battle in New York. For, in October 1873, after the House of Bishops decided precise rubrics would be futile, George D. Cummins, Assistant Bishop of Kentucky (*the* bishop lived across the river in Hoboken!), received the Communion and preached in a non-Episcopal church in the city. Bishop Potter preferred to ignore the occasion, but the outcry was so loud from the Church at large that Cummins, already seeing himself an outcast in a Church where developing liturgical practices were abhorrent to him, eventually founded the Reformed Episcopal church. (Is it not of some interest that the present Bishop of New York descends from early members of this new Church?) Bishop Potter made his expectations clear: there were to be no colored vestments, no extraordinary "demonstrations at the Holy Eucharist," no hearing of confessions "in the technical sense," no use of terms and language native to a foreign Church but not generally familiar in the Episcopal Church, such as *Mass*.[32]

FURTHER INNER CITY WORK

Episcopal Church efforts to relieve the situation of New York's poor people were as old as Neau's work with the slaves, and Elizabeth Seton's care for the ill in Trinity Parish. Bishop Potter was always aware of poverty in New York, and was probably disappointed that the Sisterhoods hadn't developed faster, for he believed them to be a potential source of much Church work. The Diocese of New York has always been a myriad of churches situated in places which might be characterized as affluent, modest, or downright poor. Of course, the city churches tried to make sure their position was maintained by occasional removals when the neighborhood showed signs of change; a few churches like St. James' and St. Michael's remained where they were founded and waited for fashion to come knocking on the door, which it did. Other churches were too slow to make the advantageous move, lost their parishioners, and slowly died. Some remained in the old neighborhoods and did the work at hand. It seems that every city has its run-down areas, and Church work among the poor and disenfranchised receives some, but never enough, notice.

"This city is the paradise of preachers," said a reporter in 1868. He was, of course, thinking of the richer churches, the more fortunate clergy, who might expect a salary of "$6,000 and a house. Magnificent presents, a tour of Europe, a life settlement, a provision for sickness and old age."[33] Such delights attract the public attention, but few eyes saw the letter of a rector who, in resigning, informed the vestry that he had at last "received an invitation to a post of duty that will enable me to provide food and raiment for my family."[34] (The vestry in question responded by making provisions that no subsequent ill-paid rector would sue the parish.) The man was simply expressing his frustration at the inadequate salaries most nineteenth-century clergymen were expected to endure. The rector of St. John's, Cornwall, wrote:

> The living here is quite as costly as in most respects as in the city, and greatly above the salary. The Carpenter who works for me in the School room earns his 22 shillings a day—$16½ a week. Mine will not reach his, even with the parsonage added, while my expenses are double his, owing to the difference of position. I mention these facts to show that I am the largest contributor to the support of the parish.[35]

But if the clergy often regarded themselves as among the poor of the diocese, they knew conditions were far worse with untold numbers of the laity. In New York City it was plain that the parishes must do more work among the poor; the Episcopal City Mission could no longer oversee all the work in the jails, hospitals, and tenements. Heroic labors had been undertaken by the City Mission: "I think it has been my privilege, both in public and private, to speak of Christ and his salvation to nearly 20,000 souls in the past year," said a City missionary, "Mr. Heath," in 1869. Trinity Church began its Mission House in 1876; two years earlier the old rectory next to St. John's Chapel had been made into an infirmary under the Sisters of St. Mary. The Sisters of St. John Baptist came over from Second Avenue at the request of Dr. Dix because he, like Bishop Potter, was convinced that the new Sisterhoods would be the greatest factor in accomplishing what could be done. The Community of St. John Baptist had been particularly effective among German immigrants on the East Side; German services were continued in Trinity Church until 1909. The Sisters of St. Margaret also became associated with Trinity in 1878, and the next year Trinity Church Association was organized to enlist influential laymen in the work. Among the young men who were charter members were James Roosevelt Roosevelt (the future President's half-brother), William Jay (whom we have already met), Elliott Roosevelt (brother of Theodore, and father of

Eleanor), and R. Fulton Cutting (who, as we shall see, became the diocese's informed conscience about the Church and society). Such other New York parishes as were able soon had "welfare" programs, fresh air homes, lodging houses, working men's clubs, and schools meeting special needs. But these reached their greatest strength in the next decade, and will be discussed later.

SISTERS OF ST. JOHN BAPTIST

Passing mention has been made of the Sisters of St. John Baptist. It is perhaps a mark of Horatio Potter's self-possession, and the respect he generally commanded, that in the midst of the ritual troubles of the 1870s he encouraged the establishment of another community of Sisters in New York. It was in 1870 that a churchwoman, Helen Folsom, acknowledged to herself and others that she was called to work for "the relief of the poor," and to gather other women of like mind in the "Religious Life" such as had been undertaken by the Community of St. Mary. Miss Folsom's idea differed insofar as she saw herself working in the Lower East Side, among the immigrants there. Even more important to her was her hope to establish there an American branch of the English Order of St. John Baptist, which she had visited in 1866. In 1871 she became a postulant of that Order; three years later, three Sisters sailed from Liverpool, appointed by Canon Carter of Clewer for work in New York. They carried a letter from the Bishop of Oxford, who commended them to Bishop Potter. Upon arrival in the city they spent a night at the motherhouse of the Community of St. Mary in 46th Street, and then moved to the Folsom house downtown. After some delay they were able to settle in their own convent house on Second Avenue below 14th Street and begin their work.

That work progressed and expanded rapidly. They began Holy Cross Mission in 1875. It was initially part of the once prosperous Church of the Nativity, which, like most downtown parishes, had fallen upon hard times. The uptown gentleman who compiled the *Centennial History* of the diocese in 1886 wrote that the Sisters' work was, primarily, "the restoration of fallen women who are either prepared to return to the world to live in it more faithfully, or else to remain secluded under religious rules, if, after due probation, they are found fitted thus to devote themselves." This was *not* meant to suggest the "fallen women" were expected to become members of the Order. The Sisters also, and increasingly, were engaged in "the instruction and training of orphans and other children."

The Midnight Mission, in which women forced into the street were gathered within the protecting walls of the Community, was particularly well publicized. Now, stories of commercialized vice and brutalization might be heard behind the closed doors of Episcopal drawing rooms. And, in the atmosphere in which they worked, the Sisters of St. John Baptist readily adopted the "tough love" image which earned them deep respect: "I would rather face all the judges in the city than the Sisters," said one who had faced both. When James O. S. Huntington and Robert Stockton determined to attempt a monastic life among the poor, they turned to the Sisters' Holy Cross mission and named their Order after the Sisters' church. Later, Huntington somewhat archly objected to the Sisters' income derived from tenement rents and moved uptown (and then to West Park, after a brief stay in Maryland). As for the Community of St. John Baptist, it maintained its Lower East Side base, with subsidiary houses in Farmingdale and Mamaroneck; the Order also had Sisters stationed at various parishes across the country, but the mother house was moved to Mendham, New Jersey, in 1915.

THREE CELBRATED RECTORS

In the last years of Horatio Potter's episcopate there were three rectors who were noteworthy in New York, renowned not only for their own abilities but because each was preceded and succeeded by men of similar caliber. They were Henry Codman Potter of Grace Church, Morgan Dix at Trinity, and Edward A. Washburn at Calvary. Henry Potter was the bishop's nephew and we shall soon hear much of him. Washburn, "regarded by his contemporaries as an intellectual giant,"[36] had as his assistant at Calvary the Rev. William Graham Sumner. Together they gathered the Club, a group of New York area clergy who were invited to meet regularly—the kind of gathering Bishop Hobart tried to forbid and his successors have occasionally deplored. The purpose of the Club was the serious discussion of religious thought in a time of profound change. Its members published a book, *Faith and Modern Opinion*.

The changes uppermost in these minds had little to do with liturgy and rubrics. They were concerned with the century's developments that seemed to undermine the Christian's beliefs. Darwin and other writers now seemed to supplement the Bible in providing thinking people an understanding of the universe and its creation. Genesis no longer stood alone, untouchable. Moreover, and partly as a response to secular poaching in what had once been the ecclesiastical preserve, the old High and Low Church parties would never again be clearly definable. "You can hardly find a representative of either among the younger men," said Phillips Brooks; "the ritualists and the Broad Churchmen divide the field." Evangelicals of the old school were unable to accept contemporary biblical inquiry and were scandalized that churchmen like Bishop Colenso would question the historical integrity of parts of the Old Testament, or that other churchmen could produce a book like *Essays and Reviews,* whose appearance in England in 1860 seemed to relish the challenge the new thinking presented Christianity.

Washburn of Calvary Church illustrates the decided shift in an Episcopal school of thought. Not interested in the trivia of church ceremony, he would once have been thought a Low Churchman; his thinking would disown the Evangelical label because a man who thought like Washburn was loath to confine God's grace narrowly or urge it excessively. Washburn and the friends who talked to him in his study or listened to him on Sunday mornings (among whom was a young girl later known to the world as Edith Wharton) viewed God's action as abundantly perceivable in much of the new discovery. They liked to be called Broad Churchmen.

In contrast, but not necessarily in opposition, there was Morgan Dix, rector of Trinity Church for half a century. Dix was a graduate of the General Seminary, was its supporter, and was much influenced by its traditionally High flavor. That older emphasis upon order in the Church received, as we have seen, new inspiration when the Oxford Movement people freely used the word "catholic" to mean something more specific than merely "universal": the Church—the Episcopal Church in particular—was divinely ordained. Men like Dix withheld their energies from intellectual inquiry into the accuracy of the new German thinking, or the tentative results of textual criticism. Rather, they saw their role as primarily priests in a Church which must *be* the Church, which must deepen the spirituality of its people and lead them to commend Christ and his Church to other people. They clearly defined what they believed: priesthood depended upon episcopal ordination; the Bible as interpreted by the Creeds and early Councils was the rule of faith; the Eucharist was the primary service of the Church, being of such divine ordinance as led to a doctrine of Real Presence in the communion bread and wine.

Morgan Dix was the champion of the High Churchmen. During his long rectorate at Trinity he lived to see men of his party far outpace him in their ceremonial preferences. Dix, like his hand-picked successor, William T. Manning, was mainly concerned about the solemnity and beauty of a church service fit for God. He made sure that Trinity and its chapels were well staffed, the preaching orthodox, the facilities available to the neighboring population. As we have seen, Trinity added the subsidiary parish activities and functions when necessity or opportunity arose, but always the prevailing principle was the Church as the wor-

shiping assemblage, complete with valid ministry, confirmed in an un-
broken tradition. It might be said that the old-fashioned High Churchman was most congenial with God in the chancel, while the Broad
Churchman more congenial with him in the study. (In New York, however, there was urgent need for those who would fit God into what was
seen on the sidewalk; the Potters knew this.)

    When Henry C. Potter became rector of Grace Church in 1868 he
almost immediately jolted that parish into a shamefaced recognition of
the shabbiness of city life only several blocks away. His successor, William Reed Huntington, inherited a church of proven involvement in
municipal affairs. Washburn's successor at Calvary was Henry Yates Satterlee. He undertook the East Side chapels that brought Calvary Church
to its greatest era and then, in advanced age, went on to be the founding Bishop of Washington.

CULMINATION OF A GREAT EPISCOPATE

Bishop Potter marked the twenty-fifth anniversary of his episcopate at a
great reception held November 25, 1879. The occasion may have witnessed the widest assortment of Gotham notables ever assembled in
one place. For the bishop had overcome whatever animosities might
have lingered from the Onderdonk days. He was admired and now, in
old age, was the revered head of a prosperous diocese in a prosperous
nation. He had used his natural geniality to smooth the way. When
someone falsely accused him of transgressions he replied, "Now, I am
content to bear my own sins, but I don't care to bear anything more."[37]
But the bishop could be quite firm, as the vestry of St. James' Church,
Goshen, learned when they received from Bishop Potter a letter saying
they could expect no more help from him if they didn't stop dallying
and elect a rector, quickly.[38] To another vestry he bluntly declared, "To
call Mr. H. to Butternuts would be to kill the parish absolutely."[39]
Speaking of the average sermon, he said, "We have so much barn door
eloquence—inflated, declamatory, high sounding, with not quite
enough of thinking and sound matter under it."[40] He once wrote to a
friend:

> We bishops, though hard working, are an uninteresting set after we
> are gone . . . Some years ago a friend said to me, "Why *will* you work
> so hard? Well, if you kill yourself we will give you an elegant funeral,
> and we will elect another Bishop as soon as we can." Alas, he has
> gone before me.[41]

Horatio Potter knew exactly who and what he was, and thus he appeared to be modest ("I always ran away from photographers," he once

said). He was somewhat less the man of New York than his nephew-successor would be. He was, throughout his long episcopate, a man who minded his own affairs. A biography summarized his life's aims as "reaching the laboring classes and the poor, to popularize the Church, to draw the plainer sort of people into her fold, and to push on home missions in the city and in the rural districts."[42]

He continued active and wise long after his twenty-fifth anniversary celebrations. He was eighty years of age when his health failed. The last public service was an evening confirmation in the Church of the Incarnation on May 3, 1883. In the days following he became so aware of deteriorating health that all engagements were cancelled. Though he would live for another four years he realized he could not bear any diocesan responsibilities. Therefore, in September he requested that the forthcoming convention elect an assistant bishop to whom he could entrust "the entire charge and responsibility of the diocese." The convention complied. So, once again the Diocese of New York had one bishop in name and another bishop in fact.

There remains for us one more aspect of Horatio Potter's episcopate, and that is the idea of a cathedral for New York. A cathedral was first mentioned by Hobart; it was, perhaps, in a moment of that Anglophilism which diminished after his European tour. Onderdonk seems to have given no thought to a cathedral church. In fact, only two of New York's bishops have devoted great energy to a diocesan cathedral: Horatio Potter and Bishop Manning; the former by urging a cathedral at a diocesan convention, and the latter because he inherited, in prosperous times, a partially built cathedral. Henry C. Potter and Bishop Greer viewed the cathedral as of peripheral importance, but it must be admitted that in Greer's time the cathedral close was developed as we now know it. Bishop Burch and Bishop Gilbert were not given the time to enter into building work, and Bishop Donegan affirmed that, in his time, other matters demanded priority. All this is in advance of the time we are now considering but is mentioned here because it was Bishop Horatio Potter who set in motion the idea of a cathedral for New York.

Many sites had been suggested. Among them was a location in Central Park (assuming the city authorities would cede such a plot), or a site on midtown Fifth Avenue (assuming the city's many Fifth Avenue rectors would be able to summon enthusiasm for the idea). Samuel B. Ruggles, one of the doughty laymen of the diocese (and father-in-law of George Templeton Strong), spoke of Morningside Heights, an idea that strained people's faith in Ruggles's accustomed perspicacity. Perhaps it was Ruggles's suggestion that led Bishop Potter to give as his opinion, "I should regret it very much if a site should be selected too high up town or too far west of the Fifth Avenue."

It is thought that Potter's formal urging of a cathedral was a response to a letter from Stephen P. Nash, a prominent layman who hoped to see a "central church" for the diocese. Bishop Potter met with a committee at his house on January 3, 1873. A charter was granted the following April 16, but there seem to have been few formal meetings of the cathedral committee from 1874 until 1886. The record, or lack of record, makes it clear that the New York clergy found it difficult to summon up interest in themselves in the cathedral project. Apart from a few, the undertaking was, in the beginning, kept alive by laymen. The most conspicuous of these was perhaps George Macculloch Miller, who was a cathedral trustee from the earliest until his death in 1917.

We will continue the cathedral story a bit further. It was well-known that the last large tracts of land available in Manhattan were those in the northwest quadrant of the city. Despite Horatio Potter's objections earlier, it was probably that part of the city that Charles F. Hoffman, rector of All Angels', and others had in mind when, in 1887, they proposed giving land somewhere in the city adequate for a cathedral "and certain other Church institutions"; St. Luke's Hospital was specifically mentioned.[43] By the end of that year arrangements had been made to purchase the Leake and Watts orphanage property on Amsterdam Avenue. A list of architects thought qualified to design a cathedral had already been drawn up—and an impressive list it was: McKim, Mead and White; Henry Vaughan; Halsey Wood; Heins and La Farge; Henry M. Congdon; Robert W. Gibson (architect of St. Michael's Church just down the avenue at 99th Street); William A. Potter (the bishop's brother, who designed St. Mary's in Tuxedo Park, St. John's in Yonkers, and St. John's in Barrytown), and Robert H. Robertson (who had just completed St. James', Madison Avenue). Perhaps because he was busy with the capitol and other public buildings in Albany, Henry H. Richardson was not listed.

One of the reasons for purchasing the Leake and Watts property was its promontory. The classic orphanage building was splendidly sited facing the city, and the architects who submitted preliminary drawings in a contest that drew much attention envisioned a great cathedral perched on Morningside Heights facing south, facing the city. The drawings of the various architects were exhibited at the Academy of Design and published in a folio volume. But Horatio Potter's original dream had gotten out of hand, for most of these designs provided for ancillary buildings—a school, a chapter house, and the like. It was probably for this reason that the cathedral was eventually located toward the north end of the plot, with the entrance on the avenue (for it appears that the cathedral trustees sold part of the land to St. Luke's Hospital).[44] Since there were as yet no immediate plans to build, the cathedral trustees offered the site for the World's Fair Columbian Exhibition set for 1892, an offer that was not accepted. During these years it was difficult to gather a quorum for any of the trustees' meetings, and the Leake and Watts site had not been paid for as late as the autumn of 1891. The orphanage authorities were very patient.

The architectural firm finally chosen after the unsigned drawings had been carefully inspected was Heins and La Farge. Their design called for a great church derived from the Byzantine. It would employ full scope for the American glass, tile, and metal work then coming to respectful attention in the art world. On January 1, 1892, the first "cathedral" service was held on the site, in a room in the old orphanage set up as a chapel. Excavations began as soon as weather permitted and, to the dismay of all, it was necessary to go down seventy-two feet before solid bedrock could be found. The cornerstone was laid on St. John's Day, 1892. Eventually the remains of Horatio Potter, who died January 2, 1887, were transferred to a sarcophagus directly behind the main altar, a site said to be the traditional burial place of a cathedral's founder.

11

Potter the Magnificent

Dr. Potter's elevation to the bishopric marked the be-
ginning of what might be called the Golden Age of
Episcopalianism.

—VALENTINE'S MANUAL

Time does not seem able to dull the luster of Henry Codman Potter's fabled years as Bishop of New York. The years of his episcopate are almost exactly those when the Episcopal Church enjoyed its storied impact upon a nation which, in fact, could record that only one out of perhaps one hundred twenty people were Episcopalians. This dispro-portionate share of public limelight, and perhaps even public acclaim, is due to a series of conditions favorable to the historic Church of the English-speaking people. The British Empire, despite the repeated fail-ure of English agriculture in the waning years of the nineteenth cen-tury, was at its zenith. Prayer Book churches were to be found all over the globe. Americans had always longed for an antiquity they could claim as their own; the search for a secure past could easily be satisfied in the cadences of Cranmer accompanied by chants said to be regularly heard in the moss-covered churches of England.

THE CHURCH IMPECCABLE

The Episcopal Church was attractive. The weavers of Wappingers said it was theirs, for were they not newly arrived from the Lancashire mills? The girl who sang in Calvary Chapel's choir, and taught Sunday school there, was the daughter of a horse importer who could point to a boy-hood in a parish in Westmoreland, and boast that his people had prayed there for five hundred years, and now prayed similarly in 23d Street. The seaman on the Church Institute's floating chapel *Sentinel* likewise knew the Prayer Book from birth; it was his way of worship.

English immigration, though diminished after the Civil War, remained a factor in filling Episcopal churches. But, as is well-known, other forces were perhaps even more active in encouraging the growth of the Episcopal Church in the East. Congregationalism, and then Unitarianism, had been dominant in Boston, just as Quakerism had once claimed Philadelphia. The Presbyterian Church in New York City benefited from its staunch patriotic record in the Revolutionary War and, under such leaders as John Mason, the reputation weathered well in the early years of the nineteenth century. In these three leading seaboard cities of the North, however, the Episcopal Church soon presented credentials admitting it to a favorable position. Native-born Philadelphian William White was patently good, wise, and able; his long years as community leader entitled him to an enviable, deserved reverence. Perhaps no other man was as responsible as Bishop White for the rebirth of the Episcopal Church in the United States following the War of Independence. Later in the nineteenth century, Phillips Brooks (after a brief time in Philadelphia) hugely commended the Episcopal Church to his own Boston. And we have already seen that Bishop Provoost sounded a positive, patriotic note for the Episcopal Church in New York. In succeeding years, immigration, the romantic revival, and the American longing for an antiquity in which it could participate—to say nothing of what came to be considered the *sensibility* of the Episcopal Church—provided an undeniable attractiveness. For these and other reasons that elude sharp description, by 1880 it was the Church of the Four Hundred (at least in New York City, where the Four Hundred were said to dwell) and, to our latter-day embarrassment, the Church basked somewhat overlong in that exalted position. Edith Wharton, baptized in her ancestors' Grace Church and introduced to Episcopal manners in a flourishing Calvary, was speaking of Henry Codman Potter's time when she wondered

> ... if those old New Yorkers did not owe their greater suavity and tolerance to the fact that the Church of England (so little changed under its later name of Episcopal Church in America) provided from the first their prevalent form of worship. ... Apart from some of the old Dutch colonial families who continued to follow the Dutch Reformed rite, the New York of my youth was distinctly Episcopalian; and to this happy chance I owe my early saturation with the noble cadences of the Book of Common Prayer, and my reverence for an orderly ritual in which the officiant's personality is strictly subordinated to the rite he performs.[1]

The piety enjoined by Hobart had probably given way to the form and prescribed rules of the later day, but even these were conducive to making the Church mystic, yet approved. The Episcopal Lent set the partying seasons, firmly. The calendar on the businessman's desk told him it was the Fourth Sunday after Trinity, as if every citizen of Gotham used the Episcopal variation of the Christian year. And Episcopalians, unlike their Presbyterian neighbors, gladly agreed that the twenty-fifth day of December was Christmas Day, though the Prayer Book in use for most of the nineteenth century seems to have preferred the title "Nativity of our Lord, or Birth-Day of Christ" over the Romish-sounding popular name.

Very memorable it is, then, that over this vaunted supremacy and popular regard for the Episcopal Church there was a man, Henry Codman Potter, who was not for one moment deceived by the appearances.

Maybe it was his Quaker background. The Potters came to New England in 1634, the same year as the Hutchisons, with whom they soon moved to Rhode Island. Anne Hutchison's enemies "were the hypocrites who masqueraded as God's elect." Henry Potter would similarly discern the hypocrites and *poseurs* of life. The family moved in 1792 to LaGrange, New York, a rural community of Hicksite Quakers near Poughkeepsie. On his mother's side were the Notts, a family of able persons presided over by the celebrated Eliphalet Nott, president of Union College in Schenectady. Henry's father, Alonzo (who later became third Bishop of Pennsylvania), married Sarah Maria Nott and was a professor at the college. An academic detachment always characterized the family. The Potters wrote and spoke with passion and conviction, but acted with the smoothness of cold steel. Young Henry was brought up in a family where the revolutions in Europe, the slavery dilemma in America, and the ritualism question in the Episcopal Church made dinner-table conversation. Later, as was then expected, Henry Potter wrote about his "conversion" and decision in 1854 to be ordained, but we are surely not far wrong when we suppose he was always destined for a life of Christian leadership.

When he went to Virginia Seminary, his father told him to beware of narrow piety; Potters never liked to be boxed and labeled. Henry filed the advice in his storehouse of wisdom, and never allowed churchmanship to overwhelm his reason or sense of perspective. Balance was his stance. His seminary days were enlightened by the stalwart professors whose Low Church reasonings were more attractive to him than the bigotry of Virginia's Bishop Meade, who had the crosses sawn off the seminary's chapel pews. One learns from such things.

Henry C. Potter was ordained in 1857, and his first assignment was in Greensburg, Pennsylvania, where he recognized his inability to readily identify with rural people—a deficiency that, as we shall see, he always tried to correct. Leaving Greensburg, he was soon in Potter country, Troy, New York. There he made a name for himself. His out-

standing good looks helped; he and his wife were a remarkably handsome couple. And he did the right things at the right time: rescued a
runaway slave from a Troy mob, and visited Gettysburg "before the
dead were buried."[2] Many earnest people joined St. Paul's, the Troy
parish, and already Henry Codman Potter was a marked man. Kenyon
College asked him to be its president in 1865, but he surely knew his
lot would be cast in a larger field. It was indeed. The next year, 1866,
two bids assured his future: he was made Secretary of the House of
Bishops, and went to Boston as assistant at Trinity Church, where the
aged bishop, Manton Eastburn, still threw cold water on High Church
pretensions. Within two years Potter was rector of prestigious Grace
Church in Manhattan.

SOME CITY CHURCHES

Grace Church had enjoyed a lengthy time of lavish prosperity, but its
reputation for opulence was somewhat belied by the fact that in 1868 it
numbered only 268 communicants.[3] Thomas House Taylor had been
rector there for many years. He had emphasized the sense of elitist
family community at Grace Church. Potter aimed at making Grace
Church a force in the broader community. His colleagues in the city at
that time were outstanding. "Ministers stood high in the community,
and most of them deserved their position," declared a knowledgeable
critic some years later.[4] There was the Congregationalist Lyman Abbott,
and the celebrated Presbyterian John Hall. Henry Ward Beecher maintained his popularity in Brooklyn. In the Episcopal churches close to
Grace there was the erudite scholar John Cotton Brown at Ascension.
Edward A. Washburn was at Calvary. Just south of Calvary was St.
George's. Its rector, Stephen H. Tyng, was fierce and forensic and unbending in his presentation of the Gospel. The Tyngs formed a clerical
dynasty; firm in their beliefs, they welcomed every challenge to their
Pauline certainties as if doing battle for the Lord.

St. Thomas Church was still on Broadway at Houston Street, but
about to move far up Fifth Avenue, for its rector, William F. Morgan,
rightly sensed the Episcopal Church's appeal to the parvenus who
would soon build notable houses along that avenue. At the Church of
the Transfiguration was its founding rector, George H. Houghton. His
readiness to officiate at the burial of an actor marked only one of the
peculiarities of that parish, for the church was open every day and
clergy available to assist anyone who came by. Such things were un-
common in city churches in mid-century. The character of the Episcopal Church then "was distinguished to a marked degree by strict con-

servatism, a dignified respectability, an acknowledged exclusiveness. It stood with emphasis for what it represented, but there was little concern for Church extension."[5] At least, it was remembered so. But at venerable Trinity, the rector, Morgan Dix, presided over a wealthy corporation already committed to building new chapels in an effort to reach Episcopalians and others who moved hither and thither in the ever growing city. Trinity Chapel in 25th Street had long and successfully challenged the prominence of its downtown mother.

The Bishop of New York was, of course, uncle to the new rector of Grace Church. Perhaps young Henry cooperated very early with his uncle in making plans and policies for the diocese. The Potters' abilities and quick rise in the Episcopal Church gave them a self-confidence and sense of mastery that probably irritated other men. For their part, both uncle and nephew had a certain disdain for clergy gatherings and clergy-inspired groups. Horatio Potter opposed the Church Congress— "a crowd of excited and declamatory spirits," he said—and issued a pastoral Letter against it in 1874. But in his dealings with the clergy, Henry C. Potter tended to be a beneficent general, organizing, directing. A story was later told of a typical evening party the bishop gave for some city clergy. When his guests assembled before dinner, the bishop announced there would be a musicale. After dinner the guests supposed there would be an opportunity to indulge in that favorite of clerical pastimes, talk; but no! Again the bishop announced music. And with the last note still in the air, he rose to bid them all good night.[6]

Henry Potter looked like a bishop. This was of great importance in a city whose citizens tended to familiarize themselves with public leaders whom they frequently saw at civic functions. New York still had a small-town feel for many of its people in the nineteenth century. Far better than his appearance, however, was the fact that Henry C. Potter had a self-assurance in the role necessarily lacking in Horatio Potter, who, after all, entered upon his episcopate with the dubious title of Provisional Bishop of New York. It was not until Onderdonk's death, in 1861, that Horatio Potter could see himself as alone on the stage; always, there was the disabled bishop who might possibly be restored.

THE POTTER PERSONALITY

Henry C. Potter never needed to pose, never needed to trim. His vision was incredibly wide, and sometimes far ahead of his own time. He could not be slotted a Low Churchman or a High Churchman, and this was a time when such labels were practically required in the Episcopal Church. Like his friend Phillips Brooks, he appreciated color in a church, and encouraged craftsmanship that might have been mistaken as supporting ritualism. In an early sermon at Grace Church he asked, "Why should not we, too, have sisters of charity?"[7] for he saw beyond his fashionable congregation to those who needed instruction, medical care, and recreation in New York slums. Ever the practical Potter, he knew the Church hadn't resources to pay salaried persons: a Sisterhood might be the answer. Yet he was not sentimental about poverty: "the deserving poor are almost as hard to find as the deserving rich," he declared.[8] He wasn't very much interested in ritual, and probably preferred the minimal ceremony found in Grace Church. As one soundly self-assured, he could welcome breadth of thought and action, but in his later years he tended to be suspicious of flamboyance or anything smacking of questionable taste. Thus, he found himself unable to encourage the Rev. Robert Paddock's methods of political and social quarreling at the Church of the Holy Apostles on Ninth Avenue.

Only rarely did Potter resort to disciplining his clergy. He insisted that political righteousness was possible in New York if leaders would use Christian conscience, and he was quick to point out that new wealth and new power seemed to prefer ostentation over decency.[9] Probably oftener than people knew, Potter was disappointed by churchpeople whom he hoped he could depend upon in his well-known efforts to make New York a better city. There is a poignant plea in his words, "No rich man has yet been found willing to try the effect of putting within reach of our poorer classes decently constructed and adequately lighted, drained and ventilated houses."[10] He doubtless had read of the indomitable English churchwoman Countess Burdett-Coutts and her housing projects in industrial England. Perhaps his loftiest view is expressed when he said his vision for all Christian churches in New York was that they "be intent not on the advancement of the parish, nor even of the denomination, nor even of the Christian Church, but on the realization of the City of God in the health, the character, and the happiness of all the citizens."[11] "Did Christ come only to teach us how to build handsome churches?" he would ask. Though he read widely, his biographer tells us Potter "had no profound social theories, but he had a firm and unfailing conviction that the parable was right when it reprobated the men who passed by on the other side."[12] The New York *Tribune* said, when he was elected bishop, that Henry C. Potter "will try to make the Episcopal Church not only the Church of the rich and learned, but the Church as well of the poor and simple." A critical, but fair, observer of the scene later wrote:

> When Potter was proposed for the bishopric some of the clergy opposed his candidacy because he went to too many afternoon teas. This was not a fair criticism because Potter liked the poor as well as

the rich . . . He frankly liked society and saw "no virtue in a life which keeps a minister apart from his neighbors." A natural capacity for work enabled him to dine out after an active day, and he was in great demand for both public and private dinners as he had a charming personality and was an able public speaker.[13]

ORDER OF THE HOLY CROSS

Quite soon after Henry C. Potter's consecration he was called upon to approve and preside at the profession of James Otis Sargent Huntington as first member of the Order of the Holy Cross. This young man Huntington—he was then thirty years old—was already on his way to becoming one of the better-known Episcopal clergymen. His father, formerly a Unitarian minister in Boston (where James was born), became an Episcopalian in 1860 and founding rector of Emmanuel Church, Boston. In 1869 he was elected first Bishop of Central New York. Young James was educated at Harvard and in his father's diocesan seminary, St. Andrew's Divinity School in Syracuse. He was ordained in 1880. Bishop Huntington assigned him to a working-class parish in Syracuse in recognition of his son's preference for that kind of ministry. But James Huntington's concerns were not fulfilled by general parish work among factory workers. He sought not to alleviate the poverty he saw, but to eradicate it by striking at its causes. He was an early single-tax enthusiast (and remained so all his life). Since the Syracuse parish did not provide the experiences of acute poverty Huntington thought he needed, in 1881 he moved to the already long-fabled Lower East Side, where the Sisters of St. John Baptist had begun their work sixteen years earlier. Bishop Huntington, partly in anguish, and partly in pride, wrote:

> James, dear boy, has gone on his way, as he believed for years God called him. With two young priests of about his own age, filled with the same purpose, he has taken an old cheap house . . . How could I hold him back, knowing his heart, seeing what he has done for me and fully believing with him that the Church sorely needs both a standard of holy living in the Ministry, and a leaven of Evangelization, supplementing our miserable, halting, half-secular Parochial system? They live in Poverty, Chastity and Obedience, with bare floors, no table cloths, scanty furniture, plain food, and seem content.[14]

It was the beginning of the Order of the Holy Cross. The Rev. Robert S. Dod and the Rev. James G. Cameron were the other two priests, but they found it necessary to drop away, so that when it came time for Huntington's formal profession he was alone. Bishop Potter agreed to preside at the ceremony; Dr. Houghton of Transfiguration was "director" of the proposed Order. The profession took place in the mission chapel of the Community of St. John Baptist, opposite Stuy-vesant Square, on November 25, 1884. "Many priests and seminary students and friends of the laity quite filled the chapel. The service was most impressive," a witness reported. "The Sisters of St. John Baptist sent a wedding cake to manifest their fellowship in our joy." [15]

The new monks had the blessing of such an unexpected person as William S. Rainsford of St. George's. Most Episcopalians, however, were puzzled or dismayed by the idea of a monastery in their communion. It should not be beyond our notice that no such antagonism met the Sisters of St. John Baptist or the Sisters of St. Mary as greeted news of Huntington's profession. Episcopalians may not have relished the communities for women, arguing that Sisters would promote High Church notions. People who could accept "pious ladies saved from wasting their time by being nuns" (it is, unfortunately, a quote from James Huntington himself!) were outraged when a man, and a very gifted, well-connected man at that, took monastic vows. "An incident is reported from the Diocese of New York that has filled the hearts of many Churchmen with anxiety and sorrow," said a Church newspaper. Another critic saw the traditional vow of chastity as an aspersion upon "the sacred mystery of marriage," and by strange logic declared that Huntington had delivered "an indirect insult to the womanhood of our mothers." [16] The new monk's kinsman William Reed Huntington, Potter's successor at Grace Chruch, wrote to deplore the "transaction" recently made at Holy Cross chapel. The *New York Times* ingenuously pleaded that monasteries need not be so terrible in Protestant America for "there are also monasteries in Thibet."

It must be said that Bishop Potter handled the "transaction" gingerly. He saw a social and practical value in James Huntington's proposed Order. Like the earlier Potter he saw that much of the Church's work simply wasn't being done because the Episcopal Church had neither the interest nor the personnel. If the idea of *someone else* working with the poor was a salve to the American conscience, at least here was a priest who *was* working in the slums of New York. For Potter, that was enough. He would give the project a chance. So, for a time, Huntington was alone. Then, with the few men who joined him there on the East Side, he worked with the Community of St. John Baptist. He was also active (disruptingly so, sometimes) in the Church Association for the Interests of Labor (CAIL). And, as was later claimed, he was "in at the birth of nearly all the social reforms safely accredited" and applauded by a later age. Distrustful of the state (but very patriotic), dramatic, romantic, occasionally playful (he was a skilled ventriloquist), something of a faddist, given to simplicity (yet remarking the minutiae of every liturgical innovation), pragmatic yet mystical, insisting on taking his meals at the kitchen table with the help, yet rejoicing in his membership in the Harvard Club: this was James Otis Sargent Huntington, prime monk of the Episcopal Church. For fifty years he was revered in the Episcopal Church by people of all shades of opinion.

But Mr. Huntington—it was only at the turn of the century that the diocesan journal allowed the "Father"—disappointed Bishop Potter. The trouble may have begun with the Sisters of St. John Baptist whose foundress had brought to the Community some family property on the East Side. Huntington questioned the Sisters' use of tenement real estate, just as he once criticized Trinity Church—everyone did—as being a slumlord corporation. More to the point, however, was the plain fact that the Order of the Holy Cross was not recruiting members. The original idea of improving the condition of the East Side poor found expression in such practical programs as Father Huntington's organization of guilds whose men members would meet shopgirls and see them safely home from work late at night. It was a program that kept the girls out of danger, but seemed far removed from the enriched "interior life" sought by the young monastics. Huntington was perhaps too practical in those days. There hadn't been enough time for the Order to become strong, to know the Eternal Will—the words are the Founder's. Therefore, to Bishop Potter's regret, in 1892 Father Huntington and the two other monks then associated with him moved to a house near 125th Street. Perhaps from there, they said, they could develop a firm communal life, explain their vocation to others, and enlist men in the Order of the Holy Cross. Thereafter the bishop was cool to the Order. When, in 1904, the monks moved into their permanent house in West Park (after some years in Maryland) it was Bishop Whitehead of Pittsburgh, not Bishop Potter, who dedicated the austere monastery designed by the gifted Henry Vaughan.

That dedication was a major, triumphal event among Anglo-Catholics. They considered it an important milestone in the developing awareness of the Church's rich and rightful heritage. Priests from all over the nation looked forward to that day in May 1904 when the monastery would be dedicated. A special train was appointed. It was filled with the leading Anglo-Catholics in the American Church, each eagerly anticipating the rites at West Park, and their enthusiasm was only temporarily dampened when a fellow passenger wondered aloud what would "happen to the Catholic movement if there should be a train wreck." [17]

It should be mentioned that while the Order of the Holy Cross ceased institutional ties in the City of New York (as, eventually, did the

Community of St. John Baptist and the Community of St. Mary), its members found individual work in the diocese, notably in Sing Sing and other prisons. And, in recent years, new work has opened. In the meantime, the legendary Father Huntington and the equally legendary Father Hughson and Father Whittemore—and many others granted grace if not legends—blessed the diocese and the Church at large with the gifts they shared.

POTTER REALISM

Henry C. Potter liked to think of himself as an "old-fashioned" American. He valued foreign traditions but believed immigrants should adjust quickly and totally to the ways of his own Anglo-Saxon forebears. This attitude is part of an emerging paternalism and, of course, it militated against the very thing that the *Tribune* writer had hoped. For most newcomers to New York now were not from the British Isles. As the origins of immigration moved more and more toward Central Europe and Russia, the ghettos of the Old World were duplicated in Manhattan. Potter thought the Jews—but not only they—were responsible for the decline in the "American Sunday." Some ecclesiastics then (and now) would have left the matter there, but not Bishop Potter. Instead of leaving the blame for desecrated Sabbaths with the new immigrants, he, very typically, made it clear that Episcopalians should set an example by walking to church on Sunday, and forgoing the huge midday meal whose preparation was often in the hands of servants. "There is a difference between Sunday and other days," he said. "In our eagerness to prove we are no longer Puritans, Sunday is less and less observed."[18] But toward the end of his life, he gave up this battle, declaring that since the population of New York City was no longer Christian, its people could not be expected to observe Sundays; the recourse lay not in legislation, he said; the fault was that of Christians who expect others to work on Sundays.[19]

Here we have an outstanding example of Potter's thinking. His native American preferences are plainly stated. Perhaps there is even a wearied satisfaction that the modes of his childhood are superior. But then there is Potter's candor: the blame isn't entirely upon the new immigrants: Episcopalians have been complacent and arrogant in their ascendency. Potter had conscience, and he was superb at inquiring into the conscience of others. And here, too, is his common sense. He knew when the battle was lost. Perhaps the most distinctive aspect of Henry C. Potter's leadership is this: he was a man of New York, able to assess the realities of its people accurately. It was not in his nature to seclude himself in the groves of academic ecclesiasticism, or to assuage his goodwill in social service, or to presume that Manhattan was an emerging City of God.

When, in 1883, the infirm Horatio Potter asked the diocesan convention to give the diocese an assistant bishop, the bishop stated he intended a "complete withdrawal from the administration of the diocese." Today, businessmen and bishops are expected, even required, to resign their responsibilities at some age tacitly understood or actually stated. In an earlier day, the resignation of a bishop implied desertion; there was something almost cowardly in the act. Even parochial clergy expected to remain in harness until they died, but in their case it was usually necessary because until the Church Pension Fund was formed in 1918 there was no adequate retirement provision for Episcopal clergy. Moreover, in the Diocese of New York, there had already been two contretemps: Bishop Provoost's resignation (never really accepted by the House of Bishops) and, of course, Bishop Onderdonk's prolonged and costly suspension. The canny Horatio Potter managed to avoid all difficulties and assured an easy transfer of office to his nephew. He was not present at the consecration in Grace Church on October 20, 1883—and it was thereafter clear that though Horatio Potter lived on, the de facto Bishop of New York would now be Henry C. Potter.

A DIOCESAN OFFICE

The Potters moved from the fabulous Grace Church Rectory to 160 West 59th Street. (It may perhaps be of interest to note here that the new rector of Grace Church, the celebrated William Reed Huntington, was already one of the prime men of the Episcopal Church in that era of Prayer Book revision and glimmerings of social awareness; and perhaps even more interesting here to note that he was among the first to locate and champion the career of a future Bishop of New York, William T. Manning.) The bishop's office—imagine Provoost or Hobart having an *office!*—was at 29 (later 416) Lafayette Place, a splendid late Federal town house that, once, proudly elbowed itself up to La Grange Terrace, the colonnaded houses built there in 1833. By the 1880s, of course, society was decidedly headed northward. Lafayette Place house became offices. *The Churchman* magazine occupied one house; the Diocese of New York was its neighbor, in the house given and endowed by Catherine Lorillard Wolfe.

Diocesan office work was minimal. Clergy and laity did not expect to meet in offices, but in churches. The bishop and his secretary (for now there *was* a secretary, the Rev. George Nelson, who served for

many years) would write to the parishes of the diocese to make visitation appointments. Everything was done by letter, or by personal interview; the word "telephone" does not appear on the records until 1901.
When the bishop went off to visit and confirm in upriver areas, he
would use public transportation, now the railroads more than the
steamboats. And many they were! It is difficult for us now to realize
how effective was the complicated system of small railroads criss-
crossing the rural parts of the diocese. Bishop Potter would probably
be amazed by our present network of superhighways. (Though, when
he saw the automobile beginning to come into use he probably predicted that someday soon such roads would be necessary; did he also
foresee the disappearance of the Hudson River steamboats?)

POTTER VISITATIONS

Bishop Potter liked to leave New York City for remote places, and his
visitations seem unhurried because they were dependent upon the
timetable of the train, day boat, or the convenience of whoever would
be taking him to the next station. (We may be certain that Henry C.
Potter never used the infamous night boats; a man as wary as he knew
what their reputation could do to an unescorted man of the cloth.) Let
us go with the bishop on a visitation to the Church of the Regeneration
in Pine Plains. He would take the New York Central to Poughkeepsie,
and then after a considerable wait (with perhaps a look-in at the
Church of the Holy Comforter near the station; if there was time, he
would surely walk across town to call at Christ Church, the Potters'
original Episcopal parish) would board a train of the Central New England Railroad, which would stop frequently between Poughkeepsie and
Pittsfield. The bishop would step off at the Pine Plains station and
probably be met by the rector and the wardens. He would dine at the
rectory, and be shown to his room by the light of a kerosene lamp. In the
morning there would be an ample country breakfast and time for a
leisurely conversation with the rector; there would probably be no
"early" celebration of the Holy Communion until that became a general custom about the turn of the century. The service would probably
be Morning Prayer and the Order of Confirmation; the bishop's sermon
would be lengthy. After the service there would be another sizable
meal at the rectory or perhaps at the home of the prosperous senior
warden. The entire village knew the Bishop of New York was present,
and here is the reminiscence many years later of a Presbyterian child:

> Bishop Potter came to confirm Fannie Eno, and a few others, too, I
> guess. We all attended the service as Mr. and Mrs. Eno were good

friends of Papa and Mama. Papa was then teaching in New York, coming up for weekends via Central New England, returning via the Sunday afternoon train. We always went down to the station to see him off. The Rev. Mr. Burroughs was at the station as he had accompanied Bishop Potter, who was on the train. Mr. Burroughs insisted we meet the bishop, so we all climbed aboard with Papa and were introduced. My memory of Bishop Potter is of an elderly gentleman wearing a funny (to me) little black cap like a rabbi. Mama said he probably put it on for traveling.[20]

Then, as now, it was often necessary for the bishop to remain overnight when he visited parishes far beyond New York City. Needless to say, over the years he might accumulate a fund of anecdotes connected with these visits. Hamilton Fish Armstrong never forgot an episode when Bishop Potter came to Christ Church, Marlboro, and dined with the Armstrongs after the service. The little boy had been warned to be particularly good and so, trying hard, "I turned to the bishop after grace and said, 'Please pass the butter for Jesus Christ's sake.' "[21]

More widely told about the diocese was the terrible time a hostess found the silver bureau set in the bishop's room missing after his departure. Finally appealing to the bishop for its return, she received a wire: "Poor but honest. Look in the wash stand."[22]

THE CITY CHURCHES

Some of the city parishes had begun one or more chapels on the East Side when Bishop Potter was consecrated. It was generally understood, and said to be mutually agreed, that poorer people would be more comfortable in "their own" chapels. Such charity-minded people as the rector might find expended their energies working with the chapel people. Nathalie Smith Dana was succinct about the arrangement. "The poor were handled separately," she said:

> Prosperous New York parishes had missionary churches suitably situated on the East Side, while the well-to-do, assisted by professional singers, worshiped in handsome edifices on Fifth or Madison Avenues. In St. James' Church the poor could sit in the gallery, but there was no room for them downstairs, as all but the back pews were rented . . . It seemed a pity that there were so many poor people, but as that was part of God's own plan what could one do about it but send them turkeys at Thanksgiving and blankets at Christmas?[23]

As might be expected, the chapels were often better attended and more active through the week than the mother churches. Work among the young was always significant. Calvary Chapel in 23d Street had sev-

en hundred children in its Sunday school in 1890. Tenement mothers
and their children were sent off to the country for a two-week "fresh air
outing." Boardinghouses—every upstate village had a dozen of them—
were rented for Calvary's people. Later, a site on Long Island was purchased for a hostel. The Rev. John Henry Hopkins has left a record of
his brief curacy at Calvary Chapel. While he was studying at the General
Theological Seminary, Hopkins worked at Calvary Church and found
the rector and people there congenial. Therefore, after ordination he
gladly accepted an appointment to Calvary Chapel. He was disappointed
that the social attention that would be extended to an assistant at the
church was not forthcoming to an assistant at the chapel.[24] The rector,
Henry Yates Satterlee (the future founding Bishop of Washington),
summered in Europe, with side trips to Twilight Park in the Catskills.
He had little to do with the day-to-day functions of Calvary Chapel. A
reasonable excuse for this might be found in Satterlee's well-known
total reliance upon able persons whom he carefully selected to do the
work at hand and then allowed free rein. Apart from the busy chapel,
Calvary maintained Galilee Rescue Mission for hoboes and alcoholics
who, in return for temporary board and lodging, were asked to pledge
total abstinence. There was also a flourishing Sunday school for Chin-
ese children. A special committee was formed to visit Blackwell's Island and treat the inmates there to tea with milk and sugar; it was said
there was never milk or sugar with tea at Blackwell's unless brought by
the women of Calvary.

In the years 1880 until about 1920 the large Manhattan parishes
published yearbooks outlining the work of the past twelve months, and
describing what might be done in the year ahead. These are fat books.
Apart from the usual financial report and rector's letter, page after page
lists schools, clubs, organizations, and committees engaged in a wide
variety of good works. The long lists of volunteers are invariably women,
married or unmarried, who found deep satisfaction, and spent long
hours, in work where thanks were sparse. The rector received the acclaim, and his more able clergy assistants may have found their positions in great parishes the gateway to future advancement. In the heady
forward rush of the Church's life in the late nineteenth century the
work of countless women volunteers received little more than perfunctory mention in a parish yearbook or a rector's thanks at the chancel
steps. Yet who can say that the strength of the Diocese in New York in
its most prosperous years was not based largely on the endless work of
these lay volunteers?

If Hopkins felt that he and his wife were socially neglected by the
people of Calvary Church, he was thoroughly satisfied about the work
done there. He was even more satisfied with his salary of $1,800 and, in

addition, the allowance of $22 granted him each month for rental of a four-room apartment on Lexington Avenue. The usual salary at that time for a city curate was about $1,000 without housing allowance,[25] which was approximately the pay of a New York City policeman. In the country, a similar stipend with rectory was regarded as quite ample.

The usual Episcopal Sunday morning schedule, in city and country, was Morning Prayer, Ante-Communion, Litany, and Sermon at ten-thirty. Some churches had an early service in Lent. When travel became easier, and Sunday observance less restrictive, people wanted an early service scheduled permanently. Sunday school was, for the same reason, gradually moved from Sunday afternoon at three to a morning hour. Evening Prayer with choir and sermon were part of the Episcopal scene until the 1920s. There were few large vested choirs in New York City when Henry C. Potter became bishop of the diocese. Choral music was rendered (judging from complaints in vestry minutes, the word is apt) by men and women choristers who formed a quartet or double quartet. In churches where the budget permitted, the singers were paid. In some churches the women were summarily replaced by boy sopranos in the now-familiar black and white vestments that the late Victorians suddenly discovered to be approximations of ancient choir garb. At the big churches the organists were apt to be celebrated musicians: Mosenthal at Calvary, Warren and Helfenstein at Grace, LeJeune and Hall at St. John's Chapel, Messiter at Trinity, and Stubbs at St. Agnes' Chapel are a few. Perhaps even more renowned in Potter's time were the sextons, who, apart from keeping the church tidy, often served as collectors of pew rents and were despotic managers of weddings and funerals. No sexton, however, achieved the status of Brown of Grace, who held that church, congregation and clergy, in thrall for thirty-five years. Sextons were nothing less than overseers who attended to the desires of the pewholders, indicated what limited seating might be available to a worthy-appearing transient who appeared unannouncd at the church door at service time, and conveyed messages to the rector, upon whose stall he kept an anxious eye during the service.

Perhaps the most enhancing role of the sexton was that of parish undertaker. One is perhaps more solicitous of a man whom he will meet some day in that capacity. Vestries often allocated a room in the church cellar where the sexton could embalm and coffin a deceased parishioner, whose remains would then be returned to the residence. Funerals were generally held in houses or tenements; church funerals were, until the end of the century, rare except for prominent people. Interments in the city were, by 1880, restricted to a few churchyards and cemeteries where the family already owned lots or vaults. Episcopal burials now were likely to be in the large cemetery Trinity Parish had laid out on Broadway at 155th Street at mid-century, or in the celebrated Greenwood in Brooklyn. Cemeteries had once surrounded the original edifices of St. Bartholomew's in Lafayette Street, St. Stephen's in Chrystie Street, and St. Luke's, Hudson Street, but the difficult process of their removal warned vestries against the time-honored practice of burying the dead near their church building. Municipal regulations also prohibited new cemeteries within the city limits, where, in any case, land was too expensive for that use. Thus, burial in the shadow of the church, so dear to Gothic revival sentiment, was eventually not practicable in the City of New York.

William A. Muhlenberg ("that grand old man who, more than any other, taught us all, minister and layman," said Henry C. Potter)[26] had been one of the foremost clergymen in advocating free churches where there was no pew rent. His Church of the Holy Communion was not alone, however. St. Mary's, Manhattanville, and the Church of the Transfiguration in East 29th Street were also early free churches. But most of the city's churches found it necessary to rent pews. Often, the family's name was engraved on a silver-plated plaque on the end, or door, of the pew. It was the custom to "sell" pews at auction when the church was built. Inclement weather or poor attendance at such a sale could be disastrous to the fortunes of a new church. Successful bidders had their choice of pews (plural here, because sometimes a second pew was selected for relatives or servants). There would be an assessment of a percentage of the purchase price each year, usually 8 percent. The proceeds were used for the basic requirements: heat, repairs, cleaning, oil or kerosene for the lamps, and so forth. Clergy salaries and other expenses were often met by special subscription. A vestryman would circulate through the households of the parish and write in a book the names of the subscribers and the amounts they intended to give for the rector's salary in the new year. The organist and choristers might be included in this book, or perhaps in a separate subscription. Offerings for urgent causes were announced and collected as needed; the "Sufferers of Kansas," for instance, was a notable special collection just before the Civil War, when the Kansas-Nebraska Act resulted in bloodshed. And, of course, the custom of holding fairs and bazaars reaches far back in Church history.

The rector was usually conceded his canonical right to use the Communion offerings. This was the primary source of what we today call the discretionary fund. Since most churches probably ended the fiscal year in deficit, the time-worn tale of the rich vestrymen dividing the red-ink sum is accurate. And it is precisely here that the city church could, and often did, succumb. For the church depended upon such frail factors as the rector's popularity, the neighborhood, one or more rich families and, above all, on its particular gifts. Among this latter might be congenial ceremony, or lack of it, remarkable music, unusually profound preaching, or spectacular philanthropic outreach. A change in rectors, the death, departure, or business reverses of a leading parishioner, or an unsightly building rising nearby could spell the doom of a city church. This instability of neighborhood is still found in Manhattan, and there are on the island former Episcopal churches now used for religious purposes by other denominations.

There were two main methods of dealing with failing churches: merger, or a move farther uptown. Thus it was that St. Luke's Church on Hudson Street became a chapel of Trinity Church. St. Luke's congregation had moved far uptown by the time of the Civil War. For many years it was assisted by Trinity, and finally taken over as a chapel when the corporation of St. Luke's decided to build a new church on 141st Street. The fine old building and its rectory were saved, and in recent years St. Luke's has again become an independent parish. This had been a pleasant episode in diocesan life despite a disastrous fire, but many parish stories are decidedly not pleasant. When a church found itself with a fine building in a good location, but with a superannuated, beloved rector who couldn't afford to retire, trouble resulted. Another parish might find itself in a soured location, but just now possessing an outstanding rector whom it didn't want to lose. Could the older man be induced to retire? Could the other congregation be persuaded to abandon their building? Truly, the gift of diplomacy was never more necessary. In the nature of things, such negotiations are left unrecorded and therefore the tangled dealings of Bishop Potter and countless committees, families, and rectors will never be known.

From the earliest times of the diocese, the Manhattan parishes adopted the simple procedure of following their notable families in their move from neighborhood to neighborhood. This usually meant a move northward, and it became risky business in the city. By Bishop Potter's time, the opportunities were nearly exhausted. Erstwhile "country" churches—and even St. Luke's, Hudson Street, had once been a country church on the outskirts of the city—now found themselves surrounded by brownstone residences built quickly by speculators. Old St. Michael's in Bloomingdale remained at the same location, but now it was called Amsterdam Avenue and 99th Street. Its church was a splendid white-framed Gothic revival building designed by the short-lived genius John W. Priest, in 1852. St. Michael's had begun in 1809 as a summer chapel for wealthy New Yorkers who fled the heat and disease of the downriver city each year. The upper part of Manhattan island was then dotted with fine Federal houses whose lawns

stretched down toward the Hudson. Now, toward the end of the nineteenth century, the West Side was developing into what promised to be
the fashionable side of town; even Bishop Potter moved to Riverside
Drive. St. Michael's now found itself a major church, and rebuilt.

St. James' across town could tell almost the same story. Founded in
1810, and often sharing ministers and parishioners with St. Michael's, it
was a chapel for families who summered on the East River bank. St.
James' barely survived after the old estates were abandoned and sold.
Fortunately, after a succession of rectors, the vestry invited the Rev.
Cornelius B. Smith to take charge. Under his gentle, steadfast ministry
St. James' was enabled to meet the flood of "chocolate sauce," as Edith
Wharton described the brownstone houses she deplored. The original
church on Hamilton Square was abandoned for a new one on 72d Street
designed by James Renwick. Soon this was too small and a third
church, designed by Robert H. Robertson, was built on Madison Avenue (the architect's idea for an extremely high tower never materialized).

A COUNTRY CHURCH

This, then, was the Episcopal Church Henry C. Potter knew in New
York City. Let us now turn to the country churches as they might have
been in the 1880s. Remember that suburbia and commuting businessmen as we know them were yet things of the future. A commuting man
in those years lived no farther away than Brooklyn or East Orange, and
it was only a man well advanced in his business who "took the cars"
into the city each day. Consider a parish in a village, say, eighty-five
miles from New York. Its church was, and is, small. Its architect, the
elder Upjohn, was inveigled by an important and able founding rector
to supply plans when the parish was formed in 1855. By 1880 the
church is already cluttered by some of the wares of the oak and brass
craftsmen which would soon, and permanently, inundate the Episcopal
Church with an incredible wash of harsh metal and grotesque wood-
work. St. Luke's (as we shall call it) had a rector and vestry who already,
in 1880, had seen fit to mutilate Upjohn's handsome wineglass pulpit.
Now there was talk of replacing his half-circle mahogany Communion
rail with a straight one made of—yes, brass and oak.

The church is illuminated by kerosene lamps that hang from the
ceiling. They are lowered every Saturday to be cleaned and trimmed. In
the chancel is a pair of elaborate candelabra. These are there strictly for
illumination, and are lit only for Evening Prayer. There is no suggestion
of their being altar lights, for while the people of St. Luke's may *think*

High Church (because some of them remembered Bishop Hobart), they and their rector do not like that label. There is no cross on the wooden altar (it *is* called an altar now) but the clever Upjohn anticipated this and provided a stained window with a clear red cross in its center immediately above the altar. The Communion plate came from Cooper of Amity Street, a firm that enjoyed Episcopal patronage for some years. The set consists of two Gothic-style chalices (as distinguished from the deeper goblet earlier used), and there are blue enamel designs on the base, with a delicate filigree in the knop. The set also includes a footed paten, and a tall wine flagon. A pair of alms basins are inscribed, "Freely Ye Have Received, Freely Give." All this is encased in a sound mahogany box kept next door in the rectory. For the Holy Communion is celebrated only once a month in this, and most, Episcopal churches.

Just south of the chancel, which Upjohn placed facing the East though the orientation was an inconvenience to parishioners, is a small room called the vestry. It takes its name from its use: here hang the rector's vestments, his short black cassock on one peg and his ankle-length surplice on another. From yet another peg depends his black stole (it is not the tippet of today), which the rector thinks he may soon retire from service. For he is hearing more and more of his clerical brethren using "preaching stoles" whose colors denote the season of the Church year. He isn't sure, however, that either he or St. Luke's is yet ready for such "advanced churchmanship." There is a small worktable in the vestry. It is covered with a white tablecloth, and on it, leaning against the wall, is a breadboard; in the drawer is a bread knife which is used, each month, to cut the bread loaf into cubes for the Communion. Wafer bread will not come into use in the Episcopal Church until well in the twentieth century—and as a matter of historic fact, at St. Luke's not until 1935, and then only over the heated objections of a prominent member of the vestry.

There is a Heppelwhite washstand in the corner, a castoff used by the leading family before taste led them to discard their mahogany in favor of oak. The rector brings water to the vestry room each Saturday afternoon, even when there is no Communion next day, because he believes there should be washing water available in the building. But the crockery pitcher on the stand is cracked because the water in it froze when the sexton, drunk again, hadn't tended the furnace in the cellar. In the other corner are two simple benches with handholds cut in the tops. These hold a coffin in the church aisle, and can be spaced according to the size of the coffin.

The sexton is expected to mow the small lawn around the church and in winter to remove the snow before service time. His wife launders and irons the rector's surplice, and for this she is paid ten dollars a year. The church has a hot-air furnace that pours its heat up through a large elaborate iron register in the aisle, and the vestrymen hope the sexton is always careful about where he puts the hot ashes. They wish they could have such confidence in the man that, like their New York City friends, they could station him near the front door on Sundays in order to remind some of the congregation that they have not yet handed in their subscriptions for the year.

There is church music of good quality, for St. Luke's has the 1874 Hymnal, and the organ is a fine Johnson, a golden-throated thing of two manuals and sixteen stops installed several years back. Its bellows are pumped by a boy who may earn as much as $20 a year for his labor. He is on the job twice every Sunday. The (unpaid) organist is very able and determined; fifty years and three rectors later she will retire. A quartet sometimes complements her ministrations, but an anthem is rendered only on special occasions, such as when the bishop visits. There is no chancel choir because the leading family in the parish has made it known it objects to anyone but the rector occupying an elevated position in the church.

Next door is the rectory, and though it wasn't designed by Upjohn it attempts to be a worthy adjunct to his church. It has suitable jigsawn bargeboards and several pointed windows. It is a large house, perhaps larger than the rector can afford. For he is expected to heat, furnish, and maintain the place from a salary of $900 a year. He must also keep the stable, for the extent of his country parish requires a horse and carriage. The rector is paid in cash by the treasurer promptly on the first day of the month and gives the treasurer a receipt in exchange. He is thankful each time that, unlike some of his brethren, he receives his salary regularly. He is also grateful that occasionally clothes and roasts and extra pocket money come his way from members of the parish who prefer to "support the church" in that way.

The rector is satisfied with his role in life. He expects the village people to defer to him and, in turn, he defers ever so slightly to the two or three estate families nearby. He is ambivalent about whether or not he should remain at St. Luke's for the rest of his life. He has put down roots in the community. There is now a public high school for his four children. His adequate salary is sufficiently augmented by gifts, and his wife finds an agreeable social life in the community, which includes frequent invitations to the big houses. The rector wonders if his friends in richer, more prominent parishes are really compensated for the additional burdens placed upon them, the books they must buy, the servants they are expected to hire and train. He has, however, one constant worry: What will happen to his family if he dies or if he is incapacitated? There is a New York Diocesan Fund for Aged and Infirm Clergy which, he knows, parcels out slim sums to disabled ministers and, sometimes, to their widows and younger orphans. But it is a hand-to-mouth affair. If anything happens to him he knows his children will not be able to complete high school. Nor is he cheered by recalling that at each diocesan convention the Fund's low resources and the many demands upon it are mentioned. But it seems that no one (not even Bishop Potter) is very much exercised about the matter, except Arthur Ritchie of Manhattan's Church of St. Ignatius, whose committee hoped that a Retiring Fund could be joined to the Fund for Aged and Infirm Clergy. That had been declared impossible by the trustees. Ritchie had responded by asking the trustees to produce "a scheme" that would commend itself to the General Convention in order that all Episcopal clergy might be protected. But this would take a long time, and the problem of money is always a present-day affair.

The rector sees as his chief duty writing good sermons for the morning and evening services every Sunday. He is particularly conscientious about preparing lectures for weekday evenings in Lent. The Sunday school meets at two thirty on Sunday afternoons. He looks in on the classes, which are held in the pews, but his wife is more directly associated with the Sunday school than he is. She is also the untitled leader of the Ladies' Group that sends boxes of handmade clothing to missionaries in Colorado. The rector is glad not to have very much to do with this group, and somewhat regrets that his wife has to bear the brunt of what is about as near to a High/Low Church argument as has yet appeared in St. Luke's. For a newcomer whose sympathies are decidedly Low Church has challenged the practice of always sending boxes to domestic missions of the Protestant Episcopal Church which are known to be in the hands of High Churchmen, and never sending boxes to foreign missions, which are usually Low Church concerns. A vote overwhelmingly confirmed the practice of sending the boxes to Colorado, but it had been unpleasant, and the matter will surely come up again.

Most marriages take place in the rectory, either in the study or in front of the parlor fireplace. There were five marriages in the years 1880–1885. Some prominent families like marriages to be in their own homes, but so far there have been very few weddings in the church itself. Baptisms are always private affairs in the church, usually following Sunday morning service. The rector tries to be conscientious about the rubric against home baptisms, but admits he has in weaker moments, agreed to baptize the grandchildren of his landed families in their libraries. He is uncomfortable about thus practicing dual regulations, but finds adequate excuse in the fact that he actually performs many home baptisms. For some of the infants of the parish never leave the houses in which they were born. He cannot think of a family in his parish that has not lost by death at least one young person.

Funerals are generally held in the houses. The undertaker comes, embalms the body in the bedroom, and disappears. Neighbors, who arrived earlier, remain to do the cooking and washing and barn chores, and some spell each other taking charge at the door. When the undertaker returns with the coffin, which he bought from a nearby carpenter but upholstered himself, the corpse is placed in it and "laid out" in the parlor. The coffin will rest on kitchen chairs, or on a pair of saw horses. The funeral service will be in the afternoon, and the house will be crowded: terribly hot in summer, and perhaps worse in winter when the wood stoves are going. Sometimes a photographer takes a picture of the deceased just before the coffin lid is screwed down for the last time. This is more often done when a child has died, and though the rector doesn't think much of the custom, it is something entirely beyond his responsibility. Then the coffin is placed in the richly decorated hearse and the long procession of horse-drawn vehicles takes its slow way to the cemetery. In the years 1880–1885, the rector has baptized thirty-four children and buried five. He is grateful that none of his own children have died young.

The clergy were careful to list the cause of death in the parish register. In the first part of the 1880s, when fifteen were buried, "congestion of the lungs" appears most frequently, followed by "Old Age," "Consumption," "Pneumonia," and "Liver Trouble." He knows these causes of death either by hearsay or personal observation; a small community soon knows what carried off its members, and the local physician rarely troubles to provide a medical name for the maladies that come to his attention.

This vignette of parish life in one New York church (which today, apart from early mortality, is remarkably like a hundred years ago) may be supplemented by recollections which have already been shared in print. At Christ Church, Marlboro, for instance, a lay reader often took the entire service of Morning Prayer in the absence of a rector. He would read one of Canon Farrar's sermons, with some portions deleted. There was

> a black walnut altar; over it a window of Faith, a long way after Reynolds; no hangings, no flowers, no ornaments . . . in the pew in front sat a large old lady in the venerable clothes of her youth—bustles, overskirts, and bonnet with streamers. She was redolent of St. Jacob's oil, supposedly potent against rheumatism, and Papa had to wear a marigold in his buttonhole and pinch it at intervals to drown the smell.[27]

We have already noted Bishop Potter's insistence upon Sunday observance. A few households tried to follow him in this, and one member of an ultra Episcopal family later recalled that on Sunday

> there were meals to cook and beds to make, but early in the day all the servants were in their Sunday best. We were not allowed to pull the bell-rope except for firewood. Servants' time was their own; they were not on call. They received family friends, they were sent to church, of course; horses were harnessed only for that purpose.[28]

In one enlightened city parish, the Ascension on Fifth Avenue:

> There was church and there was Sunday School beforehand. Sunday afternoons were sedate; games were not played . . . Lent was a slim period; candy was out for the season, but there was always the mitebox to be fed so that it would make a respectable thud when put in the plate at Sunday school on Easter morning.[29]

Another memoir sums it up decisively: "As we were an Episcopal household, formal social life was discontinued after Ash Wednesday."[30]

These quotations are from three adults who recalled the Episcopal Church of their privileged childhoods. We may be sure, however, that somber Sundays and the Lenten gloom were similarly observed in less affluent houses, for this was the teaching in the Sunday schools whose numbers increased year after year in Potter's time. And, in all probability, it was through those same Sunday schools, many of them on the East Side of New York City, that the first lapses in Sunday observance threatened the bishop's "old-fashioned American Sunday." For the dour Sunday was something purely Anglo-Saxon, and as the nineteenth century drew to a close the Sunday school rosters of St. George's, Grace Chapel, Calvary Chapel, St. Thomas Chapel, and the chapel of the Incarnation—all of these far east of Fifth Avenue—show a decided prominence of names originating in continental Europe.

The Diocese of New York was, in the 1880s, dominated by burgeoning Manhattan churches—fifty of them—and included other large well-run parish churches in such outlying communities as Newburgh, Poughkeepsie, Yonkers, and White Plains. The average number of communicants in each of the remaining churches (not counting very new missions or preaching stations) was, in 1885, probably not more than fifty. Representatives of them all gathered annually as delegates to diocesan convention. The bishop would select the meeting place, and it was now no longer the lovely St. John's, for Hudson Park had been sold to become Hudson Terminal, and the old church found itself facing a dreary railroad depot, flanked by tenements and lofts. Diocesan conventions were held in such places as St. George's Church, St. Augustine's, St. Bartholomew's on Madison Avenue, Holy Trinity on 42d Street, the Church of the Incarnation (cheek by jowl with three other Episcopal churches on Madison Avenue), or the Church of the Heavenly Rest on Fifth Avenue. The conventions ordinarily lasted two days, obliging out-of-town delegates to find lodgings. This inconvenience and expense resulted in many upstate parishes not participating in the second day of business. Clergy who attended received adequate compensation for mileage, but nothing for hotel expenses. The convention would open with Morning Prayer and the Communion. There was always a sermon by a preacher selected by the bishop. Late in the morning the convention would organize for business, and for several years after Henry C. Potter became bishop there was difficulty, as in the parable, about who should have the chief seats. While the records don't say so, it appears that the large Manhattan churches expected to sit foremost, while others, prevented from arriving early because of railroad schedules, were expected to take the remaining pews. It was once proposed that seating be by seniority. When this failed, Arthur Brooks, brother of Phillips, and beloved rector of the Incarnation until his untimely death, proposed in 1889 that seating be by lots cast. The matter seems trivial to us from this distance, but it was then something that rankled the smaller churches. It is one more indication of the tension that has always existed in a diocese as varied as New York must be.

CENTENNIAL CELEBRATIONS

In Horatio C. Potter's last year as Bishop of New York, 1886, the diocese marked its centennial. The occasion was fully anticipated, since people well remembered the nation's centennial, only a decade earlier. The centennial heightened an interest in history, in national origins, in ancient places and customs. Now the Diocese of New York could take a backward glance over one hundred years. Suddenly it seemed to have been nothing but a century of advance and—a word one uses with extreme caution in discussing the fortunes of the Church—*success.* Historic embarrassments had been generously compensated. The questionable patriotism of some early leaders of the diocese was forgotten. Provoost's alleged lethargy was, for the moment, never mentioned and, in any event, was seen as handily corrected by Hobart's energies. The Onderdonk troubles were not mentioned in the *Centennial History,* which hastened on to depict the heroic labors and early death of Bishop Wainwright, followed by the wise direction of Horatio Potter. Apart from the luster shed by this procession of notable bishops, Manhattan's own floundering General Theological Seminary (which wouldn't produce a Bishop of New York until 1947!) seemed assured a better future now that its new dean was the very rich and very generous Eugene Augustus Hoffman. It is of interest to social historians that Hoffman's importance to the seminary lay not so much with his own checkbook, but in the fact that he, of an old New York family, was able to attract less-well-connected newly rich New Yorkers who were glad, in association with him, to support the seminary. The centennial of the diocese was also satisfying to the ecclesiastical historians who, though perhaps complaining that no bishop had ever been able to oversee the Church in New York State, the territory had, by 1886, been amicably divided into five dioceses, each prospering. And also, if anyone pointed to parishes now defunct, they could now point to many more new ones that were flourishing. There were, that year, 331 clergy in the diocese, and an astounding 11,132 confirmations.

The Centennial Committee consisted of Bishop Potter, Morgan Dix of Trinity (who was then about to embark upon his own monumental history of that parish), General James Grant Wilson, Francis Lobdell, J. P. Morgan, and William H. Benjamin. Wilson had just edited Appleton's *Cyclopedia of American Biography,* and now most of the work involved in compiling a history for the diocese fell to him. Despite "the surprising apathy and neglect of a large portion of the clergy,"[31] he produced on June 1, 1886, a *Centennial History* of nearly 500 pages. It was, and remains, a most valuable book, for it has biographical sketches of the diocesan bishops, a historical essay read by the Rev. Bernard F. DeCosta at ceremonies in St. Thomas Church on Fifth Avenue, and brief histories of each parish and chapel in the diocese. General Wilson, who "liked to use the title he had picked up during the Civil War,"[32] expected the rectors to rally to his orders. He was disappointed. It seems that the clergy in the 1880s weren't very much interested in diocesan or parochial history. The general had to do what the troops wouldn't do; he riffled through diocesan journals and manufactured snippets of data for churches whose rectors had not done their homework. The result, a book of much information, causes us to forgive whatever personal foibles General Wilson may have had. It sold for $4.00 ($7.00 in half-calf) at diocesan conventions, and also at the Church bookstore, Pott and Gorham. Four dollars was a high price for any book in 1886, and the Centennial Committee members were disappointed at the slow sale of their history.

ALBANY CLAIM SETTLED

Almost as soon as Henry C. Potter became the Bishop of New York it was necessary for him to wrestle with the Albany Claim. It will be remembered that Horatio Potter (formerly of Albany) was reluctant to separate that area from the New York diocese because he doubted a new northern diocese would find adequate resources to maintain itself. He particularly feared that a disproportionate burden would be placed upon St. Peter's, his old parish. When the new diocese was formed, it was agreed that $25,000 would be given it from New York. This sum was, however, not to come from existing moneys but from donations for this special purpose. A dubious decision! Nothing is more difficult than raising money for old and, as some thought, unnecessary purposes. The Albany Claim had never been paid, though in 1886 it was nearly twenty years since the pledge had been given. But the obligation hadn't been forgotten, either, and was on the agenda for successive conventions. Surely the new bishop would not let the matter sink into oblivion, because it had been a major concern of his uncle and sponsor. Perhaps it was because of this personal anxiety of the bishop that J. P. Morgan and Cornelius Vanderbilt agreed to give the last $1,146.60 to make the Albany fund reach the required $25,000. In a moment of such playfulness as the diocese had seen before, and would see again, Vanderbilt gave one cent more than Morgan so that he could claim to be the greater benefactor. The Albany Claim was finally satisfied on November 12, 1890.[33]

ST. STEPHEN'S COLLEGE

Another perennial problem was St. Stephen's College in the hamlet of Annandale, one hundred miles up the Hudson River. The college was the ill-conceived brainchild of John McVickar, who, in his closing years, envisioned a "training school" where young men could prepare for whatever academic rigors the General Seminary might provide. Now, it happened that McVickar's nephew, John Bard, had married the very rich Margaret Johnston. The couple established themselves on a fine estate in Annandale and, by 1855, had built two schools for neighborhood children who otherwise were without any free education. Bard was a loyal, but somewhat wooly-headed, churchman, the son and grandson of distinguished New Yorkers. His wife was a true bluestocking and was ready to use her fortune in good works for the Church. In addition to the two schools, the Bards began to build an outstanding stone Gothic church designed by the noted architect Frank Wills. Bishop Wainwright had encouraged Bard to build his schoolhouses, and now his successor, Horatio Potter (with John McVickar's nudging), suggested that the Bards undertake the training school project. They agreed. A young and able priest, George Seymour, was engaged to take charge, and by 1860 there was a board of trustees, a charter from the state, and a handful of students intended for the ministry of the Episcopal Church. The Bards gave land for the college and included one of the schoolhouses and the Church of the Holy Innocents as well as the promise of a generous yearly grant.

All of this was delightful and perhaps even promising, almost a page from the English landscape so beloved by the Bards: a manor house, church, grateful villagers, diligent students, a cause nothing less than the Church of Christ—all of it woven into the fabric of high Victorianism, and in a region (the Hudson River Valley) where large land-owners consciously imitated English country life. Add a bishop or two, and the scene is perfect. But this Eden, too, had a serpent. Within a few years Mrs. Bard's fortune was exhausted. American education provided more and more opportunities that obviated the need of a training school. Other tasks claimed Horatio Potter's attention, and Henry C. Potter was never enthusiastic about St. Stephen's College. Nevertheless, it could not be gainsaid that by 1889 two hundred graduates of the college were ministers of the Episcopal Church.

Nor did the college do much to commend itself to laymen aware of educational trends in America. The faculty insisted on a form of classical curriculum that was of debatable value to a man entering seminary. Its longtime warden, Robert Fairbairn, was outpaced by educational progress elsewhere; when he retired in 1898 after nearly forty years as head of St. Stephen's, the college was hopelessly behind the times. But, "sir, there are those who love it" was as stirring a cry for St. Stephen's as it was for Dartmouth, and as alumni of the college became priests and bishops they occasionally induced wealthy Episcopalians to take up the cause. Sometimes there were as many as ninety students at the college, most of them graduating on to the General Seminary.[34] Clerical alumni are seldom able to give much financial support to their alma mater, and the conspicuous supporter of St. Stephen's was not an alumnus. The Rev. Charles F. Hoffman had been rector of St. Philip's Church in Garrison in the early years of the college. Whatever interest began then was probably later encouraged by his brother, Eugene, the fabled dean of General Seminary. Charles Hoffman gave much money for the college buildings, for endowment, and sometimes just to keep the college going one more month. Fairbairn's annual reports to the diocesan convention were faint appeals for assistance; upon reading them, one gathers the college was wary of diocesan interference and preferred to rely on the haphazard munificence of the few donors like Hoffman, or upon the steadier but limited grants provided by the Society for the Promotion of Religion and Learning in the State of New York. The SPRL was of ancient origin. No one seemed to know exactly when it began,

but its roots lay in diocesan education efforts prior to Hobart's burst of
energy for religious education. Some critics said that the Society was far
too liberal in its grants to St. Stephen's College, and in one diocesan
convention a thorough review of matters was requested.

We shall later follow the fortunes of St. Stephen's College, but for
now one thing is clear: Henry C. Potter was not much exercised about
its future. Why? Because he thought there was little value in a rural,
poor, cloistered college. Potter was a realist. He knew what was happening in the city. Between the lines of his speeches and writings he
seems to repeat the theme that "the desirable is not necessarily the
vital." St. Stephen's was never one of his major concerns, and this view
would be corroborated by his successors, as we shall see.

PRACTICES AND POLICIES

In his twenty-five years as Bishop of New York, Henry C. Potter never
cared to create a diocesan staff. His loyal secretary-cum-chaplain,
George F. Nelson, superintended what little office work Potter's style
required. James Pott was treasurer of the diocese for forty years until his
death in 1905; when money was short, Pott simply appealed to rich
acquaintances. Various Church organizations, then as now, managed
their own affairs and found their own funds. These included the City
Mission Society, the Seamen's Church Institute, the Sunday School Union, and the Society for the Promotion of Religion and Learning in the
State of New York. Like many of the city merchants of an earlier time,
Potter seemed to "keep all his business in his head."

In 1886, a year before Henry C. Potter became *the* Bishop of New
York (for Horatio Potter lingered on in an invalid state until his death
on January 2, 1887), there was a diocesan convention of extraordinary
activity. One of the first matters to come to the delegates' attention was
the prevailing practice of city churches that were caught in deteriorating neighborhoods moving uncomfortably close to parishes already established in "safe" areas. Thus, for instance, St. James' on Madison
Avenue awoke one day to the news that another vestry had quietly
negotiated to purchase a lot only two blocks away. A resolution in the
1886 convention attempted to control this by requiring that hereafter
the three nearest churches must assent to the "intrusion" before the
bishop and Standing Committee could give approval.

A Diocesan Missionary Society was outlined in the bishop's address, and was unanimously supported by the convention. That is, it
was supported in principle: no funding was asked or given. Five archdeacons were to be chosen by the bishop, and the appointments con-

firmed by the clergy in the proposed archdeaconries. Each archdeaconry was to find its own funds, and manage them in whatever mode of Church extension they agreed upon. Despite obvious drawbacks, this scheme enabled the diocese to embark upon considerable growth as improved rail service opened new residential areas and as people with newfound leisure were able to spend time in the fields of Westchester or the hills and mountains in Ramapo and Ulster.

The City Mission Society came in for special notice in that 1886 convention. In the previous year, 1,163 people had been received into St. Barnabas' House in Bleecker Street. Scarcity of money prevented serving more. "With all her claims, her wealth, her prominence," Bishop Potter said in the 1886 convention, "it is impossible that the Episcopal Church of the Diocese and in the City of New York should carry on a *little* City Mission—a little war against the vast host which Satan is daily training in our midst in the dexterous use of his own deadly weapons, is impossible for us." The appeal is ever a familiar one whenever Christian benevolences attempt to bridge the gap between the needs perceived and the funds required. But now, in the 1880s, there was an urgency, almost a despair, because the City of New York contained as much human misery as any metropolis of the Old World, and *conscientious men and women knew it.* As early as 1866—twenty years before Bishop Potter decried the notion of a *little* Episcopal City Mission—a writer had described conditions:

> Persons who perambulate Broadway on a pleasant day and who look on the elegantly-dressed throng that crowd the pavement, and through the costly plate-glass at the rich goods displayed, would be slow to believe that within a stone's throw squalid want and criminal woe have their abode. Here, in the Fourth and Sixth Wards, so famous in the history of crime in New York . . . no pen can describe the homes of the lowly where the New York poor lodge. It is a region of wickedness, filth and woe. Lodging houses are often under ground, foul and slimy, without ventilation, and often without windows, and overrun with rats and every species of vermin . . . Children are born in sorrow, and raised in reeking vice and bestiality that no heathen degradation can exceed.

This is the familiar Victorian, practically exulting in the poverty that might be found, and yet, at the same time, wishing it were not so. Perhaps accepting facts supplied by a neighborhood rescue mission, our journalist claimed that:

> Of religious faith, 118 represented the Protestant, 287 were Jews, 160 Catholics; but of 614 children, only one in sixty-six attended any school. Out of 916 adults, 605 could neither read nor write. In the

same block there were thirty-three underground lodging-houses, ten
feet below the sidewalk, and twenty of the vilest grogshops were
visited by 1054 persons—450 men and 445 women, 91 boys and 68 girls.

Henry C. Potter seems to have been the first Bishop of New York who
sensed the magnitude of New York's poverty; his uncle, Bishop Horatio, was sensitive to the problem but preferred confining the Church's
work to alleviation. For this reason he had promoted the Sisterhoods.
The younger Potter resented (and perhaps oversimplified) the *causes*
of poverty in New York.

Much closer to the diocesan convention, as it was thought, was the
condition of clergymen and their families. Most clergy salaries were
modest. An average rector must needs stay at his job until death, hoping to save something for his widow's maintenance—and maintenance
was all it would probably be. There was no nationwide pension system,
nothing resembling latter-day Social Security. Furthermore, many an
aging rectory couple lived to see their children die, which meant that
grandchildren would have to be brought in and cared for. It was announced in the 1886 convention that provisions in the Diocesan Fund
for Aged and Infirm Clergymen might now be extended to such grandchildren.

The rectors' wives were often more heroic than their husbands (an
arrangement not unknown even in these latter days). Unlike many of
the rectors' "willing workers," they had to subsist on clergy stipends
that were, at best, modest. But very often in the records we will find it
intimated that the lady of the rectory was a skilled (and unpaid) parish
worker. Sometimes they were the main evangelizing energy of the local
church. In one suburb, the scholarly rector, as well as the parish, enjoyed the ministrations of the rector's wife, who was a wise and indefatigable pastoral aide. In the 1890s there occurred an episode (surely
one of many) that was vividly recalled half a century later, for Katherine
Hoxie Hughes was not easily forgotten. She knocked at the door of a
ramshackle house in a slovenly street. There was no response until a
neighbor flung up her window and said, "If it's Mrs. Riley you're after,
she's in the jail."

"Very well," said Mrs. Hughes, "I'll call on her there." And she
did. We may be sure parallel episodes took place in many a parish in
the Diocese of New York.

Bishop Potter casually mentioned in his 1886 address that he had
"opened and set apart" the House and Oratory of the Sisterhood of the
Good Shepherd on Ninth Avenue just north of the General Theological
Seminary. This new (and short-lived) Order was committed to work in
St. Barnabas' House. (In 1900 the surviving Sisters were set apart as

deaconesses, a possibility not available to them in 1886.) Bishop Potter mentioned the good work of the Community of St. John Baptist in their Midnight Mission (a somewhat misleading name for what was in fact a twenty-four-hour refuge for destitute women). And he said he had again "visited the House of the Brotherhood of the Holy Cross."

Lest these allusions cause alarm among sensitive Protestants, Bishop Potter reminded the delegates of the recent death of the Rev. John Murray Forbes. Now, *there* was a name from the past that would remind the convention of bitter battles. Forbes was, in 1848, the rector of St. Luke's Church in Hudson Street. His gifts indicated that he was destined for a significant career—and indeed he was, though not of anyone's imagining. His admirers, and there were many in those immediate post-Onderdonk years, were dismayed when John Murray Forbes announced his conversion to the Roman Catholic Church. (They were further discomfited at reports that, the now Roman Catholic widower enlisted his sons to serve as acolytes: a pretty picture of an erstwhile Episcopal family!) Nor were Episcopalians happy to hear that Forbes's predecessor at St. Luke's, Levi Silliman Ives, Bishop of North Carolina and son-in-law of Bishop Hobart, had departed with his family to the Church of Rome. Then, years later, and after receiving singular honors in the Roman Catholic Church, John Murray Forbes returned to the Episcopal Church and, in 1869, became dean of the General Theological Seminary. It was an unfortunate appointment. Forbes's intellectual rigidity and his natural austerity, tinctured now by his disappointment with Roman Catholicism, led him to believe his greatest service to the Church of his birth would be to discover and root out anything in the seminary he thought alien to Anglican tradition. His reaction to the Roman Church was extreme, and so his deanship was a stormy three years at Chelsea Square. But he certainly managed in that brief time to assure Protestant Episcopalians that he had abandoned Romanism forever.

All this would have been known to the delegates in the 1886 convention who heard Bishop Potter speak of this "conspicuous figure in the history of this Diocese, in connection with events of which I know only the tradition."[35]

Potter's ceremonial preferences were distinctly Low, and thus he was wary of officiating in the Church of St. Mary the Virgin in New York City, where, as the diocese's *Centennial History* gingerly recorded, there was "at least one celebration of the Holy Communion every day, and where the chief service on Sunday is the high celebration of the Holy Communion." This had been the practice almost from the founding of St. Mary's in 1867. In that year the Rev. Thomas McKee Brown and Henry Kingsland Leonard, a fervent Anglo-Catholic layman, set out to establish a "Catholic Free Church." John Jacob Astor gave them three lots, with the understanding that the new church would be "free and positively orthodox." In this case, "free" meant exempt from diocesan oversight as well as having no rented pews. St. Mary's was organized under a Board of Trustees in an instrument approved by Horatio Potter on June 27, 1874. The younger Potter, like his uncle, was enthusiastic about urban Church work accomplished by any responsible Christian agency. But it was difficult for him to translate his broad-mindedness into the liturgical procedures St. Mary's people might expect when their new church, designed by LeBrun and Sons, was opened in 1895. So Bishop Henry C. Potter permitted the Bishop of Fond du Lac to preside at the Sunday service, while Potter consecrated the great new church the following Thursday. Everyone was pleased with this happy and characteristically Episcopalian solution.

Another vignette of Church life in the 1880s may be found in Bishop Potter's commendation of parochial missions. A notable mission had been held at St. Mary's Church in Cold Spring early in 1886. The bishop himself had already begun his practice of inviting his seminarians to retreats at nearby St. Philip's in Garrison at Whitsuntide. Canon W. J. Knox-Little, the celebrated retreat leader whose preaching at St. Clement's Church, Philadelphia, immediately led to James Huntington's decision to become a monk, had held a retreat in Garrison as early as 1880. "This was the first 'retreat' held in the American Church," according to a note by a later rector of that church, the historian E. Clowes Chorley.

When Henry C. Potter became the Bishop of New York, in 1887, he had been the Assistant Bishop for four years, and rector of Grace Church fifteen years prior to that. Once bishop, he moved quickly toward a position of prestige which has perhaps never been equaled by any other citizen of the city. If at one time people could say that New York stood upon the tripod of Clinton, Hosack, and Hobart, it might soon be said that now one man commanded similar respect: Henry C. Potter. And he was surrounded by able clergymen in the churches, beginning with his successor at Grace Church, William Reed Huntington. At Trinity, Morgan Dix had, as a young clergyman with excellent connections, mastered the complexities of Trinity Church and, to the astonishment of his covetous fellow curates, obtained the rectorship when ancient Dr. Berrian died. Henry L. Ziegenfuss, though received only lately from the Dutch Reformed ministry to be rector of Christ Church, Poughkeepsie, was increasingly prominent in diocesan affairs. J. Shaw Shipman, David H. Greer, Henry Yates Satterlee—all Manhattan rectors—were the rising stars. Vocal laymen included Columbia's Professor Henry Drisler, George Macculloch Miller, the now aged John Jay,

Jr., and Hamilton Fish, who, in 1890, startled people by stating that he had been at every diocesan convention since 1835.

RURAL GROWTH

The novel scheme of appointing archdeacons to plan and promote mission programs in their respective areas was initially successful, though in 1890 Bishop Potter was constrained to say "we must prosecute the work in the rural portions of the diocese with more energy." In 1890 there were eleven mission stations in Dutchess County; most of these were eventually abandoned. St. David's, Otterkill, the site of an original SPG outpost dating from 1729, was revived. There were new missions in Rifton and Rosendale for families whose breadwinners worked in the booming cement plants there. New "preaching stations" were reported in Pine Hill and Greenwood Lake. These two places were among the many developing summer resorts made accessible by superior railroad service and newfound leisure time among some people, for this was the heyday of the small woodland hotel and the rural boardinghouse. Anyone who had been aboard a Hudson River excursion boat—and many New York City people had—wondered what lay across the fields, or what was hidden in the dark, cool mountain coves they saw from deck. The dayboats and the railroads, sensing untapped wealth from vacationers, were glad to supply the answers by way of booklets and maps that were circulated on the docks and rail stations. Hudson Valley farmers and Catskill Mountain tanners whose fields and hills had been exhausted now found profits in taking in summer boarders. For thirty years this was nothing less than an industry, a reliable source of income, providing work for neighbor "help" and recreation for tired New Yorkers. Episcopal chapels and missions were well attended by that new American genus, the "summer people."

Not exactly summer people, but predominantly Episcopalian, were the inhabitants of Tuxedo Park, an "ideal" community patterned after the much older Llewellyn Park in Orange, New Jersey. The mammoth houses in rock-strewn Tuxedo had hardly recovered from their inaugural balls before St. Mary's Church, designed by the bishop's brother, was built and consecrated in 1888. Tuxedo village had an Episcopal mission for Italian laborers specially brought there to build and landscape the park. Nearby, the Harriman family soon built Arden, which had its chapel. And not far away was St. John's-in-the-Wilderness, built, maintained, and endowed by Margaret Furness Zimmerman.

A note informs us that "from Spring Valley, the Missionary extends his ministrations to the inmates of the County Poor House, and, in order to reach and touch the scattered lambs of his flock, has established a Sunday School in the woods."[36] Each archdeaconry was still expected to find funding for whatever mission work it cared to fulfill within its boundaries. This was supposed to be done through assessment of the neighboring parishes; "the apportionments are often tardily paid," said the bishop.

CHURCH IN THE CITY

About this time, the Church Club, begun about 1889, had gained a reputation sufficient to cause Bishop Potter's qualified utterance that it was an organization of "possible usefulness." The Club had already sponsored the East Side House, a "settlement" agency complete with reading rooms and gymnasium. The Church Club itself maintained clubhouse rooms, with a library for its lay members.

Three constant themes run through the later years of Henry C. Potter: the ever changing city, Church growth, and the development of the cathedral. Immigration from Europe continued, but now the newcomers were from eastern Europe, many of them fleeing persecution. Few of these immigrants had ever heard of the Episcopal Church. When, in 1901, Bishop Potter spoke of "phenomenal growth" of the city demanding new church sites he had in mind not necessarily places of worship for immigrants (such as had been Onderdonk's legitimate concern), but, rather, churches for the neighborhoods where Episcopalians were fast moving. When those summer vacationers returned from their week's sojourn in the country, they chafed under the changing conditions in their old neighborhoods. They reasoned they could "move uptown," maybe as far as Webster Avenue, and find there less congestion, more congenial people. Vacations are apt to do more to us than we realize. Now even people with modest incomes could imitate the quality, who had long ago formed the fashion of looking northward on Manhattan Island.

Toward the end of his life, Bishop Potter stated publicly what he had long known: most downtown churches faced disaster and their fate must soon be the concern of all. (Perhaps, he said in 1906, even Diocesan House in Lafayette Street should be sold because it was so far from the center of a "ganglionic city.") Changing neighborhoods, different complexions and customs, a definite alteration in accepted manners upset many churchfolk. But, at least in public, Potter showed them no sympathy: "We may look back with longing to the days and the ways of our fathers. They are passed and ended, and we shall never see them again."[37] The bishop was indisputably right, but it would seem that

New York City Episcopalians anticipated him. The sole Manhattan church to cease in his time was the Church of the Annunciation on 14th Street—ironically, it was the church Bishop Onderdonk attended regularly during his suspension. All the other churches threatened by area changes moved uptown or negotiated redemptive consolidation. The most outstanding example of consolidation is the Church of the Holy Trinity's merger with St. James' Church.

If this book had been planned along different lines, Holy Trinity would occupy at least one separate chapter. It was a pace-setting parish in all ways: pace-setting in overnight rapid growth, manner and variety of ministry, and, alas, pace-setting in decline. It was an Evangelical parish, established by Stephen H. Tyng, Jr., in 1863. Tyng seems to have thought that High Church principles were once again taking the honors after Horatio Potter became Bishop of New York. Thus, he sought by old-time Evangelicalism, and by parish programs, to build a great church in 42d Street. His efforts enjoyed (and deserved) spectacular success, perhaps unique and certainly pioneering. A year after the Church of the Holy Trinity was founded it had itself established five chapels throughout the city. But Tyng didn't end there; he

> was a forerunner of what soon came to be called the "institutional parish," and he led in the organization of an orphanage and a training school for lay preachers called the House of the Evangelists. There were also dispensaries and infirmaries, a lodging house in the city and a convalescent house in the country.[38]

In 1873, a large church designed by Cyrus L. Eidlitz (often called the Church of the Holy Oilcloth because of its fanciful red-and-yellow brickwork) was built across from Grand Central Station and was for some years filled by the 2,000 communicants of the parish. But the ominous signs were there. Hotels, competing for railroad patronage, took the places of private dwellings. Tyng resigned, believing that Horatio Potter had won the battle for Onderdonk after all. His successors were unable to maintain the house of cards he had built—the chapels, nursing homes, manual training shops, the House of the Evangelists fell one by one. Instead of all those mini-institutions, Holy Trinity now attempted the Victorian expedient of notable preachers. This failed. Luckily for the Church of the Holy Trinity, the very rich Miss Serena Rhinelander desired to build on a family property she owned uptown a church "for the poor." She had in mind a large lot of land in 88th Street, and might be induced to name the new church Holy Trinity, but the able rector of the existing parish could not be expected to move to that deprived part of the city. So, by what we may safely assume was a series of dinner-table conversations after the ladies had left the room, it was intimated to the much-loved Cornelius B. Smith, longtime rector and builder of St. James' Church on Madison Avenue, that his resignation would make it possible for Holy Trinity's rector, E. Walpole Warren, to move up to St. James'. The sale of Holy Trinity's valuable property would be an endowment for St. James', and Mr. Warren would agree to superintend the new church "for the poor" in 88th Street. It would be named the Chapel of the Holy Trinity, and would assimilate work St. James' Church had already begun in 78th Street. Perhaps the most amazing aspect of these gentlemanly dealings was the grace with which Dr. Smith and his loyal parishioners of St. James' accepted the propositions. Dr. Smith went so far as to state that he and "Bishop Potter would greatly regret to have the large value of the 42nd Street property used simply to make one rich church for rich people, with rented pews," and insisted that half the sale proceeds be used in the new Church of the Holy Trinity which Miss Rhinelander was abuilding in 88th Street (again there were notable architects at work: the firm of Barney and Chapman was engaged to do Holy Trinity).

VICTORIAN CONTENTIONS

In the 1890s biblical criticism and the implications of what was known as Darwinism replaced ritualism as a threat to the peace of the Church. Many people feared the basic things of Christianity were under assault. Nor were they placated when the clergy began to wrestle with the new thinking. Soon after Henry C. Potter became bishop, the rector of All Souls', New York City, R. Heber Newton, received considerable notoriety when he delivered a series of lectures which seemed to accept many of the conclusions of current German biblical scholarship. Bishop Potter recognized that much of the uproar that followed was the result of sensational reportage, but he was sufficiently alarmed to request that the lectures be terminated. He ignored the formal complaint lodged against Newton by Bernard DeCosta, a neighboring rector prominent just then as diocesan historian; Dr. Buel of General Seminary joined in the complaint.

At the same time, there was the Ritchie Case. Arthur Ritchie was rector of the Church of St. Ignatius and promoted ceremonies there involving sanctus bells, incense, candles, and acolytes. Potter refused to visit St. Ignatius' until Ritchie promised to desist from the service of Benediction. This "Case" also received more than its share of publicity, and it is difficult to avoid the conclusion that Bishop Potter, like Manning a generation later, enjoyed the headlines. Certainly his sojourn at the procathedral the "diocesan church" in Stanton Street in the summer of 1895 brought considerable notice. It was reported that the bishop, despite his statement, "I don't like slumming," lived among the poor for a month, taking a share of the services at the church. The episcopal diary published in the *Journal* is not clear about the event, but public attention was aroused by the unusual episode.

But perhaps the greatest publicity was reserved for the Briggs affair in 1898–99. Charles A. Briggs, a Presbyterian minister, was a professor at the Union Theological Seminary whose biblical studies led him to a point of view incompatible with those of his colleagues (one gathers that Briggs's personality could add to that incompatibility). He was suspended from the ministry by the General Assembly of his church in 1893. Several years later it was announced that Dr. Briggs was seeking ordination at the hands of Bishop Potter. This was challenged by several prominent churchpeople, including, again, Dr. DaCosta and Admiral Mahan. They were countered by Dr. Huntington, who offered Grace Church for the occasion. Dr. Smith, retired rector of St. James', Madison Avenue, renewed his proposal to present Briggs for ordination. The shrewd bishop archly noted that the canon stated the bishop, after appropriate approvals had been received, *shall,* not *may,* proceed to ordination. This was the line Onderdonk had taken, with somewhat less success, at the Carey ordination. The rite accordingly took place in the procathedral on May 14, 1899; the ensuing uproar carried DaCosta into the Roman Catholic Church.

Bishop Potter's oft-stated preference for simpler days and an uncomplicated life contrast with his amazing forcefulness in a city where he moved among an opulence and power he frequently criticized. He was not afraid to lash out at the Republican Party, American "imperialism," race prejudice, and the evils of company towns. He believed in consumers' leagues, trade unions, the complete assimilation of immigrants in the social fabric. He believed with Tocqueville that American mobility fostered envy and competition resulting in a "brutal and socially destructive" civilization. His participation in the Church Association for the Interest of Labor (CAIL) is well-known. He served as chairman of the mediation board which ended the New York lithographers' strike in 1896 by setting a minimum wage and abolishing piece work. At the same time, he was president of the Century Club!

ANOTHER DIVISION?

Public transportation was well developed in the Diocese of New York by 1900. Telegraph service had long been efficient, and was now gradually supplanted by telephones: that word first appears in diocesan records in 1901.[39] The Hudson River passenger boats were a leisurely convenience between all major river docksites. The 391 clergymen serving 239 churches and chapels in 1900 would seem united by such excellent communication in a diocese led by one of the most respected bishops in the United States. But in the 1900 diocesan convention there was a resolution, followed by "considerable discussion," that the diocese be divided yet again. The motion aimed at exactly what Professor Samuel Roosevelt Johnson of General Seminary predicted in 1865: the Diocese of New York would be reduced by division to "the city and its vicinity."[40] The motion was not carried, but it is evident that then, as later, the idea had been privately argued and favorably received by many New York churchmen. One plan called for the Diocese of Albany to relinquish some of its vast territory in the creation of a new Episcopal Diocese of Ogdensburg. Then, perhaps, Albany could extend itself downriver, leaving the Diocese of New York with Manhattan and Westchester. So persuaded were many delegates that a motion advising new boundaries was carried, and a committee appointed. The next year, 1901, no one troubled to revive the question or the committee. Why? Probably because Henry C. Potter had quashed the idea. *He* had no difficulties with a populous diocese that stretched a hundred miles upriver and as far west as Pike County in Pennsylvania—he and the visiting bishops he called in to assist him: the Bishop of Nebraska was in New York every winter and spring. In the 1890s there had been an average of 4,315 confirmations each year. The Potters always had things very much under control. Very adroitly, the bishop vested a sense of responsibility and prestige in his archdeacons. They responded by extending the diocesan presence in their five regions. Why, then, should the Diocese of New York be divided in 1900?

But William Reed Huntington of Grace Church, Manhattan, was adamant. In 1902 he moved that division again be pursued, and correspondence be initiated with other dioceses. The old committee was reactivated and, in 1903, reported division inadvisable. Huntington gamely presented a minority report. He said that if all the territory beyond the city limits were made into a separate diocese, that diocese would rank twelfth in the American Church. So cogent was Huntington's argument that the committee was yet again continued, and four more members added to it. In 1905, thirty-six clergy (of more than 400 in convention that year) presented a petition that General Convention be asked to take preliminary steps for a new diocese. A long debate ended in a refusal to comply with the request. It is noteworthy that in this 1905 convention there were almost as many non-Manhattan clerical delegates present as there were city clergy. And in that year lay delegates from upstate outnumbered those from Manhattan. One of the reasons Manhattan was not made into a separate diocese was later touched upon by the bishop coadjutor when he said, "Rapid transit to the Bronx is now an accomplished fact." Nonetheless, the question of dividing the diocese would arise again and again.

THE BISHOP NEEDS ASSISTANCE

The growth of the Church required sustained assistance to Bishop Potter. Mention of a bishop coadjutor brings to the fore the question, When would there be adequate episcopal help? In 1902 Henry C. Potter was sixty-seven years of age and had been Bishop of New York for fifteen years—and what halcyon years they had been! Potter was called upon for hundreds of tasks never contemplated by the canons of the Church. No cornerstone was set in place, no public building opened, no civic meeting gathered, without the bishop's presence. Editors were keen to hear Potter's pronouncements upon political and social upheavals. He was known to walk with the great. Thus, when the 1901 convention met just after the assassination of President McKinley, the delegates thrilled to hear the kind words of Potter, who, of course, had been an intimate of the man everyone now mourned. The bishop spoke of the President's "dignity of presence, and a candor, openness, and sympathy of mind which made his personality one of charm and loveableness." The bishop confined himself to McKinley's personal characteristics and never touched upon the public ones. But he did enlarge upon the somberness of the moment to say that

> the assassination of three presidents in less than forty years, however
> different may have been their immediate causes, presents a situation
> that practically arraigns before the bar of the world's judgement civic
> and social conditions that we dare not ignore.[41]

It was the next year, 1902, when the convention was sitting in Holy Trinity Chapel, 88th Street, that Bishop Potter asked that a coadjutor be considered. He offered one-half his salary to meet the increased expenses. (This, too, was a Potter trait: the gratuitous gesture in the presence of fifty millionaires who, the bishop knew, would instantly see that funds for a coadjutor would be forthcoming: Potter, with his astuteness, could afford to be playful.) A committee was formed to facilitate the bishop's request. The idea of a coadjutor, an assistant bishop who automatically succeeds, was not then fully acceptable in the American Church. The following year, in the Church of the Heavenly Rest, then at 551 Fifth Avenue, Bishop Potter referred to the matter, and the committee moved the convention proceed that day to an election. Upon motion, nominations were made "without any debate, in accord with the precedent of the Convention of 1883."[42] After silent prayer, five names were placed in nomination.

Those five may serve as a summary of prevailing concerns in the Diocese of New York toward the end of its era of greatest prominence and influence. First, as was expected, the name of David Hummel Greer was heard. He had been rector of St. Bartholomew's in 42d Street since 1888. Here he had developed the "parish house movement" into one of the city's great institutions. St. Bartholomew's classrooms, gymnasia, and medical clinics were known far and wide. Greer's preaching was said to be intellectual and up to date. He was a much respected man.

William Reed Huntington of Grace Church was also nominated. Often mentioned for the episcopate in scattered dioceses, he fell more comfortably into the role of "first presbyter" of the Episcopal Church. Though his forcefulness was well appreciated in New York, Huntington seems never to have separated himself from the New England background that bade him stand independent, perhaps aloof, from the everyday concerns of a great diocese.

William Mercer Grosvenor, rector of the Church of the Incarnation, was nominated and many people believed him to be Potter's choice. Grosvenor was then forty years old, and had been rector of the Incarnation for six years, and had already received an honorary doctorate from the University of New York and been elected a deputy to General Convention; obviously, a comer.

The Rev. John C. Roper, slightly younger than Grosvenor, was a Canadian who had come to the General Theological Seminary as a professor in 1897. His ability brought him to notice sufficient to nomination. (In 1912 he became Bishop of British Columbia.)

We have already met the fifth nominee: Archdeacon George F. Nelson. He had long been Bishop Potter's lieutenant, having been a curate of Grace Church, and secretary in what passed for a diocesan office. Both he and Huntington withdrew their names—and then Greer proceeded to take the election in both orders on the first ballot. By any standard, New York was indeed a unified diocese in an age when electing conventions were frequently prolonged and acrimonious; that same year, 1903, the Diocese of Newark across the river endured its "all night" convention in which, finally, Low Church Edwin S. Lines was elected bishop of a diocese hitherto decidedly otherwise marked.

Nowadays, the election of a coadjutor bishop signals the last act of the bishop of the diocese. For a coadjutor has the right to succeed, unlike a suffragan, whose functions are those assigned from time to time by *the* bishop. The Episcopal Church was slow to adopt the principle of assisting bishops. No diocese was more reluctant than the Diocese of New York, whose corporate memory harkened to the time of Benjamin Moore, when three bishops claimed authority, or, later, when visiting bishops and "provisionals" invited near anarchy.

Potter's decision to ask for a coadjutor was based on the clear fact that as he aged he needed episcopal assistance in a diocese too large for one bishop, and too small to be divided again. He had suffered some kind of collapse about 1900[43] and now that Greer was there to visit churches and confirm, Potter assigned him the oversight of the city churches, while he, Potter, would look after those in the rural sections. This peculiar arrangement, which was entirely satisfactory to Greer, worked well, and made all the more certain the statement that "the country clergy knew Potter best"[44]—a strange assessment of the man who was generally considered Manhattan's first citizen.

Honors had come abundantly to Henry C. Potter. Apart from the constant flood of invitations to be present at every significant civic occasion in New York City, he received doctorates from Cambridge, Oxford, and St. Andrew's, as well as from American colleges. It was coincidental that he delivered his last sermon in the Church of the Incarnation, Madison Avenue, where his uncle's last public appearance had been in 1883. He died, quite unexpectedly, in Cooperstown, where he was vacationing, on July 21, 1908. Since Bishop Greer was then in England and many prominent people out of the city, there was a small burial service in the crypt of the cathedral; a great public funeral was held at Grace Church in October. Potter's sarcophagus is now in St. James' Chapel, a portion of the cathedral built in his memory and consecrated in 1916.

12

La Belle Epoque

The Absolute was born at Bethlehem,
The Perfect died on Calvary,
The Omnipotent rose at Easter,
The Infinite ascended from Bethany, and
The Eternal came down at Pentecost.
                    —David Hummel Greer

When Henry C. Potter was elected Assistant Bishop of New York in 1883, there were more than 1,500,000 people living in what was the Diocese of New York, and nearly 40,000 of them were reported to be communicants of the Episcopal Church. In 1908, the year that Bishop Potter died, there were 87,248 communicants in an area with 3,521,000 persons. In 1883 there were 144 incorporated churches and chapels and 318 clergy in the Diocese of New York. To give further perspective to his episcopate, let it be noted that the Brooklyn Bridge was opened the year Henry C. Potter was consecrated, and in the year of his death the East River subway tunnel connecting Manhattan's Bowling Green with Brooklyn's Borough Hall was made available to a public demanding quicker transportation. Also in that year, the world's tallest building, the Singer Building at Broadway and Liberty Street, was completed. The Queensboro Bridge would soon be ready for use, and the Pennsylvania railroad's tunnels under the Hudson and East rivers united New Jersey and Long Island. People of poetic temperament might muse that, truly, Manhattan was no longer an island; the more prescient, however, saw the bridges and tunnels as opening vast new areas which must be considered part of a greater New York. Bishop Greer was among those who saw the responsibilities as well as the wonders. His successors, alas, would learn that bridges and tunnels also made it possible for Episcopalians to flee the city and its parish churches. For in 1908 motorized traffic was here to stay. Just before Bishop Potter died, the last horse stages were taken off Fifth avenue, and some cabs installed "taximeters." But the country clergy would yet depend upon the older mode; in 1908 the rector of Millbrook, the Rev. Charles K. Gilbert, was presented with a horse and carriage.

THE CATHEDRAL AND ITS CLOSE

Perhaps the most opulent days of the Episcopal Church in New York came, paradoxically, immediately after Bishop Potter's death. Just ahead lay great construction on the cathedral grounds at Morningside. Amazingly, the bishop least interested in the cathedral idea, David H. Greer, was the very man under whose aegis all the ancillary buildings on the close were erected. When he became the diocesan, there was only the great cathedral apse and its beautiful Tiffany crypt chapel (now gone). Within twelve years, all the present structures were built, and since each has its own legends it is well to consider them here separately. Each suggests the popular (and wistful?) view of the Episcopal Church in the lingering twilight of the *belle époque*.

First of all, there was St. Faith's House, designed by the original cathedral architects. Heins and La Farge. It was designed to be a training school for deaconesses, and was built in 1911–12, the gift of Archdeacon Charles C. Tiffany. Its library was a memorial to William Reed Huntington; it was filled with the books bequested by him. Huntington was Potter's successor at Grace Church, and he championed the idea of deaconesses in the Episcopal Church. His influence was crucial in seeing the enabling canon through General Convention in 1889. St. Faith's House was a substantial facility in a prominent location. It was a focal center of the Episcopal Church's somewhat ambiguous attempts to incorporate the ministry of women into its total mission. Between 1890 and 1930, deaconesses were to be found in many of the larger parishes. At first, the idea of women workers, "set apart" in the Church, and garbed in a conventual habit yet not confined to the precincts of a convent, unsettled many Episcopalians as being distinctly Anglo-Catholic. But William Rainsford's early employment of deaconesses at St. George's, and William Huntington's arguing for them, made it clear this was not a party issue. For some, indeed, deaconesses were seen as an alternative, a counteraction, to the growth of sisterhoods in the Episcopal Church. Time has shown that the deaconess idea was a milestone along the way toward full historic ministry for women. But long before the ordination of women was permitted in the American Church, St. Faith's House ceased to be a training school. It is now the diocesan library and office building. But an aura of its original use remains, and there are those who say that, in the twilight of a midwinter afternoon, the apparition of a black-garbed, long-deceased instructor deaconess

may be seen scurrying down the narrow corridor toward a distant class-
room.

While St. Faith's was abuilding, work was proceeding on Synod
House and the Deanery, both designed by Cram and Ferguson. Again,
stories abound—and they are repeated here only to illustrate how difficult it is for historians to wrest fact from oft-repeated fiction. The Deanery was given by Mrs. Clinton Ogilvie, a devoted member of Grace and,
later, St. Thomas Church. Mrs. Ogilvie is one of the legendary rich
ladies of the Potter and Greer years who made life a trifle easier and
prettier in the Episcopal Church. According to the accepted tale, a
portrait bust of Mr. Ogilvie was to adorn forever a niche over the portal
of the Deanery's drawing room.

Entirely untrue is the story that Ralph Adams Cram planned Ogilvie House with two separate apartments on the second floor because
Dean Grosvenor and his wife didn't speak to each other. Grosvenor was
never married. His maiden sisters acted as hostesses in the public
rooms downstairs, but understandably preferred an apartment for themselves on the second floor.

The Synod House was built for the General Convention held in
New York City in October 1913. Here, the fable is that J. Pierpont Morgan wanted to provide the building for the conventions he enjoyed
attending. He was infuriated when he heard another "eminent layman," R. Fulton Cutting, had already contracted to build Synod House-
—and he never again spoke to Cutting. Which may in fact be true, for
Morgan died in 1913. He provided in his will a generous bequest to St.
George's, Stuyvesant Square, and another bequest for diocesan missionary work. Once Synod House was empty of the bishops and deputies of General Convention, it was to serve as diocesan offices for the
bishop and whatever assistance was thought required. Since 1910 there
has usually been at least one suffragan bishop.

Most splendid of all is the Bishop's House, also designed by Cram
and Ferguson. The tired old story, which seems to have no foundation
whatever, is that this elaborate house was built by J. Pierpont Morgan
"so that the Bishop of New could live like everybody else." Morgan was
no buffoon, and in its elaborate entrances, if not its size, the Bishop's
House exceeded any the elder Morgan himself owned. Moreover, Morgan didn't pay for the Bishop's House, nor was he even the most generous of the contributors who gave toward the $135,375 cost of its erec-
tion. When Bishop Greer said he thought the house of the Bishop of
New York should be near the cathedral, the cathedral trustees gave use
of the land the house would occupy. Proceeds from the sale of the
"Episcopal Residence" at 7 Gramercy Park added $52,000. The Episco-
pal Fund (of which the now deceased Morgan had been a trustee) was

expected to pay for the house, which was said to be "a commodious and suitable residence" for the Bishop of New York. As late as 1920, $32,000 was still owing on the place.[1] It cost $253 to move Bishop Greer into his new house.

If you were to call on Bishop Greer in those first years he occupied the Bishop's House, you would pass through a great stone archway into a vaulted reception room. A porter would indicate "retiring rooms" for ladies and gentlemen. Then, having been announced, you would be escorted up a long flight of stone steps to the paneled upstairs passage which gave on to a pair of parlors, later made into one large drawing room. Or, if yours was a more intimate gathering, you might be taken to the bishop's study, a huge room—one of the finest in the city, surely—whose eight tall windows facing three directions invite the streaming sun. Dinner would be served down the hall in an ample wainscoted dining room. A safe in the adjoining butler's pantry held whatever episcopal silver was not then in use. At one end of the dining room is a dais which had its own small family table. Now the room is used for conferences. An imaginative guide might tell you that once the bishop dined there at a high table while his lesser guests feasted at the lower table—something like the arrangements at the General Seminary refectory downtown. You will also be shown an iron-grilled aperture high up in the northeast corner of the dining room, and be told it was the minstrels' gallery from which gentle music might soothe the bishop and entertain his guests after a tiring day. Such tales are expected of extraordinary houses and the people who once inhabited them. There is the tale that a ghost inhabits the third floor of the bishop's house. It is said to be the wraith of a curate who, deposed because he stole Bishop Greer's jeweled pectoral cross, hanged himself in shame and returns to search for the purloined pendant. We will do well to remain with the fact that none of the three bishops of New York who lived in the entire "palace" ever played the role envisioned by the architects. The Greers, with their daughter Daisy as hostess, may have enjoyed the new house in a time when domestic help was available and perhaps suitable. But the place put Bishop Burch in debt[2] and the maintenance of six servants "impaired" Mrs. Manning's fortune. Bishop Gilbert and Bishop Donegan chose to live in the more sensible Ogilvie House, and Bishop Moore elected to take the bedroom floor of the Bishop's House which Dean Pike had made into a large and convenient apartment.

The final building on the close was completed the year Bishop Greer died. It is the Cathedral School, designed by Cook and Welsh, and given by Mrs. J. Jarrett Blodgett. It was intended to be a choir school for the boy choristers of the cathedral, and it served as such for almost fifty years. By the time Bishop Greer became diocesan, the choir of men and boys had become a fixed and popular feature at the cathedral. The bishop made no secret of his preference for a chorus of men and women, such as he had had at St. Bartholomew's. But the rule of male choristers prevailed at the cathedral until recent times, and the choir school was a significant part of diocesan life, enrolling boys "from all parts of the United States."[3]

BISHOP GREER

Bishop Greer was fifty-nine years old when elected to assist Bishop Potter, and almost sixty-five when he became the seventh Bishop of New York. He retained his administrative ability and prophetic vision, but diocesan work proved to be for him a prolongation, not a deepening, of his powers. In a sense, he transferred his ideals from St. Bartholomew's on Madison Avenue to the Diocese of New York: the diocese might be the parish writ large. Greer had awakened at St. Bartholomew's a concern for the poor and forgotten people who lived not far from the church. This concern was translated into "rescue" chapels and the well-equipped parish house and clinic on 42d Street. Nor did the rector merely direct his curates working in unfashionable places; it is said David Greer spent much time himself in that work, and went so far as to learn to speak Yiddish. Not many New York rectors cared to make that claim! Like Potter, Greer wasn't "churchy." But in his seeking to extend the Gospel in all areas of city life, he depended far more upon Episcopal institutions than his predecessor had done. In Potter, one finds a certain weariness, almost a sense of futility, about ecclesiastical organizations—the societies and guilds that Hobart, for instance, relied upon and aggressively directed. Bishop Greer would value Church organizations more highly than did Potter. Another difference between the two men is that they read different kinds of books. Greer read deeply in philosophy and theology; Potter preferred to keep up with political and economic thought. A correspondent wrote, in 1974, "I attended Columbia ('13) and had a slight acquaintance with Bishop Greer in the Brotherhood of St. Andrew, I admired him very much, and considered him the leader of the Broad Church School of the Frederick Robertson type. He seldom wore clericals, and generally had a bright red tie, whose effect he missed for he was totally color blind."

In yet another way the two bishops differed. Potter loved the country, while Greer preferred the city. This was an important difference in a diocese as varied as New York, and explains why Bishop Potter assigned his assistant charge of the city churches while he, the bishop of the diocese, remained responsible for the rural churches.

Bishop Greer acknowledged his preference for the city in his address to the diocesan convention in 1910. He said, "There is something in me that keeps making me want to do things I am not very good at, and of course the country is the ideal place for that."[4] Perhaps rural New York reminded him of his unhappiness in his first parish in Kentucky, which he quit amid questioning of his own belief. It was at Grace Church in urban Providence that David H. Greer hit a stride and effectiveness that made people compare him with his friend and admirer Phillips Brooks. Again, it was in midtown New York City that he accomplished the greatest work of his life. His election to be assistant bishop at the age of fifty-nine cannot be said to be a mistake; it simply came too late for the Diocese of New York to gain the maximum benefit from this great man. His sermons were considered profound, yet "eminently practical," and fired by his own personality drew large numbers to his church. Although devoted to his calling, he was thoroughly human and without professional self-consciousness. He rarely wore clerical garb on the street, and was friendly to all sects and classes. He was broad in his churchmanship but nonpartisan, liberal in his views, and alive to the problems created by modern science. A colleague compared Greer with Potter by stating that Potter looked like an autocrat and was a democrat, while Greer looked like a democrat and was an autocrat. He was firmly in charge of the diocese until age and near-blindness diminished his energies.

Once he was Bishop of New York, Greer made it clear that he wanted to strengthen Church institutions and interpret the Christian faith in "modern" terms as he had done at St. Bartholomew's. This he would do not only by his remarkable and memorable extemporaneous sermons, but also in a series of convention addresses, usually titled, which are today notable mainly for their datedness. So evanescent is modernity! As for institutions, Bishop Greer eagerly pursued his dream for two: the Bronx Church House, and Hope Farm.

The Bronx Church House was part of Bishop Greer's overall enthusiasm for providing new churches in the Bronx, an area made accessible by new rapid transportation. The Greater New York Charter united Brooklyn, Queens, Staten Island, Manhattan, and the Bronx in 1898, giving the city a population of more than three million. Though there was now a Tenement House Department in the city promising improved multiple housing, subways pushed farther and farther out of the city, making new lots available to those who had hitherto lived in the old-style airless tenements. Soon there was an uptown rush much greater than the accustomed middle-class migration that had crept northward, block by block, in Manhattan. This removal of families from downtown parishes was probably felt very early in the century; by 1908

it was so urgent a matter that the diocesan convention acted favorably
upon a motion asking families to obtain a Letter of Transfer when they
moved, with clergy expected to inform the prospective rector. We need
not speculate how effective this resolution was. When, for instance, a
family abandoned its East 26th Street flat for a new apartment in Webster Avenue, Calvary Chapel in 23d Street lost one more family. Bishop
Greer wanted that family to find an Episcopal church ready for them in
their new neighborhood. He aimed to strengthen existing parishes, and
there were some that had been founded when the shady lanes there
were thought to be far beyond the city's rough intrusion. Some were
very old parishes; St. Peter's, Westchester Square; Grace Church, West
Farms; St. Ann's, Morrisania; and St. James', Fordham, come to mind.
But apartments and single-family houses were also built in new neighborhoods where there was no nearby Episcopal church. Bishop Greer
begged his rich friends to give sites for new churches; the location for
St. Simeon's on Carroll Place was given by John Jacob Astor, for instance.

BRONX CHURCH HOUSE AND GREER SCHOOL

In his autobiography, Bishop Thomas March Clark of Rhode Island
declares that the "parish house movement" must be regarded as one of
the significant developments of the American Church during the nineteenth century. The Church, in Europe and here, had always used
buildings adjoining the church for educational or charitable purposes,
but in the second half of the century "parish houses" were used for
outright nonecclesiastical purposes. They were equipped with stages
for plays, ranges for cooking classes, rooms for social meetings, even
health clinics and, of couse, classrooms for Sunday school. Offices for
the clergy came very late. St. Bartholomew's had a very notable parish
house, but Bishop Greer realized it would be impossible for every new
church in the Bronx to build such a facility, and he therefore planned
one great parish house for the borough churches to share. This was
called the Bronx Church House. It was built in 1908 and at first had a
resident priest and deaconess. In 1914 the Church House was turned over
to the Board of Managers of the Missionary and Church Extension Society. Soon after, the neighborhood was deemed to be "non-Episcopal"
and the building was sold; the proceeds remain marked the "David H.
Greer Fund" for Episcopal churches in the Bronx.

Early in his episcopate, Bishop Greer decried the failure of New
York Protestants to provide a "protectory" for young people, as the
Roman Catholic Church had done. Almost immediately, for such was

the bishop's power of command, Episcopal-sponsored Hope Farm came into existence. The bishop was able to use the Priory Farm of the Episcopal Brothers of Nazareth in Verbank, near Peekskill. That Order had been founded in 1886 by Gilbert Tomkins of the Church of the Holy Comforter, Poughkeepsie. Tomkins, like James Huntington, was professed at the Holy Cross Mission Church of the Community of St. John Baptist, but the purpose of the Brothers of Nazareth from the beginning was to provide for destitute men and boys—in part, something Bishop Greer had in mind when he called for a "protectory." The Verbank property was eventually abandoned in favor of a site near Millbrook, where Hope Farm is now located.

FATHER WATTSON AND GRAYMOOR

Less successful as far as the Episcopal Church is concerned, but far more notable in the annals of the Church at large, was the Society of the Atonement in Garrison. It was founded by Lewis T. Wattson in 1898. Wattson was a graduate of St. Stephen's College and the General Theological Seminary. For a time—a somewhat stormy time!—he was rector of St. John's Church in Kingston. Finding the parishioners of St. John's reluctant to accept the liturgical changes he required, he founded the Church of the Holy Cross in Kingston in 1891. "Father" Wattson was one of the first to be called so in the Diocese of New York. Even James O. S. Huntington is listed as "Mr." in diocesan journals until the turn of the century. The Church of the Holy Cross was established as an Anglo-Catholic alternative to St. John's. Wattson's purpose in founding the new church was that Kingston might "have an Episcopal Church as he thought an Episcopal Church should be," and while he remained rector of the older parish, he installed the Rev. Charles Mercer Walker in charge of Holy Cross. An Ulster County tourist guide of the time reports that services in the Church of the Holy Cross "are maintained daily, and other chief services every Lord's Day. They are performed with the full use of the beautiful and ornate ritual of the Episcopal Church. The work of the parish is chiefly amongst the poorer classes."

Father Wattson left Kingston for a brief time as part of an associate mission in Omaha, Nebraska. He was drawn back to the Hudson River Valley by the vision of founding a Franciscan Order. Land was available on a hillside south of Garrison, where a small mission of St. Philip's-in-the-Highlands, named St. John's in the Wilderness, remained and was then unused. The Society of the Atonement was begun there in 1898, a mixed Order for men and women. Neither Bishop Potter nor Bishop Greer appears to have taken the new Order very seriously. Just before

Potter died, Father Paul—as Wattson was now known—organized a meeting of about twenty-five Episcopalians who formed what they called the Anglican-Roman Union, looking to the "ultimate reversion of the Episcopal to the Roman Church." Such announcements made headlines in those days, but did not endear the participants to the bishops of the diocese. The next year, 1909, the Vatican's Apostolic Delegate arranged for the two friars, the five sisters, and the ten terti-aries to be received into the Roman Catholic Church. The diocesan *Journal* for 1917 simply states that the property of St. John's, founded in 1878, had been "seized by the Roman Church and is now in litigation." That statement is misleading. Only a small portion of the Society of the Atonement's land belonged to the Episcopal Church. Most of the land had been purchased after the Society was established at Graymoor, and the courts confirmed the possession of the Society of the Atonement there.

SEAMEN'S CHURCH INSTITUTE

Another Church facility was very old, and safe in the fold: the Seamen's Church Institute. It traced its beginnings back to Onderdonk's concern for immigrants and sailors in the city. Church services were held by the Institute from its earliest days, and facilities for sleeping, eating, and banking were provided. The floating chapels were a picturesque part of the city's maritime life. In 1913 the Seamen's Church Institute moved into its new building at 25 South Street. Beds were available for 15¢ and an average of 411 men slept there each night the first year. At the same time, the Institute's new boat, the *J. Hooker Hamersley,* was built to replace the old *Sentinel.* The New York waterfront now had new docks, due to a report of the City Improvement Commission advising the con-struction of uniformly designed piers along the rivers. But in any case, New Yorkers were generally conscious of the importance of the port and its maintenance.

BISHOP GREER AT WORK

The official headquarters of the Diocese of New York was now called See House in Lafayette Street. Bishop Potter had kept an office there only for formal interviews, but most of his desk work was carried on in the various houses he occupied in the city during his episcopate. Bishop Greer lived at 7 Gramercy Park; his office was in his house, though Archdeacon Nelson continued to use See House for diocesan business and the bishop had office hours there on Wednesdays and Fridays from ten to noon. The suffragan bishop had office hours on Tuesdays and Thursdays.[5] Bishop Greer's style is suggested in the following incident, related by a young man:

> I went to see the Right Rev. David H. Greer, Bishop of New York. The butler at last showed me into Bishop Greer's study, and there the great man was, looking somewhat like a handsome, prosperous farmer, and wearing a frock coat and a red tie. He glared at me. I explained, as well as I could, that I was an Englishman who had married an American girl, and was expecting to live in this country.
>
> "What do you want?"
>
> I said I wanted to be ordained.
>
> "Where were you educated?" he asked.
>
> I told him I had been at Clifton and Trinity College, and that I held an Honorary Degree in Classics and Philosophy from Oxford University.
>
> "Where is that?" he demanded.
>
> "Where is what?" I whispered.
>
> "The degree," he snapped, while his hand reached out for the bell. Now this was a poser. I do not think Oxford ever gives degrees in the sense of written or printed certificates. . . . I explained as well as I could. He glared at me.
>
> "Well, go get it," he commanded.[6]

NOTABLE LAITY

Bishop Greer was assisted by such able laymen as J. P. Morgan (who usually presented the diocesan financial report to the convention), Roswell P. Flower (governor of New York in the early 1880s), Nicholas Murray Butler (the promising new president of Columbia University), Seth Low, and R. Fulton Cutting. Less conspicuous were the women who provided great sums of money for the Diocese of New York: Georgia E. Morris, Helen Slade Ogilvie, Mrs. E. W. Coles, Mary A. Edson and Mrs. J. Jarrett Blodgett, to name a few.

THE *TITANIC* AND ITS PORTENTS

For New York Episcopalians, the *Titanic* disaster in 1912 had particular significance. The liner symbolized Anglo-Saxon predominance and excellence. Its passenger list included Episcopalians whose names appeared in one or another columns of the daily papers. Aboard the *Titanic* (as the public soon discovered) were also hundreds of steerage passengers. Captain Smith, a typical British seadog, delayed retirement to take the great ship across the water on its maiden voyage. It was all part of the glorious Edwardian scene in which many people in New York unashamedly insinuated themselves. News of the tragedy was on the streets early Saturday morning. At first there were rumors and wild tales of heroism, together with the fears that were soon proved justified. We now know the ship's insufficiencies and feckless management, but the churches that Sunday and for weeks thereafter savored the horror. It was a disaster that equaled the awful *General Slocum* calamity on the East River in 1904. Then hundreds of Sunday school children and their mothers were lost. The *General Slocum* had been chartered by a group of Lutheran churches, but the *Titanic* seemed peculiarly Episcopalian: the ship's chaplain was Church of England, the hymns reportedly played by the band as the ship foundered were known to Episcopal churchgoers, and the ship emanated from that country to which the Episcopal Church looked to its origins—England. What we see is a contradiction to the then prevailing belief in the inexorability of progress, or as an overture to what would soon be a wailing chorus of catastrophe in war-torn Europe.

ARCHITECTS AT WORK

The poignance of this failure of technology, human valor, and empire was at least partially offset in those halcyon days of Edwardian splendor by magnificent churches built in New York City and in nearby towns. We need look no further than the grounds of the Cathedral of St. John the Divine to see what grandeur, what spaciousness, men and women of the Episcopal Church thought appropriate. There were some Episcopalians, a minority to be sure, though sometimes they don't appear to be a minority, who were building houses so that they could live like the Bishop of New York. By 1910 the taste for putting up pretentious houses on Fifth Avenue had just about run its course; easier transportation made it possible to spend long weekends in a country house on Long Island, or in Westchester or New Jersey. The homes of the Episcopalians who lived in the Fifth Avenue châteaus were devised by George B. Post, Richard Morris Hunt, the Herter brothers, and the firms Lord, Hewlett and Hull, and McKim, Mead and White. They might be expected to rival but, like Solomon's Temple, not exceed those of the proprietors in opulence.

In 1906 Trinity Church absorbed the impecunious Church of the Intercession on the upper end of the island at the prompting of its rector, the Rev. Milo Hudson Gates. Gates knew that Trinity had long planned a chapel in its uptown cemetery, at Broadway and 155th Street. The old church was sold, and Gates became vicar of what would be the Chapel of the Intercession. Bertram Grosvenor Goodhue was engaged to design the new building, which, when it was consecrated in 1915, was loudly acclaimed.

Earlier, St. Thomas Church on Fifth Avenue had selected Goodhue to replace its Richard M. Upjohn church, destroyed by fire in the summer of 1910. The flames had swept away works by LaFarge and St. Gaudens but—somewhat more to the point at the time—the vestry hoped the congregation wouldn't also be swept away by Leighton Parks, the new rector of St. Bartholomew's on Madison Avenue. Therefore, a neat wooden church was built amid the ruins of the burned church, and the congregation was able to note, week by week, the progress of the splendid new church rising about them.

St. Bartholomew's was practically forced to abandon its Renwick-designed Tuscan building when structural problems were discovered in 1914. Ten years earlier there had been discussions about changing neighborhoods, but the beautiful Vanderbilt entrance designed by McKim, Mead and White was too good to abandon. Now it was thought the portal could be moved and incorporated in a new building. The northeast corner of Park Avenue and 51st Street was purchased in 1914, and work went forward on another Goodhue Byzantine-style church which would soon become a New York landmark. While it is certainly true that the Episcopal Church ornamented many a New York State community with buildings of architectural distinction, it was the metropolis itself that was able to command the finest.

TYPICAL PARISH LIFE IN 1916

Let us look in again on our "St. Luke's," the rural parish eighty miles distant from New York City. We will find the same Upjohn building in use, but by 1916 there are significant changes in the church and its congregation. The former incumbent has died. His widow lives with an unmarried daughter in the city, where teachers are able to earn salaries considerably higher than those paid in the country. A parish house, shingled in the Queen Anne style, was built next to the church in 1890. It is a popular place for many townspeople and, despite some objections, there have even been dances held there. It has no plumbing, and water for the kitchen is carried in pails from the rectory well. (The rectory itself has water, but the present rector's wife has made it known she doesn't like "strangers filing through the kitchen." The lady attends church infrequently and, it is said, she "reads books.")

The parish had a very brief rectorate at the turn of the century. The man seemed all right when interviewed by the vestry. The only drawback was that he had attended a seminary none of them had heard of "somewhere out West," and Bishop Potter had seemed somewhat reserved about him. Also, the gentleman was unmarried, but that wasn't entirely negative inasmuch as he would accept the $1,000 salary the vestry offered him (though they were prepared to pay a married man as much as $1,200). This new man came, but things didn't turn out well. He was "a good caller," and his enthusiasm for renovating the church had at first been infectious. One of the wealthier parishioners paid for a New York architect's designs aiming at "making this church up-to-date." But it was all too elaborate and, frankly, strange. Nobody wanted a rood screen in that small church, and "all that business back of the altar" reminded people of St. Anthony's on Prince Street. The only "improvements" carried out were a brass-and-oak credence table (for the alms basins), an elaborate altar cross, and a pair of tall vases with a PX monogram in front. People didn't want candlesticks. (But they were later accepted when given as a memorial to a popular young man of the parish who died in the First World War.)

This short-lived rector was the one who sometimes wore Russian-looking white robes for the Communion service. He took them away with him when he left, which was all right with everybody. It was a sudden departure; he simply wrote a letter to the vestry regretting that there had "been disappointment on both sides," and by the first of the next month he was gone to be chaplain at the convent in Peekskill.

The interior walls of the church were painted a buff color in 1912, covering what remained of the original Upjohn stencils. As if to make up for the loss of that maroon and gold scroll motif, several windows from Louis Tiffany's studio are now in place. Several years ago the choir was moved from the floor of the nave to the chancel: the two front pews were placed on the higher level and served as the stalls. There is always an Offertory anthem during "the collection," and at its end the organist shifts into Old Hundredth, which the congregation sings, rising in waves as the ushers-vestrymen carrying the brass basins past successive pews. This is a liturgy, firmly fixed. The choir, about sixteen men and women, boys and girls, uses the Hymnal approved by General Convention in 1892; ordinarily, six hymns are sung during the customary ten-thirty service of Morning Prayer, Litany, and Ante-Communion. The choir does not now sing at Evening Prayer.

The rector in 1915 wears colored stoles for the Communion as well as at Morning and Evening Prayer. His black cassock buttons down the front, and his surplice reaches almost to his ankles. He brings his sermons down from the rectory in one or another of the "sermon cases" presented to him from time to time by needleworking women of the church; since the manuscript has been rolled tightly in the cylindrical case it is necessary for him to flatten it out on the pulpit desk before the service begins. The new electric lights in the church are turned off during the sermon, and the only light to be seen is that which streams down on the sermon manuscript from a brass pulpit lamp specially adapted: it was a kerosene lamp in former days.

The afternoon or evening service has been maintained despite clear evidence that whole families who once attended them are now touring back roads in their new Ford motorcars. Some people say the later service is a thing of the past, and a waste of the rector's effort, but he feels that as long as the cathedral keeps an afternoon service, the churches should do so, too.

After service, the rector now stands at the door to shake hands with the departing congregation. His parishioners at first thought this was undignified, though several New York City rectors are known to stand at or near the church door after service to be available to the flock. St. Luke's rector took up the custom after the new suffragan, Bishop Burch, insisted upon thus greeting the congregation.

St. Luke's has recorded thirty-three infant baptisms and fifteen adult baptisms in the years 1910–1915. In that time, fifty-one persons have been confirmed and twenty-one couples married; two infants and fourteen adults have been buried.

ELECTING A SUFFRAGAN

Bishop Greer was more prominent in the House of Bishops than Potter had been. When the canon permitting suffragan bishops was finally enacted in 1910 by General Convention, Greer called for a suffragan in New York. "I am permitted to ask for two suffragan bishops. I ask for one. That, for the present at least, is in my judgment enough," he said.[7] The next day, November 10, 1911, the Diocese of New York elected its first suffragan bishop, Charles Sumner Burch. He was nominated by the rector of Trinity Church, William T. Manning. This was a memorable occasion if only because, for the first time since 1784, the convention elected as a bishop in New York a man not associated with a "cardinal" parish.

Bishop Burch was a genial man, and he was warmly welcomed in a diocese whose bishops had seemed to be elderly, an irony since Burch was fifty years old when ordained to the priesthood. He was born in 1855, attended the University of Michigan, and was for years a newspaperman. At the time when most successful men thought of retiring,

Burch entered Western Theological Seminary in Chicago. After ordination he became rector of St. Andrew's Church, Staten Island, with eventual oversight of Stapleton and other nearby parishes. He was appointed an archdeacon and widened his work and his reputation as a man of acumen and good nature. He was a particular favorite of Bishop Greer,[8] and the two men were together in Oxford when word came that Potter had died in Cooperstown. It is certain that they then discussed what Greer should do, now that he was eighth Bishop of New York and, as it happened, so far away from his see. The business experience and popularity of Burch would be a great help. When it came to electing a suffragan in two years' time, he was overwhelmingly elected after his name was placed in nomination by Manning.

We detected scant alteration since the 1880s in a small country parish immediately prior to the First World War. But we will find changes much deeper in the diocesan conventions. The Potter legacy demanded close scrutiny of the contemporary scene, and to this Greer lent a forceful intellectual approach as well as administrative abilities Potter never possessed. In the years immediately before World War I there was a very great concentration of spiritual, commercial, and political ability at diocesan conventions. A synopsis of convention discussions indicates the breadth of diocesan concerns. Dr. Manning of Trinity offers a cogent resolution respecting arbitration between the United States and Great Britain as a major step toward settling international disputes (imagine such a resolution in a Hobart convention!); the Floating Church is gone after sixty-seven years; there had been three such boats, but the Seamen's Church Institute will henceforth have much more opportunity to serve the Port of New York through the new building rapidly rising on Spring Street; there are sixty-four students at St. Stephen's College, most of them studying for the ministry (and the college now has electric lights); a special diocesan commission proposed salaries of $1,200 for bachelor rectors, and $1,500 for married ones; another special commission recommends that there be three archdeaconries, "New York" (Manhattan and Staten Island), "East Hudson" (Westchester, Putnam, and Dutchess), and "West Hudson" (Rockland, Orange, Ulster, and Sullivan counties).

In a resolution he might one day regret, Manning asked that the diocesan canons be altered "to give due and suitable recognition to the Bishop Suffragan of this diocese." There was now a diocesan Social Service Commission, and it sent questionnaires to parochial clergymen asking if they belonged to any organization for social betterment (presumably meaning other than the Episcopal Church!)? what work was done in the parish for such betterment? was the parish house a "socializing" agency in the community? did the parish or community have a district nurse, or a neighborhood clinic, or trained workers among foreign-speaking people? was there a parish committee on legislation? affiliation with labor organizations? (three respondents replied Yes).

These questions are valuable to us who look at the Episcopal Church seventy years later. The clergy were moderately favorable to the ideals of the Social Service Commission. Half the respondents thought the parish house could be "a strong social factor in the community," and "a few of the clergy are alive to matters of local health," but "Sunday Schools are doing very little regarding social things." One reply read, "Never are such subjects spoken of" (but another man said he "used every sermon" to speak for social concerns). Yet another said "No politics" were wanted in this parish. "Apparently, few seem to know how far their parishioners are interested in national or state organizations for social uplift and betterment. We wonder if this is due to the lack of sympathy on the part of the clergy with such movements," mused the Commission chairman.[9] In summary, it was declared the Church should be alert to "vicious legislation," should supply clergy and laity plenty of information about social matters, should formulate a "suggested social program," and urge the clergy to become involved "in outside organizations." Alexander Griswold Cummins of Poughkeepsie gave this summary: "The Church should inspire every individual member to take an active, intelligent interest in all movements of social betterment,"[10] and offered as a bibliography books by Jacob Riis, Jane Addams, Walter Rauschenbusch, and Shailer Matthews.

The diocesan Social Service Commission found a warm friend in Robert Fulton Cutting. He was a vestryman and warden at St. George's Church and, like many of the delegates to the annual conventions, possessed great inherited wealth and a lineage considered impeccable (if not absolutely necessary!) for a layman of top-level diocesan importance in those days. But he was one of the few men of inherited wealth who studiously considered poverty in the city. He was president of the old Society for Improving the Condition of the Poor and the New York Trade School; in addition, he served on the boards of a dozen other organizations that sought to understand the causes of poverty as well as to alleviate it. New York Episcopalians remember him as the man who vied with Pierpont Morgan in building the Synod House. Both men had attended General Conventions for the past twenty-five years.

DAILY BUSINESS OF THE DIOCESE

As we have seen, in Potter's time the diocese maintained an office in a fine old house at 416 Lafayette Street. This writer once worked in that house and remembers it as much above the average New York City town house; its double parlors seemed grander, and its massive elliptical stairs more graceful than most such houses of mid-nineteenth-century New York. It had been the gift of Catherine Lorillard Wolfe and was to be used for any offices required by the Diocese of New York. It was used by the diocese and by Church-related agencies for more than fifty years. Even after the cathedral close began to fill up with buildings, Archdeacon George F. Nelson kept his office in Lafayette Street, though Bishop Greer, after he moved from Gramercy Park and temporary quarters in lower Fifth Avenue, used Synod House, and particularly Bishop's House, as his offices.

It should be remembered that comparatively few clergy expected to have offices in those days. The rector of St. James', Madison Avenue, for instance, never required an office until after World War I. Even the Bishop of New York quite casually received any callers in his study two or three afternoons a week "between the hours of two and four." Nevertheless, Bishop Greer was aware that contemporary demands upon the Church required new methods of doing business. His 1911 address to diocesan convention, titled "The Church Getting Ready for Work," has an almost ominous sound about it, for it practically puts into discard all the management customs of the past. The bishop claimed—in that heyday of metropolitan life, 1913—that spiritual realities are now required more than ever because materialistic values have proved wrong and inadequate. He saw the cathedral as a monumental witness to Christ in the city and, moreover, a center of Christian energy in the whole diocese. In his time the older ideal of the convention being the missionary society of the diocese was supplanted by the more efficient system of three archdeacons. There were men who, like Charles Sumner Burch, were rectors of substantial parishes now given additional responsibilities of supervision (unpaid) over an assigned area.

The archdeacons were expected to seek out promising places for new Episcopal congregations, and find clergymen to organize services there. It was a significant and, on the whole, generally successful undertaking. At the eve of World War I the Diocese of New York had eighty-seven missions and preaching stations and seventeen assisted parishes representing 5,653 communicants. Simple arithmetic made many of these outposts of the diocese impractical; a mission of sixteen communicants could not long exist unless it grew rapidly, or was richly endowed. The motorcar very soon closed many preaching stations, for it was now easier to consolidate four congregations in a central place.

It was not only the small rural missions that troubled the Diocese of New York, however. "Each year thousands of families are pushed out of the heart of the city," and the strength of the Episcopal Church was, by 1914, said to be in the circumference of the city. This meant far uptown, the Bronx and Westchester County. The considerable emigration to Long Island and the dioceses in New Jersey enriched the Church there. City churches now heard the call to establish chapels far removed from the mother church. Unfortunately, they were unable to respond. Churches such as Calvary, Grace, Incarnation, and St. George's were already committed to large and expensive programs and buildings in their East Side chapels. The handwriting was sadly discerned when Calvary Chapel on 23d Street, thronged in 1895, was declared derelict in 1904. So fast were neighborhoods changing. Even Calvary Church on Fourth Avenue had by 1914 declined far from the crowded congregations of Washburn and Satterlee. Only Trinity Church was able to respond to the call to do great things in a chapel beyond the heart of the city when it adopted the failing Church of the Intercession and built, as we have already noted, the glorious building in the corner of Trinity Cemetery at the corner of Broadway and 155th Street. This, however, was not a chapel for the poor, but rather for the well-to-do whose grandparents had lived downtown.

RAPID CHANGE

Many people said World War I put an end to the old era; others saw the demise clearly marked by the *Titanic* disaster. Perhaps Bishop Greer and other astute Episcopalians saw it in what must soon be a decline of Manhattan churches *if* they remained in their accustomed neighborhoods. It is one thing to buy and sell church buildings of indifferent architectural character, but quite another when your church is an acknowledged part of the city's beauty; even St. Bartholomew's on 42d Street delayed its move uptown because its people did not want to abandon the great portal. Manhattan's churches had, of course, followed the churchpeople in the steady uptown migration. Much money was spent in the process, and many feelings hurt as vestries surreptitiously took options on sites only a block away from other Episcopal churches. The difficulties of what we now call "inner city" churches, perhaps more than any other single factor, plainly spelled the end of the old era when the European war broke out so suddenly in the summer of 1914.

Bishop Greer was thought to be something of a pacifist; certainly (unlike Manning then and later) he was remote from the war: "A new, or rather an old, unexpected force . . . a throwback to a savage and barbarous age [that] does not express or typify the sober thoughts of the people," is how the bishop described what would soon become the worst carnage in the history of mankind. The bishop believed world crises gave Christianity a better hearing, that Christian *service* would in wartime commend the Christian faith, and doubted that the war would spread. The long late afternoon of Victorian "progress" was slow to fade into darkness. But as American casualties, and the Bolshevik successes, bore down upon the national consciousness, Greer took a more measured view: the war must be won because it is "a destructive force which has broken in upon our modern world and threatened the destruction of our modern civilization." Bishop Greer was a man of his own age who now, in his last years, was obliged to deal with public issues heretofore esoteric or easily dismissed.

Prohibition, for instance. For years there had been a vocal group in diocesan convention, headed by Bishop Frederick Courtney, rector of St. James', pressing for total abstinence. In the precocktail age, "social" drinking was just that: good dinner wines such as certain New Yorkers had always liked to think they could put on their tables; beer at corner saloons for German and English families; whiskey (for the Irish, it was said), available at five cents a glass. Since New York Episcopalians had long included "foreigners" (especially people of German, English, and Irish background) as well as old-name families, there probably wasn't much enthusiasm for Prohibition among the people of the diocese. But war does things: it had suddenly made Bishop Greer seem old and outdated, and with equal rapidity it made Prohibition respectable, even patriotic. The diocesan convention of 1917 asked Congress to prohibit the "manufacture and sale of alcoholic beverages during the war."

There were other sobering signs of the times. The convention opposed the so-called liberal Sunday, and remarked that "the moving-picture houses, at least in the city, lawlessly continue their Sunday exhibitions." President Wilson sent a telegram to the convention when it assured him of support in the war effort. Parish clergy in considerable numbers volunteered for chaplaincy duty in the reserve (Manning was conspicuous among them), and many went overseas; war had indeed come to the diocese when it was learned of the death of the first Episcopal priest to be killed in the war, the Rev. Henry P. Seymour of Christ Church, Piermont.

DEATH OF BISHOP GREER

When the diocesan convention met in May 1919, Bishop Greer was not present. He was a patient in St. Luke's Hospital, and sent a letter to the delegates saying that he would soon be "on my feet again, as good as or better than new": an optimistic statement for an overworked man of seventy-five who had been almost completely blind for several years. (It was necessary to paint on the cathedral floor white lines for the bishop to follow during services.) The bishop asked for a second suffragan, but would not want a coadjutor. The convention voted to proceed to election the next day but, on motion of Dr. Cummins of Poughkeepsie's Christ Church, instead of a suffragan, Bishop Greer was provided with a generous fund with which he could procure episcopal services (Bishop Lloyd, for instance, had just left his Domestic and Foreign Mission Society position, and would be available). It is entirely probably that Cummins and his friends, satisfied with the ascendant Low Church aspect of the diocese, feared the election of someone like Manning, who would disturb the status quo. He was right but, as events unfolded, probably regretted his successful motion to his dying day.

For, six days after the convention of 1919 adjourned, Bishop Greer died. He was buried immediately in the cathedral crypt. The Standing Committee of the diocese (all Manhattan men likely to depart soon from the city for the summer) arranged for a special convention early in September which would elect a new bishop for New York. In the meantime, Mrs. Greer died, less than a month after the bishop, and thus the great Bishop's House so recently completed and occupied was empty.

ELECTION OF BISHOP BURCH

The Standing Committee fixed September 17, 1919, as the day for the election. Needless to say, there had been discussions among Episcopalians all summer. Once gathered in the cathedral nave, not in Synod House, the amenities were first observed. Stephen F. Holmes, senior presbyter of the diocese and recently retired rector of St. John's, Pleasantville, was invited to take the chair until the permanent chairman, the Rev. Harry Peirce Nichols of Holy Trinity, Lenox Avenue, was appointed. It was resolved that nominations would be by name only; as in 1883 and 1903, there would be no speeches promoting candidates. The nominees were soon apparent: Manning of Trinity (popular with the clergy); Stires of St. Thomas, Fifth Avenue; Slattery of Grace Church; Nathaniel S. Thomas, Bishop of the Missionary District of Wyoming; and, of course, New York's suffragan, Charles S. Burch. Later, it was remembered that

> Bishop Burch had been devoted in his work as Suffragan Bishop, and had greatly endeared himself to the up-state clergy to whom he had ministered: they came down to the Harlem River like a tidal wave, met there with support from the "High Church" group on Manhattan Island, and the result was a foregone conclusion.[11]

Burch had a lay majority all along, and easily took the clerical vote to win on the third ballot. The special convention adjourned at four thirty, unmindful that the new diocesan was not provided an adequate salary, housing expenses, and episcopal assistance. Nevertheless, Bishop Burch entered eagerly into his new responsibilities. And he was surrounded by active laity of very high caliber. Bertram Grosvenor Goodhue and Mrs. William Halsey Wood (whose late husband had been notable runner-up in the competition for designing the cathedral) served on a commission for new church buildings. Franklin D. Roosevelt was a cathedral trustee on the "Estate and Property" committee, and a provisional deputy to General Convention. Nicholas Murray Butler was also a cathedral trustee, as were Ogden Reid and August Belmont. J. P. Morgan the younger continued his father's participation in the Episcopal Fund, and Alton B. Parker (unsuccessful presidential candidate against TR in 1904) was chairman of the committee on diocesan boundaries. Celebrated attorney George Zabriskie, banker Stephen Baker, and insurance magnate Haley Fiske were prominent in various committees, year after year.

The new bishop sounded a certain trumpet. Forsaking Bishop Greer's profundities, Burch was decidedly "churchy" in his address to the 1920 convention. He said the diocese needed more postulants for the ministry. There was need for more preaching stations, and automobiles to facilitate diocesan mission work (there were already eleven such cars in use). Clergy salaries should be set no lower than $1,500. The cathedral construction would soon resume. At the bishop's urging, the old Fund for Aged and Infirm Clergymen was consolidated with the Church Pension Fund recently formed by the national Church. Bishop Burch announced that he would not ask for episcopal assistance in 1920 except for what might be given by Bishop Lloyd and visiting missionary bishops.

"281"

Every missionary bishop in the Episcopal Church came to New York because the Domestic and Foreign Missionary Society had its headquarters at 281 Fourth Avenue. The Society was established by General Convention in 1820 in order to strengthen and unify the missionary work of the Episcopal Church. The Presiding Bishop was to be its president; bishops, members of the House of Deputies, and anyone else contributing $3 or more each year could be a "member." Auxiliary organizations, aiming at assisting the main body, were formed in various dioceses and churches. The leadership of women in these was conspicuous, none more so than that of the Emery sisters, who were salaried officers of the auxiliary they had helped establish in 1872. Thereafter, an impressive proportion of missionary support came from the women's auxiliary of the Board of Missions (as it was often called).[12]

The address 281 Fourth Avenue was familiar in the Episcopal Church long before General Convention formed the National Council in 1919, for it was at the Church Missions House that missionary policies determined at the triennial were carried out. The new canon providing a central organization with various departments meant that now the Episcopal Church in the United States had a headquarters, and the Presiding Bishop had an office (though it would be nearly another twenty years before he was required by canon to relinquish his diocesan duties). The Rt. Rev. Arthur Seldon Lloyd, formerly Bishop Coadjutor of Virginia, was general secretary and president of the older organization, the Board of Missions, and as consolidation drew near he graciously resigned. Much to everyone's surprise, this bishop known to all Episcopalians inquired of a mission church, St. Bartholomew's in White Plains, if he could be their minister. Needless to say, he was engaged immediately. Meanwhile, the name National Council was adopted in 1922. Thereafter, the Presiding Bishop of the Episcopal Church found himself on Fourth Avenue in New York City more and more as expanding Church affairs demanded the attentions of a presiding officer. And, as we shall see, Bishop Lloyd was not allowed to remain long in White Plains.

The years immediately following World War I saw also the Nation-Wide Campaign. This was an attempt, on the whole successful, to "bring the spiritual and material resources of the Church to bear most effectively and adequately upon the whole task of witness to the Master." The campaign, and the formation of the National Council, had a unifying effect upon the entire Episcopal Church. Diocesan lines and loyalties were, perhaps for the first time, seen as secondary to the interests of the whole national Church. The Nation-Wide Campaign also utilized laity as leaders, and within a year many dioceses had heard of the Episcopal Church's work from expert speakers from distant places. A direct outgrowth of this was the Every-Member Canvass and the ideal of diocesan quotas. This latter may have been unfortunate, because many people came to associate the campaign with money raising, forgetting that its original purpose had been a broad reawakening and education of churchpeople after a terrible war had shaken the foundations of what had been considered "Christian" civilization.[13] Nonetheless, the underlying reasons and ideas of the Nation-Wide Campaign were not irrelevant when it came to raising funds for the Cathedral of

St. John the Divine in the 1920s. And there was an undeniable increase of Episcopal awareness of perceived mission, and money to support that mission. Perhaps never before had so many Episcopalians recognized their responsibility in the welfare and witness of the Church.

Both the formation of the National Council (with its displacement of Bishop Lloyd) and the Nation-Wide Campaign helped determine the future of the Diocese of New York. Bishop Burch, in his only address to the convention as Bishop of New York, said that the Campaign had, so far, been salutory for the diocese. He also was pleased with the apparent effectiveness of the "archdiaconal system," which, he said, was responsible now for 127 assisted parishes and missions and preaching stations; in 1911 there had been less than half that number. The diocesan missioners now had eleven motorcars, a figure beginning to spell doom for those little railroads Henry C. Potter had known so well— and, as a matter of fact, doom also for many of those missions and preaching stations the cars were expected to serve. The bishop was glad that the salaries of diocesan missionaries had much improved, though whether or not they had kept pace with prevailing inflation was questionable. The bishop looked forward to a reinvigoration of diocesan morale by a program he called Bishop's Weeks, during which he would reside in various parts of the diocese and be accessible to local clergy and laity. He was optimistic about urban ethnic groups, mentioning specific diocesan work with people from Italy, Poland, Japan, China, and Sweden. He was especially enthusiastic (as well he might be) about the growth of Negro churches. The cathedral services were "thronged"; completion of the building "soon" was now urgent, and entirely feasible. The trustees were about to proceed.

On the negative side, Bishop Burch said he and the Standing Committee would continue to resist disposing of old churches, nor would mergers of existing Manhattan parishes be encouraged: the Church should minister in the neighborhood where it found itself. The bishop also decried individual liturgical practices, High or Low. Sensing for some reason that the diocese was reluctant to elect a suffragan at that time, he said he could handily depend upon visiting bishops for assistance, as well as have the help of Bishop Lloyd. It was a robust address, optimistic, looking forward to advances the Great War had merely postponed. Perhaps the delegates present wanted to hear such a sanguine word from their genial bishop, but certainly there were some men present who saw the late war not as an interruption, but the end of much that had been accepted as the deserved portion for New York Episcopalians. Perhaps the diocesan convention of 1920 was a watershed, running fast toward the future, yet coursing back to the days of "Wise Potter" and all the promise of the turn of the century when the Episcopal Church was, at least in the East, prestige and power at prayer.

In that 1920 convention there were motions to allow women to serve on vestries and as delegates to diocesan conventions. The former was soon determined to be a matter of local preference, but it would be many years before women were accepted as convention delegates. There was also solemn concern with irresponsible churchpeople and church papers which "directly or indirectly countenance any propaganda, party, or individual advocating disorder or violence in effecting economic or governmental changes." [14] This was the Big Red Scare as expressed by some New York Episcopalians. There was also a motion approving the Eighteenth Amendment "as a great moral advance, a help to clean thinking and clean living and a strong bulwark against many of the ills which society has been heir to in the past." [15] (How many of the gentlemen delegates voting for such national high-mindedness had already made private arrangements to slake their own thirst?) The regrettable Amendment was, at the least, an inconvenience for rectors who now had to obtain Communion wine by individual bottle, through local purveyors. Here evolved another lay task: the city businessman or the faithful communicant stenographer, regularly carrying a carefully wrapped parcel to church. And that led the mind to an ancillary problem: intinction, dipping the Communion bread in the wine, practically unheard of prior to the great flu epidemic of 1918–19. Some churches began communicating entirely by intinction, using specially designed vessels. Others said that in time the common cup would be made illegal, and one senior warden spent his whole term in the Legislature at Albany lobbying for such a measure. [16]

The convention of 1920 heard a resolution that Congress be urged to extend food relief in Europe "even at the expenditure of the large sums of money required," and yet another asking that convention assist people in the knowledge of basic "economic processes" so that Christian principles and social justice might prevail. There was mention of the need to "calm agitation," and the "rehabilitation of wounded servicemen," a complaint (heard since) that the Post Office was declining in efficiency, a warning that trouble between England and Ireland might lead to prolonged bloodshed, and a plea for "education in social hygiene" as the best way to combat venereal disease. [17] Toward the end of the convention it was noted that all five dioceses in the state would have to agree before women could be included in diocesan conventions.

Postwar years are always intoxicating, as proved literally true in the 1920s. Restrictions are thrown off. One thing becomes certain: old verities are scrutinized. In 1920, when the people of the Diocese of New York questioned their politics, their moral outlook, their neighborhood, they may well have paused to give an estimate of their former bishops in light of the prevailing attitudes. "Up-to-date" was the new watchword, as Sinclair Lewis so aptly noted in *Main Street*. If Greer's infirmities cast a shadow on his undeniable ability, nothing seemed to dull the luster of Potter's reputation. And now there was Bishop Burch. He had not been the first choice of the Manhattan rectors, who had for so long taken it upon themselves to determine who would be the next Bishop of New York (generally, one of their own number). But Burch won the respect as well as the affection of churchpeople. He remembered their names, had been a working newspaperman "out in the world," and was—to put it plainly—as different from Potter and Greer as their times were from his time. Though sixty-five years old in 1920 (Potter was seventy-three when he died, and Greer seventy-five), Bishop Burch seemed much younger, and with his vigorous six-foot-two stature and open, genial nature, he promised much.

Unfortunately, he died nineteen months after his election as diocesan. The sad event was seen as a parallel to the early death of Bishop Wainwright in 1855. Both men had assumed great burdens, Wainwright a diocese that had had no active bishop for eight years, Burch a diocese long presided over by elderly predecessors. Both Wainwright and Burch made superhuman efforts to "catch up," Wainwright by arduous visitations throughout his huge diocese, and Burch by particular attention to administration and cathedral fund-raising. Now that the war was over, he was certain the diocese could find $500,000 each year until the nave was complete.

On Sunday, December 19, 1920, Bishop Burch went to the Women's Bedford Reformatory and there confirmed eleven "penitents." The authorities allowed them to wear white dresses instead of the usual prison denim. The bishop presented each confirmand with a cross and spoke to them about the Summary of the Law. The occasion was considered noteworthy enough for the *New York Times* to provide it full coverage.

The next day dawned sunny in Manhattan and toward noon the bishop (who had been suffering a sore throat for more than a week) took the opportunity of a fine day to stroll along Riverside Drive. There, near Grant's Tomb, he was stricken with a heart attack. Minutes later, he died in the home of a friend who had summoned help from St. Luke's Hospital. The Standing Committee was immediately notified.[18] The sudden death of the new bishop came as a keen disappointment to all who had heard of him; one newspaper stated that the bishop's early death was caused "by the strenuous labors on plans to rush the work of the cathedral . . . he had no Suffragan or Coadjutor to share the burdens with him." A *Times* editorial said, "He reminded many of Bishop Potter."

New Yorkers who read of the bishop's sudden death were further stunned to read, next day, that a man and woman were found murdered in the bishop's car. The automobile had been stolen from the bishop's chauffeur, and the crime committed some place distant from the cathedral. The Standing Committee, whose president was Ernest M. Stires, rector of St. Thomas Church, and whose leading layman was then George A. Zabriskie of Calvary, asked Bishop Lloyd to take visitation appointments already made and, soon after Bishop Burch's burial in the cathedral crypt, arrangements were made for the election of his successor.

13

The Reign of Manning

*Bishop Manning extended his religious ministry
beyond the walls of his beautiful cathedral, and beyond the confines of his denomination. He brought
the message of religion to our city, and to our
country as a whole.*

—RABBI DAVID DeSOLA POOL

Bishop Burch had given promise that the Diocese of New York would
cease its "policy of drift"—these words occur forcefully in the record—
and enter upon a new era. His death seemed to end these auguries of
improvement. The picture probably appeared bleak to some observers:
postwar changes in conduct, signs of urban disintegration, the antique
modes of Church management, the faltering of once-prominent city
parishes (Epiphany and Calvary come immediately to mind)—these
certainly troubled anyone concerned with the Church's future in Manhattan. As for the rest of the diocese, much promise had yet to be
translated into reality. The delegates who gathered in January 1921 on
Morningside Heights to elect Burch's successor seemed to have been
charged with one great task: choose a man who will stop this drift.

THE ELECTION

Three Manhattan candidates were waiting to do that: William Thomas
Manning, rector of Trinity Church; Charles Lewis Slattery, rector of
Grace Church; and Ernest M. Stires, rector of St. Thomas. All were capable, and all would soon be bishops of great dioceses. The Special Convention was scheduled for January 26, less than five weeks after Bishop
Burch died. Manning led early and was elected on the third ballot after
the Stires enthusiasts threw their votes in his direction. Though Slattery
had been their candidate, intense Low Church people never forgave
him for not withdrawing: "his faculty for political advanture in the

church was highly developed, due perhaps to his Irish lineage," sniffed a critic long after.[1]

The argument was that, had Slattery withdrawn, Stires would have been elected. But others said Manning's triumph was due to the affront offered convention delegates when minions of William Randolph Hearst handed them newspaper editorials condemning Manning. During the war, Manning had fiercely criticized the Hearst papers for their neutral stand at a time when the future bishop urged the United States to assist the Allies. One thing was sure: Manning was not entirely the candidate of the High Church people. He had "lost much of the Catholic vote: because of his interest in the Faith and Order movement which, in time, developed into the World Council of Churches."[2] On the whole, when the convention adjourned, church people of every shade of belief were quite sure the right man had been elected.

Who was this man who would dominate the Church in New York in such a manner that reasonable observers a generation after his time would speak of his twenty-six-year "reign"? What qualities in him led men and women either to adore or to detest him? He was indeed most remarkable, though not all would agree even there; "a little man in a big job," commented one critical colleague. "I venerate his memory," says another. Between these extreme assessments might be found the opinions of many who, especially on Monday mornings after the newspapers had been delivered, read what the bishop had said or done the day before. Bishop Manning recognized the importance of the city's flourishing newspapers. He was skilled at publicity releases, and was an energetic writer of letters to the editor. His cathedral sermons were often printed and available beforehand to the reporters who sat at a large table near the pulpit.

There was near unanimity that Bishop Manning was remote, inaccessible, forbidding. One man, today a judge, says he will never forget the Sunday he was an acolyte in his Mt. Vernon parish when the bishop made a visitation. The dignified wardens, themselves so intimidating, trembled as they handed the alms basons to the bishop at the Offertory. Perhaps it was the bishop's appearance. He was short (five feet four and a half inches) and slight (130 pounds), astonishingly so for a man of his reputation, but his frame was well put together and in the early days of his episcopate suggested the muscular agility one associates with the Hobart portraits. His skull seemed oversize, but it was his death-mask visage that made him look like a censuring prelate who would be more at home in the fourteenth century than in New York in the 1920s.

The comparison is not far from the mark, for the new bishop would insist on orthodoxy, as he understood it. "If you threatened him or his convictions, you were in trouble," recalls one admirer.[3] He used the word "catholic" rather more often, and somewhat more particularly, than his predecessors had done. A leading Evangelical layman, banker Stephen Baker, wrote to congratulate Manning on his election, stating that the new bishop's businesslike methods were much needed by the diocese, but Manning himself saw his task of tightening up ecclesiastical practices as equally important. Two famous examples will interest us here, for they confronted Manning—or rather, Manning confronted *them*—soon after his consecration.

EARLY CONFLICTS

At St. Mark's-in-the-Bouwerie the rector, William Norman Guthrie, had promoted what seemed to many people to be strange liturgical practices, accompanied by harp. "There, over the graves of some of the city's most esteemed forefathers," the services were "danced out" by professional artists, who, coached by Guthrie, saw their roles as an authentic religious expression. Many people in the congregation thought otherwise. When these liturgical oscillations came to the notice of Bishop Greer, he remonstrated with the rector—unsuccessfully. Manning, however, was not to be so easily deterred. He and Guthrie had known each other at Sewanee and in Cincinnati. Guthrie came to downtown St. Mark's when Manning had been rector of Trinity three years. It is doubtful that they were congenial colleagues. The battle lines, then, were probably already drawn when the bishop was consecrated. Though Guthrie was a prolific writer, he never offered the public a cogent apologia for the goings-on he promoted at St. Mark's, and therefore the matter was publicly reduced to Manning vs. Dancing-barefoot-in-church. Today, such art forms are frequently accepted in liturgical settings, but in 1921 the public was decidedly on the Manning side of the argument, and enjoyed the quarrel, too. Guthrie wouldn't promise to end the dancing, and Bishop Manning refused to visit St. Mark's for some years.

Even more troublesome for the bishop and equally diverting to the public was Percy Stickney Grant, at the Church of the Ascension on Fifth Avenue. Here was a longtime rector who, for years, had publicly advocated some ideas the bishop was bound to oppose. Grant had followed E. Winchester Donald at Ascension. Donald was a most capable man whose succession to Phillips Brooks at Trinity, Boston, undid his fine reputation (for who *could* follow Brooks?). While at Ascension, Donald had firmly set that parish toward social action, discussion of contemporary problems, and bringing the Gospel to bear upon modern

developments, as Brooks had long done at Boston. It was later said of
Dr. Donald, "Of the Church as an institution whose object it is to keep
the Spirit of Jesus Christ in touch with human life, and to put as much
goodness into life as possible, he was tremendously hopeful."[4] Percy
Stickney Grant enlarged upon this ideal at the Church of the Ascension.
He had begun by refusing to come to the parish unless the vestry declared the pews free. Almost immediately after, Grant moved toward
merging some of the weak neighboring Episcopal parishes with the
Ascension. He was a decisive leader who spoke often about the Gospel
and society.

He was apt to be impatient with Episcopal customs. For instance,
he advocated the use of little cups for the Communion.[5] This would
have been enough to arouse Bishop Manning, but it was Grant's strong
and strange views of Christian marriage that brought him into direct
conflict with the bishops of New York. He favored the marriage of
divorced persons, and was thought to have officiated at such services.
Bishop Greer had confronted him about this.

Now, Percy Stickney Grant was himself handsome, popular—and
unmarried. Romantic stories had long circulated about him, and from
the record it looks as if he enjoyed being the talked-of Fifth Avenue
bachelor rector. If this is true, he received full measure for his taste
when it was announced that he would soon marry a divorced "New
York Society Beauty." The city papers assumed at first an unwonted
discretion, despite the news value of orthodoxy vs. liberal views in the
1920s. The newspapers in distant places, however, were soon in full
cry, for this was the era of the Scopes Trial, and a time when indecency
was said to have invaded even the churches: was not New Jersey's Reverend Mr. Hall recently found murdered with his mistress? The headlines told what editors thought of Percy Stickney Grant: A GOOD MAN
GONE WRONG, lamented the Lockport *Journal;* another *Journal* (Spar-
tanburg, South Carolina) simply said, KICK HIM OUT, BISHOP. Many people wrote to Manning and demanded that Grant be deposed. It was
remembered that he seemed to deny the divinity of Christ, had scoffed
at such ecclesiastical practices as the consecration of church buildings,
and had implied the New Testament miracles were mere autosugges-
tion. The Walden (N.Y.) *Herald* declared, THE MAN SHOULD RESIGN. Father Huntington of the Order of the Holy Cross volunteered to present
Grant for trial; Billy Sunday wrote, praising Bishop Manning's sound-
ness.

The bishop, who relished publicity as much as the rector of Ascension did, resorted to what became a characteristic approach: he sent
Grant a list of questions, demanding either satisfactory answers to each

or a resignation, and the letter appeared in the New York papers the next morning. Grant outwitted the bishop by replying in a defense so lengthy that it bored the public and took the sting out of the bishop's confrontation. The bishop then adopted an attitude of waiting to review Grant's future "conduct"—meaning, of course, would he or would he not marry the Society Beauty. The bishop further righted himself by challenging Grant, at a Church Club dinner address, to deny the Creeds flatly and make himself clear.[6] The antagonism ended in a standoff in which neither principal was the winner. That means, in effect, the bishop was the loser, for he would have to bear the burden of the trouble, while Grant, soon to retire, could bask in the delights of a joust with the Bishop of New York. A sagacious observer was accurate when he wrote, "When the Rev. Dr. Grant created so much excitement on Fifth Ave. he finally wrote a rather vaguely worded letter to Bishop Manning, saving the bishop's face for not proceeding against him as a "'contumacious heretic and defiler of the shrine.'"[7]

Nevertheless, the persona of Bishop Manning was so indelibly cast in his confrontations with Guthrie and Grant that it ever after tended to place him in the role of an unbending and rigid monarch of a diocese. This was commonly perceived by those who knew Manning's strict views on divorce and remarriage, and his firm refusal to allow non-Episcopal clergymen to participate in marriage services in Episcopal churches. When in 1926 he declared that the Marlborough-Vanderbilt marriage performed in St. Thomas Church in 1895 was still valid, despite a much publicized Vatican decree to the contrary, he was generally applauded. But, again, Manning's apparent severity was the enduring memory. And, after the Judge Lindsay controversy, Bishop Manning's reputation was forever tarnished.

THE REGRETTABLE MOMENT

Ben Lindsay was an elderly jurist and Methodist layman whose humaneness and experience at the bar led him to sympathize with those people who, in increasing numbers, were seeking divorce. His remedy was a legally respected period of "trial marriage," a solution that brought him the dubious "appreciation" of Havelock Ellis.[8] Lindsay's writings and speeches had received national notoriety for four years when, early in 1930, the Churchman's Association in New York City asked him to be a luncheon speaker on December 1 of that year. "The Institution of Marriage" was the announced title of Lindsay's address. Bishop Manning heard that the judge would speak to the association of Episcopal clergymen. He demanded that the engagement be canceled, and even announced that he and Bishop Gilbert would be the speakers that day. The Association's program chairman, the Rev. Eliot White, refused to accede to the bishop's demand, whereupon the truculent Manning girded himself for battle. It was the most unfortunate single event of his episcopate.

Canceling his participation in a memorial service for the Rev. Dr. Mottet, for fifty years Muhlenberg's successor at the Church of the Holy Communion on Sixth Avenue, the bishop made it known that he would preach about Judge Lindsay's notions at the afternoon service in the cathedral. The nave was well filled, and the congregation expectant. The bishop began his sermon by denouncing those who had been cordial to Judge Lindsay: "There is in this diocese a little group of churchmen who, with what motive I do not venture to say, have been doing whatever lay in their power to make difficulties for their Bishop, and to place him in embarrassing situations," he declared.[9]

The London *Times* reported what followed:

At Sunday morning's [sic] service, detectives mingled with the congregation and stationed themselves near Judge Lindsay, who took up a position immediately behind a press table. Hardly had Bishop Manning begun the Benediction after the sermon when the Judge leaped on the press table and began shouting at Bishop Manning, demanding five minutes to refute "the lies" levelled at him. Members of the congregation (of 3,000) began to shout, urging those in front to kick the Judge and throw him out. Detectives removed the judge from the cathedral and took him to the police station where, in the absence of anyone willing to charge him with disorderly conduct, he was released and ordered to appear in court on the following morning. Judge Lindsay showed signs of the beating he received in the cathedral.[10]

The bishop was not spared excoriation. The conservative New York *Herald Tribune* said, "There has seldom been an episode in the city more completely disheartening than the Manning-Lindsay confrontation in the cathedral . . . Bishop Manning's unseemly utterance was a grievous wrong to the communion and to the community which he serves."[11] Heywood Broun, then columnist on the *Telegram,* came down hard on the bishop:

Dr. Manning was at his worst, moved to undignified fury by a revolt within the clergy of his diocese. . . . The quality of the bishop's spiritual leadership may be checked by the fact that members of his congregation cried out "Lynch him" (i.e. Lindsay) and that several beat a small, defenceless man severely. . . . The edifice which was to be a place where all might come to find spiritual solace, according to their lights, has become all too palpably the lodge room of one of the smallest bishops who ever issued an imperial edict.[12]

It was not true that there was a "revolt" in the Diocese of New York. Rather, the bishop had several able, vocal challengers. Among them at the beginning of his episcopate were Leighton Parks and Robert Norwood, rectors of St. Bartholomew's Church on Park Avenue. Another was that one clergyman who was ever a thorn for Manning: the celebrated Rev. Dr. Alexander Griswold Cummins of Christ Church in Poughkeepsie. Cummins had been rector there for twenty years before Manning became Bishop of New York. Many people considered him "First Citizen" of Poughkeepsie, as Potter had been similarly regarded in New York City. He was usually in the foreground of every worthy civic movement. An outdoorsman, Cummins seemed more at home with his English rifles and bird dogs than in ecclesiastical councils. Cummins delighted in showing off his bird dogs. Meeting a visitor, he would say to the setter on his left side, "What does Bishop Manning think of Dr. Cummins?" and the dog would give a piteous wail. Turning to the dog on his right, he would say, "And what does Dr. Cummins think of Bishop Manning?" and that dog would growl ferociously.[13]

Cummins was nevertheless remarkably akin to Manning on many issues. This is amply proved by reading his editorials in his *Chronicle,* a church magazine he published monthly for many years. Ostensibly aimed at preserving Low Church verities endangered by the Manning onslaught, the *Chronicle* and its editor were exactly and early right as regards Prohibition, some Anglo-Catholic schemes for "reunion" with the Roman Catholic Church, Soviet despotism, the rise of Hitler ("an Austrian military adventurer"), Buckmanism, and Father Coughlin. Bishop Manning would have nodded agreement, if indeed he ever perused the *Chronicle.* Theirs was a conflict of personalities as well as churchmanship. Cummins wrote of the indecencies of injustice while Bishop Manning often preached against the sweatshop, racial prejudice, and persecution in Europe that both he and Cummins perceived early.

It was Cummins's practice to send "spies" (as some people said) to evaluate what was happening in the New York churches now exposed to the influence of Manning's alleged High Church intolerance. It is fortunate for us that he did so, because if the aforementioned spies counted correctly, we have an important picture of church life in the city. The following is what the *Chronicle* reported in 1930:

	Communicants Reported	Summer Attendance	Winter Attendance
Church of the Heavenly Rest	989	120	350
St. James'	1206	52	400
St. Bartholomew's	3825	106	2000
St. Thomas	1915	450	500
St. Mary the Virgin	1040	330	450
Transfiguration	682	450	500
Calvary	741	104	250
St. George's	2518	54	400
Grace	1947	150	550
Trinity	1179	200	150
Intercession	3322	200	600

If this table does nothing else, it suggests which Manhattan churches continued to be attractive to visitors to the city. And it is worth mentioning in this history where we have already noted prolonged slights to the Negro churches, that Cummins overlooks in his list St. Philip's, though by 1930 that parish was probably already larger than any other in the diocese, excluding only the sum of Trinity and its chapels and possibly St. Bartholomew's.

It has been necessary for us to consider the early controversies of the Manning episcopate. Our digressions, however, neglected two important events which must now be discussed: the election of two suffragans, and progress toward completing the cathedral.

TWO SUFFRAGANS

Bishop Manning's concept of an adequate episcopate for New York required two suffragans. Remembering that Bishop Burch's death was hastened by the lack of episcopal assistance, the diocese readily provided for two suffragan bishops in a resolution at the 1921 convention which followed immediately the consecration of Manning. Bishop Arthur Seldon Lloyd was easily elected. The second man elected that day was Herbert Shipman, who had been rector of the Church of the Heavenly Rest since 1907, and before that one of the long line of chaplains at West Point in the days when the military academy seemed to appoint only Episcopalians as chaplains. Shipman's election as a suffragan for New York occasioned something of a mild outcry among some churchpeople because he had officiated at the marriage of a divorced person; Shipman also served on the board of the *Chronicle*. He was elected on the fifth ballot, and the election prompted a pamphlet war about the "Case Against Herbert Shipman." Bishop Manning, however, seemed satisfied with Shipman, and he was duly consecrated.[14]

It is worth noting that neither suffragan held Manning's rigid views. And, as the years went on, neither suffragan found his work entirely congenial. No administrative responsibilities were given these men, though both had proved to be supremely able in their former work. Moreover, Bishop Manning had a flair for the dramatic (which he was the first to acknowledge). He besought himself readily to the cathedral pulpit or some other public rostrum on a Sunday when his appointments lay elsewhere. This meant that the suffragans might receive last-minute calls to adjust their own scheduled appointments. And, since the bishop was *the* bishop, "he had to authorize everything," recalls one observer.[15] Sometimes the suffragan learned of appointments by happening to read the daily papers.[16] This was frustrating. And, of course, there were those who tried to drive a wedge between Manning and his assistant bishops for their own purposes; fortunately, neither encouraged this. But Bishop Shipman broke down at least once under the strain before he died in 1930, while Bishop Lloyd (who died in 1936) maintained a stoic resignation. "Lloyd's unqualified support of Bishop Manning against all detractors played a considerable part in preserving the unity of the diocese in the troubled first years of the Manning episcopate," declares one historian.[17]

THE CATHEDRAL

The greatest portion of Manning's energies in those "troubled first years" were devoted to completing the cathedral. It has been noted that to this man of strikingly small, almost gnomelike stature, fell the task of building one of the world's largest cathedrals. He always said he was reluctant to enter upon the work, that it was something handed on to him by his predecessors.[18] It was often remembered and held against him that, while rector of Trinity, Manning had shown singular lack of interest in the cathedral. But no one who reads his convention addresses can doubt his dedication to a task that soon became nothing less than devotion to the cathedral and all it might represent in the great city of New York. "It will speak to men of the permanent amid the transitory," he said.[19] One of the means used to communicate the "cathedral idea" to the diocese was the beginning of the *Diocesan Bulletin* in April 1924; at first, it was edited by the bishop himself.

When Manning became the Bishop of New York in 1921, the cathedral consisted of an unfinished choir and the great dome executed according to the plans of the initial architects, Heins and La Farge. The choir and two ambulatory chapels had been consecrated April 19, 1911;

soon after, the trustees exercised the rights accorded them by the original contract and terminated the appointment of La Farge (Heins having died). Ralph Adams Cram was thereupon engaged as architect, and his designs envisioned a great Gothic structure rather than the "Romanesque, with a Byzantine influence," earlier contemplated. Other notable architects had done work on the cathedral. The firms of Cram, Goodhue and Ferguson, Carrere and Hastings, Warren and Wetmore, and Henry Vaughan designed parts that were built. But the new Cram drawings provided a cathedral larger and far different from that proposed in July 1891 when the cathedral's Committee on Architecture accepted the competitive designs of Heins and La Farge.

In 1921, the west end of the dome area was walled off; outside lay little more than the rough foundations of the nave. Among the cathedral trustees were James Roosevelt and his half-brother Franklin, now stricken by infantile paralysis. This was not the future President's first involvement with Episcopal business; he was elected a vestryman of St. James' Church, Hyde Park, in 1906 and a cathedral trustee as early as 1911. Franklin Roosevelt managed the great mass meeting at Madison Square Garden in January 1925 that initiated the funds appeal when building recommenced. Now that the original LaFarge plans had been abandoned in favor of those by Ralph Adams Cram, it was expected that the great Gustavini dome would be removed so that the redesigned upper ranges of the choir might result in a vaulted ceiling flowing from altar to the completed west end. It was said that $15,000,000 was needed to finish the entire cathedral; in 1925 Bishop Manning declared that two-thirds of that sum was "assured."[20] Work on the nave had then begun, and the bishop expected it would be completed in 1929. Each year, convention delegates heard the bishop's view of cathedral progress, and it was not a view unanimously shared by those present. In 1925, Bishop Manning thought it necessary to defend the costly project because "some have feared that our work for the cathedral" diminished the receipts for other Church organizations. Two years later, he noted signs that contributions to the cathedral had begun to dwindle. The rector of St. James' Church, the Rev. Frank W. Crowder, was urged by his vestry to move that building be suspended when the funds already in hand were exhausted, but the convention proved docile to the known will of Bishop Manning, and he was able to announce in 1926 that both towers had been promised—a gift unfulfilled when the stock market collapsed in late 1929 developed into the Great Depression.

The Depression slowed, but did not stop, work on the cathedral. When people questioned spending money on bricks and mortar while people were homeless, it was argued that construction gave employment to men who would otherwise be out of work. But the bishop's optimism about those towers, the uninterrrupted nave, and the "women's transept" faded as, year after year, he had to reckon with lessened contributions. But the construction work never ceased. The west front rose fairly rapidly, the Amsterdam Avenue steps were finally set in place and, in a great service on the last Sunday in November 1941, the long cathedral nave was opened in a triumphant service. Events the next Sunday meant that Bishop Manning would never see a completed cathedral.

For the first ten years of Manning's episcopate, the cathedral dean was the gifted Howard Chandler Robbins; formerly rector of Manhattan's Church of the Incarnation, he was appointed in 1917. Robbins's intellect was congenial with Bishop Greer's wide-ranging mind of inquiry. He was impatient with what he considered Manning's cut-and-dried orthodoxy. Having been longer on the close, and probably rankling because of the bishop's obvious lack of interest in the cathedral prior to his consecration, Robbins bristled at the new bishop's ecclesiasticisms. That there was a great gulf fixed between Manning and his dean was implied in a letter James O. S. Huntington wrote the bishop at the time of his election; he said, "Who but you could save us from Dr. Stires or Dr. Robbins?" [21] Several contretemps widened the breach between the two men. One is worth relating because it is one of the cathedral legends that happens to be true. The Deanery had been built by funds given by Mrs. Clinton Ogilvie as a memorial to her husband. His sculptured bust was to be enshrined in a niche over the drawing room portal. But other people's ancestors are not always pleasant to live with, and it became the custom in the Deanery to remove the portrait bust, replacing it when Mrs. Ogilvie announced a forthcoming call. As always happens when we "practice to deceive," the arrangement led to trouble. One afternoon, Mrs. Ogilvie came, unannounced, with her daughter Ida (a distinguished anthropologist who, unfortunately for the Diocese of New York, was concerned for ancestors remote as well as near). The Robbinses were not at home, and the maid, when asked about the empty niche, gave the honest but lamentable explanation that "the statue is *never* there." The Ogilvies left.

Somewhat less amusing was the matter of a large bequest to Dean Robbins. Bishop Manning was convinced it rightfully belonged to the cathedral, that Robbins had influenced the testator to leave the money to him, not to the Church. But the intention of the deceased was plain: the money was indeed left to the Dean; "Now I can have a new razor blade every morning," he exclaimed. Bishop Manning was not amused. This is not to say the bishop was without a sense of humor. He delighted in showing callers the letter addressed to him: "Dear Bishop Manning: I am a Christian woman, which it is obvious you are not . . ." [22]

In the 1920s many Episcopalians moved from lower Manhattan into the northwest quadrant of the island and found in the cathedral services similar to those they had known in their former churches. Dean Robbins's ecclesiastical preferences, and those of his predecessors, Grosvenor and Gates, were generally central—neither High nor Low. The bishops wore black chimeres until Bishop Gilbert's consecration in 1930, when Bishop Manning wore a red chimere—and preached a sermon on "apostolic succession" that many people in and beyond the Episcopal Church found offensive. White linen chasubles were used in the cathedral services soon after Manning's consecration.[23] Toward the end of his episcopate he wore cope and miter, sparingly.[24] Even Bishop Lloyd could sometimes be persuaded to wear the full Episcopal vestments. Bishop Manning was often accused of promoting Anglo-Catholicism in the diocese. This was untrue. He was thoroughly "Prayer Book" in taste and belief, cared little for ceremony one way or the other, and was far quicker to attack what he held to be wrong thinking than he was to lay siege upon chancel peculiarities.

THE DIOCESE IN 1926

Now let us turn to the Diocese of New York as it appeared to the general public in the late 1920s. Everyone knew a cathedral was abuilding, and that it was probably not quite as fully a "House of Prayer for All People" as its proprietors claimed. And every reader of the daily press was aware that Bishop Manning was in frequent debate with his clergy or with others whom he considered to be public malefactors. One reporter, giving his opinion about the Diocese of New York in 1926, wrote:

> No one has been openly called heretical, no one has held Morris dances in sacred buildings, there have been no open rows between bishops and clergy; there has been a temporary let-up in propaganda. In fact, everybody has been quiet and outwardly peace-loving and well-behaved.[25]

Just a month before this appraisal, the *American Mercury*, edited by H. L. Mencken, printed a memorable article about "that most baffling of all mysteries, the Protestant Episcopal Church."[26] It was asserted that only one out of every seventy New York City persons was an Episcopalian, and though numerically weak, "the Episcopalians are the religious aristocrats. Just as the hoi polloi cannot hope to contend with the 400 in the Sunday supplements, so neither can the outcast religions cope with the Church of the Vanderbilts and Morgans." In New York City "there are a number of parishes paying their rectors well over

$10,000 a year," though the average salary in the East was $1,500 (if married), plus rectory and a car. New York City was seen as the fountainhead of Episcopalianism because here, at 281 Fourth Avenue, "the budget is made out, and the sums to be raised apportioned among the dioceses."

Not everything in 1926 was "peace-loving and well-behaved" among Episcopalians in New York, however. Bishop Manning was opposed to any anti-evolution law. He, with Bishop Brent, urged President Coolidge to join the Permanent Court for International Justice, and continued (with Greer and Burch) Potter's sympathy with CAIL. Charles Slattery of Grace Church opposed ousting elected Socialists from the legislature in 1920, and his successor, Walter Russell Bowie, questioned the true patriotism of the DAR and other organizations, and was active in the Scottsboro Case. Bishop Shipman said white people owe the Negro a great debt, and Bishop Manning demanded the impeachment of the California governor who excused a lynching. This was what the Episcopal Church in New York looked like to the *American Mercury* reporter.

In 1926, our pilot year, there were 409 clergy connected with the Diocese of New York, 272 parishes and chapels, 4,492 confirmations, and 93,387 communicants. There were thirty diocesan organizations and institutions. Among them were the cathedral, Trinity School, St. Agatha's School for Girls on West End Avenue, St. Stephen's College, St. Luke's Home for Aged Women, the Sheltering Arms on Amsterdam Avenue at 129th Street, the Home for Incurables on Third Avenue at 182d Street, the Hospital of Rest for Consumptives on 209th Street, the House of the Annunciation for incurable and crippled girls on Greystone Avenue, St. Faith's House in Tarrytown "for the rescue, shelter and training of young girls who have fallen for the first time," the Home for Old Men and Aged Couples across the avenue from the cathedral, the Peabody Home for Aged and Indigent Women, the Orphan's Home and Asylum on Convent Avenue at 135th Street, the Society for the Relief of the Destitute Blind on Grand Avenue, and the City Mission of Help. In addition, there were the Seamen's Church Institute and the Episcopal City Mission Society, which traced their histories back to Onderdonk's time. The Community of St. Mary had its motherhouse at Peekskill, and maintained its schools and its hospital in the city; the St. John Baptist Sisters had long since moved motherhouse and school to Mendham, New Jersey, but in the 1920s still continued some of the work they had begun in New York many years before. St. Faith's House on the cathedral close, designed to be a training school for the Order of Deaconesses also continued, but there were signs that its great days were past, partly because the Episcopal Church as a whole had never fully accepted this type of women's ministry.

The year 1926 might also be called the peak year for St. Stephen's College in Annandale as far as its connection with the Church is concerned. In 1919 the Rev. Bernard Iddings Bell had become president. His energy, intelligence, and nationwide reputation brought immediate results. Within a year the college had begun a building program that vastly increased its potential; leading laypeople argued for the college, and Bell himself challenged the diocese to support what he insisted was a major Church institution. Unfortunately, Bell also insisted that the small college be run entirely according to his own will, a policy that tended to exclude able people who desired to help the school. It is ironic that at the very time Bell should have been able to congratulate himself on his undeniable building success, he met his Waterloo in the form of a student strike. It was springtime 1926, and the president found occasion to offend the students in an impromptu speech. They directed their exuberance to cutting classes and chapel; it became front-page news and in the end the college trustees (including Franklin D. Roosevelt) were obliged to step in and make peace. Bell believed it was all caused by two or three disgruntled faculty members bent on his removal, and he was perhaps partly right. In any event, two years later St. Stephen's College became part of Columbia University. It is said that Nicholas Murray Butler had long wanted a campus of Columbia to be located in a pleasant rural area to attract again the "sons of New York gentlemen" who were now forsaking the university for other Ivy League colleges. Bell became warden of the absorbed college, and resigned five years later. In 1934 the name was changed to Bard in honor of its founders, and ten years later the connection with Columbia was severed. The college continues its Episcopal Church connection by means of its chapel and chaplain; and its education system, tracing its ideas back to those of Bell, is now widely shared by other colleges.

Did the Church withdraw from the college or did the college withdraw from the Church? Both. Episcopalians are not notably enthusiastic about Church institutions. They support their home parish and whatever charities appeal to their interests. St. Stephen's College was unable to command the attention of a wide circle of churchpeople. A noted Anglo-Catholic, Bernard Iddings Bell, alienated many alumni and erstwhile loyal supporters; his temperament alienated many others. The college found funding elsewhere and gradually drifted away from Church auspices, though all the bishops of New York have been trustees. The same process might be seen in others of the "Church" institutions listed above; they were established by Church people, were known as Church organizations, and over the years drifted away from Church control. The real cause is the lack of Episcopal Church money:

but some people found it easier to blame Bishop Manning. It was thought he wanted funds for the cathedral instead of various institutions, a charge he refuted annually in his convention addresses.

In a 1920s survey of the Episcopal Church in New York City, E. Clowes Chorley, rector of St. Philip's, Garrison, and longtime historiographer of the diocese, asserted that *"The Church has gradually withdrawn, or has been driven out* from the still densely-populated territory below 14th Street" (italics original). Why? Mainly because "the privileged classes moved uptown and then parish churches followed them."[27] In all, twenty-one Episcopal churches south of 14th Street had disappeared: between 15th and 72d Streets, eight had gone, plus five north of 72d Street. These figures do not include churches merged with others, nor do they include the ten churches, quickly defunct, that were organized soon after Bishop Onderdonk's suspension. (Lack of episcopal authority and admonition appear to have permeated new churches that probably had better not have been formed.)

In 1926 St. Bartholomew's Church on Park Avenue was the largest congregation in the diocese, claiming 4,000 members. Grace Church, St. George's St. Philip's, the Chapel of the Intercession, and St. Agnes Chapel each listed nearly 3,000, while other Manhattan parishes reported numbers nearly as impressive: St. Andrew's, 1,193; St. James', 1,050; Holy Trinity Chapel, 1,000; St. Mark's (now recovering from the dance), 1,543; St. Mary the Virgin, 1,447; St. Michael's, 1,157; St. Thomas, 1,322; and Trinity Church, 1,100.

Parishes of noteworthy size outside the city were St. Luke's, Beacon (542); Christ Church, Bronxville (902); Grace Church, Middletown (545); Ascension, Mt. Vernon (998); Trinity, Mt. Vernon (840); Christ Church, Poughkeepsie (901); Holy Comforter, Poughkeepsie (512); St. Paul's, Poughkeepsie (634); Good Shepherd, Newburgh (986); St. George's, Newburgh (584); Trinity, New Rochelle (935); Grace Church, Nyack (600); Trinity, Ossining (525); St. Peter's, Peekskill (651); St. Peter's, Portchester (801); Grace Church, White Plains (980); St. Andrew's, Yonkers (1,096); and St. John's, Yonkers (1,658). The fact that each of these parishes now reports significantly fewer members is due in part to the redefinition of the word "communicant" and the new custom of charging $2.00 for each communicant: parish treasurers tend to make rectors honest! While it is true that these parishes now record fewer members, there are other churches in the Diocese of New York, small in 1926 and much larger now. Nonetheless, the diocese listed 93,387 communicants in 1925 and 47,846 in 1980. And more than forty chapels and churches outside the city listed in 1926 have since then been merged with other churches and are now nonexistent. In 1925, 272 were reported in the Diocese of New York; in 1980, 190.[28] The national Church in 1925 claimed 1,193,321 communicants, and 2,018,870 in 1980.

People always want to be shown the high peaks of a storied past. The ferment and creativity abounding in New York City in the 1920s are generally acknowledged, perhaps not so much for the cathedral abuilding on Morningside Heights, as for Scott and Zelda Fitzgerald's celebrated plunge in the fountain on Grand Army Plaza. It was now a city of wonderful buildings, imposing civic monuments, manicured parks; there were even "parkways" for automobiles. Though the predicted demise of the East Side never took place, there was a persistent airy luxurious ambience about Riverside Drive, not far from the cathedral. In 1926, the Diocese of New York was creeping toward its largest number of communicants, which would be reported at 112,174 ten years later in 1936, when the world was much changed by Depression. Confirmations in the 1920s never quite reached their consistently high level of the early years of the century.

THE DEPRESSION OF THE 1930s

The Great Depression that began soon after the Wall Street collapse of October 1929 is clearly reflected in the annals of the Episcopal Church.

> Parish after parish report financial agony. In many cases rectors are taking a voluntary cut, or are being forced to take a 10% reduction of salary. Many parishes carrying a debt were having a hard struggle in good times but now their position parallels the experience of many business and industrial organizations. Frequently we hear of parishes that are defaulting on their rectors' salaries. In not a few instances, parishes will probably have to go into mission status.

Such was the gloomy assessment of one knowledgeable reporter, in 1932.[29]

In one church, the deaconess was funded by a wealthy layman who, when his textile-related firm was shaken (but by no means toppled) by the crash, simply went to the rector and said, "Get rid of her." Since those in the Order of Deaconesses had no job security, they were often the first casualty of the Depression in the Church. It may be said that one of the significant effects of the Depression on the Episcopal Church was the demoralization it wrought among many of those selfless women who had given their entire working lives to the Church, and could be dismissed so easily. It is no wonder, then, that St. Faith's House—the "training school" for deaconesses on the cathedral close—barely survived the Great Depression, and soon after closed forever.

THE BISHOP IN A CHANGING DIOCESE

In the 1930s, two main facts were clear to anyone who observed the Episcopal Church in New York: its bishop made frequent pronouncements, and its parishes were undergoing rapid change. In 1937, even before the nave was opened, Bishop Manning proved the potential importance of the cathedral as an awakener of the public conscience by having an authentic slum flat set up in the cathedral. New Yorkers flocked to see how their neighbors were living. Several years later, the bishop again conspicuously displayed a righteousness he genuinely felt. The story is well-known. When a Bronx rector welcomed black worshipers with a cordiality whose warmth dismayed his vestrymen, those gentlemen attempted to prevent the new neighbors from worshiping in that church by declaring the building closed for redecoration; the locks were changed and the rector was not given a new key. This was entirely uncanonical as well as patently un-Christian. Therefore, when the rector appealed to Bishop Manning, the bishop was at his most resourceful. He canceled existing Sunday appointments and, by prior arrangement, met a locksmith—and a corps of press men!—at the church steps. The church doors were opened, and the divine worship was uninterrupted.

Changes in the churches? Probably no more change, by proportion, than in the nation. But Manning's character was such that he stood to be blamed for anything that struck an unaccustomed note among churchpeople. Intinction, for instance, remained a sensitive Episcopal issue. Bishop Manning would not approve intinction, but permitted communion in one kind.[30] Was not this sheer Romanism? people asked. Similarly, Manning's reluctance to allow ministers of other churches to participate in Episcopal services was reminiscent of Hobart. The appearance of red chimeres, or purple cassocks, upset some people. And, when the church furnishings house, Morehouse-Gorham in 41st Street, published the *American Missal* in 1931, Bishop Manning was thought to be a promoter, though in reality he discountenanced anything other than the Book of Common Prayer. (Those who knew the bishop best were well aware that, when officiating, his practice was always to insist upon holding the Prayer Book, or appearing to be reading from it, even though he knew its words by heart—for *this was the book of the Church.*) The fact that Manning showed sympathy with the Oxford Group in its earlier manifestations, that he rehired as secretary a priest he had just deposed, and as early as 1921 approved the removal of the word "male" from the legal clauses providing parochial electors shows a breadth of mind his detractors often denied. Nevertheless, he *did* seem forbidding, remote, dictatorial. And the public never forgot those early skirmishes he had seemed to relish heartily.

One more fact caused observers to think Bishop Manning espoused Anglo-Catholicism in the diocese, and that was his knowledge of Catholic practice, and his willingness to participate in any ceremony not inimical to the Book of Common Prayer. In this he differed from the Potters, or Bishop Greer, who were simply uninformed about some traditions, and preferred to remain uninformed. Manning, for instance, knew how to consecrate holy oil, and was willing to supply it to parishes when requested.

Manning's rigidity may be seen in the following anecdote. A rector, new in his Manhattan parish, discovered many of the members had never been confirmed. When the bishop came for the rite, more than one hundred persons came forward, and the rector announced that after the first two candidates had been confirmed the congregation— many of them elderly—might be seated. Later, in the sacristy, the rector waited for Bishop Manning to commend him upon such a large confirmation class. Instead, Manning demanded to know "who gave you permission to evade the rubric and allow the people to be seated, Mr. Donegan?" The bishop was emphatic about this. "If there are more than 150 candidates, the class can be divided and the two sections can be confirmed on different days or at different hours on the same day, but it will be understood that the congregation should stand," he declared in a *Bulletin* editorial.[31]

After his death, an editorial said that despite the bishop's many controversies, time usually proved he was right in his stands. This generous appraisal is probably true. One of the gentler skirmishes involved the relocation of the Church of the Epiphany. Here was a midtown parish that traced its beginnings to City Mission enterprise under Onderdonk. The loyal congregation, living in other neighborhoods, in 1937 determined to sell the old church and build elsewhere. The bishop agreed that Epiphany should move, but refused permission for the proposed site. He wanted an Episcopal church on the far East Side near the York Avenue hospitals. "Your arguments leave me decidedly unconvinced," the bishop told Epiphany's vestry, and those gentlemen eventually capitulated to the bishop's requirements. The new church, designed by Wyeth and King, was built on York Avenue.

All the churches were called to broader considerations in World War II. Again, as in the First World War, Manning was truculent. The bishop's well-known disgust with Hitlerism won him notice in *Der Stuermer* in 1937 as "a two-fold child of hell, and a wolf in sheep's clothing." The United States is "directly concerned" with the Allied cause, he told the convention delegates in 1940. He urged that "fullest help, at once" be offered England. "There can be no compromise between Democracy and Hitlerism—we are already in the war," he declared the next year. He decided not to spend his vacation in Soamesville in 1941, preferring to remain close to the city. Despite his age, the world crisis was bracing to him. War meant extraordinary decisions: there would be no more building at the cathedral, and the steel scaffolding was eventually given to "the war effort"; there would be a one-day diocesan convention. Bishop Manning was aware that there was a fresh importance of New York's Negro Episcopalians, many newly arrived in the city. He urged housing and health and recreational facilities for "our Negro population" (though in his own manuscripts, the bishop wrote "Coloured"). There were then more than 10,000 black communicants in the diocese.[32]

Another minority (at least as far as the franchise was concerned) were Episcopal Church women. When, in 1942, Mrs. E. H. Paddock was listed on the printed ballot as a candidate for the diocesan Board of Religious Education, it was probably the first time a woman was accorded that privilege. Her election merely pointed out that in times of national emergency decent things can happen. War has its uses. One wonders now at the absurdity of reading off, year after year in diocesan convention, the names of prominent Episcopal laymen who had died in the previous twelve months, with no mention of lay women who (as everyone present knew) meant so much to the diocese. Yet it was not until 1954 that women were allowed on mission advisory committees, 1957 allowed on vestries in the Diocese of New York, and 1958 permitted to be delegates to diocesan conventions. "The Vestry is the last vestige of the male sex in this day and age," declared the Rev. Dr. Fleming of Trinity Church in 1935.[33] "Soon there would be nothing to stop them from the priest's office," warned another observer, who was wiser than he knew.[34]

Nonetheless, if the Diocese of New York deprived itself of recognizing the long years of women's service, full acknowledgment was given the men who annually appeared in convention. Monell Sayre, Stephen Baker, and R. Fulton Cutting were diocesan familiars; Baker's Church responsibilities began in the old Church of the Holy Trinity in 42d Street, and ended just about the time his rector, Horace W. B. Donegan of St. James', was elected suffragan bishop of New York in 1946. In the 1930s the diocesan business structure was reorganized by Edward K. Warren (whose father had also been rector, successively of Holy Trinity and St. James'), Richard Mansfield, G. Forrest Butterworth, and Clarence Michaelis.

NOTABLE CLERGY AND LAITY

The New York Episcopal clergy in Bishop Manning's time, apart from the controversial Guthrie and Grant, included an assortment of notable scholars, preachers, and pastors. At the General Seminary there was Hughell E. W. Fosbroke, formidable dean and teacher of Old Testament; his celebrated profundity seldom appeared in bound books, much to the loss of Christendom. Burton Scott Easton, General's New Testament giant, was a recognized author. At Union Seminary there was the great Folkes-Jackson, whom generations of seminarians learned to know early in studying for the ministry. Robert Norwood held crowds at St. Bartholomew's spellbound; rumor said he went directly from the pulpit to a couch in his study where a masseur stood ready to massage and relax his taut body. At St. George's there was Karl Reiland; he was skilled at extemporaneous preaching, and lost no opportunity to goad Manning into controversy. He was one of those "always gunning for Manning," as Bishop Donegan remarked later. Frank Crowder, rector of St. James', and Donald Aldrich of Ascension were skilled and beloved pastors; when Aldrich resigned to enter the navy as a chaplain in World War II, his parishioners thought they had done far more than their duty to their country in allowing him to leave them.

Interesting lay persons helped promote the Episcopal Church's "image" throughout Manning's time. Apart from the old Knickerbocker families (whose prominence and ability to bestow funds steadily declined toward mid-century), there was, for instance, the longtime mayor, Fiorello La Guardia. He was an Episcopalian, as truculent as the bishop, and of about the same stature. Together they engaged in some badinage about their similar height on the dais of Synod Hall when the mayor appealed to diocesan convention to have the cathedral nave open for public symphonies by the time of the 1939–1940 World's Fair. Very soon after this, the appointment of Bertrand Russell as a professor in the city's college aroused the bishop's opposition; blasts from the close were a major factor in preventing the British philosopher from coming to New York. And, in 1944, two New York Episcopalians opposed each other for the Presidency: Franklin D. Roosevelt and Thomas E. Dewey were from the same county and archdeaconry.

RETIREMENT?

The question of Bishop Manning's retirement was discussed even before World War II. Once, in a pointed reference to President Roosevelt's attempt to "pack" the Supreme Court, the bishop told convention delegates that neither judges nor bishops need retire because they had passed a certain age. The convention applauded. From time to time, he would declare that he had no retirement plans, and at least once he was given a standing ovation when he said he expected to remain bishop indefinitely. But General Convention had other plans; in 1943 the convention passed the first reading of a new canon obliging bishops to retire at age seventy-two; if passed in the succeeding General Convention, it would be the rule of the Church. Bishop Manning was extraordinarily hale and hearty in 1943, and he fought against the new canon, arguing that the national Church's organization was subsidiary to the diocese which had elected and supported its bishop as father-in-God. He never regarded the national Church as having special sanctity. In his view, the bishop-diocese relationship, and the priest-parish bond were of divine provenance and must be safeguarded, a view in which he was supported by a varied group in the House of Bishops. But the new canon passed into law after the 1946 General Convention. Bishop Manning was advised that the canon couldn't be made retroactive, but as the year drew toward its close he announced he would retire at the end of December.

The bishop's resignation was sudden, and his departure quiet. He moved to a house in Washington Mews owned by Bishop Gilbert (who, in turn, moved to Ogilvie House on the close). There, in that tiny house in the Mews, Manning continued to be active. He wrote spirited letters to the *Herald Tribune* and the *Times,* explaining why a Unitarian ought not to read the Epistle in an Episcopal church, or why the ambience of Washington Square must be preserved. His study was cluttered with mementos of his busy life, and above his desk was an altar that had been designed by Canon West; it could readily be lowered into position for daily use. Nearby on the wall was a photograph of a large confirmation class prepared by the bishop back in his Sewanee days— "and they knew their catechism," he would tell a visitor, for the bishop was ever a teacher.[35] And of equal significance, there was a photo of William Thomas Manning in World War I uniform. He lived nearly three years after his resignation.

14

Bishop Gilbert: A Brief Interlude

We live in strange and perilous times.
—Charles K. Gilbert

It is worth noting that at Bishop Manning's last diocesan convention a knowledgeable speaker referred to the atom bomb as capable of mass destruction. The speaker warned the delegates that "the trend toward such catastrophe is unmistakable."[1] The possibility of worldwide horror was only one of many modern developments the Manning years had witnessed, and at first it appeared to be almost an avoidance of a dangerous future that led the Episcopal Church in New York readily to elect its longtime suffragan to be bishop of the diocese. When Manning resigned, two New York City rectors were put forward as possible successors; and, claiming that the rural churches had been neglected, the rector of Millbrook moved into position as a dark horse in what might have been a prolonged election. But then Charles Gilbert, suffragan since 1930, quietly said yes, of course he would like to be Bishop of New York. It was a possibility not hitherto seriously considered, for Charles Gilbert was close to the age of mandatory retirement. But his expectations were not to be denied. He was elected on the first ballot in a special convention held less than a month after Manning retired. The other candidate was Claude W. Sprouse of Kansas City. The convention delegates were satisfied that Bishop Gilbert would, for a few years, prolong the Manning regime while new long-term leadership might emerge. This is exactly what happened. Within a year names such as Donegan and Pike were frequently heard; a seminarian named Moore was a teller at convention.

Bishop Manning was certain that, had he called for a coadjutor before his retirement, Charles Gilbert would have been the person elected.[2] But now that the aging Gilbert was the ordinary of the diocese, it was clearly necessary to find a suffragan who would stand ready to become diocesan if, after several years of trial, he appeared to be suitable. Let it not be thought the clergy are unaware of such contingencies. Very soon after Bishop Gilbert's institution, the two prominent Manhattan rectors mentioned earlier were viewed as active contenders. They were Horace W. B. Donegan and Louis W. Pitt. Donegan had been a New York rector since 1933, and had brought St. James', Madison Avenue, into the forefront of the city's churches. The "St. James Lessons" for Sunday schools were significant in the Church prior to the National Council's expanded Church Teaching Series. Horace Donegan, like Horatio Potter at St. Peter's, Albany, had "minded his own business" in the parish (which then included the large Holy Trinity Chapel, whose vicar was the beloved James Paul). St. James' churchmanship was central.

On the other hand, Louis W. Pitt maintained the older "liberal" stance of Grace Church, Broadway, at a time when, in those postwar years, churchpeople tended toward a redefinition of orthodoxy, with revived interest in tradition. The rector of Grace Church was decidedly not in sympathy with Anglo-Catholicism. Without the principals' encouragement, lines were drawn, sides were chosen, adherents enlisted—and bitter things said. Then both Donegan and Pitt withdrew their names. This meant the diocese was effectively deprived of two good candidates, and others must be found. Easier said than done! It was soon apparent to the Donegan people that they could find no one his equal. "Fourteen magnificent years at St. James' were a matter of record. No one could be more presentable—he had presence—he had shown administrative skill, pastoral concern, he had never promoted himself, could proclaim the Word of God with power," said one of the Donegan supporters long after the election.[3] Some of those supporters met at the University Club on May 5, 1947, and after long discussion someone went to telephone Donegan and importune him to allow his name to be put in nomination at the electing convention, which was exactly a week away. Donegan agreed, absented himself from the election, and won on the first ballot.[4] In 1949 he was elected Bishop Coadjutor by acclamation, and in 1950 became the twelfth Bishop of New York.

Horace William Baden Donegan was born in Derbyshire, England, in 1900 but came to this country at a very early age. He attended St. Stephen's College in Annandale, but soon applied successfully for admission to Oxford. Bernard Iddings Bell, always resentful of any student's desire to leave his tutelage, advised the Oxford authorities that their new charge hadn't the "intellectual capacity" to undertake the rigors of an education there—an appraisal, as it turned out, that was more a reflection upon Bell than it was upon Donegan. For, despite Bell's pessimism, the future bishop managed to do well at Oxford and later at the Episcopal Theological School in Cambridge, Massachusetts.

He was ordained by Bishop Slattery in 1927, and served with distinction as an assistant at All Saints', Worcester, and rector of Christ Church, Baltimore. He was called to St. James' in 1933 and very soon that somewhat somnolent neighborhood church was faced with a difficulty every vestry dreams of: how can all the congregation find seats?

Bishop Gilbert, a widower, chose to avoid the huge episcopal residence. Mrs. Manning had said it required "six people to keep that four-storied forty-room palace going." [5] The new bishop elected to live in Ogilvie House; the last dean to live there had been James P. DeWolfe in his brief term prior to becoming the Bishop of Long Island. (When Dean Pike came to the cathedral, he and his family lived very comfortably on the third floor of the Bishop's House.) There was a vague understanding that the new suffragan would live "in the country," so at first Bishop Donegan lived in Westchester County. Very soon, however, he was back in Manhattan, confirmed in the belief that he was not a country boy.

MAKING CHANGES

These sensible housing arrangements are symbolic of the three-year episcopate of Bishop Gilbert. It was a time of neatly folding up the garments of the past, and it was a time of recognizing what new things were required. The Depression and Second World War had prevented the building of new churches in the diocese. At the same time, if our deductions from the records are correct, it had delayed removals from the city and thus had tended to keep the metropolitan churches full. Now that prosperity was evident and population changes obvious in new housing developments, it would be necessary to build new churches. It would also mean that some old churches must be abandoned, but the Church is always loath to face that cold fact. The "cornerstone campaign" initiated in Bishop Gilbert's time was intended to collect capital funds for new churches in the diocese. Prefabricated mission churches caught the imagination. The campaign was moderately successful, and several new churches were built, the last being St. Luke's, Williamsbridge, in 1952.

In 1949 there was a new Committee for College Work. This, too, was a sign of the times. Formerly, Episcopalians were said to attend the church near the college campus and be identified with the life of that parish. Of course, college students required a somewhat feistier fare than a local parish might offer, and in those postwar days there was a host of college chaplains, some of them directly out of the armed services, ready to offer what was wanted: relevant religion. That was the word: *relevant.* Not unrelated to the existentialism of the most popular books and cocktail conversation of the time, there was abroad in the land a suspicion that the Christian religion did, after all, have something to say about everyday life.

The "strange and perilous times" to which Bishop Gilbert often referred in his addresses and private talks helped foster the search for bedrock realities. For very soon after the peace of 1945 it was plain that civilization was imperiled by the capitalist-Communist tension, which itself might be viewed as proof of God's creation smeared by the waywardness of free will gone awry. The world situation seemed to restate a basic Christian belief. It made earnest college work inevitable. The Episcopal Church's Canterbury Club on the campus, and the chaplain there, found a new respectability. With an arch tolerance of the sweet hymns of his youth, the college student might now engage in long evenings of intellectual wrestling with the topics those same hymns had obliquely mentioned. Everyone knew about discussion groups. There was an undeniable magnetism about many of them. Sometimes beer and sherry were served; four-letter words were often acceptable, even necessary.

DEAN PIKE

The postwar Western world was plainly tired of a futile idealism which the threat of another war made empty and even foolish. Perhaps religious traditions might say persuasively what secular idealism could not. The names of the Niebuhr brothers and Paul Tillich were known to men and women who never darkened a church door. Reinhold Niebuhr and Paul Tillich lived in New York. And upriver, Cummins's successor at old Christ Church would, in time, be as well-known as those two scholars. This was James A. Pike. Brought up in the Roman Catholic Church, and a lawyer with a doctoral degree, Pike was ordained an Episcopal priest in 1944. In the two years he was rector of Christ Church he had discomfited the Vassar College authorities in a public row over their stand on religion on the campus and, as partial retaliation for what Pike regarded as Vassar's old-fashioned restrictions against religious groups in the college, he organized a popular weekly discussion session for Vassar undergraduates. His weekend seminarian assistant, Paul Moore, Jr., was not a negative influence in these novel developments at Christ Church. The old church buzzed with "relevant" activities, and a Bryan Green mission there toward the end of 1948 made that parish, and neighboring ones, too, aware of a genuine spirituality among churchpeople who—though they were Episcopalians—

were not fearful of coming forward to sign a pledge of deepened faith.

Clearly, Pike was going places, and the next place was Columbia University. The chapel and university chaplain were yet Episcopal (though the college ceased to be listed as "Episcopal" in the Church yearbooks after 1908). The next move was across Amsterdam Avenue to be dean of the cathedral, to whose wide forum was soon added a Sunday afternoon television program. At the same time, Pike became a member of the Standing Committee, for he was in these days thoroughly involved in the day-by-day concerns of the Church.

The Pike years in the Diocese of New York overlap the episcopates of Gilbert and Donegan, but are discussed here because the career of that fabled man may be seen, in retrospect, as a symbol of Christianity in America during those years now under our scrutiny. Coming from agnosticism (for he gave up his Roman Catholicism early in life) to an enthusiasm about religion in the last years of the Second World War, Pike possessed a unique (there is no other word) ability to commend the faith of the Church to thinking men and women. He had *charisma*—an old Christian word rapidly coming into renewed use by 1950. Some years later, one bishop glumly admitted that a simple announcement on a three-by-five card posted on a college bulletin board would bring crowds of college students to a remote meeting place whereas large posters failed to gather a respectable audience for a better-equipped theologian. He was a wonderful example of the new type of apologist who made the Church heard and pondered in unaccustomed ways, unaccustomed places. "A better class of men is now going into the ministry," sniffed one snobbish layman, unaware that it wasn't the class of men, but the prominence of the subject, that was making the Church not only acceptable but—well, *relevant.* What other reason maintained the Pike television program so long?

Now, years after, we tend to dismiss the postwar "return to religion." The tide did ebb, but who can deny that "authentic Christian spirituality flowed among the more ephemeral streams so deeply entangled with cultural realities," as one historian has asserted?[6]

SAM SHOEMAKER

It should not be thought that James A. Pike was the original pied piper of Episcopal college students in New York. That honor might be claimed by a long line of distinguished Church people, including Provoost and Morgan Dix, and none with more credentials than Samuel M. Shoemaker of Calvary Church. Here was a man far different from Pike. When Calvary's membership was decreasing, despite the pastoral abilities of its former rector, Theodore Sedgwick, the senior warden, George Zabriskie, convinced the vestry to call Shoemaker to the parish. Desperation proved fruitful. Very soon Calvary Church and its new multifloor parish building became what the rector liked to call a power house. He also liked to be called Sam, and though his preaching was consistently strong through the years, and his administrative abilities far above average, he was at his best in informal sessions with undergraduates at Ivy League colleges. He spoke of lives being "changed" by Christ; his publication, *The Evangel,* was likely to be a somewhat fundamentalist appeal to men and women of his own privileged background. This "mind set"—another Shoemaker term—enabled him to be congenial with the first stages of Frank Buchman's Oxford Group. It also equipped him, a nondrinker, to be an originator of Alcoholics Anonymous. Sophisticated churchpeople were prone to scoff at Shoemaker's simplistic approach to Christianity, but its positive results could not be denied: a prosperous parish church, many men (of various denominations) led to the ministry, and a laity rededicated to faith in Christ. One of the more conspicuous signs of the latter was "Red Cap 42" at Grand Central Station; this was Ralston Young, a longtime railroad employee, who held regularly scheduled prayer meetings in a Pullman car laid over in the terminal. He, too, was part of Sam Shoemaker's widening circle of influence. The Pullman car meetings drew thousands of people over the years. The Shoemaker era was long lived; it began in Manning's early years and grew in strength through Bishop Gilbert's time and into the first years of Bishop Donegan. Unlike Pike, however, Sam Shoemaker could never claim to be symbolic of an era.

We have seen, then, that the Shoemaker meetings at Calvary House had an enduring effect on the Church. And the wide publicity accorded Pike represented an intellectual respectability, nay, invincibility, that commanded wide attention. There was yet a third postwar development, and it was to be perhaps the most influential of all: work in the inner city. There had been a long and honored Anglican tradition of a few priests spending their lives ministering in deprived places: Wilson at Haggerston, Hook of Leeds, the long procession of future notables who served at Stepney and London Docks. In New York, such work had been spasmodic, and probably met with instant discouragement. The English Church, after all, is national and produced more ready-made clients and appreciative witnesses than the Episcopal Church could find in New York. Even the devoted work of the Sisters of St. Mary and the Community of St. John Baptist aroused less public attention than, say, the Episcopal boys' choirs that sprang up in the later years of the nineteenth century at fashionable churches.

Now, however, and partly because of Michonneau's widely read

Revolution in a City Parish, translated into English in 1949, renewed work began in far-deteriorated and forgotten places in cities. Churches there had perforce been forgotten during the Depression and during the war. Bishops in the metropolitan area cooperated with the new spirit because, along with the much-trumpeted "return to religion," they had on their hands dozens of once-prosperous brownstone churches that would never regain a vestige of their gilded past. Trinity Church, always a power in the Diocese of New York, responded in particular by sponsoring vigorous activity in its St. Augustine's Chapel, whose vicar then was Kilmer Myers.

COMMUNITY OF THE HOLY SPIRIT

Bishop Gilbert's three-year episcopate was drawing to a close when the Community of the Holy Spirit established itself in New York. Its story is as interesting as that of the other two distinctly New York Orders for women, the Community of St. Mary and the Community of St. John Baptist, and like them it was founded by a native of the city. Ruth Younger was born and grew up in New York City; she attended St. Philip's Church and St. Luke's, Hudson Street. Later, after her family moved to Canada, Miss Younger realized her life's vocation would be in a teaching Order, an ideal she fulfilled for many years in Canada. But when her Order decided to terminate its teaching work, Sister Ruth found it difficult to enter other pursuits, for she knew her gifts. She was given leave by her Order to come to New York. Bishop Gilbert extended a cordial permission; "he was so kind and so good and so understanding of what we were up to," recalled Mother Ruth many years later[7] (for, in time she became Mother Superior of the new Community of the Holy Spirit). Canon Green at the cathedral suggested the Canadians begin a kindergarten on Morningside Heights, for he thought there was great need for the children of the many professional people connected with Columbia University, Union Theological Seminary, St. Luke's Hospital, and the other expanding facilities near the cathedral. Canon West helped locate a house in 113th Street, and the school— soon to be St. Hilda's and St. Hugh's—began with eight little children.

The Order became autonomous in 1952, and the name was chosen partly because it was plain to the original Sisters that their move to New York, and their subsequent activity there, had been Spirit-led. The Rule of the Community of the Holy Spirit is based on traditional monastic lines, with close alignment with that of the Oxford Mission to Calcutta. The Community's school building in 114th Street was made necessary several years after that first class of eight met, and all grades through high school were added year by year. In fact, the New York school was so successful and so busy that the Sisters wondered if their corporate spiritual life was not endangered. Therefore, it was determined to purchase a place of retreat in the country and, after some search, a fine place in Brewster was chosen. Now, it too has a school as well as houses for retreats and conferences.

The founding of the Community of the Holy Spirit was a quiet episode in the history of the diocese. There were no fierce Protestant objections in the Church. Bishop Gilbert did not feel obliged to make excuses for what the Sisters were doing, and who they were; those troubles which Horatio Potter and Henry C. Potter had to confront were now absent. This in itself does much to describe the Episcopal Church in New York (and probably elsewhere) at mid-century, and is underscored by the fact that Bishop Gilbert would never label himself either High Church or an Anglo-Catholic.

His three years and more as Bishop of New York were exactly right in preparing for the long episcopate of his successor that lay ahead. It is tempting to compare the brief Wainwright period with that of Gilbert—and we shall give in to temptation! For both men in their brief times were enabled to be effective bridges between one definite period and another. Had there been no bridge, there would have been unnecessary abrasions for the man to follow. The "mildness and grace" of Wainwright proved to be a reconciliatory factor that bade people forget the past acrimonies. Bishop Gilbert's frank lack of interest in administrative tasks and his keen awareness of present-day difficulties enabled the diocese to realize that the Bishop of New York could well delegate his important work among capable persons. The stage, then, was set for Horace W. B. Donegan.

15

Horace W. B. Donegan: Changing Fortunes of American Christendom

Bishop Donegan has the spiritual care of the wealthiest diocese in the church embracing 225 parishes and missions in Manhattan and six upstate counties. One of his consuming passions is the ministry to the city dwellers.

—NEW YORK TIMES,
MAY 11, 1960

In 1950, when Horace W. B. Donegan became the twelfth Bishop of New York, it was clear that, despite the much touted "return to religion," the tide was a good deal more conspicuous in the suburbs than in the city churches. True, "inner city" work was noted and applauded. The presence of the Episcopal Church was seen in its magnificent churches with music of undiminished standards; it was also to be seen in its Youth Consultation Service, the Seamen's Church Institute and, especially in the Episcopal City Mission Society, which was just completing a new building at the old address, 38 Bleecker Street in 1950 (that new building was sold in 1983). The sports announcer "Red" Barber was prominent among the promoters of the City Mission.

The new bishop was greeted by the 380 clergymen of the Diocese of New York, 221 congregations, and slightly less than 100,000 communicants. An examination of these figures is important. The number of clergy in the diocese would grow steadily throughout Bishop Donegan's episcopate to nearly 500 by the time of his retirement in 1972. This suggests the evolving significance of nonstipendiary and part-time clergy in the Church. It may also signify that inflation and varying, competing interests were cutting into the ranks of those whose sole life occupation would be the priesthood; now, for instance, you might find a pharmacist or a schoolteacher who, thoroughly trained, spent Sunday in the chancel.

It was anomalous that a diocese whose membership was declining should show a marked increase in ordained persons. For, alas, the Diocese of New York continued its slide of communicant membership since the peak of 110,800 reached in 1938. The number of confirmations increased to 4,115 in 1957. This was about the number confirmed in 1938, and similar to the annual number throughout the late Potter and Greer years. But there is a constant decline after 1962 (3,939) to 1972 (1,990). Much of this may be due to the Prayer Book studies that questioned the heretofore accepted Biblical basis of the Confirmation sacrament, or the value of the event as a traditional rite of passage for youngsters in their early teens. It is also important to remember that the word "communicant" was defined along the way, and rectors making out the annual parochial report now had a standard: some were quick to blue-pencil names on their lists.

As for the number of very small congregations, this continued to be a problem born of the preautomobile or rigid-churchmanship past. Far more sensitive and difficult to manage were the churches founded according to social preferences that no longer existed. It sometimes happened that a once prosperous parish now began to envy the activity and crowded congregation it had scorned: the exalted were humbled, as the Gospel tells us will be the case. The new bishop was forthright in stating that, as there is a time to begin a mission, there is also a time to end mission work when there seems to be no further promise of accomplishment. The peak point of congregations in the diocese came probably about 1874 when there were 313, but since that figure probably includes estate chapels, institutional chapels, and seasonal preaching stations, we will do well to accept the 297 given as the number of congregations in 1920. There were 198 congregations in the Diocese of New York in 1983.

The fact that confirmations and the number of communicants in the diocese declined in the face of the much heralded interest in religion was attributed to Episcopal families continuing to quit the City of New York for suburbs, which, in this case, might mean the dioceses of New Jersey, or Long Island, or Connecticut. Therefore it must be understood that the Diocese of New York never reaped its share of what optimists like the aging Bishop Manning perceived to be a "turning of the tide." Bishop Donegan seemed to be attuned to the real situation when, in his first convention address, he stated, "I wish to make it clear that it is my earnest desire to be first and foremost a pastor to the clergy." He was able to underscore this sentiment almost immediately, for in a moment when it seemed possible to recommence building the cathedral the bishop discouraged the trustees from doing so because clergy salaries remained far below what they should be. This decision, perhaps not too reluctantly agreed to by the cathedral trustees, seemed to establish as fact what many people already suspected: at contemporary prices the Cathedral of St. John the Divine could not possibly be completed.[1]

The first notable Donegan move was a restructuring of diocesan administration. It had been years since administrative procedures had been analyzed; had Bishop Potter and Archdeacon Nelson returned in 1950 they could easily have resumed their routine, such as it was, for the bishop of the diocese was still the linchpin upon whom all business depended. Bishop Gilbert had not cared to alter administrative methods in his brief time, but in those days of burgeoning business people became aware as never before of professional efficiency. According to the New York plan, which had already been adopted by some other dioceses, there would be a "Bishop and Council." Most of the Council members would be elected by the diocesan convention; some might be appointed by the bishop. This plan—and here was the selling point—could draw many talents into the decision-making process, and Council members might be assigned to one of the departments envisioned by the plan. There were four: Missions (which included aided parishes, established missions in the diocese, and mission strategy), Christian Education (most important in those days of revived interest in what the Church believed), Christian Social Relations (which would become of unprecedented importance as the Western world began to wrestle with injustice and ungodly complacency), and Finance. Later, the Woman's Auxiliary was added. These departments would be financed by the Council with moneys authorized by the annual diocesan convention. For example, thirty diocesan missions required about $300,000 a year. Christian Education was no longer a matter of colorful leaflets, and required substantial funding; in time, that department was able to bring from Canada an expert, J. Stuart Wetmore.

Laymen Clarence G. Michaelis and Edward S. S. Sunderland were now frequently seen and heard in diocesan affairs. Theodor Oxholm, proficient in finance, was engaged as a full-time diocesan treasurer and, once settled in the job, managed diocesan finances with an iron hand which lost no power because of his devotion to the Church. The bishop was said to be "at home in any parish in the diocese" insofar as ceremony was concerned; "I'll do it the way you do," he is reported as saying to an incumbent whose preferences were decidedly not those of St. James', Madison Avenue, where the bishop had been for so long.[2]

HOME ON THE CLOSE

Bishop Donegan, a bachelor, lived with his mother in Ogilvie House, the pleasant residence built for the cathedral's dean. It seemed to be a sensible place for the bishop of the diocese, especially when there was, in 1950, no dean. The bishop's refusal to encourage further cathedral construction might have sent a chill through the close were it not for the obvious fact that he was otherwise quick to promote varied activities there. Now, life on the close seemed more ebullient than ever it had been when Manning was arguing the need for a cathedral. The installation of the organ's "state trumpets" was perhaps symbolic, for after James A. Pike became dean the cathedral could offer one of the most publicized apologists the Church has ever known. He wanted, very much, to complete the cathedral, but Donegan's principle must be respected.[3]

Pike, and the Church, were lucky in the able assistants at the cathedral. Canon West knew how a cathedral in New York should be run, and lent a spirituality to his undoubted managerial gifts. Darby Betts was headmaster of the Choir School, and if nothing else, demonstrated that paddling miscreant pupils could be part of the school's regimen in New York; the ensuing publicity reminded New Yorkers that the school still flourished on Morningside Heights. It is now remembered that the cathedral close in the 1950s was the scene of profound creative hilarity among Pike's priest colleagues; it is also remembered that the wives of those colleagues had a far less fulfilling time of it, inasmuch as the standards of the day discouraged them from having remunerative jobs of their own.[4] Moreover, the Pike team's heady sense of ascendancy was always tempered by knowing that the churches downtown were facing bleak times of attrition and circumstance; they were not replenished by new churchgoers.

In 1951 the Right Rev. Charles F. Boynton, Missionary Bishop of Puerto Rico, was elected Suffragan Bishop of New York in a contest that was marked by overtones of bitter churchmanship. There was no doubt that Bishop Donegan needed episcopal assistance. One of the leading candidates was Samuel Shoemaker. His ministry at Calvary had been effective for many people, and his radio meditations made him well-known. But the Shoemaker point of view, political as well as ecclesiastical, failed to commend itself to many others, who (as it now seemed to "Sam") allied themselves against him. A last-minute letter appeal from St. Thomas's rector, Roelif Brooks, probably added votes to the Boynton column, and he was elected. Shoemaker was understandably offended by the concerted opposition to him, and left Calvary Church soon after—a somewhat unfortunate conclusion to a notable career in the city, and ironic, inasmuch as Shoemaker was probably never overmuch interested in being a bishop.

Bishop Boynton was of decided Anglo-Catholic point of view, and as such probably reflected the rank-and-file clergy taste in the diocese at that time. He later said that the Suffragan is primarily supportive. If he and his Diocesan respect and love each other (which was our case) things go smoothly and one is not sure who suggests what to whom. My eighteen years were extremely happy ones and Bishop Donegan and I worked like hand in glove; and that was also true when Bishop Wetmore served as second Suffragan after his election.[5]

In 1959 Bishop Donegan called for another suffragan, and at a special convention on December 15 J. Stuart Wetmore was elected. He came to New York from Canada, (whence his Tory ancestors had fled at the Peace of 1783) to be diocesan Director of Christian Education. The runners-up on that occasion were Dillard H. Brown, Albert A. Chambers, and John M. Burgess, who all subsequently became bishops. Bishop Wetmore was himself a nominee when Paul Moore, Jr., was elected Bishop Coadjutor in 1970.

Bishop Donegan proposed to make full use of the convocations which had replaced the archdeaconries. In those days of keen interest in Christian Education, the convocations were an excellent practical vehicle for bringing the Church's teaching to the parishes, which sent representatives to area meetings. It is said that more than a hundred clergy and lay persons were at one time involved as leaders in the convocation all-day training conferences.

The Deans of Convocation were ex officio members of the Department of Missions, and were always priests. Convocation meetings of the clergy and elected representatives from the area's parishes took place two or three times a year, and it was expected that diocesan staff people would attend them. This aimed at a close connection between the diocesan offices, and was particularly useful when individual churches needed help in organizing their Every Member Canvass. For the diocesan treasurer, Theodor Oxholm (now salaried), kept a watchful eye on parish finances. He centralized diocesan moneys and sternly overhauled mission budgets. This new approach had the bracing effect of sharply reducing the number of aided parishes, practically forcing them to self-supporting status. In 1947 there were seventy-one aided parishes; in 1962 there were thirty-seven. Thirty-one churches had become self-supporting in that time. In the same period, the average stipend for a mission priest rose from $2,750 to $5,700.

There were times when Bishop Donegan seemed in danger of repeating the recognized preference for the city and its concerns. Now, in the late 1950s, it was difficult to know where to draw the line between urban, suburban, and rural places. "The urbanization of suburbia is upon us," said the bishop. But what he did not say was that it was an unattractive urbanization. He mentioned Mount Vernon, New Rochelle, and Newburgh as changed places having blighted slum areas; he might soon add Poughkeepsie and Beacon.

There was a salutory effect here, however, for there were priests who were led to work in these inner cities. They tended to form a bloc assuring that the Diocese of New York retained a concern equal to that we have noted from time to time in its past. Very often the Department of Christian Social Relations was a focal point for organized protest. For instance, the General Convention of 1955 was scheduled for Houston, a city then not racially integrated. There was an uproar from New York's Christian Social Relations department that led directly to the convention's being transferred to Honolulu. It was a small step from the protest in diocesan convention to firm stands on civil rights, capital punishment, poverty in the cities, and black clergy placement.

Nonetheless, it was easier to make arch pronouncements about the lack of civil rights in Houston than to enact them at home. Even as late as the diocesan convention of 1957 no woman in the Diocese of New York was allowed to be a delegate to those conventions, or to sit on a vestry, despite Bishop Donegan's plea in 1955 that an enabling resolution be approved. The laity—men only!—were notably more conservative than the clergy in this matter.

Another effect of the diocesan awareness of urbanization was the realization that a conference center was needed in a central location not far from the city. The modern method of conducting the Church's business seemed to assure conferences into a long future. There had never been a diocesan facility for meeting and housing large groups. The first clergy conferences were held in the late 1920s in a hotel at Lake Mahopac, and meeting there was considered quite an outing. Other locations were tried, and for some years West Point's Hotel Thayer was used. Then, in 1955, Myron C. Taylor, former United States minister to the Vatican, presented his commodious house in Locust Valley to the Diocese of New York. It was to be the much-sought-for conference center, and was accepted as such. Wise second thoughts, however, barred such use of the Taylor house, because it was in another diocese and eminently inconvenient for those who lived north of Westchester. More to the point, another house was now in sight and, after negotiations conducted by Bishop Donegan, the former Tilford place in Tuxedo Park was purchased in 1957. It was named for the bishop and for about twenty years served as a diocesan home away from home; the Taylor house was sold as, eventually, was the Tuxedo location.

Also in 1957 it was proposed that the Diocese of New York embark on a gigantic capital-funds drive to mark its 175th anniversary year. Other dioceses had raised very large amounts in professionally conducted intensive drives aimed at collecting money for "advance" work in an expensive age. Bishop Donegan mentioned a goal of five million dollars but, for reasons perhaps at least partly owing to a reversal of the popularity of American Christianity, the campaign was a disappointment to its promoters. By the end of 1958 barely half the expected five million had been pledged or received.

CLERGY CLUBS

Along with the heightened interest in Christian education throughout the national Church, and the impressive numbers of Church school students of all ages meeting in buildings recently erected, there were clergy social and study groups throughout the diocese. These clergy associations have been organized from time to time, and a few have had a long history. We have seen that Bishop Hobart distrusted such groups and asked their members to disband. Perhaps his suspicions were not entirely unfounded, for the clergy at such gatherings have been known to discuss matters other than, say, the new lectionary or the Filioque Clause of the Nicene Creed. But the clergy clubs were an early attempt at what we now call continuing education and they have not been irrelevant to the thinking and speaking of many diocesan clergy. There is the Rectory Club in the Westchester area, and the Monday Club in the upper Hudson Valley; both groups assign books or topics to their members, expecting papers adequate if not profound. (The clergy are remarkably generous in their estimates of each other's scholarship, as this writer gratefully concedes.)

Sigma Chi was an interchurch discussion group founded in 1866. It met for many years at St. Bartholomew's Church in New York City; it ceased in 1973. Almost as old is The Club, whose organizing about 1871 has already been noted. It was founded to thrash out the emergent theological problems of the time. Another group, called Kilin, was founded in 1921 for a specific purpose: "to continue the education of Bishop Herbert Shipman when he became Suffragan in New York."[6] William Norman Guthrie was one of the founders; apparently he suspected Shipman would require continuing education when he became Manning's suffragan. Kilin continues to be active. The Church Club was founded, about 1887, on more ambitious lines. For some years it maintained club rooms in midtown Manhattan. Formal dinners with prominent speakers have been the main attraction of the Church Club in recent years. Bishop Manning often used it as a forum for presenting his position on civic and ecclesiastical issues.

ORDER OF ST. HELENA

Another religious Order for women joined those already working in New York when, in 1954, the Order of St. Helena moved to Vails Gate near Newburgh. The Order had begun at Margaret Hall in Versailles, Kentucky, a school then operated by the Sisters of St. Anne. When that Order decided to end its work at the school, some of its teaching Sisters determined to begin a new Order. In 1947 they were permitted to adopt the Rule kept by the Holy Cross Fathers and, eventually, they became a sister community, wearing the white habit and the plain black cross of the West Park house. After a brief time in the Diocese of New Jersey, the Sisters of St. Helena purchased an old house in Vails Gate and began their work in New York. Very soon they were conspicuous at St. Augustine's and St. Christopher's, two inner city churches maintained by Trinity Church and staffed partly by seminarians from Chelsea Square. Later, the Order of St. Helena opened a branch convent at Calvary House, an event that would have astonished its builder, Sam Shoemaker, had he been yet alive. Finally, the Order moved to its own house in the city in East 28th Street. It is perhaps worth noting that three of the Orders discussed—St. Mary's, St. John Baptist, and Holy Spirit—owed their beginnings to New York City women; and the fourth, St. Helena's, looked to an original New York Order, Holy Cross, for its beginnings.

Proof of how complicated the demands upon the churches might become can be offered at St. Philip's, Harlem. The rector there for many years was the Rev. Shelton Hale Bishop and he, above all, was responsible for making it one of the nation's notable churches. Toward the end of his ministry, Dr. Bishop was joined by the Rev. M. Moran Weston. It was Weston's idea that such a firmly established parish should undertake to build and maintain a great community center in the environs of the church. Through slow and demanding negotiations, land was purchased, plans drawn, money allocated, and in 1969 construction began. The result was facilities for all ages, a pleasant episode in a decade that was decidedly unpleasant for much of the nation.

For, while St. Philip's, St. Martin's, St. Paul's, and many other urban churches were pursuing visions of a better neighborhood made that way by the Church, there occurred the student riots at Columbia University. The cathedral had always enjoyed a warm neighborliness with the university, but this time the relationship was perhaps too warm for comfort. The rights and the wrongs of the riots will long be debated, but it was clear to Bishop Donegan that there was a breakdown of business at the university and a stalemate that displaced its personnel and students. While maintaining an appropriate neutral stance, the bishop opened the cathedral buildings to student strikers—and to any others who might require the proffered hospitality. The Columbia chaplains were thought to have sympathized with the strike. Whether or not this was true, the last vestige of official Episcopal Church connection with the university was severed soon after, when Bishop Donegan was informed by letter that henceforth there would be no university chaplain at Columbia.

A FINAL VISIT TO "ST. LUKE'S"

Let us make a 1966 visit to our "St. Luke's" which we last saw in 1926. A rector was called there in 1928 and remained twenty years. Only several years after his retirement and removal to Maryland people seemed to have a hard time remembering what he was like. "Colorless," said one woman. Another *thought* he was a charter member of the Rotary Club, and was certain he was president at the time of Pearl Harbor. What people did recall was that his small daughter was struck and killed by an automobile on the street outside the rectory.

St. Luke's seemed untouched by the Depression. While there was never a "discretionary fund," the rector was able to supply food and used clothing to the several families in chronic distress during those years. He was also able to supply them coal by simply adding the cost of a quarter ton to the church's bill. When World War II came, ten men served overseas. None were killed, but one returned "shell shocked," to use a term carried over from the former war, and was thereafter frequently a patient in the Castle Point Veterans' Hospital.

When the rector retired in 1948 you could still see in the vestibule of the church the little black metal box suggesting alms for building the Cathedral of St. John the Divine; whatever might have been slipped into that pence box was casually added to the loose plate offerings on Sunday mornings, for neither the rector nor the vestry cared whether or not the cathedral was ever finished. You would also see in that vestibule a pile of magazines (for the shut-ins), an altar flower chart seldom changed from year to year, the "Roll of Honor" of those who had served in the world wars, Sunday school leaflets, and old Forward Day-by-Day booklets that had never been discarded.

But the rector who came in 1949 changed all that, and a lot of other things, in St. Luke's. To begin with, he was thought to be very "High," and was impatient with anyone who wouldn't call him Father. He claimed oversight for everything: Sunday school, Women's Auxiliary, even the Every Member Canvass. Some people stopped coming to St. Luke's, but it couldn't be denied that the man was popular down at the fire house and in the Businessmen's Association. In the five years he was at St. Luke's he overhauled everything, and when he left some smart people were amused that the parishioners expected to call their new rector Father whether he preferred the honor or not. It was also a fact that the finances of the parish were now sound because annual pledging was very much increased. Perhaps one reason for this was that the last inhabitant of the big house now a nursing home—she who had "run the church" for years—was dead. Now it was plain that all the people of the parish must support the church.

The new rector in 1955 was a veteran married to a nurse who substituted in the Sunday school when she wasn't doing private duty at the hospital eight miles away. This couple remained at St. Luke's nearly ten years, made a host of friends in the community, and then moved to a church in Connecticut. The people of St. Luke's were saddened to hear they later were divorced, and their former rector was now in personnel work in Stamford.

The rector who came in 1965 was also married to a nurse, and it was no secret she expected to be full-time at the hospital; her mother (who moved with them, and soon found a part-time job) kept house at the rectory and looked after the three children when they were not in school. The vestry were satisfied that the rectory was fully occupied and felt justified in not negotiating seriously with two of the candidates Bishop Donegan had recommended for the rectorate. Both those men refused outright to live in the old rectory and wanted a housing allowance. This seemed impossible to the vestry because, first of all, rectors had always lived in that house and, secondly, it was a landmark practically adjoining the church.

There is a rotating vestry now, and two women serve on it. The Sunday school is considerably smaller than it was in the 1930s but, for some reason, the parish house seems busier than it was then. There is a senior citizens club, a nursery school, a weekly meeting of Alcoholics Anonymous, and an aerobic dancing group Wednesday mornings. The Women's Auxiliary was finally declared defunct after a succession of poorly attended meetings; several of its members now meet in the parish house to tie a quilt, which is raffled off; others join in holding an annual rummage sale, but this gets more and more difficult each year because everyone seems to be saving her rummage for her own yard sale. Gone are the days of the turkey suppers and beef barbecues— events that meant long hours of preparation. Crowds always came, and St. Luke's was famous for its feasts; but the profit diminished annually in the wake of high food prices. For now very little by way of vegetables and dairy produce would be donated.

People are quick to say the church isn't "what it used to be" in the community. The rector and his family are no longer set apart as they were formerly. There are a lot of things giving Sunday competition: the A & P is open, the firemen schedule practices, the Little League has a game. But at the same time, more people, people of all religious commitments, cross the threshold of St. Luke's buildings these days. Many do not come to worship; they come to use the facilities built by St. Luke's people. Nowadays more people than ever before have a proprietary interest in St. Luke's as a good place. And, for reasons nobody can explain, every year the budget is more than met.

Sunday morning changes have been subtle. The choir is smaller than it was in 1926 and seldom attempts an anthem except at Christmas and Easter; the old pipe organ was literally discarded in 1959 and an electronic one purchased. Most people now suspect the exchange was unwise. There is at least one acolyte at every Sunday service; the celebrant wears Eucharistic vestments. Morning Prayer is scheduled for the second and fourth Sundays of the month, and some people think that maybe when the new Prayer Book finally "comes in," the rector will want to have the Eucharist every Sunday at both morning services. The church looks about as it did in 1926 except that there are new bronze chandeliers, suspended over the pews so that the congregation can see the pages clearly. The same walnut altar, brass credence table, and dark oak choir stalls are there. An ambry is set in the north wall of the sanctuary, and a brass lamp with a clear glass globe signifies the Sacrament is reserved there. The old branch candlesticks are gone now, and in their place are six lights on the retable; the retable itself is new and was handily made by one of the vestrymen.

The pews still have maroon cushions, but old carpet hassocks are gone: no more sawdust to clean up. Instead of hassocks to kneel on, there are low benches covered with a red plastic. However, most people still adopt the "Episcopal crouch" while at prayer. In the book racks people expect to find *The Hymnal 1940* and the Book of Common Prayer. There is a leaflet for each Sunday, run off by the part-time secretary on the duplicating machine in the corner of the parish office in the rectory. A funds drive in 1967 enabled the parish thoroughly to refurbish the old parish house, but there was not enough money to build the office wing that had been planned.

The rectory family spend a month at their newly bought camp in New Hampshire. The rector has heard that there was a time when the parishioners begrudged his predecessors a month's vacation, but he has the feeling now that people want him to get away and relax. He appreciates this, for while he has much spare time, he is on constant call. He is seldom able to take a whole day off during the week. (He wryly chuckles about the "reading days" he planned as a self-discipline. They never materialized.) Nor does he often see his Episcopal colleagues, though he attempts to meet with them at their monthly Eucharists on Friday mornings at the only "cardinal" church in the area. After the service, which is one of the trial use services approved by the Standing Commission of the national Church chosen by the celebrant, there is coffee and Danish and an hour or so of small talk before some of the men go out for lunch. It adds up to a valuable support group that wasn't available to clergy until recent years. Such support seems necessary now in 1966, when there seem to be many negative factors suddenly militating against the Church—or at least the Episcopal Church. Those who attend the Friday meetings are eager to hear what might be done to perk up their parishes; the old formulae seem to have little viability now.

The rector makes few house calls because almost everyone below retirement age has a full-time job. His calls are limited to shut-ins or to those in hospital. He spends many hours counseling and acknowledges that this is probably the most rewarding aspect of his work. He gets in his weekly tennis game—at a renovated theater in winter, the public recreation park in summer. He also jogs. He meets with his colleagues of the other churches in the local "Ministerium," which is now a far more congenial group because the Fundamentalist minister has, to the unspoken satisfaction of the other members, refused to rejoin them after an argument over prayer in the school. The rector expects to remain at St. Luke's because his wife has a supervisory position in the hospital; her salary is considerably greater than his. Their combined salaries and perquisites add up to a comfortable life, and from the looks of things, and with care, they will be able to send the children through college. Nevertheless, he has moments of distaste at the prospect of remaining at St. Luke's for the rest of his working life. The parish isn't really growing, and in any case it is always hard to see parishioners transferred summarily by IBM or Texaco: they go on to something probably exciting and certainly higher-paying, while he remains to look for people to take their places.

In this vignette, which is not contrived beyond reason, may be seen the joys and the disappointments of the rector toward late century. But the disappointments seemed overwhelming to many priests in the 1960s. The roots of dissatisfaction lay not so much in the frustration born of Vietnam times as in the geography of the Diocese of New York. The diocese encompassed what is probably the most cosmopolitan and the richest city in the world. It also had its share of failed towns and villages whose principal source of income vanished years before; one upstate community, for instance, has steadily declined in population since 1890. As we have seen, even in Manhattan the Church knows

poverty, always has known poverty, and must live with its conse-
quences. The protests of the 1960s, whatever their other causes, arose
from a rising generation that was enraged by what was perceived to be
the futility of the existing order. Christianity was very much involved in
this. It teaches a distrust of the world around us, and yet enjoins that we
labor in that world. It has been wryly suggested that the Church's
Teaching Series of the 1950s did entirely too good a job, for it resulted
in young people's demanding in practice much that was taught when
they attended Sunday school. The suggestion is at least true in the
sense that often the Church was too uncritical of its surroundings.
Those who thought about Christ at all wondered if the Church hadn't
abandoned him. "Organized" Christianity—is there any other kind?—
was under siege. In this ferment there was much that was true, and
there was much that was unthinking, but one of its effects was to suggest that the clergy in their work were isolated, that perhaps the world
was passing them by.

Isolated and forgotten! There were clergy in various pockets of the
diocese who used those words, but if memory serves, those in Ulster
County were particularly beset by feelings of neglect. They worked far
from New York City. They seldom saw more than a handful of their
colleagues. Their salaries were modest, and their parishes in remote
places not likely to grow. Was there any guarantee that they would
really be considered for another parish? How could their situation improve when they had little to do with the decision-making process? At a
spontaneous meeting in Kingston, followed by yet another one in the
same city, men poured out their complaints about a diocesan system
that wasn't serving the days of adversity as well as it had served the days
of prosperity.

"The pressure for reorganization began to be felt about 1968, and
Bishop Donegan was amazing in his ability to accept proposals for
change, and even provided the funds by which the reorganizers were
able to continue their countless meetings." So wrote Bishop Wetmore
some years later.[7] He was one of the participants in some of those
"countless meetings." Other clergy leaders were Richard Gary, then
rector of St. Mary's, Manhattanville; Michael Allen of St. Mark's in-the-
Bowery; David Bronson, rector of Holy Cross, Kingston; and David
Wayne of St. Edmund's in the Bronx. The result, helped along by "position papers" ranging in color from purple to tangerine, provided for a
three-region division of the diocese, each having its "Regional Officer"
(a designation later abandoned in favor of the traditional "Archdeacon"). Each region was itself divided into clusters of parishes that were
expected to send their clergy and appoint lay representatives to meetings that would be called Interparish Councils. These councils would

have a direct voice in the spending of moneys pledged by the parishes for local and other benevolences. And each Interparish Council was to be represented on the Council of the diocese, the authoritative deliberative and deciding body created in Bishop Donegan's first years as bishop.

As Bishop Wetmore stated, Bishop Donegan encouraged the research and discussions that led up to the final recommendations, and he welcomed what he hoped would be as near as possible a solution to some of the problems the Diocese of New York has always encountered. During the restructuring discussions the idea of dividing the diocese into two or more separate new dioceses was pondered. There was no proposal to do this, and some years later a study committee appointed by Bishop Moore once again—as so many times previous— made a prolonged examination of the possibilities by corresponding with adjoining dioceses, asking advice from the Bishop of London, and considering suffragans permanently resident upriver. The result was the same conclusion reached earlier: it is best for the Diocese of New York to remain as it is and enjoy the urban-rural diversity it must always have.

Bishop Donegan announced in 1969 that, the House of Bishops permitting, he would call a special convention to elect a bishop coadjutor. The bishop was not slow to intimate that he intended to remain ordinary of the diocese until he must retire at age seventy-two. The fact that he had so openly and enthusiastically promoted the ideas for restructuring the diocese indicated he had not become fixed in the mold of recent prosperity. He remained eminently respected by his people. They seemed to take pride in the honors that came to him. Bishops always gather unto themselves honorary chairmanships, presidencies, and doctorates; even early in his episcopate, Bishop Donegan could add the initials of the Order of the British Empire and wear the rosette of the Légion d'Honneur with his other honors. Bishop Donegan would be firmly Bishop of New York until he retired.

A committee appointed to submit the names of candidates announced that John M. Krumm and Paul Moore, Jr., would be names on the slate; later, the name of Suffragan J. Stuart Wetmore was added. John Krumm had come to New York City in 1952 to be chaplain of Columbia University; later he became rector of the Church of the Ascension. Paul Moore had been made deacon in the Cathedral by Bishop Gilbert, and was, in 1969, Suffragan Bishop of Washington. He was elected Bishop Coadjutor of New York on December 12, 1969 (John Krumm was the next year elected Bishop of Southern Ohio; in 1980 he became Suffragan Bishop for Europe). One well-wisher sent Paul Moore a telegram asserting it was, after all, his wife's recent book *The*

People on Second Street that won him the election. There was much delight that this couple would be coming to New York. Unfortunately, Jenny Moore became ill and died without ever having the opportunity of entering the work of the Church, and all people, in New York as she had done on Second Street in Jersey City. In 1975 Paul Moore and Brenda Hughes Eagle were married.

An Epilogue:
Paul, Our Bishop

He is the man for New York.
—J. STUART WETMORE

The chronicler of the distant past tends to become less a historian and more an editor as his narrative approaches recent times. He hastens to appraise events and decisions that have not yet had time to resolve themselves, and he is likely to do this by a rigid interpretation, using the history he has been writing. This is unjust to the subject, and unfair to the trusting reader. It is particularly hazardous in the case of the current Bishop of New York, Paul Moore, Jr., who is probably the most controversial man on the bench. This chapter, then, will attempt little more than a description of what has so far happened in the current episcopate. Perhaps the historian who writes about the next century of the Church in New York will find the few tentative statements here helpful a hundred years from now.

When Paul Moore came to New York as coadjutor in 1970, he had credentials that immediately invited interest, beginning with an ancestor who was a Trinity vestryman in the mid eighteenth century. The future bishop was born near Morristown, New Jersey, in 1919, educated in a somewhat prim local school there, and went on to St. Paul's, Concord, New Hampshire, and then to Yale. While at St. Paul's he perceived and pondered the disparity between the goodness ascribed to the Creator and the suffering in creation. Five years' military service in the Marine Corps during World War II (in which he was seriously wounded) deepened Moore's reflection, as it did to many other men, who, weighing the alternatives, saw the Church's ministry as their most positive response to the human predicament they surveyed. For at St. Paul's School a remarkable master, Frederick Fox Bartrop, aroused in Paul Moore a vocation to the priesthood. In 1946 he entered the General Theological Seminary in downtown New York City.

At the seminary, then in the last year of the redoubtable Dean Hughell E. W. Fosbroke and the first years of his able successor, Lawrence A. Rose, Moore's vocation became focused on work with people who lived in what were then called slums, but which soon came to be known, more accurately, as the inner city. For it was already plain that rich cities were neglecting conditions at their core. The inner city was deteriorating, and so were the lives of the people who lived there. The seminary's Chelsea area was identifiably shabby, but there were much worse conditions in other parts of the city, and in most cities across the land. It happened that two young members of the faculty were also drawn to inner city work. Together with Paul Moore, Kilmer Myers and Robert Pegram believed the only authentic ministry in decayed urban areas was to live with the people in those poor neighborhoods. If the priests were married, as was Paul Moore, then their families would become part of the neighborhood.

The three men sought an existing church in a run-down urban area by inquiring of those bishops whose jurisdictions included cities that might have such a chruch. It is perhaps indicative of the Episcopal Church at that time that there were few responses. The only viable reply came from right across the Hudson River. Bishop Washburn of Newark had, in Jersey City, exactly the place the men were looking for: Grace Church in the VanVorst section of that decayed, politics-racked city.

The rest of the story has become an epic in the Episcopal Church. Those of us who worked at "Grace, VanVorst" recall an excitement and sense of purpose that neither scrutiny of method nor archcriticism can diminish. Very soon, the parish came alive with all manner of activity; even more, however, it was a respected statement of purpose. Episcopalians need not abandon their old churches in the dark streets. Paul Moore remained in Jersey City eight years, went on to be Dean of Christ Church Cathedral, Indianapolis, and, in 1963, was elected Suffragan Bishop of Washington. As we have seen, he was elected Bishop Donegan's coadjutor and came to New York in 1970.

Paul Moore was installed thirteenth Bishop of New York on September 23, 1972. The city then was a dispirited place. Whole neighborhoods in the Bronx were a wasteland. Apartment house after apartment house was abandoned, burned out, which meant less tax revenue for municipal purposes. Businesses threatened to leave the city, and many had already done so. The city's credit rating slipped downward. There were few newspapers, crime statistics mounted, and one failure seemed to follow another. The pervasive discouragement invaded the churches. In more than one city parish, the forbidden question was at last spoken: How long can this church survive?

Others were asking an even bolder question: *Should* the Church survive? Maybe there *ought* to be empty pews in American churches, perhaps bare ruin is deserved in those old choirs that lulled a citizenry into a pretense of a religion whose God must be dead: so ran the general argument of some thinkers. The nation's spiritual fabric took on a tougher, less comforting texture in the late 1960s and early 1970s. Traditional American Christianity was cross-examined as perhaps never before in our history. There was a new, optimistic, and often naive interest in other religious traditions, particularly those of the East. Astrology assumed an unwonted respectability. The older professions of ministry, law, and medicine began to question basic premises and practices; in the Episcopal Church, people even began to ask what theological reason prevented women from ordination.

The Episcopal Church was not alone in feeling the cold winds of unfavorable change. All the mainline denominations, not excluding Roman Catholic, could look back to those recent days that now seemed better than they probably were, and most certainly appeared to be fast fading in a remote past. The Episcopal Church, however, probably had more than its share of troubles because, at this most inopportune time, it was in the midst of a long-projected revision of the Prayer Book. The revisions of 1892 and 1928 had been mild updatings of the 1789 book, which itself wasn't far different from the English Prayer Book of 1662. Even so, 1892 and 1928 had seen some reluctant rectors and sullen laypeople who did not want public worship altered in any direction. Now, in the 1970s, it was plain that the revisions were going much further than most Episcopalians at first realized, and would add to the anxieties of the times. Then there was the sexual revolution everyone was, at last, talking about openly: clergy divorcing and remarrying, homosexuality identified, churchgoers living together without benefit of the marriage vows. If ghosts laugh, there was a constant chortle from the shade of old Onderdonk.

Paul Moore moved into this farrago when he succeeded Bishop Donegan in 1972. A large portion of the new bishop's first problems were, inevitably, inherited from an old past, and they often involved a sensitive issue: parish loyalty. While our religion presupposes the use of buildings, our Lord never promised lovely structures in perpetuity. The historian is especially aware of this as he reviews what once was and today is not. The disappearance of old St. John's Chapel, one of the finest buildings ever put up in New York City, must always be an embarrassment to us. Its destruction in 1918 was a mistake.

The disappearance of Christ Church as a separate parish placed in jeopardy its fine building at Broadway and 71st Street. The church was designed by Charles C. Haight. The parish itself laid claim to be the second oldest of the city's Episcopal churches. It had had its share of migrations: from Ann Street to Worth Street, then to 18th Street, and on again to Fifth Avenue. Finally, in 1886, the vestry of Christ Church chose a site on Upper Broadway. The new and expensive location seemed worth the gamble, but Christ Church never enjoyed the flood-tide of West Side prosperity. It was in decline by the 1920s, and finally merged with St. Stephen's Church, several blocks away. The church building was left to whatever fate might befall it. Those who are intrigued by Episcopal Church peregrinations will be interested to know that Christ Church, begun in 1793 by a former Methodist itinerant minister, Joseph Pilmore, was the congregation from which in 1871 the rector, Ferdinand Ewer, led a group of people to found the Church of St. Ignatius.

Of parallel interest is the fate of the Church of the Holy Communion on Sixth Avenue. This was the church of William Augustus Muhlenberg. The building was one of the elder Upjohn's finest town churches. In the 1840s that part of Sixth Avenue did have a small-town flavor about it, but quite soon this was succeeded by fashionable stores that, in time, became lofts and warehouses: not a promising neighborhood for a parish church. Nevertheless, Muhlenberg's spiritual legacy, the loyalty of the small congregation, the extraordinarily long rectorate of Dr. Mottet, and a substantial endowment kept the church alive. During the 1920s the Canadian virtuoso organist W. Lynwood Farnum attracted crowds of people to the old church (which must have tried Dr. Mottet's patience, because rectors never like to have congregations gathered for that sole purpose). Farnham and Mottet died about the same time, in 1930, and there remained only a dwindling congregation. Soon after Bishop Moore came to New York there were conversations beween the authorities of the Church of the Holy Communion and Calvary Church, which was then in process of merging with old St. George's, Stuyvesant Square. The result was a combination of the three congregations under one rector. The old church on Sixth Avenue was sold and, eventually, the name Holy Communion ceased to be listed with the associated parishes. It is a poignant loss, made harder by the subsequent use of Upjohn's exquisite building as a disco. But it is further proof that very few churches can escape the plain fact that they must be located in an area where people live. It is a principle directly related to the idea of the Incarnation itself.

These are examples of two old and prominent city parishes that ceased to exist as separate corporations. Their disappearance is not necessarily the result of modern faithlessness. The latter-day disappearance of Episcopal churches is small compared to the rise and fall of parishes in what we wistfully suppose was the heyday of churchgoing. The diocesan historiographer in 1910, E. Clowes Chorley, declared that in the past fifty years—that is, between 1860 and 1910—forty-four Episcopal congregations in the Diocese of New York became extinct. In addition, ninety-one chapels, missions, and preaching stations were similarly pronounced defunct in that fifty-year period. These statistics should silence those who pine for the good old days.

The fact is that the first archdeacons of the diocese did their work too assiduously. They established places of worship where they supposed Episcopalians might be found. They themselves officiated at, or persuaded neighboring clergy to take charge of, what they optimistically declared would probably become a full-fledged parish. Their hopes led them to establish missions in such unheard-of places as Princes Bay, Garrettson's, Linoleumville, Hitchcock's Corners, Mabbettsville, Quaker Hill, Rochdale, Bangall, Spuykenkill, Tioranda, Reynoldsville, Attlebury, Vosburgh, Chapel Corners, Satterlytown, Sparrowbush, Huguenot, Moodna, Lincolnville, Montana Mills, Pochuck, Dean's Corners, Breakneck, Milltown, New Landing, Mead's Corners, Chichester, LeFever Falls, Gleneria, and Centerville. What antiquarian today can identify half of these places? Many were rural railroad stops, soon to be ended by the automobile.

For by 1910 the motorcar had begun to change church life. Churchgoing thereafter was more and more restricted to Sunday mornings. Families could now drive past the once-dear mission chapel at Budds Corners and worship in a larger church where there was a choir, electricity, and central heating. In one rural area, there were in 1910 *nine* Episcopal churches and missions within a radius of ten miles. Eight of them existed until Bishop Donegan's time, and it was his distasteful task to urge the cessation of four; those surviving seem to have a viable future.

This digression concerning the rise and fall of churches in the Diocese of New York has been necessary because each bishop as he arrives at the responsibility to which he has been elected must grasp the salient facts underlying every congregation. The other clergy, too, must be aware of history. In 1983 an assortment of priests thought to be representative of diocesan clergy were asked to look back across the years since they began their ministries in the diocese and list what they believed to be "the most important developments." The responses were remarkably similar. Most important seemed to be the reorganization of the diocese in Bishop Donegan's final years. A few respondents thought reorganization was important because it was a mistake, but most were convinced it did something to correct long-standing problems.

Those who were thus polled thought the ordination of women to the priesthood ("which did not upset the diocese") a major event. The introduction of the 1979 Prayer Book was seen to be of only slightly less importance than reorganization and women's ordination, and it *has* been somewhat unsettling, a few parishes (encouraged by recalcitrant rectors) refusing to discard their 1928 books.

Slightly less significant also seemed to be the choice of a black suffragan bishop in 1974, when Harold L. Wright was elected and consecrated. His early and unexpected death occurred in 1978; he was succeeded by Walter D. Dennis, also black. The resumed building of the cathedral was also seen as important. This decision was announced by Bishop Moore in a letter sent to the clergy in December 1978. He said, "The Trustees of the Cathedral have just met in special session to take an extraordinary and historic step: to resume construction of our Cathedral after a cessation of 37 years." The plan was—and still is—to employ young people as apprentice and expert stonecutters working under the direction of J. R. Bambridge, who had just finished working on Liverpool Cathedral. Completing the southwest tower of the cathedral was to have priority, and by our Bicentennial year one could see the new courses rising high above Amsterdam Avenue.

Also offered as important recent events were social concerns "in all areas of our diocese": the Gay Movement, the trend away from conservatism, the heightened city ministry, the abolition of "aided" parishes ("no more second-class citizens"), crises in the lives of the clergy such as low salaries, decline in their prestige, and especially a perceived "decline in the morality and integrity of the clergy." The Church was seen as hard hit by the rise in oil prices and the economic malaise of the Northeast. And there was said to be a "liberalization" of the life of the clergy inasmuch as they are (if only because of the ordination of women!) no longer obliged to fulfill the role of the correct man in the dark gray flannel suit.

Each bishop who has been called to lead the Diocese of New York has probably had an aim which compelled him to work toward a goal. Samuel Provoost, for instance, saw his task as saving the Episcopal Church in New York from the ravages of the Revolutionary War, and in this he succeeded admirably. Hobart popularized the Church and promoted its historic claims; Onderdonk had a genius for administration and organized Hobart's legacy. The Potters, each in his own way, sought to widen the Church's social influence, just as Greer, also a superb administrator, strove to provide an intellectual apologia for the Church. Manning insisted that the age-old Church had a right to speak to modern times, and was jealous that spiritual prerogatives not be neglected. Bishop Donegan had thrust upon him the need to reconcile diverse Protestant and Catholic points of view in his diocese, while at the same time streamlining its administration.

What, then, was the goal of Paul Moore when he accepted election as New York's thirteenth bishop? There is no question that it was an effective ministry to the poor. He was convinced that the Church should do its utmost to expose reasons for poverty, and then go on to alleviate the results of poverty. This should be achieved in the parishes, expected by the diocese, and made exemplary in the cathedral and the Episcopal City Mission Society.

Almost as important for Bishop Moore was his belief that, as he said, there must be "a continual hammering away for justice and peace" in the world. If his celebrated visit to Vietnam (1970) and to the Soviet Union (1982) failed to make clear his ideal of negotiated détente and the employment of international resources to promote human welfare, the giant Peace Rally at the cathedral in June 1982 made his mind plain to all observers. The Diocese of New York is on record about these things. If those who responded to the question about important developments failed to be explicit about Bishop Moore's well-known beliefs, it is probably because they are so obvious—and have roots in the words and acts of former bishops.

The historian of the next hundred years will note that his century began soon after two epochal moments in Episcopal Church history: the ordination of women, and the settlement of the 1979 Prayer Book. Bishop Moore's apparent casual manner, complemented by a barbed directness, will be seen to have helped New York steer a remarkably steady and tranquil course throughout these proceedings. He did not ordain women until it was permitted by canon law, though some people predicted he would be among those who acted before the appropriate legislation was enacted. The new Prayer Book has been accepted in the Diocese of New York with far less difficulty than that experienced by many other dioceses. In this connection, it is worth noting that New York has had no conspicuous defections to "Anglican" splinter churches, despite the fact that its bishop is generally considered a protagonist of that which has disturbed the peace of the national Church in his generation.

Perhaps one reason for New York's sparse defection to those other churches may be that the Episcopal Church here has been both sophisticated and wounded. Sophisticated, because of cosmopolitan Manhattan; wounded, because (as we have already noted) the tide of statistics has been running against the Diocese of New York since the late 1930s. When the communicant lists of the Diocese of New York slipped year by year, those of the dioceses in New Jersey, Long Island, and Connecticut grew. The graphs marking the post–World War II "return to religion" simply don't show growth in New York's communicant strength, though it is indisputable that in some Manhattan parishes *attendance* improved in those years. A special committee appointed by Bishop

Moore was charged with probing the patterns and reasons for growth and decline in the diocese. It reported in October 1983 that, while baptisms in the diocese have lately kept up at the same rate, communicant numbers have decreased in all three regions. Surprisingly, the decrease rate is less in Manhattan, where there has been a notable resurgence and activity in such parishes as Trinity, Grace Church, St. Thomas, Heavenly Rest, St. Bartholomew's, and St. Michael's—all of them old-line churches hard hit by the times. Ironically, All Angels' Church razed its building of absurd proportions, and presently finds itself very much in need of some of the space thus destroyed. The National Council of Churches noted at the end of 1983 that membership in the Diocese of New York had probably bottomed out in 1981–82 while other mainline denominations continued to decline.

Our historiographer of the year 2085 will weigh these facts, and will know better than we how deep was a sense of despair in the late twentieth century. The apparent faithlessness and dominant materialism of our century will be seen in perspective then. On the other hand, it will be easier then to assess the long-range appeal of the Fundamentalist churches. The future historian may also be able to provide reasonable answers to questions that have been only implicit in this history: How important has "class" been in the life of the Episcopal Church in New York? How much did the distinctive teachings of the Episcopal Church foster its growth and retain the loyalty of its adherents? How much did the fortunes of the Episcopal Church depend upon its traditional liturgy? Was the "bridge church" ideal nurtured by Bishop Manning a reality or an illusion? These are moot points today; the future will reveal their answers.

Much more certain, as these pages have implied, is a sense of unity in the Diocese of New York as it approaches the beginning of its third century. The future historian may identify the reasons for this: the bishops are accessible to all the people of the diocese, the Interparish Councils appear to be excellent modes of communication, the old "churchmanship" tensions are gone, and there is a sense of having weathered the worst of the storm—indeed, at this writing signs are good.

As for us who have been writing and reading this history of the first two centuries and more, we can look back across that expanse of time to a distant day when some unnamed Englishman had in his kit a Prayer Book as his ship came up the Narrows toward Manhattan. From that moment on, there has been a long procession of people, men and women, who worshiped "according to the usage" of that book, and so planted the Church in this place. That procession has included governors and missionaries whom we have named: bishops, other clergy, prominent layfolk (including a criminal or two) by whom the Church spread from the banks of the Hudson to the Falls of the Niagara. We have seen varying modes of worship, a few of the customs, and some of the varying degrees of concern for human need felt by these church-people. We began with a near-wilderness and saw it become an Empire State; with a handful of Church of England people who must have been aware that their prestige was far less than that of their brothers and sisters in the province of Virginia, but who built the Church here into what they liked to think was a premier diocese. We have seen our share of failure, and remembered that, by God's grace, the future builds on mistakes, too. Inspired human gifts such as music, sculpture, architecture, and scholarship have accompanied our story, for people of diverse and great ability have been in that long column. Whether or not they have been adequately noted here is not our present concern.

For what has been inadequately described, and perhaps must always remain so, are the countless unnamed people who are the substance of the history of the Diocese of New York. Whoever writes this history is constantly aware of that which is not, can not, be written: the prayers gone up, the lives enriched, wrongs confessed, compassion enacted, human dignity asserted, wisdom gained, the Christ seen and God praised. That is, and must ever be, the history of the Diocese of New York.

Appendix I

Bishops of the Diocese of New York

1. Samuel Provoost, bishop 1787–1815; resigned 1801. Born New York City 1742, died New York City, 1815.
2. Benjamin Moore, consecrated 1801 to serve in place of Samuel Provoost, resigned; became diocesan at the death of Provoost in 1815. Born Newtown, Long Island, 1748, died New York City, 1816.
3. John Henry Hobart, consecrated 1811 to serve in place of the disabled Bishop Moore; became diocesan 1816. Born Philadelphia, 1775; died Auburn, New York, 1830.
4. Benjamin Treadwell Onderdonk, Bishop of New York 1830–1861 (suspended 1845–1861). Born in New York City, 1791; died New York City, 1861.
5. Jonathan Mayhew Wainwright, consecrated 1852 to serve as Provisional Bishop in place of Bishop Onderdonk. Born in England, 1792; died in New York City, 1854.
6. Horatio Potter, consecrated 1854 to serve as Provisional Bishop in place of Bishop Onderdonk; became diocesan in 1861 at death of Bishop Onderdonk. Born LaGrange, New York, 1815; died New York City, 1887.
7. Henry Codman Potter, Acting Bishop 1883–1887 in place of Horatio Potter, his uncle; Bishop of New York 1887–1908. Born Schenectady, N.Y., 1834; died Cooperstown, N.Y., 1908.
8. David Hummell Greer, Bishop Coadjutor 1903–1908, Bishop of New York 1908–1919. Born Wheeling, [West] Virginia, 1844; died New York City, 1919.
9. Charles Sumner Burch, Bishop Suffragan 1911–1919; Bishop of New York 1919–1920. Born 1855 in Michigan; died New York City, 1920.
10. William Thomas Manning, Bishop of New York 1921–1946. Born Northampton, England, 1866; died New York City, 1949.
11. Charles Kendall Gilbert, Suffragan Bishop 1930–1947, Bishop of New York 1947–1950. Born Bainbridge, N.Y., 1878; died New York City, 1959.
12. Horace William Baden Donegan, Suffragan Bishop 1947–1949, Bishop Co-

adjutor, 1949–1950; Bishop of New York 1950–1972. Born Derbyshire, England, 1900.
13. Paul Moore, Jr., Bishop Coadjutor 1970–1972, Bishop of New York 1972–. Born Morristown, New Jersey, 1919.

Appendix II

Assisting Bishops of the Diocese

1. Benjamin Moore was elected in 1801 to act for Samuel Provoost, resigned; he subsequently became second Bishop of New York.
2. John Henry Hobart was elected to act for the invalid Benjamin Moore, and succeeded him in 1816 as third Bishop of New York.
3. Jonathan M. Wainwright was consecrated Provisional Bishop in 1852 to act in place of Benjamin T. Onderdonk, suspended.
4. Horatio Potter was elected Provisional Bishop in 1855 to act in place of Benjamin T. Onderdonk, and succeeded as sixth Bishop of New York at Bishop Onderdonk's death in 1861.
5. Henry Codman Potter was Bishop Coadjutor 1883–1887, and succeeded to become seventh Bishop of New York at the death of his uncle, Bishop Horatio Potter.
6. David Hummell Greer was Bishop Coadjutor 1903–1908, and succeeded Bishop Henry C. Potter in 1908 to become eighth Bishop of New York.
7. Charles Sumner Burch was elected Suffragan Bishop in 1911 after General Convention enacted a canon providing for suffragan bishops; he was elected ninth Bishop of New York upon Bishop Greer's death in 1919.
8. Arthur Seldon Lloyd, Suffragan Bishop of New York 1921–1936. Born Loudon County, Virginia, 1857; died Darien, Conn., 1936.
9. Herbert Shipman, Suffragan Bishop 1921–1930. Born Lexington, Kentucky, 1869; died New York City, 1930.
10. Charles Kendall Gilbert, Bishop Suffragan 1930–1947; elected eleventh Bishop of New York City, 1947.
11. Charles F. Boynton, Bishop Suffragan, 1951–1969. Born Geneseo, N.Y., 1906.
12. James Stuart Wetmore, Bishop Suffragan 1959–. Born 1913, Hampton, New Brunswick, Canada.
13. Harold Louis Wright, Bishop Suffragan 1974–1978. born Boston, Mass., 1929; died East Elmhurst, Queens, 1978.
14. Walter Decoster Dennis, Bishop Suffragan 1979–. Born Washington, D.C., 1932.

Appendix III

Members of the Standing Committee

In the diocesan conventions of 1785 and 1786 the delegates to General Convention probably assumed the responsibilities of what soon became the Standing Committee of the diocese. In the diocesan convention of June 1787, a committee was "appointed, with all power to call a special convention, should the episcopate become vacant by the death or removal of the Bishop." Thereafter, a Standing Committee became a fixed part of the structure of the Diocese of New York.

Clerical Members

Joshua Bloomer, 1787–1790
Benjamin Moore, 1787–1800
Abraham Beach, 1787–1793
Jeremiah Leaming, 1790–1791
Thomas Moore, 1790–1791
Thomas Ellison, 1791–1792
Elijah D. Rattoone, 1791–1792
William Hammel, 1792–1793
John Bissett, 1793–1796
George H. Spier, 1794–1796
Elias Cooper, 1797–1801
John H. Hobart, 1801–1811
Cave Jones, 1801–1811
William Harris, 1802–1828
Nathaniel Bowen, 1811–1817
John Bowden, 1811–1815
Thomas Lyell, 1817–1824,
 1831–1847
Thomas Y. How, 1817–1818
Samuel F. Jarvis, 1818–1819

James Montgomery, 1818–1819
William Berrian, 1820–1862
Henry U. Onderdonk, 1820–1826
William Creighton, 1825–1836
Benjamin T. Onderdonk, 1827–1830
Jonathan M. Wainwright, 1829,
 1844–1848
George Upfold, 1830
John McVickar, 1834–1868
Henry Anthon, 1836
Francis L. Hawks, 1837
Thomas H. Taylor, 1838–1844
Benjamin I. Haight, 1848–1860
Samuel Seabury, 1848–1853
Samuel R. Johnson, 1854–1863
William E. Eigenbrodt, 1861–1885
Edward Y. Higbee, 1863–1867
Morgan Dix, 1864–1908
William F. Morgan, 1867–1890
Isaac H. Tuttle, 1868–1884

Thomas Richey, 1884–1892
William J. Seabury, 1887–1893
Henry Y. Satterlee, 1889–1894
Thomas M. Peters, 1892
Frederick B. VanKleeck, 1893
Octavius Applegate, 1894–1906
Thomas R. Harris, 1895–1908
J. S. Shipman, 1896–1900
William M. Grosvenor, 1901–1911
Amos T. Ashton, 1906–1912
William T. Manning, 1908–1912,
    1915–1918
Frank H. Clendennin, 1909–1915
Alexander G. Cummins, 1910–1914
Herbert Shipman, 1912–1916
Leighton Parks, 1914–1916
Arthur H. Judge, 1915–1923,
    1924–1928
Frank Heartfield, 1916–1919
Ernest M. Stires, 1917–1920,
    1922–1925
Theodore Sedgwick, 1918–1922,
    1927–1930
Charles L. Slattery, 1919–1923
William M. Gilbert, 1921–1924
Milo Gates, 1923–1933
H. Percy Silver, 1924–1926,
    1928–1934
Robert S. W. Wood, 1926–1929,
    1935–1936
Frank W. Crowder, 1928–1932
R. Townsend Henshaw, 1931–1934
Caleb Stetson, 1932–1933
Thomas McCandless, 1933–1936
Frederick S. Fleming, 1934–1938,
    1945–1949
H. Adye Prichard, 1934–1938
Roelif F. Brooks, 1937–1939
Donald B. Aldrich, 1937–1941
Frank D. Gifford, 1938–1942
J. H. Randolph Ray, 1939–1943,
    1945–1946, 1949–1953

Harold F. Hohly, 1942–1946
Horace W. B. Donegan, 1943–1945
Louis Pitt, 1947–1951
Samuel M. Shoemaker, 1948–1952
Shelton H. Bishop, 1952–1954
James A. Pike, 1952–1956
John Huess, 1953–1957
J. Howard Johnson, 1955–1957
John A. Bell, 1956–1959
Albert A. Chambers, 1957–1960
John Ellis Large, 1958–1961
George W. Barrett, 1959–1962
Leslie J. A. Lang, 1960–1963
Bernard C. Newman, 1961–1964
Arthur L. Kinsolving, 1962–1965
Charles H. Graf, 1963–1966
John V. Butler, 1964–1967
John M. Krumm, 1965–1968
J. Norman Hall, 1966–1969
David B. Weden, 1967–1968
Clarke K. Oler, 1968–1969
Clifford S. Lauder, 1969–1970
Leopold Damrosch, 1969–1970
Thomas F. Pike, 1970–1973
Walter D. Dennis, 1971–1972
Reid Isaac III, 1971–1973
Lloyd Uyeki, 1972–1976
John Murdock, 1973–1975
John B. Coburn, 1973–1975
Arthur Hargate, 1974–1977
John L. Kater, 1975–1979
Carol Anderson, 1976–1980
Christopher Webber, 1976–1980
Charles Colwell, 1977–1981
Frederick B. Williams, 1977–1981
Walter D. Dennis, 1979
William C. Heffner, 1980–1983
Jay H. Gordon, 1980–1984
Alanson B. Houghton, 1981–1983
George Zabriskie, 1982–
Fred Hill, 1983–
Joel Novey, 1983–

Lay Members:

James Duane, 1787–1791
John Jay, 1787–1789

John Alsop, 1787–1788
Richard Harison, 1788–1792

William Laight, 1789
Hubert VanWagenen, 1790
Aquila Giles, 1791–1793
William S. Johnson, 1792
Robert Watts, 1792
Josiah O. Hoffman, 1793
Matthew Clarkson, 1793, 1797–1821
Cadwalader Colden Sr., 1793–1797
———— Stevenson, 1793
R. H. Augustus VanCortlandt, 1794
Philip S. VanRensselaer, 1794–1796
John Charlton, 1796–1806
Guert VanSchoonhoven, 1797–1800
William Ogden, 1801–1824
John Onderdonk, 1806–1814
Robert Troup, 1814–1817
Nicholas Fish, 1817–1833
Henry Rogers, 1821–1834
Jacob Lorillard, 1825
Edward Lyde, 1826–1834
Thomas L. Ogden, 1826–1845
Peter A. Jay, 1832–1836
Floyd Smith, 1832–1874
William A. Duer, 1834–1838
Murray Hoffman, 1838–1863
Gulian C. Verplanck, 1838–1853
Samuel Jones, 1845–1853
Gerrit G. VanWagenen, 1853–1861
Gouverneur M. Ogden, 1854–1860
Stephen P. Nash, 1861–1897
George Templeton Strong, 1864–1874
Edward Jones, 1868–1870
Lloyd W. Wells, 1870–1880
Henry Drisler, 1870–1889
George Macculloch Miller, 1874–1914
Hamilton Fish, 1881–1885
David Clarkson, 1886–1893
S. Nicholson Kane, 1890–1905
George Zabriskie, 1893, 1898–1911, 1913–1921
———— Guion, 1894–1895
Herman C. VonPost, 1894–1895, 1897–1910
Cornelius Vanderbilt, 1895

Charles H. Russell, 1906–1913
Seth Low, 1910
Ambrose S. Murray, 1911–1913
Edmund L. Baylies, 1914–1918
Thaddeus R. Beal, 1916–1920
John L. Sague, 1919–1921
Thomas S. McLane, 1921–1923
Vernon M. Davis, 1921–1925
Robert W. B. Elliott, 1922–1925
George W. Wickersham, 1925–1928, 1932–1934
Augustus N. Hand, 1926–1929
James A. Hamilton, 1929
Samuel Thorne, 1930–1933
J. Mayhew Wainwright, 1934–1936
William Mason Smith, 1934–1935
Charles H. Tuttle, 1935–1937
Charles C. Burlingham, 1936–1940
G. Forrest Butterworth, 1937–1940
R. K. Kane, 1939–1943
Marsden B. Candler, 1940–1946
Charles A. Houston, 1940–1944
Clarence G. Michaelis, 1941–1955
Stephen F. Bayne, 1944–1948
Clifford P. Morehouse, 1949–1953
Charles M. Walton, Jr., 1952–1956
Douglas M. Moffat, 1952–1956
George W. Burpee, 1955–1959
Ludlow S. Fowler, 1956–1960
J. Taylor Foster, 1958–1962
Andrew Oliver, 1959–1963
Linden H. Morehouse, 1960–1964
Russell E. Aldrich, 1961–1965
Robert H. E. Elliott, 1962–1966
Willis L. M. Reese, 1963–1967
Thurgood Marshall, 1964–1965
John C. Pierson, 1966–1968
W. N. Seymour, 1966–1970
James M. Hubball, 1967–1971
Samuel G. Welles, 1968–1972
Margaret Lawrence, 1969–1973
Samuel Brookfield, 1970–1974
Archibald Murray, 1971–1975
Lucia Stich, 1972–1975
Sister Andrea, OSH, 1973–1977
Marshall Green, 1974–1978

George Browne, 1974–1979, 1981
Madeleine L'Engle Franklin, 1976–
  1980
Jane S. Auchincloss, 1977–1981

Richard E. Jacker, 1979–1983
Gwendolyn Simmons, 1980–
Diane Pollard, 1982–
John Miles Evans, 1983–

Appendix IV

Churches in the Diocese
of New York 1984

Symbols used: fs = first services; inc. = date of incorporation; org. = date congregation was organized; un = date of union with the diocese; SPG = known missionary station of the S.P.G.

Cathedral of St. John the Divine
Cathedral Heights, NYC
  fs 1892

New York City

All Angels Church
251 West 80 Street
  fs 1846, un 1859

All Saints Church
230 East 60 Street
  fs 1858, un 1965
  (formerly St. Thomas' Chapel)

All Souls' Church
88 St. Nicholas Avenue
  fs 1887, un 1890

Church of the Ascension
Fifth Avenue and 10 Street
  fs and un 1827

Calvary, Holy Communion and St. George's Church
East 16 Street (St. George's)
Gramercy Park (Calvary)
  a consolidation of St. George's Church (fs 1752), Calvary Church (org. and un 1836), and the Church of the Holy Communion (org. 1844)

Chinatown Mission Inc.
48 Henry Street
  worship in Church of Our Saviour
  (formerly St. Christopher's Chapel)
  fs before 1977

Christ and St. Stephen's Church
120 West 69 Street
  a consolidation of Christ Church (fs 1793) and St. Stephen's (fs 1805, merged with Church of the Advent, fs 1847)

Church of the Crucifixion
459 West 149 Street
  un 1930

Church of the Epiphany
1393 York Avenue
  fs 1833 as a chapel of the Episcopal City Mission Society; consolidated 1893 with St. John Baptist Church; un 1845

Church of the Good Shepherd
236 East 31 Street
   formerly Chapel of the Incarnation,
   and prior to that Church of the
   Reconciliation (un 1863); org. c.
   1860

Grace Church
802 Broadway
   fs 1804, un 1809

Haitian Congregation of the
Good Samaritan
Worship in Church of
St. Edward the Martyr
14 East 109 Street
   fs before 1978

Church of the Heavenly Rest
2 East 90 Street
   fs 1868, un 1870; consolidated with
   the Church of the Beloved Disciple
   (fs 1873)

Church of the Holy Apostles
296 Ninth Avenue
   fs 1836, un 1845

Holyrood Church
715 West 179 Street
   fs 1893, un 1900

Church of the Holy Trinity
316 East 88 Street
   fs 1895, un 1951 (formerly a chapel
   of St. James' Church)

Church of the Holy Trinity, Inwood
20 Cumming Street
   fs 1868, un 1874

Church of the Incarnation
Madison Avenue at 35 Street
   fs 1849, un 1852

Church of the Intercession
Broadway at 155 Street
   formerly a chapel of Trinity Church,
   and prior to that the Church of the
   Intercession (org. 1847); un 1976

Church of Our Saviour
48 Henry Street
   presently the Chinatown Mission,
   Inc.

Church of the Resurrection
115 East 74 Street
   fs 1865, un 1866 (formerly the
   Church of the Holy Sepulchre)

St. Ambrose Church
9 West 130 Street
   fs 1905, un 1928

St. Andrew's Church
2067 Fifth Avenue
   fs 1829, un 1829

St. Ann's for the Deaf
209 East 16 Street
   fs 1898

St. Augustine's Church
333 Madison Avenue
   fs 1869; formerly a chapel of Trinity
   Church

St. Bartholomew's Church
Park Avenue at 51 Street
   fs and un 1835

St. Clement's Church
423 West 46 Street
   fs 1830

Church of St. Edward the Martyr
14 East 109 Street
   fs 1883, un 1888

Eglise de St. Esprit
111 East 60 Street
   formerly a Huguenot church, org.
   1687; un 1804

Church of St. Ignatius
552 West End Avenue
   fs 1871, un 1874

St. James' Church
Madison Avenue at 71 Street
   fs and un 1810; consolidated with
   Church of the Holy Trinity, 1895

St. John's in the Village
224 Waverly Place
  fs and un 1853; also known as the
  Wainwright Memorial and the
  Church of St. John the Evangelist,
  successor to St. Jude's Church

St. Luke's Church
Convent Avenue and West 141 Street
  fs 1820, un 1821 (congregation
  moved from Hudson Street, 1892)

St. Luke's in-the-Fields
487 Hudson Street
  originally St. Luke's Church, whose
  congregation moved to Convent
  Avenue; then a chapel of Trinity
  Church, and now again a parish; un
  1976

Church of St. Luke the Beloved
Physician
28 Edgecombe Avenue

St. Mark's Church
Second Avenue at 10 Street
  fs 1799, un 1801

St. Martin's Church
230 Lenox Avenue
  un 1940

St. Mary's Church (Manhattanville)
521 West 126 Street
  fs 1820, un 1824

Church of St. Mary the Virgin
145 West 46 Street
  fs 1868, un 1874

Church of St. Matthew and St.
Timothy
26 West 84 Street
  a consolidation of St. Matthew's (fs
  1887), St. Timothy's (org. 1853, un
  1854), and Zion Church (inc. 1810)
  which was a consolidation with the
  Church of the Atonement in 1880

St. Michael's Church
Amsterdam Avenue at 99 Street
  fs and un 1809

St. Peter's Church
346 East 20 Street
  fs 1827, un 1831

St. Philip's Church
204 West 134 Street
  services held continuously since
  c. 1809; un 1853

St. Thomas Church
Fifth Avenue at 53 Street
  fs 1823, un 1824

Church of the Transfiguration
1 East 29 Street
  fs 1848, un 1849

Trinity Church
Broadway at Wall Street
  probably the successor
  congregation to that worshiping at
  "the Fort" since the English
  accession of 1664; Royal Charter
  1697 (St. Paul's Chapel, built 1765,
  was long a separate and sometimes
  competing congregation within the
  Trinity Parish)

Bronx

Church of the Atonement
1344 Beach Avenue
  fs 1900, un 1946

Christ Church (Riverdale)
5030 Henry Hudson Parkway
  fs and un, 1866

Church of the Good Shepherd
4401 Matilda Avenue
  fs before 1916, un 1924

Grace Church (City Island)
104 City Island Avenue
  fs 1862, un 1880

Grace Church (West Farms)
1909 Vyse Avenue
  org. 1844, un 1848

Church of the Holy Nativity
3061 Bainbridge Avenue
  fs 1900, un 1908

Church of the Mediator
260 West 231 Street
  fs before 1855, un 1858

St. Andrew's Church
781 Castle Avenue

St. Ann's Church
295 St. Ann's Avenue
  fs 1704, un 1841

St. David's Church
384 East 160 Street
  fs 1896

St. Edmund's Church
1905 Morris Avenue
  fs 1892, un 1928

St. James' Church (Fordham)
2500 Jerome Avenue
  fs and un 1853

St. Joseph's Church (Co-op City)
171 Dreiser Loop

St. Luke's Church
777 East 222 Street
  un 1952

St. Margaret's (Longwood)
940 East 156 Street
  fs 1899, un 1903

St. Martha's Church
1858 Hunt Avenue
  fs 1901, un 1946

St. Paul's Church
489 St. Paul's Place
  fs 1849; named 1853

St. Peter's Church
2500 Westchester Avenue
  fs 1702, Royal Charter 1762;
  un 1790, SPG

St. Simeon's Church
1020 Carroll Place
  fs 1899, un 1906

St. Stephen's Church
Vireo Avenue at East 238 Street
  fs 1897, un 1945

Trinity Church
698 East 166 Street
  fs 1868, un 1869

Staten Island

All Saints' Church
2329 Victory Boulevard
  fs 1891, un 1906; formerly Church
  of Our Father

Church of the Ascension
1 Kingsley Avenue
  fs 1800, un 1870; formerly Trinity
  Chapel, Factoryville

Christ Church
76 Franklin Avenue
  fs 1849, un 1851

St. Alban's Church
76 St. Alban's Place
  fs c. 1865 as Church of the Holy
  Comforter; consolidated 1951 with
  St. Anne's, Great Kills; un 1952

St. Andrew's Church
40 Old Mill Road
  fs c. 1702, Royal Charter 1713,
  un 1785

St. John's Church
1331 Bay Street
  org. and un 1843

St. Mary's Church (Castleton)
347 Davis Avenue
   fs 1848, un 1851

St. Paul's Church
225 St. Paul's Avenue
   fs and un 1833

St. Simon's Church
1055 Richmond Road
   fs 1854, un 1855

St. Stephen's Church
7516 Amboy Road
   fs 1872, inc 1887, un 1946

Farther North

Amenia Union
St. Thomas Church
   fs 1847, un 1849

Arden (formerly Greenwood)
St. John's Church
   fs 1852, un 1868

Ardsley
St. Barnabas' Church
   fs 1914, un 1958

Armonk (formerly Northcastle)
St. Stephen's Church
   fs 1840, un 1844

Barrytown
Church of St. John the Evangelist
   inc 1874, un 1888

Beacon (formerly Fishkill Landing)
St. Andrew's Church
   fs 1871, un 1900

Beacon (formerly Matteawan)
St. Luke's Church (formerly St.
Anna's)
   fs 1832, un 1833

Bedford
St. Matthew's Church
   fs 1704, un 1787 (originally
   included in the parish of Christ
   Church, Rye), SPG

Brewster
St. Andrew's Church
   fs 1873, un 1882

Briarcliff Manor
All Saints' Church
   fs 1848, un 1869

Bronxville
Christ Church
   fs 1853, resumed 1900; un 1903

Callicoon
St. James' Church
   fs and un 1874

Chappaqua
Church of St. Mary the Virgin
   fs 1874 (family chapel), un 1944

Chelsea (formerly Carthage Landing)
St. Mark's Church
   fs 1865

Chester
St. Paul's Church
   fs 1895, un 1901

Cold Spring
St. Mary's in the Highlands
   fs 1826, un 1840

Cornwall (formerly Canterbury)
St. John's Church
   fs and un 1858

Cragsmoor
Chapel of the Holy Name

Croton-on-Hudson
St. Augustine's Church
   fs 1756, resumed 1852; un 1855

Dobbs Ferry (Greenburgh)
Zion Church
   fs 1833, un 1834

Dover Plains
St. James' Church
   fs 1836, resumed 1892

Eastchester
St. Luke's Church
un 1953

Ellenville
St. John's Church
fs 1849, org. 1865, un 1892
(formerly St. Paul's)

Elmsford
Church of St. Joseph of Arimathea
fs 1883 (family chapel); un 1931

Fishkill
Trinity Church
fs 1755, un 1787 (originally shared
priest with Christ Church,
Poughkeepsie), SPG

Fort Montgomery
St. Mark's Church
fs 1915, un 1978

Garnerville (formerly Haverstraw)
Trinity Church
fs c. 1847, un 1847

Garrison
St. Philip's Church
fs 1768; a chapel of the Peekskill
parish, but possessing its own Royal
Charter, 1770; un 1840, SPG

Goshen
St. James' Church
fs 1793, un 1802 (probably
succeeded defunct churches in
Coldenham and Washingtonville)

Granite Springs
Church of the Good Shepherd
fs 1902, un 1958

Greenwood Lake
Church of the Good Shepherd
fs 1855, resumed 1873; un 1942

Harrison
All Saints' Church
fs 1898, un 1916

Hartsdale
St. Andrew's Church
fs 1910, un 1951

Hastings-on-Hudson
Grace Church
fs 1856, un 1917; formerly Zion
Chapel

Highland
Holy Trinity Church
fs 1870, un 1876; shares priest with
Church of the Ascension, West Park

*Highland Falls (formerly Fallsville,
or Buttermilk Falls)*
Church of the Holy Innocents
fs 1841, un 1850

Highland Mills
St. David's Church
fs 1896, un 1935; the name is said
to be taken from the pre-
Revolutionary church at Otterkill;
Royal Charter 1770

Hopewell Junction
Church of the Resurrection
fs 1886, un 1974

Hughsonville
Church of St. Nicholas on-the-Hudson
fs 1897; until 1983 a chapel of Zion
Church, Wappingers Falls

Hyde Park
St. James' Church
fs 1811, un 1812

*Irvington-on-Hudson
(formerly Dearman)*
St. Barnabas' Church
fs 1852, un 1859

Katonah
St. Luke's Church
fs 1914, un 1958

Kingston
Church of the Holy Cross
fs 1891, un 1898

Kingston
St. John's Church
services attempted 1704, resumed
1832; un 1832

Lake Mahopac
Church of the Holy Communion
  fs 1860, un 1881

Larchmont
St. John's Church
  fs 1891, un 1892

Lithgow (formerly Washington)
St. Peter's Church
  fs 1801, un 1834

Mamaroneck
St. Thomas' Church
  fs 1704, resumed 1797; un 1817,
  SPG

Marlboro
Christ Church
  fs 1836, un 1837

Middletown
Grace Church
  fs 1843, un 1845

Millbrook (formerly Hart's Village)
Grace Church
  fs before 1845, org. 1864; un 1882

Mohegan Lake (formerly Yorktown)
St. Mary's Church
  fs before 1867; un 1870

Monroe
Grace Church
  fs 1825, un 1887

Montgomery
St. Andrew's Chapel
  fs 1842, resumed 1900

Monticello
St. John's Church
  fs 1816, un 1817

Montrose (formerly Cortlandt)
Church of the Divine Love
  fs 1854, un 1906

Mt. Kisco
St. Mark's Church
  fs 1772, resumed 1848; un 1851
  (originally St. George's Church,
  Newcastle)

Mt. Vernon
Church of the Ascension
  fs 1887, un 1892

Mt. Vernon
Church of Saints John, Paul, and
Clement
  a consolidation of St. John's Church
  (fs 1851), St. Paul's Church (fs
  before 1700), and St. Clement's
  Church

Mt. Vernon
Trinity Church
  fs 1851, un 1857

New City
St. John's Church
  fs 1854, resumed 1866; un 1867

New Paltz
St. Andrew's Church
  fs 1844, resumed 1873; un 1873
  (formerly St. Athanasius' Church)

New Rochelle
St. John's Church
  fs 1858, un 1861

New Rochelle
St. Paul's Church
  fs 1910, un 1911, SPG

New Rochelle
Church of St. Simon the Cyrenian
  fs 1915, un 1955

New Rochelle
Trinity Church
  originally a Huguenot
  congregation; conformed to the
  Prayer Book 1709; Royal Charter
  1762; un 1785

New Windsor
St. Thomas Church
  fs 1733, inc. and un 1818; shared a
  Royal Charter with St. George's
  Church, Newburgh; SPG

Newburgh
Church of the Good Shepherd
  fs 1871, un 1891

Newburgh
St. George's Church
  fs 1729, Royal Charter 1770;
  un 1785; SPG

North Salem
St. James' Church
  fs 1725, un 1787

Nyack
Grace Church
  fs 1856, un 1862

Ossining (formerly Sing Sing)
St. Paul's on the Hill
  fs 1833, un 1834

Ossining
Trinity Church
  fs 1868, un 1869

Patterson (formerly Franklin)
Christ Church
  fs 1844, un 1897

Pawling
Church of the Holy Trinity
  fs 1816, un 1957

Pearl River
St. Stephen's Church
  fs 1887, un 1953

Peekskill
St. Peter's Church
  fs 1744, Royal Charter 1770,
  un 1791

Pelham Manor
Church of Christ the Redeemer
  a consolidation of Christ Church
  (fs 1695, resumed 1840) and the
  Church of the Redeemer (org.
  1872)

Pine Plains
Church of the Regeneration
  fs 1818, resumed 1850; un 1860

Pleasant Valley
St. Paul's Church
  fs 1836, un 1837

Pleasantville
St. John's Church
  fs 1852, un 1853

Port Chester
St. Peter's Church
  fs 1836, un 1852

Port Jervis
Grace Church
  fs 1853, un 1854

Poughkeepsie
Christ Church
  fs 1795, Royal Charter 1773;
  un 1785

Poughkeepsie
Church of the Holy Comforter
  fs 1859, un 1866

Poughkeepsie
St. Andrew's Church
  fs 1889; org. 1900 as St. John's
  Chapel

Poughkeepsie
St. Paul's Church
  org. and un, 1835

Red Hook
Christ Church
  fs 1850, org. 1854, un 1895

Rhinebeck
Church of the Messiah
  fs 1831, un 1852

Rye
Christ's Church
  fs 1702, Royal Charter 1764, un
  1786 (once known as Grace
  Church)

Saugerties
Trinity Church
  fs c. 1827, un 1831

Scarborough
St. Mary's Church
  fs 1839, un 1895

Scarsdale
Church of St. James the Less
  fs 1724, resumed 1849; un 1849

Somers (formerly Stephentown)
St. Luke's Church
    fs 1704, resumed 1830; un 1839

South Fallsburg
St. Andrew's Church
    fs 1913

South Salem (Lewisboro)
St. John's Church
    fs 1759, inc. 1811, un 1853, SPG

South Salem (Lewisboro)
St. Paul's Chapel
    cornerstone: 1871; served by
    St. John's, South Salem

Sparkill (Piermont)
Christ Church
    fs 1847, un 1848

Spring Valley
St. Paul's Church
    fs 1854, un 1868

Staatsburgh
St. Margaret's Church
    fs 1857, un 1882

Stone Ridge
Church of Christ the King
    a consolidation of St. Peter's
    Church, Stone Ridge (fs 1845, un
    1846), All Saints' Church,
    Rosendale (fs 1835, resumed 1874;
    un 1893), and St. John's Church,
    formerly St. Paul's, High Falls (fs
    1874)

Stony Point
St. John's in the Wilderness
    fs 1880

Suffern
Christ Church of Ramapo
    fs 1853, un 1860

Tarrytown (formerly Mt. Pleasant)
Christ Church
    fs and un, 1836

Tivoli (formerly Red Hook)
St. Paul's and Trinity
    a consolidation of St. Paul's
    Church, Tivoli (fs c. 1788, un 1817)
    and Trinity Church, Madalin (fs
    1854)

Tomkins Cove
Church of St. John the Divine
    fs and un, 1871

Tuxedo
St. Mary's Church
    fs 1888, un 1890

Valley Cottage
All Saints' Church
    fs 1915

Walden
St. Andrew's Church
    fs 1733, un 1785; formerly in
    Coldenham, moved to Walden in
    1833; Royal Charter 1770

Wappingers Falls
Zion Church
    fs 1833, un 1834

Warwick
Christ Church
    fs 1853, un 1866; formerly St.
    Alban's. There was probably a pre-
    Revolutionary congregation in
    Warwick

Washingtonville
St. Anne's Church
    org. 1957, un 1978

West Park (formerly Esopus)
Church of the Ascension
    fs c. 1840, un 1841 (presently
    shares rector with Holy Trinity,
    Highland)

White Plains
Grace Church
    fs 1724, resumed prior to 1824;
    un 1824

White Plains
Hispanic Congregation
    at Grace Church since 1978

White Plains
St. Bartholomew's Church
fs 1915, un 1916

White Plains
Church of St. Francis and St. Martha
a consolidation in 1968 of St.
Francis' Church (1951) and St.
Martha's Church (1935)

Woodstock
St. Gregory's Church
fs 1892, resumed 1952; un 1980.
Formerly known as Christ Chapel

Yonkers
Church of the Holy Cross
a consolidation in 1976 of Christ
Church (1872) and St. Augustine's
Church (c. 1909); un 1976

Yonkers
St. Andrew's Church
(Iglesia San Andres)
fs 1894, un 1895

Yonkers
St. John's Church
fs 1702, un 1787

Yonkers (Tuckahoe)
St. John's Church
fs 1789, un 1853; originally a
chapel of St. John's, Yonkers

Yonkers (Nepera Park)
St. Mark's Church
fs 1897, un 1952

Yonkers
St. Paul's Church
fs 1858, un 1859

Notes

The following abbreviations have been used in the Notes:

NYDJ — The *Journal* of the proceedings of the annual conventions of the Diocese of New York. In the very early years there appears to have been no Journal. In 1844 the Minutes and the printed *Journal* were published in one volume; thereafter, a separate bound volume has been published each year.

NYDA — The Archives of the Diocese of New York are under the care of the registrar of the diocese, and are located in Cathedral House, 1047 Amsterdam Avenue, New York, N.Y.

MDA — The Archives of the Diocese of Maryland are on deposit in the Maryland Historical Society, Baltimore, Maryland. They contain a wealth of New York material because William R. Whittingham, once librarian of the General Theological Seminary and rector of St. Luke's Church, Hudson Street, later became Bishop of Maryland and left his correspondence to that diocese.

GTS — The diaries of George Templeton Strong were edited by Allan Nevins and Milton Halsey Thomas and published in 1952 by the Macmillan Company, reprinted 1974 by Octagon Books, New York. A citation appears once in the following pages, and thereafter the symbol GTS because the manuscript as well as the published volumes have been consulted.

1 The Beginnings

1. Gerald F. DeJong, *Dutch in America*, Twayne Publishers, Boston, 1975, p. 68.

2. Samuel Eliot Morison, *The European Discovery of America: The Southern Voyages*, Oxford University Press, 1974, p. 35.

3. Ibid., p. 90.

4. Ibid., p. 301.

5. Samuel Eliot Morison, *The European Discovery of America: The Northern Voyages*, Oxford University Press, 1971, p. 1423.

6. Gerald F. DeJong, op. cit., p. x.

7. Ibid., p. 8.

8. Ibid., p. 10.

9. Robert T. Handy, *A History of the Churches in the United States and Canada,* Oxford University Press, 1977, pp. 13–14.

10. Fitzsimon Allison, "Toward an Historical Hermeneutic for Understanding PECUSA," *Historical Magazine of the Protestant Episcopal Church,* Austin, Texas, March, 1979, xlviii.

11. Robert T. Handy, op. cit., p. 74.

12. Ibid.

13. E. Clowes Chorley, "Beginnings of the Church in the Province of N.Y.," *Historical Magazine,* XIII, p. 10 ff.

14. Ibid.

15. Norman Sykes, *From Sheldon to Secker,* Cambridge University Press, 1959, p. 143.

16. Ibid., p. 147.

17. C. J. Stranks, *Anglican Devotion,* SCM Press, 1961, p. 291.

18. Norman Sykes, op. cit., p. 149.

19. John R. H. Moorman, *A History of the Church in England,* 1953, p. 267.

20. E. Clowes Chorley, op. cit., p. 13.

21. Robert T. Handy, op. cit., p. 61.

22. Cf. Gerald F. DeJong, op. cit., p. 62.

23. Robert T. Handy, op. cit., p. 62.

24. John W. Davis, *Dominion in the Sea,* Hempstead, N.Y., 1977, p. 33.

25. Malcolm Freiberg, ed., *The Journal of Madam Knight,* David R. Godine, Boston, 1972, p. 30.

2 "Come Over and Help Us." The SPG

1. C. F. Pascoe, *Two Hundred Years of the S.P.G.,* London, 1901, p. 2.

2. William W. Manross, *Fulham Papers,* Oxford, 1965, xviii.

3. William Stevens Perry, *History of the American Episcopal Church,* Boston, 1885, Vol. I, p. 138.

4. C. F. Pascoe, op. cit., p. 7.

5. Willis T. Hansen, *History of St. George's,* Schenectady, 1919, p. 10.

6. Antonia Fraser, *Royal Charles,* Alfred A. Knopf, 1979, p. 432.

7. Carl Carmer, *The Hudson,* New York, 1939, p. 69.

8. *Ecclesiastical Records,* Albany, 1902, Vol. III, pp. 1738–39.

9. Ibid., p. 1813.

10. Ibid.

11. Ibid., p. 1862.

12. C. F. Pascoe, op. cit., p. 61.

13. Guildhall Library, Manuscripts 9535/3, pp. 143–44.

14. Quoted in *St. James' Eightieth Anniversary,* St. James' Church, Fordham, 1933, p. 6.

15. *Ecclesiastical Records,* Vol. III, p. 1872.

16. Ibid., p. 1880.

17. Ibid., p. 2059.

18. Ibid., p. 2002.

19. Ibid., p. 2113.

20. Ibid., p. 2118.

3 An Era of Expansion in Manhattan and Westchester: Growth Around New York City

1. William W. Manross, *Fulham Papers,* Oxford, 1965, p. 87.

2. C. F. Pascoe, *Two Hundred Years of the S.P.G.,* London, 1901, p. 58.

3. Van Wyck Brooks, *The World of Washington Irving,* World, New York, 1944, p. 36.

4. Robert Bolton, *History of the Protestant Episcopal Church in the County of Westchester from Its Foundation,* Stamford and Swords, 1855, pp. 16–17.

5. Malcolm Freiberg, ed., *The Journal of Madam Knight,* David R. Godine, Boston, 1972, p. 33.

6. Robert Bolton, op. cit., p. 142.

7. William Stevens Perry, *History of the American Episcopal Church,* Boston, 1885, Vol. I, p. 173.

8. C. F. Pascoe, op. cit., p. 58.

9. Ibid., p. 62.

10. William Stevens Perry, op. cit., p. 171.

11. William W. Manross, op. cit., p. 83.

12. William Stevens Perry, op. cit., p. 72.

13. Frank J. Klingberg, "The S.P.G. Program for Negroes in Colonial New York," *Historical Magazine,* VIII, 1939, p. 307.

14. William W. Manross, op. cit., p. 86.

15. Ibid., p. 319.

16. Edward Midwinter, "The S.P.G. and the Church in the American Colonies," *Historical Magazine,* IV, 1935, p. 70.

17. William W. Manross, op. cit., p. 86.

18. C. F. Pascoe, op. cit., p. 66.

19. Malcolm Freiberg, op. cit., p. 28–31.

20. Robert Bolton, op. cit., *passim.*

21. NYDA, St. Peter's Church, Westchester box.

22. Ibid.

23. Ibid.

24. Robert Bolton, op. cit., p. 18.

25. Ibid., p. 19.

26. Ibid., p. 366.

27. Ibid., p. 370.

28. Ibid., p. 398.

29. Ibid., p. 406.

30. Ibid., p. 402.

31. Ibid., p. 695.

32. Ibid., p. xix.

33. Ibid., p. 44.

34. Elizabeth L. Gebhard, *Parsonage Between Two Manors,* Hudson, N. Y., 1925, pp. 22–23.

35. Arthur Pierce Middleton, *Amiable Dwellings,* Springfield, Mass., 1976, pp. 10–11.

36. Edward N. West, "History and Development of Music in the American Church," *Historical Magazine,* XIV.

37. Ibid., p. 20.

38. George W. Shinn, *King's Handbook of Notable Episcopal Churches,* Boston, 1889, p. 33.

39. A. P. Middleton, op. cit., p. 13.

40. I am indebted to the Rev. Wayne Schmidt for bringing the subscription paper to my attention.

41. There is reason to believe an Episcopal Church existed in Warwick prior to the Revolutionary War. However, the present Christ Church there (formerly St. Alban's) commenced services about 1853 and was probably a missionary enterprise of St. Thomas, Vernon, in the present Diocese of Newark.

42. George Woodward Lewis, "Clergymen Licensed to the American Colonies by the Bishops of London: 1745–1781, *"Historical Magazine,* XIII, 1944, p. 129.

43. Arthur Sandys, "Reminiscences," unpublished manuscript in Bard College Library, p. 28.

44. C. F. Pascoe, op. cit., p. 67.

45. Ibid., p. 69.

46. Ibid.

47. William W. Manross, op. cit., p. 87.

48. Willis T. Hansen, *History of St. George's,* Schenectady, 1919, p. 16.

49. William W. Manross, op. cit., p. 146.

50. W. Max Reid, *The Mohawk Valley,* Putnam, 1917, p. 114.

51. William W. Manross, op. cit., p. 123.

52. Theodore Sedgwick, *A Memoir of the Life of William Livingston,* New York, 1833, p. 79.

53. James Thayer Addison, *The Episcopal Church in the United States,* Scribner's, 1951, p. 45.

54. William W. Manross, op. cit., p. 86.

55. *Gazette or Weekly Post Boy,* July 1, 1754.

56. Herbert and Carol Schneider, eds., *Samuel Johnson,* Vol. IV, Columbia University Press, 1929, *passim.*

57. Cf. Eben Edwards Beardsley, *William Samuel Johnson,* Hurd and Houghton, 1876.

58. Herbert and Carol Schneider, op. cit., p. 372.

59. Ibid., p. 293.

60. Theodore Sedgwick, op. cit., p. 64.

61. Ibid., p. 9.

62. Jacob Judd and Irwin H. Polishook, eds., *Aspects of Early New York Society and Politics,* Sleepy Hollow Press, 1974, p. 201.

63. Arthur W. H. Eaton, *American Loyalists,* T. Whittaker, New York, 1892, *passim.*

64. E. Clowes Chorley, *Quarter of a Millennium,* Church Historical Society, 1947, p. 29.

65. John N. Norton, *Samuel Provoost,* Protestant Episcopal Sunday School Union, New York, 1861, p. 39.

66. Morgan Dix, *Parish of Trinity Church,* G. P. Putnam's Sons, 1901, Vol. II, p. 36.

67. Ibid., p. 37.

68. William Smith, *Historical Memoirs,* ed. William H. W. Sabine, New York, no date, p. 260.

69. Ibid., p. 125.

70. Ibid., p. 194.

71. Ibid.

72. Agnes E. Kirkwood, *Church and Sunday School Work in Yonkers, N.Y.,* New York, 1889, p. 28.

73. Bernard Barlyn, *Ideological Origins of the American Revolution,* Belknap Press, 1967.

74. Ibid., p. 312.

75. Ibid.

76. Ibid., p. 137.

77. Reginald V. Harris, *Charles Inglis,* Toronto, 1937, p. 40.

78. Frank J. Klingberg, "SPG Program," *Historical Magazine,* IV, 1939, p. 80.

79. Ibid., p. 79.

4   After the Peace

1. Alexander C. Flick, ed., *History of the State of New York,* Columbia University Press, 1933, p. 253.

2. James T. Flexner, *States Dyckman,* Little, Brown, 1980, p. 7.

3. Ibid., p. 23.

4. John C. Fitzpatrick, *Writings of George Washington,* Washington, D.C., 1931–44, XXXI, p. 336.

5. Sidney I. Pomerantz, *New York, an American City,* New York, 1938, p. 19.

6. Reginald V. Harris, *Charles Inglis,* Toronto, 1937, p. 60.

7. Ibid., pp. 61–62.

8. Duane Papers, New-York Historical Society.

9. Lorenzo Sabine, *American Loyalists,* Boston, 1847, p. 18.

10. Clara O. Loveland, *The Critical Years,* Seabury Press, 1956, p. 66.

11. Morgan Dix, *Parish of Trinity Church,* G. P. Putnam's Sons, 1901, Vol. II, p. 14.

12. Duane Papers, 12/22/1783.

13. Harold C. Syratt, ed., *Papers of Alexander Hamilton,* Columbia University Press, 1962, II, p. 164.

14. Morgan Dix, op. cit., II, p. 19.

15. Samuel White Patterson, *Horatio Gates,* Columbia University Press, 1941, p. 383.

16. George Dangerfield, *Chancellor Robert R. Livingston of New York,* Harcourt, Brace and Company, 1960, summarizes the Tory-Whig contest, pp. 199ff.

17. *Country Life,* London, 1980, CLXIX, 4351, p. 67.

18. Alexander Coventry, *Memoirs,* Albany, 1978, p. 69 and *passim.*

19. Edward Midwinter, "The S.P.G. and the Church in the American Colonies," *Historical Magazine,* IV, 1935, p. 81.

20. Agnes E. Kirkwood, *Church and Sunday School Work in Yonkers, N.Y.,* New York, 1889, p. 30.

21. Horatio O. Ladd, *Founding of the Episcopal Church in Fishkill,* Fishkill, N.Y., 1895, p. 25.

22. Ibid., p. 36.

23. Helen Wilkinson Reynolds, *Records of Christ Church,* Poughkeepsie, N.Y., Frank B. Howard, 1911, p. 50.

24. Lorenzo Sabine, op. cit., p. 636.

25. Ibid., p. 704.

26. Ibid., pp. 683–84.

27. Horatio O. Ladd, *Origins and History of Grace Church, Jamaica, N.Y.,* Jamaica, N.Y., 1914, p. 48.

28. Ibid., p. 102.

29. Richard N. Ruedger, "Founding of St. Peter's Church at VanCortlandtville," 1967, *passim.*

30. Allan Nevins and Milton Halsey Thomas, eds., *The Diary of George Templeton Strong,* Octagon Books, New York, 1974, I, p. 40 (hereafter cited as GTS).

31. Ibid.

32. William W. Manross, *A History of the American Episcopal Church,* Morehouse Publishing Co., 1935, p. 193.

33. The records of the early conventions of the Diocese of New York were published in one volume in 1844; see p. iv (hereafter cited as NYDJ).

34. William W. Manross, op. cit., p. 131.

35. NYDJ, 1844, p. 6.

36. E. Clowes Chorley, "The Election and Consecration," *Historical Magazine,* III, 1933, p. 188.

37. NYDJ, 1844.

5 A Bishop for New York

1. Edward Midwinter, "The S.P.G. and the Church in the American Colonies," *Historical Magazine,* IV, 1935, p. 257.

2. Bissett to Kemp, April 28, 1796, MDA.

3. Morgan Dix, *Parish of Trinity Church,* G. P. Putnam's Sons, 1901, Vol. II, p. 109.

4. Clara O. Loveland, *The Critical Years,* Seabury Press, 1956, p. 215.

5. Act Book, 1787, Lambeth Palace Library, p. 33.

6. John W. Francis, *Old New York,* New York, 1866, p. 163.

7. I am indebted to E. G. W. Bill, Librarian of Lambeth Palace Library, for a photocopy of the consecration record, sent to me April 14, 1981.

8. New-York *Packet,* June 22, 1787.

9. E. Edwards Beardsley, *William Samuel Johnson,* New York, 1876, p. 133.

10. Robert T. Handy, *A History of the Churches in the United States and Canada,* Oxford University Press, 1977, p. 153.

11. Frederick V. Mills, "The Protestant Episcopal Church in the United States 1783–1789: Suspended Animation or Remarkable Recovery?" *Historical Magazine,* XLVI, June 1977, p. 156.

12. "Empire State Mason," December 1978, p. 2.

13. Robert T. Handy, op. cit., p. 155.

14. Ibid.

15. Frederick V. Mills, op. cit., *passim.*

16. Henry Anstice, *History of St. George's Church,* Harper & Brothers, 1911, p. 99.

17. Lockwood Barr, *History of the Ancient Town of Pelham,* Dietz Press, Richmond, Va., n.d., p. 50.

18. Ibid., p. 14.

19. Helen Wilkinson Reynolds, *Records of Christ Church,* Poughkeepsie, N.Y., Frank B. Howard, 1911, p. 97. This would be the beginning of the present St. Paul's, Tivoli.

20. John W. Davis to the author, July 16, 1981.

21. Henry M. MacCracken, *Old Dutchess Forever,* Hastings House, 1956, pp. 222, 235.

22. George DeMille, *History of the Diocese of Albany,* Philadelphia, 1946.

23. NYDJ, 1844, p. 24.

24. Clara O. Loveland, op. cit., p. 184.

25. Sidney I. Pomerantz, *New York, an American City,* New York, 1938, p. 64.

26. Ibid., p. 41.

27. Ibid., p. 224.

28. Ibid., p. 203.

29. Ibid.

30. Duane Papers, New-York Historical Society.

31. Bissett to Kemp, MDA.

32. Duane Papers, New-York Historical Society, April 12, 1794.

33. David Freeman Hawke, *Paine,* Harper & Row, 1974, p. 142.

34. Levinus Clarkson's Cash Book, unpublished manuscript in the possession of a descendant.

35. William A. Duer, *Reminiscences of an Old New Yorker,* New York, ed. 1867, pp. 17–18.

36. George DeMille, op. cit., p. 40.

37. Henry M. Onderdonk, *History of the Protestant Episcopal Church in the City of New York,* New York, 1845, p. 58.

38. John N. Norton, *Life of Samuel Provoost,* New York, 1859.

6 Benjamin Moore: Benign Bishop

1. John W. Francis, *Old New York,* New York, 1866, p. 168.

2. Ibid.

3. Ibid., p. 52.

4. NYDJ, 1844, pp. 90–91.

5. Morgan Dix, *Parish of Trinity Church,* G.P. Putnam's Sons, 1901, Vol. II, p. 180.

6. Ibid.

7. Ibid., p. 132.

8. John W. Francis, op. cit., p. xvi.

9. Broadus Mitchell, *Alexander Hamilton,* Macmillan, 1962, p. 537.

10. J. Newton Perkins, *History of St. Stephen's Parish,* Gorham, 1906, p. 32.

11. NYDJ, 1844.

12. George DeMille, op. cit., p. 35.

13. Ibid., p. 49.

14. "The Act of 1819 required the captain or master of a vessel arriving from abroad to declare to the local collector of customs a list or manifest of all passengers taken on board," and this list was to include the "country to which they severally belonged"; prior to 1819 there was no record of an immigrant's native land. Cf. *Historical Statistics of the United States,* Department of Commerce, Washington, D.C., ed. 1961, p. 48.

15. John Henry Hobart to John Moore, September 1, 1801, MDA.

16. John McVickar, *Professional Years of Hobart,* New York, 1836, p. 205.

17. Ibid., p. 201.

7 The Heritage of a Great Bishop: Hobart

1. Alexander Coventry, *Memoirs,* Albany, 1978.

2. Joseph I. Dirvin, *Mrs. Seton,* Farrar, Straus and Cudahy, 1962, p. 80.

3. Mary Kathleen Flanagan, "Influence of John Henry Hobart on the Life of Elizabeth Seton," Union Theological Seminary thesis, 1978, p. 84.

4. Ibid.

5. J. P. K. Henshaw, *Memoir of the Life of the Right Reverend Richard Channing Moore, DD,* Philadelphia, 1842, p. 26.

6. Mary Kathleen Flanagan, op. cit., p. 230.

7. J. P. K. Henshaw, op. cit., p. 73.

8. Edward N. Cox to Thomas John Claggett, April 1, 1811, MDA.

9. John Henry Hobart to Joseph Jackson, September 23, 1807, MDA.

10. Cave Jones to Claggett, November 12, 1811, MDA.

11. Hobart to Kemp, May 3, 1811, MDA.

12. Quoted by William Stevens Perry, *History of the American Episcopal Church,* Boston, 1885, Vol. I, p. 158.

13. Morgan Dix, *Parish of Trinity Church,* G.P. Putnam's Son's, 1901, Vol. III.

14. William White to Claggett, June 5, 1811, MDA.

15. White to Claggett, April 20, 1811, MDA.

16. White to Claggett, December 2, 1811, MDA.

17. Joseph Bend to James Kemp, January 27, 1812, MDA.

18. Bend to Jackson, December 10, 1810, MDA.

19. Hobart to John Moore, September 1, 1810.

20. Bernard M. G. Reardon, *Religious Thought in the Nineteenth Century,* Columbia University Press, 1966, p. 26.

21. Ibid., p. 27.

22. Robert T. Handy, *A History of the Churches in the United States and Canada,* Oxford University Press, 1977, p. 162.

23. Bernard M. G. Reardon, op. cit., p. 1.

24. J. Brett Langstaff, *The Enterprising Life, John McVickar,* St. Martin's Press, 1961, p. 342.

25. John Henry Hobart, ed., *Companion for the Altar,* preface to the 14th edition, New York, 1843.

26. Hobart to Kemp, June 6, 1808.

27. Quoted in John McVickar, *Professional Years of Hobart,* New York, 1836, p. 351.

28. Quoted in John McVickar, op. cit., p. 339.

29. John McVickar, op. cit., p. 342.

30. James Thayer Addison, *The Episcopal Church in the United States,* Scribner's, 1951, p. 99.

31. John Ireland to Claggett, November 9, 1814, MDA.

32. Ibid.

33. Hobart to Kemp, July 20, 1814, MDA.

34. Hobart to Kemp, June 14, 1814, MDA.

35. Nelson R. Burr, *The Anglican Churches in New Jersey,* Philadelphia, 1954, p. 488.

36. *The Evergreen,* New Haven, 1845, p. 290.

37. John McVickar, op. cit., p. 356.

38. J. Brett Langstaff, op. cit., p. 25.

39. Hobart to Kemp, February 2, 1818, MDA.

40. Powel Mills Dawley, *The Story of the General Theological Seminary,* Oxford University Press, 1969, pp. 77–78.

41. John McVickar, op. cit., p. 359.

42. Ibid., p. 394.

43. Charles G. Finney, *Memoirs,* New York, 1876, p. 279.

44. J. Newton Perkins, *History of St. Stephen's Parish,* Gorham, 1906, p. 29.

8   Onderdonk: Triumph and Tragedy

1. Morgan Dix, *Parish of Trinity Church,* G.P. Putnam's Sons, 1901, Vol. IV, p. 70.

2. James Franklin Beard, ed., *Letters and Journals of James Fenimore Cooper,* Harvard University Press, 1964, p. 447.

3. Benjamin T. Onderdonk to Hobart, November 17, 1828, Howard Chandler Robbins Collection, General Theological Seminary library.

4. William Francis Brand, *Life of William Rollinson Whittingham,* New York, 1883, p. 359 and *passim.*

5. "Laicus," *The Trial Tried,* New York, 1845, p. 22.

6. George DeMille, *History of the Diocese of Albany,* Philadelphia, 1946, p. 56.

7. Thomas March Clark, *Reminiscences,* New York, 1895, p. 32.

8. James Franklin Beard, op. cit., pp. 4–5.

9. Allan Nevins, ed., *Diary of Philip Hone,* New York, 1927, p. 78.

10. Ibid., p. 209.

11. Quoted in Lucius A. Edelblute, *History of the Church of the Holy Apostles,* New York, 1949, p. 7.

12. Thomas March Clark, op. cit., p. 52.

13. Thomas Hunt, *History of Clermont,* Hudson, N.Y., 1928, p. 123.

14. Thomas March Clark, op. cit., p. 55.

15. Levi Silliman Ives to William R. Whittingham, January 16, 1832, MDA.

16. Ibid.

17. William Francis Brand, op. cit., Vol. I, p. 104.

18. Ibid., p. 118.

19. Auburn (N.Y.) *Gospel Messenger* (edited by Bishop Hobart's host), September 13, 1830.

20. Ibid.

21. William Francis Brand, op. cit., Vol. I, pp. 61ff.

22. Hobart to Kemp, July 11, 1826, MDA.

23. Onderdonk to Whittingham, May 14, 1840, MDA.

24. NYDJ, 1832, p. 5.

25. Matthew Hale Smith, *Sunshine and Shadow in New York,* Hartford, 1868, pp. 581–82.

26. NYDJ, 1833.

27. Ibid.

28. James Fenimore Cooper and George Templeton Strong believed the trial so disastrous that it would be impossible for Bishop Onderdonk to resume the role of Bishop of New York.

29. NYDJ, 1834.

30. NYDJ, 1833.

31. Ibid.

32. NYDJ, 1835.

33. NYDJ, 1836.

34. NYDJ, 1841.

35. George Washington Doane to Whittingham, October 3, 1836, MDA.

36. Doane to Whittingham, February 15, 1845, MDA.

37. NYDJ, 1834.

38. NYDJ, 1837.

39. NYDJ, 1838.

40. Ibid.

41. John H. Hewitt, "The Sacking of St. Philip's Church," *Historical Magazine,* XLVIV, p. 17.

42. Doane to Whittingham, March 18, 1833, MDA.

43. Archives of the Diocese of Maryland on deposit in the Maryland Historical Society, Baltimore, Md.

44. Ibid.

45. Albert Bushnell Hart, ed., *Hamilton's Itinerarum,* Arno Press and the *New York Times,* 1971, p. 53.

46. Manuscript record, St. Paul's, Eastchester, NYDA, n.d., p. 10.

47. Helen Wilkinson Reynolds, *Records of Christ Church,* Poughkeepsie, N.Y., Frank B. Howard, 1911, p. 162.

48. J. Newton Perkins, *History of St. Stephen's Parish,* Gorham, 1906, pp. 30–31.

49. George W. Shinn, *King's Handbook of Notable Episcopal Churches,* Boston, 1889, p. 39.

50. NYDJ, 1832.

51. Ibid.

52. NYDJ, 1836.

53. NYDJ, 1839.

54. Christopher W. Knauff, *Dr. Tucker,* New York, 1897, p. 101.

55. NYDJ, 1841.

56. Ibid.

57. William Francis Brand, op. cit., p. 356.

58. George DeMille, op. cit., p. 57. See also the results of annual diocesan elections as appearing in the *Journals.*

59. Manton Eastburn, *Tribute to the Memory of the Rev. Henry Anthon, D.D.,* New York, 1862, p. 13.

60. Matthew Hale Smith, op. cit., p. 582.

61. Henry Anthon to Francis L. Hawks, August 19, 1844, NYHS (italics added).

62. Ibid.

63. Milton Rugoff, *The Beechers,* Harper & Row, 1981, p. 283.

64. For a full treatment of the hearing, see John E. Lawrence, "The Episcopate of Benjamin Treadwell Onderdonk," unpublished thesis, General Theological Seminary library (1970).

9   Interregnum

1. NYDJ, 1848.

2. Robert A. West, *Record of the Proceedings,* New York, 1845, *passim.*

3. Ibid., p. 99.

4. Robert B. Croes to William R. Whittingham, November 7, 1825, MDA.

5. GTS, *passim.*

6. George Washington Doane to William R. Whittingham, November 3, 1836, MDA.

7. NYDJ, 1845, p. 19.

8. NYDJ, 1848, p. 28.

9. NYDJ, 1845, p. 69.

10. NYDJ, 1845, p. 72.

11. NYDJ, 1847, p. 74.

12. NYDJ, 1848, p. 12.

13. NYDJ, 1849, p. 57.

14. GTS, Vol. II, p. 29.

15. Scot Alexander Mackay, 1846, quoted in Perry Miller, *The Raven and the Whale,* New York, 1956, p. 15.

16. GTS, Vol. II, p. 24.

17. Ibid., p. 57.

18. Andrew B. Myers, ed., *The Knickerbocker Tradition,* Tarrytown, N.Y., 1974, p. 37.

19. Ibid., pp. 122–23.

20. Walter F. Willcox, ed., *International Migration,* New York, 1929, p. 380.

21. GTS, Vol. II, p. 106.

22. Ibid., p. 69.

23. William Rhinelander Stewart, *Grace Church and Old New York,* E. P. Dutton, 1924, pp. 115–16.

24. Perry Miller, op. cit., p. 157.

25. Van Wyck Brooks, *The World of Washington Irving,* World, New York, 1944, p. 31.

26. Perry Miller, op. cit., p. 15.

27. Robert W. July, *Essential New Yorker,* Duke University Press, 1951, p. 211.

28. Perry Miller, op. cit., p. 23.

29. Ibid., p. 24.

30. Andrew Jackson Downing, *Rural Essays,* ed. George William Curtis, New York, 1881, p. 263.

31. Don E. Fehrenbacker, *Dred Scott Case,* New York, 1978, p. 117.

32. Bayard Tuckerman, *William Jay,* New York, 1893, p. x.

33. Ibid., p. 145.

34. Leonard L. Richards, *Gentlemen of Property and Standing,* Oxford University Press, 1970, p. 121.

35. Bayard Tuckerman, op. cit., p. 145.

36. Ibid., p. 148.

37. NYDJ, 1846, p. 76.

38. Ibid., p. 73.

39. Ibid., p. 78.

40. Bayard Tuckerman, op. cit., p. 167.

41. "John Jay's Attack upon the Rector of Christ Church of Rye, New York," New York, 1863, p. 14.

42. George Templeton Strong manuscript, January 29, 1854, and November 26, 1853.

43. George Templeton Strong manuscript, February 2, 1854.

44. Allan Nevins, ed., *Diary of Philip Hone,* New York, 1927, p. 689.

45. William A. Duer, *Reminiscences of an Old New Yorker,* New York, ed. 1867, p. 13.

46. Christopher W. Knauff, *Dr. Tucker,* New York, 1897, *passim.*

47. Richard Upjohn, *Upjohn's Rural Architecture,* New York, 1852, Preface.

48. Everard M. UpJohn, *Richard Upjohn, Architect and Churchman,* Columbia University Press, 1939, pp. 77–80.

49. Ibid.

50. Ibid.

10   Horatio Potter: From Farm to Fifth Avenue

1. Correspondence of Robert Cambridge Livingston, New-York Historical Society.

2. David M. Ellis et al., *Short History of New York State,* Cornell University Press, 1957, p. 265 and *passim.*

3. Morgan Dix, *Parish of Trinity Church,* G. P. Putnam's Sons, 1901, Vol. II, pp. 188–89.

4. NYDJ, 1855, p. 76.

5. NYDJ, 1856, p. 87 (italics added).

6. NYDJ, 1856, pp. 102–04.

7. NYDJ, 1859, pp. 100ff.

8. NYDA.

9. GTS, Vol. II, p. 460.

10. Ibid.

11. NYDA Onderdonk box.

12. Ibid.

13. *Obsequies and Obituary Notices of the Late Right Reverend Benjamin T. Onderdonk,* New York, 1862, p. 23.

14. Onderdonk to Adam Badeau, April 7, 1851; Howard Chandler Robbins Collection, General Theological Seminary library.

15. New York *Express,* May 8, 1861.

16. George Templeton Strong manuscript, April 30, 1861.

17. NYDJ, 1863, p. 256.

18. Archives, Community of St. Mary, Peekskill, N.Y., Letter 16, sheet 1, p. 29.

19. Archives, Community of St. Mary, Letter 22, sheet 1, p. 43.

20. NYDJ, 1864, pp. 91–93.

21. Ibid., p. 94.

22. Samuel M. Shoemaker, *Calvary Church Yesterday and Today,* New York, 1936, pp. 103–04.

23. George DeMille, *History of the Diocese of Albany,* Philadelphia, 1946, p. 75.

24. Louis H. Gray, *History of the Parish of St. Ignatius,* New York, 1946, n.p.

25. J. H. Randolph Ray, *My Little Church Around the Corner,* Simon and Schuster, 1957, p. 106.

26. Ibid., p. 287.

27. Matthew Hale Smith, *Sunshine and Shadow in New York,* Hartford, 1868, pp. 281–82.

28. Ibid., p. 494.

29. GTS, Vol. IV, p. 144.

30. Ibid.

31. Manuscript in the Archives of the Community of St. John Baptist, Mendham, N.J.

32. Horatio Potter to Mother Harriet, CSM, November 22, 1870; Archives, Community of St. Mary.

33. Matthew Hale Smith, op. cit., p. 82.

34. Manuscript edited by Margery Taylor providing vignette episodes in the history of St. Mark's Church, Mt. Kisco.

35. "St. John's Church, Cornwall, N.Y.," 1958, n.p.

36. E. Clowes Chorley in a paper read at the 70th anniversary of The Club in 1941; NYDA.

37. NYDA, January 20, 1860, Horatio Potter box.

38. Archives, St. James' Church, Goshen, N.Y.

39. NYDA, letter August 8, 1864.

40. NYDA, letter February 3, 1873.

41. NYDA, letter January 10, 1874.

42. Article by Morgan Dix, *Centennial History of the Protestant Episcopal Church in the Diocese of New York,* D. Appleton and Co., 1886, p. 793.

43. NYDA, George Macculloch Miller Letterbook.

44. Ibid, April 9, 1891.

11 Potter the Magnificent

1. Edith Wharton, *A Backward Glance,* Scribner's, 1933, p. 2.

2. George Hodges, *Henry Codman Potter,* Macmillan, 1915, p. 45.

3. Ibid., p. 70.

4. Nathalie S. Dana, *Young in New York,* Doubleday, 1963, p. 114.

5. Quoted by Vida Scudder, *Father Huntington,* E. P. Dutton, 1940, p. 88.

6. William H. Owen, *I Remember,* privately printed, 1939, p. 16.

7. George Hodges, op. cit., p. 78.

8. Ibid., p. 87.

9. Ibid., p. 64.

10. Ibid., p. 102.

11. Ibid., p. 112.

12. Ibid., p. 117.

13. Nathalie S. Dana, op. cit., p. 113.

14. Vida Scudder, op. cit., p. 76.

15. Sturges Allen manuscripts, Archives, Order of the Holy Cross, West Park, N.Y.

16. Vida Scudder, op. cit., p. 76.

17. The Rev. Charles Townsend to the author; Charles Townsend was aboard the special train.

18. NYDJ, 1899.

19. NYDJ, 1905.

20. Grace Hoysradt MacDaniells to the author.

21. Hamilton Fish Armstrong, *Those Days,* Harper & Row, 1963, p. 39.

22. William H. Owen, op. cit., p. 84.

23. Nathalie S. Dana, op. cit., pp. 114, 4.

24. John Henry Hopkins, *Life of Marie Moulton Graves Hopkins,* privately printed, 1934, p. 24.

25. Ibid., p. 25.

26. George Hodges, op. cit., p. 109.

27. Hamilton Fish Armstrong, op. cit., p. 41.

28. Margaret C. Aldrich, *Family Vista,* New York, 1958, p. 22.

29. Hamilton Fish Armstrong, op. cit., p. 49.

30. Nathalie S. Dana, op. cit., p. 30.

31. NYDJ, 1886.

32. Nathalie S. Dana, op. cit., p. 32.

33. NYDJ, 1891.

34. This author, graduated from Bard College in 1952, was the last in a near annual line of alumni to proceed to the General Theological Seminary;

since that year only a few Bard graduates have matriculated at General.

35. NYDJ, 1886, p. 94.

36. NYDJ, 1890, p. 71.

37. NYDJ, 1906, p. 196.

38. James Elliott Lindsley, *St. James' Church,* New York, 1960, p. 48.

39. NYDJ, 1901, p. 116.

40. Samuel Roosevelt Johnson to William R. Whittingham, April 1, 1865, MDA.

41. NYDJ, 1901, p. 111.

42. NYDJ, 1903, p. 72.

43. George Hodges, op. cit., p. 358.

44. Ibid., p. 358.

12   *La Belle Epoque*

1. NYDJ, 1914, 1920.

2. William Dudley Hughes, *Prudently with Power,* Holy Cross Press, n.d., p. 107.

3. NYDJ, 1915.

4. NYDJ, 1910.

5. *Chronicle,* Poughkeepsie, N.Y., October 1912.

6. Helena Rutherfurd Meade, *St. Mark's,* Mt. Kisco, N.Y., 1967.

7. NYDJ, 1910, p. 173.

8. Charles Lewis Slattery, *David Hummell Greer,* Longman's, 1921, p. 224.

9. NYDJ, 1911, pp. 180ff.

10. Ibid., p. 185.

11. Howard Chandler Robbins, *Charles Lewis Slattery,* Harper & Brothers, 1932, p. 212.

12. For a recent perspective on women's work on the national level, see Mary Sudman Donovan, "Zealous Evangelists," *Historical Magazine,* LI, December 1982, pp. 371ff.

13. Alexander C. Zabriskie, *Arthur Seldon Lloyd,* Morehouse-Gorham, 1942, *passim.*

14. NYDJ, 1920, p. 68.

15. Ibid., p. 69.

16. This was Robert R. Livingston, of St. Paul's Church, Tivoli.

17. NYDJ, 1920, p. 85.

18. *New York Times,* December 20, 1920, *et seq.*

13   The Reign of Manning

1. *Chronicle,* July 1932, p. 252.

2. Leslie Lang manuscripts, NYDA.

3. George W. Wickersham to the author.

4. James W. Kennedy, *The Unknown Worshipper,* Morehouse-Barlow, 1964, p. 63.

5. Ibid., p. 83.

6. William Thomas Manning manuscripts, General Theological Seminary library.

7. *American Mercury,* October 1926, p. 36.

8. William Thomas Manning manuscripts.

9. *Chronicle,* January 1931, p. 82.

10. *Times* (London), December 11, 1930.

11. New York *Herald Tribune,* December 9, 1930.

12. New York *Telegram,* December 9, 1930.

13. Horace W. B. Donegan to the author, June 9, 1983.

14. Stuart L. Tyson, *Case Against Herbert Shipman,* n.d., privately printed.

15. Thomas Muncaster to the author, November 12, 1979.

16. Alexander C. Zabriskie, *Arthur Seldon Lloyd,* Morehouse-Gorham, 1942, p. 248.

17. Ibid., p. 250.

18. William Dudley Hughes, *Prudently with Power,* Holy Cross Press, n.d., p. 132.

19. NYDJ, 1924.

20. NYDJ, 1925, p. 94.

21. William Dudley Hughes, op. cit., p. 69.

22. Ibid., p. 197.

23. Ibid., p. 119.

24. Leslie Lang manuscripts.

25. *Chronicle,* November 1926, p. 13.

26. *American Mercury,* October 1926, pp. 129ff.

27. NYDJ, 1917, p. 286.

28. The *Living Church Annual* has been used for the 1926 and 1980 statistics.

29. *Chronicle,* June 1932, p. 209.

30. William Dudley Hughes, op. cit., pp. 196–97.

31. Horace W. B. Donegan to the author, and the *Bulletin,* Lent, 1938, p. 12.

32. NYDJ, 1942, p. 50.

33. *Chronicle,* 1935, p. 211.

34. Ibid.

35. William Thomas Manning to the author, January 1949.

14   Bishop Gilbert: A Brief Interlude

1. NYDJ, 1946, p. 57.

2. Leslie Lang to the author, February 23, 1983; Lang manuscripts, NYDA.

3. Ibid.

4. *New York Times,* May 6, 1947.

5. Frances Manning to Leslie Lang, NYDA.

6. Robert T. Handy, *A History of the Churches in the United States and Canada,* Oxford University Press, 1977, p. 399.

7. Mother Ruth, CHS, to the author, October 11, 1983.

15   Horace W. B. Donegan: Changing Fortunes of American Christendom

1. *New York Times,* May 11, 1960.
2. Leslie Lang manuscripts, NYDA.
3. Interview with Darby Betts, August 10, 1982.
4. Ibid.
5. Charles Francis Boynton to the author, May 25, 1983.
6. William Howard Melish to the author, May 25, 1983.
7. J. Stuart Wetmore to the author, July 29, 1983.

Index